Power and Politics
in Africa

Power and Politics in Africa

Henry L Bretton

*State University College
at Brockport, SUNY*

ALDINE PUBLISHING COMPANY / CHICAGO

ABOUT THE AUTHOR

Henry L Bretton received his B.A. from Yale University and his M.A. and Ph.D from The University of Michigan. He presently holds the rank of University Professor (Political Science) at the State University College at Brockport, SUNY, and has been Visiting Professor at the Universities of Ghana and East Africa (Nairobi). He has published articles in professional journals, and has authored several books, two of which are *The Rise and Fall of Kwame Nkrumah* and *Power and Stability in Nigeria*.

First published 1973 by
Aldine Publishing Company
529 South Wabash Avenue
Chicago, Illinois 60605

ISBN 0-202-24131-9 Cloth
      0-202-24132-7 Paper
Library of Congress Catalog Number 72-78212

Printed in the United States of America

To the victims of Power and Politics

It is hard to avoid the banal wish that economists and students
of politics could share a little of the tradition of the other:
this is the chimera, or the lost continent, of Political Economy.

BERNARD CRICK

Contents

Figures

Currency Chart

Franc Zone	CFA (Communauté Financière Africaine) August 1969: 1 US\$ = CFA 277.710 Before: 1 US\$ = CFA 246.85
Ghana	New cedi N₵1 = US\$ 0.98 (as of December 1, 1971)
Nigeria	Nigeria pound 1 £N = US\$ 2.80 (as of December 1, 1971)
Zambia	Kwacha 1 K = US\$ 1.40 (as of December 1, 1971)
Kenya	Kenya shilling 1 US\$ = 7.143 sh. (as of December 1, 1971)

Preface

Not too many years ago, the study of politics in Africa was conducted within an exceedingly narrow conceptual framework. The focus was on the legal-constitutional developments surrounding independence, the doings of individual political leaders, the political parties, and the nationalist movements from which they sprang. This work was essential, for the long night of colonial rule had distorted and obscured *political* Africa; one had to be brought back to realization that there was a political universe other than that depicted by French, British, Belgian, Portuguese, Spanish, German, Italian, or American observers, most of whom were prone to rationalize European rule and its consequences.

Some of the one-country studies published during the first decade after independence still are unsurpassed, and some of the compendiums on the politics of independence and related subjects were most timely and valuable. One major gap, however, remained to be closed. Although widely recognized as crucial to an understanding of politics, the economic dimensions of the events unfolding on the continent were studied quite separately from the political, social, and sociopsychological dimensions. This book seeks to fill that gap. In so doing, it seeks to lay bare the raw structure of politics: resources, production and distribution of wealth and income, public and private resource management, public finance, and administration. Reflecting the inseparable linkages between internal and external power and politics, analysis is conducted at two levels, national and international. But the book attempts more than that.

A Brazilian archbishop, Helder P. Camara, addressing himself to the political future of his country and in particular to the constant danger of dictatorship, offered this advice:

I am not a technician, not in economy or sociology or politics . . .
Now I am always urging the youth of my country, the young university
students and professors, to join interdisciplinary teams and to look for a
model that will not be a servile copy of either capitalism or the present
Socialist model. (*New York Times,* October 1970, 6.)

This book was conceived and written not so much to produce a new model
as to provide a basis for broad-gauge and interdisciplinary discussion and
study of the most pressing social, economic, and political problems facing
the less developed parts of the world today and tomorrow; in fundamental
respects there are no significant differences and distinctions among Asia,
Latin America, and Africa.

Professors and students in all social sciences are ever more urgently demanding recognition of the fact that nothing we discuss or study can
actually and meaningfully be compressed into one single, narrowly defined
discipline. The political scientist knows in his heart that he is working a
good part of the time in neighboring disciplines. As we demonstrate
throughout this book, economists, sociologists, and anthropologists share
the same insight; yet we have few published works on which to base the
kind of discussion Archbishop Camara has in mind. This book is intended
and was designed to serve that purpose.

Another source of inspiration for this study has been the debate between
radicals and establishment-oriented scholars and other conservatives, between social revolutionaries in the United States and in Africa and the
defenders of the status quo. These debates often seem little more than
dialogues of the deaf, mainly because of a near-total lack of commonly
understood and accepted reference points. It may well be urgent to attempt
to discover a common ground. Political economy commends itself superbly
if updated and adjusted to contemporary conditions. Although social relevance is not easy to achieve — it is a relative term through and through —
this study should offer something of value to those who are persuaded that
too much of contemporary social science research and writing fails to
establish contact with any known social reality.

The central concern of this study is power and influence, a twin concept. One aim of this effort is retrieval of the concept, or concepts, from
the quicksands of social science theory and practice. Both concepts are
deeply embedded in social mythology to the point where it is impossible
at times to distinguish fact from fiction, shadow from substance. Transfer
of the concepts of power and influence from the plane of theory to that
of social practice should render a service to those in search of greater social
relevance in social science as well as to those seeking an improved, more
precise, and intellectually more manageable and intelligible frame of reference for power, evidently the core of most if not all of the social sciences.

There is an urgent need for viable social programs to improve the chances for solution of social ills on the continent of Africa. 2 years of sustained service on the continent and 16 years of intermittent research in or about Africa have revealed a dearth of social theory germane to social problem-solving in Africa. It is hoped that the present effort will assist Africa's theorists and practitioners in their search for realistic and viable answers to their problems.

In the main, research was based on African economic and development surveys and reports, budget estimates and budgets, hard data extracted from development plans, United Nations surveys and commission papers, country and international organization statistical compilations, and census reports. The reliability of these sources, it is fully realized, ranges from substantially accurate to fictitious. Extensive interviews in the several countries in Africa, in France, in Britain, at the United Nations, and in United States public and private circles concerned with and knowledgeable on Africa, as well as the fruits of my own research over the decades, should be adequate to assure necessary corrections and adjustments.

The greater part of the evidence was gathered systematically in six countries — namely Senegal, Ivory Coast, Ghana, Nigeria, Kenya, and Zambia. Where appropriate, illustrations are drawn from other countries. This sampling includes unitary and federal states and states of different religious and cultural orientation and different racial composition. The economies range from substantially dependent to substantially independent, from those dominated by agriculture to one based mainly on mineral extraction. Not at all considered where those states about which reliable data cannot be obtained. The evidential base for any generalizations offered should therefore be sufficiently broad to assure a high degree of authenticity, (Studies purporting to deal with all of Africa rarely if ever do; frequently they are based merely on information gathered in very few countries, probably only in portions of countries.)

To achieve our objective, the book is divided into seven major parts. Part I is concerned with the more basic problems of perception of what it is we are trying to see and study, and Part II offers a general overview and outlines a grid that to an extent regulates the flow of international and national power and influence. To provide a basis for what is to follow, Part II includes political-economic profiles of the principal countries chosen to illustrate the general problems. Part III examines the international universe, assesses the respective bargaining positions of the contending forces — the former colonial powers and their associates versus the new states — and attempts to draw a balance. Part IV begins the more extensive analysis of the new states themselves, in general terms, identifying the principal sources of power and illustrating their uses. This sets the stage for consideration of the power and influence structure from the rulers and governors (Part V) through the pressure and interest groups that cluster and flow around them (Part VI), to the eventual payoff in the power and politics game that centers on individual and group shares of available wealth and income.

It is our conviction that the fundamentals here discussed and analyzed will govern power and politics in Africa and relations between the new states and the outside world, regardless of which individual ruler or group of rulers may be in control of the governmental and administrative apparatus at any given time. Put differently, no matter who seizes power in a given African country tomorrow morning, and regardless of his ideology, the reality here discussed will have to be contended with. Although none of the following should in any way be held responsible for the study, special credit for making it possible go to the Rockefeller Foundation, the Ford Foundation, the University of Michigan, and the State University of New York. A Rockefeller Foundation grant to the University of Michigan, transferred subsequently to the State University of New York (at Brockport), enabled me to find the time to continue my research and begin writing. The Ford Foundation grant to the Developing Areas Study Program at the University of Michigan helped to finance several trips to Africa and to support summer research and writing. A modest grant from the University Awards Committee of the State University of New York helped to finance acquisition of needed materials and typing of the manuscript.

I

Problems of Perception

> Let us say you cut an automobile in half down the middle.
> In that case, you could guess the complete, 'whole' structure.
> But if you cut a very thin slice from the automobile, and
> if you cut it on a strange angle, it could be more difficult.
> In your slice, you might have only a bit of bumper, and
> rubber tire, and glass. From such a slice, it would be hard
> to guess the shape and function of the full structure.

MICHAEL CRICHTON
THE ANDROMEDA STRAIN

Shadows and Illusions

The Myth of the Potent Organization

We are all familiar with the phenomenon. Someone describes what he perceives, honestly, sincerely, though it is but an illusion. Once in print it turns into an unassailable fact, defended vigorously by its own adherents, a literary reality. All of us, or most of us at any rate, are struggling continuously to discover the true reality behind what we know or suspect may be a mirage, an error, or at best a very tenuous proposition. Continuously we are searching for unassailable proof. Our personal involvement and our commitments are of no help. Even the most sophisticated method does not seem to spare us the embarrassment of confusing, on our own, fact with fiction.

The challenge seems to be most severe where ascertainable reality is remote from us in space and time, or where it is obscured by thick layers of propaganda or myth. One of these myths, which we want to examine briefly in the way of an introduction to our particular mode of analysis, is the myth of the potent political organization as applied to the study of power and politics in Africa.

One illustration of that myth, applied on a colossal scale, represents all of Africa as one solid, homogeneous organizational entity. Another endows the newly independent nation-states with a potency only a few actually possess. At yet another level the myriads of large and small political parties competing for control of the embryonic states are credited with far greater potency than their actual performance tends to support. Similarly, influence and influentials are all too often accepted on face value, frequently solely on the strength of a precarious reputation or just self-proclamation. Among prime beneficiaries of this misassessment are the once powerful but now virtually impotent African chiefs and religious leaders.

The developing administrative structures and bureaucracies, though capable of generating considerable power at their apex, do not, as a rule, warrant the broad ascription of organizational effectiveness that characterizes much of the literature on the subject.

METHODOLOGY OF ILLUSION

A prime source of our analytical difficulties in getting at the core of social behavior and of power and influence in particular lies in the nebulosity of the terms we use. Foremost among these is the term *political*. Robert Dahl should have prefaced his brilliant *Modern Political Analysis* with a frank admission that he was not at all clear on what he meant by *political*. To be sure, the lack of clarity on this point becomes apparent from a careful reading of the book.

One consequence of our insistence that a political structure or hierarchy may be found in every society, separate and distinct from economic structure and hierarchies, has been our fascination with neatly contrived schemes, sets of concentric circles, pyramids, and the like. This has facilitated conceptualization of thoroughly integrated, mutually dependent segments of state and society as evolving within clearly defined, generally understood, and recognized boundaries.

If in addition to admitting our definitional difficulties we could free ourselves from conceptual restraints that compel us to think only or exclusively in traditional and well-established terms, a breach might be effected in the disciplinary prison that now confines us and prevents us from broadening our perspectives. Abandonment or revision of time-honored ways of viewing things may be in order generally but may be mandatory in the study of the less developed states and societies of Africa.

A hint of what might be required may be obtained from what a computer "saw" when it was fed data from a spacecraft surveying sections of the moon during the early stages of lunar exploration from afar. The computer image made our satellite appear very much like a potato, a smaller portion broadening out into a larger one. The image was produced by computation of the different gravity actions of the moon's internal mass. The peculiar shape represented the moon as seen by a computer programmed by reference to a mathematical model of the moon's odd gravitational field, which is caused by uneven concentrations of mass below the surface.[1]

We might ask how a human computer or political analyst might see the social African landscape if freed from traditional conceptional restraints. How would he see a nation, a social organism, even a human being? It may well be that the seemingly distorted image of the moon is a far more useful model for viewing social Africa. Instead of the symmetrical pyramid normally thought of — a concept where a narrow apex rests on a broad base — a more realistic perception might take into account the "odd gravitational fields caused by uneven concentration of (power and influence) beneath the surface?" An African state then might be represented by this shape.

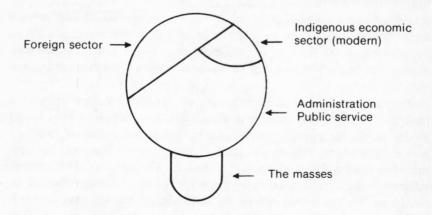

Our willingness to consider odd and unusual — that is, unconventional — relationships, to digest and integrate economic data along with non-economic, so-called political data, and to arrange these in novel formats toward equally novel hypotheses and generalization is severely crippled by a chronic disinclination to look in certain directions. We do not like to venture into the highly charged zone of economic reward and punishment. We do not see the critical gravitational mass below the surface of what we call the polity. But when we plead inability to cope with this mass we do not admit our real reasons for reticence.

We argue that data on the more crucial, if not central, aspects of what we set out to study are difficult to come by. James K. Pollock, pioneer in the study of money in politics, observed years ago: "The financial operations of political parties have always been more or less shrouded in mystery." Arnold Heidenheimer, assessing availability of data on party finance, reports that such information "is always fragmentary."[2] Actually, these comments apply with equal force to everything else we study. Yet it does not seem to trouble us that all of man's motivations in politics are very much shrouded in mystery, that what we assert about the behavior of individuals, groups, or even states is both mystery laden and always, by its nature, fragmentary.

What the experts on party finance are really saying is that it is more difficult, because it is downright hazardous, to speculate where the money used in politics originates and where it goes.

The fallacy of the nonavailable documentation becomes apparent when one examines the extent to which generalizations on other subjects are made without documentary support. A cursory examination of any standard text in comparative politics will support this contention. What, for instance, has been the documentation to support the theses on nation-building in developing areas? What are the documentary foundations of the theses that seek to ascribe to government officials a primary dedication to the public interest? What is the documentary evidence to support the contention that in a given electoral campaign X amount has been spent and not Y amount?

A plea that relevant documents are not available reflects in part a notion that all relevant spheres of knowledge have been considered, and all are within the purview of the analyst. We know, of course, that the economist tends to stop at the disciplinary boundary that separates his discipline from political science and vice versa. The usual pleas of research difficulties simply reflect acceptance of the wholly arbitrary division of society into sectors determined by the exigencies of our academic trade. It is difficult to locate the original architect of the division. It is possible that in modern times Talcott Parsons nudged us toward separatism when he referred to his "polity" as "a primarily functional subsystem of a society, strictly parallel in theoretical status to the economy, as that concept is broadly used in modern economic theory."[3] This is tantamount to saying that in the human system blood represents a functional subsystem strictly parallel in theoretical status to the living organism through which it runs.

The argument that certain economic questions cannot be researched because of insufficient or unreliable documentation implies a dedication to methodological rigor, to objectivity, to flawless scholarship. This posture is characteristic especially of modern political science, mistakenly but commonly referred to as the behavioral study of politics. In that study, gone are the fallacies that troubled social studies for ages. Gone are the conceptual errors and the methodological imperfections, and reality is contacted at long last. We are putting an end to the literary universe. Or are we?

The real center of social science is man. He may be a political animal, but he is most certainly also an economic one. How dependable is any documentation, how reliable are any results if the spheres of man's activity are abstracted from the total environment and compressed into quite artificial and arbitrary topical or subject-matter compartments? Some pertinent observations on this problem are offered by R. D. Laing, a psychoanalyst.

The theoretical and descriptive idiom of such research in social science adopts a stance of apparent "objective" neutrality. [But] we have seen how deceptive this can be. The choice of syntax and vocabulary is a political act that defines and circumscribes the manner in which "facts" are to be experienced. Indeed, in a sense it goes further and even creates the facts that are studied.

The data [given] of research are not so much given as taken out of a constantly elusive matrix of happenings. We should speak of *capta* rather than data. The quantitative interchangeable grist that goes into the mills of reliability studies and rating scales is the expression of processing that we can do *on* reality, not the process of reality.

Natural scientific investigations are conducted on objects or things, or the patterns of relations between things, or on systems of "events." Persons are distinguished from things in that persons experience the world. Things-events do not experience. Personal events are experiential. Natural scientism is the error of turning persons into things by a process of reification that is not itself part of true natural scientific method. Results derived in this way have to be dequantified and dereified before they can be reassimilated into the realm of human discourse.

Fundamentally, the error is the failure to realize that there is an ontological discontinuity between human beings and it-beings.

Human beings relate to each other not simply externally, like two billiard balls, but by the relations of the two worlds of experience that come into play when two people meet. This should dispense with claims to objectivity, of methodological rigor, of scientific detachment as a means of uncovering social reality.[4]

If a reasonable degree of objectivity and detachment is to be achieved, it is clear that the entire matrix of human experience must be considered relevant. If our intellectual and physical limitations dictate subject matter, epistemological selectivity reorientation is indicated, not shortsightedness.

Economists are not immune to the problems of perspective, and literary universes are not unknown in that field of study. Economics also has its internal and external jurisdictional disputes and the inevitable theoretical and methodological controversies. Some conceptual frameworks used by economists are extremely rigid and unrelated to observable reality.[5]

Whatever the perspective or conceptual framework, reliable information on economic relationships also is at times most difficult to come by. Seemingly accurate data on production processes, trade flow, revenue collection, and income are known to have been substantially or wholly invented. As can be expected, this phenomenon is most acute in less developed areas; in Africa the condition is notorious. Relevant statistics, in French-speaking Africa for example, may range from speculation or guesswork to meticulous and reasonably reliable compilations. Often the data may have been produced in Paris by public servants innocent of all contact with reality overseas. The margin of error may reach 100 percent. Reliability of data differs from country to country or from sector to sector, depending on such accidental variables as availability of competent personnel. The desire to protect critical sectors from prying foreign — that is, non-French —

eyes is known to have been a prime factor effecting the dependability of economic data on French-speaking Africa.

Informational deficiencies are not confined to French-speaking Africa nor to public officials. Academic economists are inclined to exaggerate the importance of whatever data they happen to have obtained, usually overlooking such variables as differential quality of data and regional or sectoral differences caused by the accident of governmental change, for example. Assuming availability of reasonably accurate information in government archives, the sheer accident of an investigation and publication of a report on one single ministry may flood the literary market with studies and analyses of that one set of data. In the process, an entirely false picture of economic conditions and relationships in Africa generally may be conveyed. In Nigeria the accident of the 1962 move by a coalition of two regions and the federal government against a third region produced a veritable avalanche of data on one region alone. That region, and in particular its capital, Ibadan, suddenly was bathed in stark, revealing light while capitals of the other regions in the north and east remained discretely in the dark. The inundation of the data bank with information on the Western Region tended to color economic views on Nigeria generally for years to come.[6] The overthrow of Nkrumah in Ghana, and of Margai in Sierra Leone produced similar informational imbalances when series of official inquiries focused attention on certain sectors and not on others.

For a variety of reasons African states feature a relatively large public economic sector. Public finance, therefore, occupies a far more crucial, if not controlling, position than is so in the more highly developed system. The growth of the public sector, however, is not matched by a corresponding development of fiscal and financial statistics.[7] Consequently, most plans, programs, and budgets, and most development plans in particular, are shots in the dark; some may be very far off the mark. Considering the central position of the public sector especially in centrally planned and directed economies, the importance of fiscal and financial statistics can scarcely be exaggerated. The methodological problems in attempting to cope with the inevitable disparities and analytical dislocations and in attempting to compensate for the inevitable errors and misjudgments are staggering. It is doubtful that economics has developed techniques adequate for the task.[8]

SUBSTANCE: POWER AND INFLUENCE

Like its adoptive parents *political* and *politics,* power has been a much abused word. In current use it appears to be synonymous with ability to do something, to act, to impress, influence, reward, or punish, to war or mediate — in short, it is a word used to connote any extension of will or physical ability beyond an individual or group to effect certain goals in relation to other individuals or groups. As commonly used, the term is ascriptive; it usually is not really defined, though ritual bows toward definition are made. Attempts to reduce it to its multiple components are amazingly few, considering its wide and common use. It is a very large — in international relations studies (Hans Morgenthau, for instance) an enormously large — black box, a zone of uncertainty if not ignorance. One might suspect from examination of professional literature that many a social scientist *thinks* of power when he uses politics and vice versa.

Anthropologists such as Balandier, Fortes, and Evans-Pritchard use power but apply it within a narrowly defined social sphere. In *Anthropologie Politique,* Balandier categorizes the traditional systems of government by reference to diverse segments of activity, which leads him to treat power in separate categories: political power, kinship power, social stratification power, religious power. It is apparent that he uses power to identify an area of activity, of influence, which he suspects exists but on which he lacks concrete evidence. (Significantly, the economic or subsistence power crucial in traditional society is not one of the categories used.) Balandier's problem stems from the difficulty of distinguishing varying degrees of evidence on the presence and actual operational relevance of power. That power is there he knows; what it does exactly, he does not. The problem is endemic to social science, but we can gather rather strong and convincing circumstantial evidence. To do that, however, the search must concentrate on discovery of concrete and substantive sources of human behavior. Religion, lineage, even authority — a much favored concept in political and legal parlance — are poor and unrewarding analytical reference points. It is not at all surprising that Balandier finds *power* an ambiguous term.[9]

If *power* is to be made less ambiguous, central or crucial variables must be separated from purely peripheral ones. Scales or rank orders must be developed to allow us to distinguish several magnitudes or degrees of potency. The accumulated fallout from excessive use of the term has created a climate where invocation of *power* has become a ritual exercise, a reflex action. (It is not unlikely that man derives vicarious pleasure from use of the term.) If it is to have any value, along with its companion, *influence,* a determined effort must be made to endow the word with substance. Universal misuse makes that most difficult.[10]

Within the social sciences the most intensive and extensive work on power has been done by political scientists and sociologists. The sociologists, as will be pointed out, explore the subject to greater depth, and their research product therefore tends to be more convincing.

The problem has been recognized, though without the obvious conclusions being drawn, by several theorists. It is possible that Dahl is correct when he refers to the study of power alone as being "a bottomless swamp."[11] Cartwright notes that "theorists who have attempted to impose some order upon (the literature on social influence) have found it exceedingly intractable."[12] March and Simon have not discovered a more reliable method of identification or delimitation.[13] Significantly, Cartwright himself while discussing influence seems to stray into the adjacent precinct of power.[14]

One of the basic deficiencies in the use of power and influence is lack of discrimination about weight and importance. Scholars use various criteria — for example, geographic location, GNP, economies, organization — as though they are of equal weight in all systems and in all parts or sections of a system. Recognition of important differences usually are made only by verbal means. The military factor, for instance, is automatically evaluated as a source of power, as a physical force, when there may actually be no proof of force potential. Often, economic resources are given equal weight as sources of power when, as noted, in certain instances there may actually be little or no justification for such a conclusion.

Max Weber's treatment of power, though stimulating, is not too helpful. He identifies power derived from economic means, from social prestige, from legal positions. Any of these forms of power may generate any other, and he does not provide a clue to which of the several forms will prevail in the event of conflict. Social prestige as a source of power and influence always poses problems. In the African context the nexus is easily lost. At first glance prestige derived from social status appears to have helped some traditional rulers to accumulate modest means. It is doubtful, though, whether sufficient wealth was acquired through the medium of social prestige to tip the scales of power in important respects. More likely, traditional rulers obtained only initial capital through use of their chieftaincy positions, and acquired more substantial rewards by other, nontraditional means such as land scale, speculation, sale of favors, or sale of influence.[15]

Our purpose, then, is to outline the nature, quality, and quantity of the power resources and the limits governing their growth, including generation of additional units by artificial means (mythmaking). This is a most dependable point of departure for a realistic assessment of what is possible in developing Africa.

Concentration on material resources does not require abandonment of other avenues of inquiry. The less tangible reputed sources of power and influence, such as quality of leadership, trust and confidence, or charisma, certainly can be kept in view. Reliance on concrete substantive sources simply is an elementary precaution to correct the notorious open-endedness of political inquiry. Analysis on wholly or substantially intangible grounds usually renders intelligible discussion, hence definitive determination, impossible.

In his comprehensive survey of definitional efforts, Cartwright concludes that "most theories of social influence assert the ability of an agent to exert influence arises from the possession, or control, of valued resources." He notes that Dahl refers to these as the base of an "actor's power," which consists of "all the resources — opportunities, acts, objects, etc. — that he can exploit in order to effect the behavior of another."[16] Cartwright reports that lists of resources contain such items as wealth, military capabilities, prestige, skill, information, physical strength, and even personal rewards like recognition and affection." Ownership or, more recently, management of economic resources, means of production of wealth, do emerge, however, as the resources identified most frequently. This was to be expected, and leads us to consideration of that branch of social science that precedes by several decades the formation of the discipline of political science — namely, political economy.

Political Economy or Economy of Power and Influence

Whatever we may have in mind when using political economy, the adjective *political* poses an immediate obstacle. The accumulated ambiguity contained in political theory and method merely contaminates and beclouds what could otherwise be a relatively lucid subject matter. It is doubtful whether the loss of the adjective will be irreparable. "Economy of power and influence" should be an adequate substitute, provided, of course, that the terms power and influence are not left in their usual confused and confusing state.

In his characteristic manner, while attempting to link influence — political influence in this case — to economic reality. Parsons demonstrates the hazards inherent in the use of *political* as an adjective.

> [Political] influence ... [is] influence operating in the context of the goal — functioning of collectivities, as generalized persuasion without power or direct threat . . . used, on the one hand, by units either exercising or bidding for leadership positions and, on the other hand, by non-leaders seeking to have an effect on the decisions and orientations of leaders. Though political influence is analytically independent of power, we conceive the two to be closely interconnected.

One must doubt that the author really expected his readers still to be with him at the end of that thought.[17] In any case, a few passages later one of the roots of our problem with power and influence is laid bare. There Parsons argues that it is necessary to raise political influence to the level of "symbolic generalization" in order to avoid reduction "of the power relation to a barter basis." This means that to avoid clarity at all costs we must seek refuge in nebulosity and ambiguity — for example, "goal-functioning or collectivities." With such assistance, clarity may well be beyond our reach. Fortunately, light is being cast into this otherwise obscure corner.

It is precisely the barter aspect that occupies Cartwright, Simon, and others, and has enabled them to dynamically conceptualize the power and influence relationship. Once we accept that material resources and values derived therefrom are at the root of the power and influence tree, terminological formulation can be held to a level of clarity that permits intelligent discussion. Social reality, socially meaningful relationships as Weber might put it, then cannot be too easily pushed aside in favor of elaborate, superficially persuasive verbal constructs.

If we accept that ownership and control of resources are not fixed, a market analogy would seem appropriate. Cartwright speaks of expectations of gain as an element in the calculation of influence. He also distinguishes between influence or mere contagion. The expectation of reward alone, Cartwright notes, can be the equivalent of reward, hence can be regarded as influence and eventually as power. (This is a familiar concept in international relations where the expectation of a military assault by a hostile nation can have the same effect on the potential victim as an actual military action.)[18]

Cartwright's point is clear. If concepts like the exchange of power and influence are used too broadly, the need for specifics concerning the type of resource exchanged, for example, does not rise. Another elegant generalization may have been coined, but nothing has really been learned about power in influence. Actually, what is being exchanged or bartered in its final form — that is, the form in which it is actually exchanged — usually is quite concrete and specific. More often than not it relates to money in one form or another.

Simon, ever in quest of precision while struggling with the problem of measuring power and influence comes down in the same general area. "To the extent to which we can establish empirically the condition for the exercise of power, these conditions, or influence bases, provide an indirect means for measurement." Having established a respectable premise, he proceeds to identify not a bartering process but an "asymmetrical relation between the behavior of two persons."[19] The stage is set for an economic interpretation of power and influence.

Frey, discussing power on a communitywide or systemic level, speaks of a rise in the level of overall power in the society as possibly more important for analytical purposes than determination of distribution of power. Either of these two, or any similarly formulated generalization, must remain vague unless related to firm and concrete values.[20]

R. Harrison Wagner acknowledges the central importance of power in the study of politics. "If 'politics' could be defined by 'power,' then political science could be given clear boundaries (assuming one can define 'power'), and a theory of power might be a general theory of politics."[21] While it is not my purpose here to develop such a general theory, I hope to contribute to its development by outlining the basic parameters of power and influence in one geographic area.

It is entirely possible that the term *political* in political economy has little if anything to do with what modern political scientists are thinking of when they use that adjective. Oscar Lange suggests that:

the term political economy was first used early in the 17th century by Montchrétien in his *Traité de l'économie politique,* published in 1615. In that context, "political" really means state since Montchrétien was mainly interested in state finance. Later the term "political economy" was widely used to denote research on problems of social economy.

Lange also suggests that perhaps *social* economy might convey a better idea of what is meant by that subject matter. Lange further notes that "in English-speaking countries, the term 'political economy' is used almost exclusively in Marxist literature, which consciously opposes the political economy of the classical school and of Marx and Engels to contemporary academic "economics.""[22] It is conceivable that the formulation "economy of power and influence" might be used to distinguish contemporary academic consideration of politics — shorthand for the field of political science — from more substantive analysis.

ON RATIONALITY, POWER, AND INFLUENCE

Rationality has not yet been treated adequately or convincingly in political science, partly because that discipline is concerned more with aggregations than with man, even though the term *behavioral* is employed by some practitioners. Rationality, however, cannot be assessed at the group or aggregate level of analysis. (That this is attempted — in certain international relations analyses, for example — does not mean that it can be done successfully.) Rationality is assessible only at the level of the individual.

The individual is infinitely complex; it might be said that he is complex to the point of being beyond systematic assessment. He exists in several worlds and is of several minds. The worlds he relates to, or thinks he exists in, may be any one of a large number of or combinations of make-believe worlds. The events he thinks he relates to, or that his observers believe he relates to, may be pseudoevents — that is, events that occurred largely or entirely within his imagination. To describe man as schizophrenic may be one of the kindest things one can say. Yet the social analyst need not despair.

If the conceptual sweep is restricted to the relationship of man to economic environment, specifically to his material needs and expectations, some contact with substance can be established. Of course, we will probably never lay bare all of man's behavioral and mental secrets. It is within our capability, however, to develop an improved sense of the outer parameters that govern man's behavior, of the range of real and concrete, empirically ascertainable options before him.

The possibility that irrationality is a major, possibly even crucial variable need not be denied. We need only investigate what forces, or stimuli, if any, tend to control or govern man's behavior. It is entirely likely that economic stimuli relating to subsistence and survival interest may act very much like an electrified fence. Irrational man is transformed into a more rational being as he comes into contact with the fence. Within the area bounded by the fence man is free to behave quite irrationally and unpredictably; he may even run amok.

What we so lightly call personality, or prestige, or lust for power undoubtedly has some empirical basis and may effect man's behavior to an extent. Still, it is likely that in the final analysis all of these factors may be subject to modification under the impact of material consideration. The individual may change his tastes; a leader's style of rule may change, at times dramatically. Yet the material environment, used by man at times for devious purposes, remains substantially unchanged. Even where drastic measures are taken — as, for example, when industries are nationalized — no basic changes need occur. If the direction of external trade is shifted massively, or if the distribution of wealth is changed substantially (given the African patterns within limits, of course), in all probability the material environment will remain unaltered structurally as well as substantively. If it changes, it will do so only slowly, in certain cases agonizingly so. The potential of technological innovation as an instrument of social change, is easily exaggerated in Africa. The mainstream of economic life flows on inexorably, creating eddies here and there, an island now and then, but altering the configuration of the shoreline only slightly.

A common source of confusion on rationality is failure to distinguish between make-believe and real worlds as reference points for decision. The African decision maker and policymaker, more likely than not of limited education and training, cannot be thought of as reacting typically to the abstractions conjured up by social scientists. To be sure, he may say that he does, especially if his public addresses are prepared by a sophisticated speechwriter. Actually decisions are made on a different basis, especially when — as is true of most decisions on public matters — money is involved. It is most unlikely, for instance, that many African decision makers decide on budgetary questions in terms used by social science theorists concerned with nation-building. The immediate frame of reference is likely to be far more down to earth. (R. D. Laing mentions the situation one may encounter in the clinical environment familiar to the psychotherapist — in an asylum, for instance. There the less imaginative observer, or therapist, may posit certain types of behavior as normal, no matter how absurd or unreasonable these might be on reflection, and then faults the helpless inmate for failing to live up to his expectations.)[23] There is much of that in social science treatment of rationality in politics.

A sense of proportion regarding discussions of rationality can be maintained only if a healthy scepticism is observed whenever the subject is raised. Some social scientists, such as Parsons, have posited a wholly unrealistic set of standards, or goals, to determine rationality. Olson reminds us that the Parsonian concept of social consensus, vague and nebulous as it is, has been used as a test of rationality. A decision maker is said to be nonrational if he ignores the reputed or alleged consensus. We know, of course, that social consensus is a social fiction, and a Parsonian theorist can manipulate the master's words very much as he pleases. Consensus means that a majority of the people concerned essentially want the same thing at the same time. In the world of politics that state of affairs, we well know, can be achieved only if the object of the consensus majority's desire is held sufficiently vague and ambiguous. In economics, though, an erroneous assertion of consensus on the availability and distribution of goods, for example, cannot be maintained beyond the next consumer index.

Lange warns that application of the economic principle to human behavior is unreliable unless it is considered in the wider context of underlying social relationships.[24] He distinguishes between two kinds of rationality, factual and methodological, citing Kotarbinski's illustration. "Someone bases his plan of travel on the official time-table but fails to reach his destination, because contrary to the information given, the train does not stop there."[25] The illustration shows methodological but not factual rationality. We shall return to this crucial distinction later. Of relevance at this point is the probability that regardless of the typology of rationality and regardless of all additional considerations that come to mind as one contemplates the possibilities open to man, especially at a decision or policy-making level where power and influence are wielded in large quantities or units, the matrix of economic factors, forces, and relationships is more dependable than the shifting sands of political theory or what may go under that name.

MONEY, POWER, AND INFLUENCE

Among the few who seriously investigated the role of money in state and society, James K. Pollock, Alexander Heard, and more recently Arnold Heidenheimer (excluding his work on corruption cited below) offer the most useful insights. None of these analysts, however, carry his inquiry far enough. They are concerned with either electoral or public finance — public finance very much as traditionally viewed, strictly as defined by statute. The subject of corruption is rarely touched. Where it is examined, the inquiry is not carried far below the surface. There is little indication that public and private finance may be indistinguishable in strategically important respects and that money may flow through society essentially independent from the structural-functional systems identified in social science. Writers on the subject seem unaware of the possibility that in numerous instances distinction between economic and political uses of money may indeed be quite meaningless.

One of the more significant references to money in politics was made by Spengler and is cited by Pollock in his pioneering study, *Money and*

Politics Abroad. Spengler wrote: "Democracy is the complete equating of money with political power."[26] The passage is exceedingly interesting, for it reflects probably a century of misunderstanding of the relationship between money, democracy, and power. With reference to the economically underendowed societies, the Spengler formulation might be altered to read: Influence is the complete equating of money with social power.

If inquiry on money is to extend beyond conventional political analysis, several notions about its uses may have to be abandoned. Private money may be socially effective. Public money may have controlling impact on private interests. Declared funds — for example, those raised for political party support — may be no more than the visible portion of the iceberg; in any case, declared funds are not necessarily employed as stated. No practically significant dividing line may exist between legitimate and illegitimate use of public or private money, between honest and corrupt use. Here Parsons is helpful when he notes that "money becomes the most important allocative mechanism, not only over commodities, but over human services." Again, services must be thought of as spanning both public and private spheres.[27]

II

The Power and
Influence Grid

Anyone who wishes in the name of independence to
become free, may do so, providing that he considers suicide as the
supreme act of independence.

MARCHÉS TROPICAUX

2

The International Environment:
Independence or Dependence?

Poverty and Power

Two conditions that affect the fortunes of the new states can be indisputably debited to their colonial past. While many of their social and economic problems may be endemic and in some cases clearly antedate the colonial era, the condition of grinding, at times paralyzing poverty and the eviscerated legal status they are said to "enjoy" as "sovereign and independent" states are not of their own making. The two conditions are, of course, linked. Today, sovereignty and independence are economic functions in the first instance and military functions in the second. The weaker a state is economically, the more fragile is its independence. Although this relationship should be quite obvious, this simple truth is not recognized as a valid principle in the governance of the international community. In the United Nations, for example, all states from Fiji to the Soviet Union are officially equal.

Little of any consequence in this world can be attained without payment of an economic price. If at times fiery oratory appears to achieve the impossible, the event is more apparent than real and of short duration in any case. Few of the new states are capable of maintaining their current position in the international rank order; to score net gains seems to be well-nigh impossible for many. Because the capacity of the several economies to generate adequate financial support for their needs is severely limited, their capital resources must constantly be augmented from outside. For instance, after current obligations have been met most of the development plans depend on outside assistance to assure even a reasonable degree of success. Basic consumer goods and virtually all vitally needed capital goods must be imported and at constantly rising prices. Unless very substantial and liberal credit facilities are opened, imports for current and development needs require foreign exchange. That commodity is notoriously scarce. The situation is deteriorating.

As a general proposition one might say that *independence varies in direct proportion to ability to generate capital resources on a sustaining basis.* In classifying countries, or economic systems, by reference to investment financing alone, an interesting pattern emerges. A United Nations report suggests three broad categories.

The first includes countries that have relied essentially on domestic savings, but gradually switched from net saving surpluses to using up past savings through the period under consideration. This has been the case of the sterling countries, particularly Ghana and Nigeria.

The second category comprises the large net recipients of private foreign capital, namely Liberia and Mauritania, which now draw a major share of their investment from foreign official aid, having run down the savings that they once accumulated. This category also includes all French-speaking countries, except Mauritania.

In the third category of countries, recourse to external finance for domestic investment takes a special form, heavy inflows of public funds coinciding with a high level of remittances abroad on private accounts.[1]

Given the tendency of most of the governments concerned to increase public expenditures, at times spectacularly, one can see how independence is governed by availability of capital, in particular by the methods by which capital must be raised.

A useful set of indexes of African independence has been developed by an unidentified economist. He posits the following criteria as minimum gauges of effective independence.

1. Concentration of trading relationships by commodity and foreign country.
2. Average size of trading partners' economies in relationship to that of the African country studied.
3. Ratios of exports and imports to GDP.
4. Percentage of total manufactured goods consumption supplied by imports.
5. Ratio of foreign to total high-level manpower.
6. Concentration of sources of both capital and personal transfers.
7. Percentages of public and private investment dependent on foreign finance.
8. Percentages of sectors' total outputs or turnovers attributable to foreign-controlled enterprises in export production and marketing, importing banking insurance, construction, manufacturing, and domestic trade.[2]

The *Economic Indicators* published by the UN Economic Commission for Africa (ECA) in 1968 reveal the extent of Africa's financial procurement problems.

In 1966, the GDP of Brazil alone was 50 per cent of that of Developing Africa as a whole; and the products of the UK, the USSR, and the USA were about 2.5, 6 and 19 times greater than the African product respectively.

The Report goes on:

This contrast becomes the more striking when it is remembered that the population of Brazil, the UK, the USSR and US are but 28, 18, 85, and 80 per cent respectively of the population of Developing Africa. This point established, it may further be remarked that the increase in the American market (as measured by GDP) in 1966 was 50 per cent greater than the total size of the Developing African market in the same year.

In 1966, the Republic of South Africa accounted for some 24 per cent of the GDP of Africa as a whole. Even South Africa, however, is smaller economically than Brazil; and among developing countries, in Africa the two largest economic units — the UAR and Nigeria — were about one-quarter and one-fifth of the economic size of Brazil in 1966. In the same year, the UAR represented a market which was some six per cent of the total market in the UK, less than three per cent of the market in the USSR, and less than 1 per cent of the total market in the USA.

Perhaps the most telling comment on the poverty of Africa is contained in the following passage.

Even if this kind of comparison is extended to include all countries in Developing Africa with a GDP in 1966 of more than US $1,000 million — that is, Nigeria, Algeria, Morocco, Ghana, Libya, Sudan, Ethiopia, Congo (Kinshasa), Kenya, Zambia, Ivory Coast and Rhodesia — then, although such countries together with the UAR accounted for 72 per cent of the total product of developing Africa, the aggregate market size of these countries was still little more than 60 per cent of aggregate pre-tax incomes of less than four million income earners who in 1966 fell into the lowest income group assessed for tax purposes in the United Kingdom.[3]

Although Africa's share in the world trade of certain crops is substantial, many of these crops are in danger of being replaced by synthetics and are subject to other hazards. There is actually very little capability on the African continent to compel the richer economies of the world, singly or jointly, to provide substantial portions of the financial resources required.

From Colony to Satellite?

The precariousness of the new states and the fragility of the African regional power grid have been obscured by the lore surrounding what is commonly described as decolonization. To an extent the notion that something significant occurs when a new national flag is run up a pole or a new delegation makes its appearance at the United Nations is a product of a cultural commitment. We prefer to view the event as significant even though, on reflection, the value of what is a mere symbolic act must pale if compared to, let us say, the act of nationalization of a major mining industry. Also, fascination with the ritual surrounding the grant of nominal independence diverts our attention from the transition stage when a state may be for all practical purposes neither dependent nor independent. Progression from one stage to the other is not inexorable, and alternatives exist.

In the course of a debate on decolonization and the lack of progress toward that objective in southern Africa, the UN representative of the United Kingdom, responding to charges against his government on that count, offered this argument.

> His Government's policy regarding decolonization was clearly demonstrated by the succession of former United Kingdom colonial Territories which had become independent States Members of the United Nations during the past ten years. In his view there was no evidence to support the theory that the presence of foreign economic interests impeded the colonial peoples' progress towards independence and the administering power's political will to grant it. For example the fact that foreign interests had exploited important mineral resources in most of the thirteen former United Kingdom colonial Territories in Africa had not prevented those Territories from becoming independent.[4]

The fundamental flaw in that reasoning lies in the very wide interpretation attached to decolonialization. The degree of economic power at the disposal of the decolonizing state vis-a-vis the nominally independent one is not considered. The political influence that flows from that power is not even remotely acknowledged.

On a different level, J. P. Nettl subjects the term *state* to a more critical and sophisticated analysis but ends up nevertheless with a generalization intended for but not applicable to the majority of the states today.

> . . . the concept of state, in addition to being a unit, also generates the almost exclusive and acceptable locus of resource mobilization. Whatever the state may or may not be internally . . . there have in the past been few challenges to both its sovereignty *and* its autonomy in foreign affairs . . .
> . . . for almost all intents and purposes, the state acts for the society internationally, and internal matters relating to foreign affairs are a state prerogative (including interpretations of sovereignty—limiting norms emanating from supranational arrangements). In short, the state, is the gatekeeper between intra-social and extra-social flows of action.[5]

If the state in tropical Africa is indeed the gatekeeper, the state will be extremely frustrated, for the fences are either nonexistent or in extremely poor condition. Over the fences and through the gates pour foreign bearers of power and influence. The international power and influence flow is indeed so massive, concerning as it does the major share of the national resources available to the new rulers, that in many instances it is not possible to determine where national prerogatives end and foreign ones begin. The flow of authoritative decisions on matters of strategic importance to the former colony, to cite but one test of sovereignty, in many instances may be far heavier between the metropolitan centers of economic and political power and the new rulers than within the former colony itself. To an ever-increasing extent the political survival of the new rulers depends on the scope and timing of decisions made by foreign interests. These decisions do not necessarily reflect African interests.

While membership in the UN is determined by reference to standard or irregular political tests, other bodies in the UN recognize the limitations on sovereign status. A resolution adopted by the General Assembly of the United Nations noted that sovereignty cannot be safeguarded unless, first, the natural resources are permanently within that sovereignty (not outside it as is so under so-called political sovereignty) and, second, these resources can be exploited with a view to contributing to the highest possible growth rate of the developing country.[6] Of course, this is the crux of the matter.

Natural resources could well be located within a sovereignty and yet remain absolutely worthless to the sovereign, or they could have some value but so little that it would not pay to extract them. Perhaps Soviet academician Potekhin's comments are pertinent.

> Achievement of economic independence means the establishment of a system of economic relations with foreign countries which precludes first, the possibility of dictate on the part of any country or group of countries, and secondly, the possibility of some part of the national income leaving the country without its equivalent in one form or another being received in turn. In other words, economic independence *strengthens* a country's sovereignty and delivers it from plunder by other countries.[7]

Plunder may be too strong a word, for not all movement of goods or funds from Africa necessarily constitutes plunder. But Potekhin recognizes that what he posits cannot guarantee absolute sovereignty, hence absolute independence; it can only contribute to a strengthening of sovereignty and independence. A different point of view suggests that the best we can hope for might be modification of a rather ambiguous, malleable concept. With a view to the popular desire in Africa to press for rapid industrialization, W. A. Lewis cautions that "in industrialization, one has to cross a desert to get to the promised land."[8] In that desert, sovereignty and independence are of little substance.

One of the more imaginative among the students of modernization, Soja, writes:

> In its most pervasive form modernization operates within the confines of a state to create a new behavioral system, mobilizing the population into independent positions in empathy with a central government and sufficiently united to preserve stability and technological progress. This new system is based upon the nation-state, which has been recognized almost universally as the most potent organizational form for the initiation, dissemination, and perpetuation of modern ways of life. Indeed, the belief that the nation-state

is the pivotal unit of a human social organization lies at the heart of the spreading world culture.[9]

There can be little doubt that nationalism constitutes indeed a potent force. What must be doubtful, and increasingly so, especially with regard to conditions prevailing in the Third World, is the potentiality of that force to effect concrete achievement. Though faith may move mountains in the proverb, the nation-state system may not be capable of assisting the enfeebled remnants of former colonial empires to overcome the handicaps with which they have been saddled. In any case, a high degree of caution is indicated in any attempt to apply to Africa the generalizations on the nation-state and nationalism that have been developed with regard to other areas of the world.

Instead of the nation-state we may have series of systems and subsystems, linking groups, trends, technologies, religions, civilizations, and so on, in clusters of objectives, all within the nation-state *nominally,* formally, but not essentially. What is the "primary function of a political system," as Soja puts it? The answer may provide the key to his perception of the nation-state. If the primary function of what traditionally has been called the political system relates to distribution of wealth and associated functions, then in the cases here analyzed that function can manifestly not be performed by or exclusively within the nation-state.

The controlling position of the older states is acknowledged by exponents of nation-oriented theories and concepts, but only inadequately so. Lucien Pye, for example, recognizes that "[The] formation of new states is profoundly influenced by the existence of old states."[10] Neither he nor other writers on the subject allow that acknowledgement to lead them to the logical question of how precisely an old state might influence the formation of a new one. Could it be that the influence is of the magnitude of body on organ, or of mother on child?

It may well be that the flow of power and influence from the established to the yet-to-be-established new state may be assessed more accurately within a tri, or triple, level system: the nation-to-nation diplomatic level; the national level, facing out as well as in; and the purely internal local one. The first may be the level at which the internally most consequential battles are fought out; the second may be a mere fulcrum of what we may call the politics of support, the activities required to keep a group of rulers in power. The third level serves mainly to satisfy the internal circle of consumers by providing goods and public services; this is the level for therapeutical social mythmaking.

Instead of nation-states, we then may have systems in which economic forces push and pull, exert magnetic power, and repel, and in which all of this transpires across national boundaries in visible but most likely invisible ways. (One reason these ways are not always visible is that social science has so signally failed to draw them firmly on the map.) We may have patron-client relationships that transcend national boundaries in all materially consequential respects, as against ritualistic respects. We may have a series of satellitic systems in which groups exist and function in tow of groups elsewhere. While the formal efforts to fashion transnational organizations founder and fail, the informal invisible or less visible forms prosper: transnational behavior patterns are formed, transnational value systems, loyalties and commitments, *weltanschauungs* and cultures. The political culture, of so much interest lately, appears to be a veritable and impenetrable thicket of ethereal concepts and ideas, of little practical value to the analyst. It may be a different story if behavior patterns, institutions, and processes are extrapolated from economic relationships.

In the world of economics, options open to governments are far more limited than those in the world of politics. Leaving aside chance occurrences and the possibility of economically irrational behavior at the leadership level, as a rule the scarcity of resources dictates rather specific fiscal policies, socioeconomic policies, patterns of resource allocation, and so on. Since the larger share of ready resources is either directly or indirectly controlled by interests beyond the jurisdiction of local leaders, social policy decisions cannot be viewed as originating always at the African government level. The policy source may well be situated abroad. The extent of foreign policy influence becomes quickly apparent if a few production and trade data are reviewed.

The preponderance of one or two commodities among the exports of 19 African states illustrated in Table 2-1 tells part of the story of African independence.

The prospects of escape from dependency are further dimmed by the uneven distribution of prime resources among the new states. All too easily lost in the rhetoric of African unity are the sources of disunity. Conflicting interests and competition orient states differently in more critical respects at a time when in relatively unimportant matters government spokesmen may firmly proclaim devotion to what is declared to be the common cause.

A prime source of inequality is the accident of mineral deposits. These deposits, in turn, shape the economies, hence societies, in certain instances overwhelmingly so. In particular, the social importance of ore mining industries within certain economic systems is commonly underrated. In conditions favorable to the industry, the role of a single corporation can far exceed that of the dominant political party, and it may exceed or at least rival the power of the local government. Consequently, the mining industry's ties within the international web of commerce, finance, and industry, the relative position of a particular mineral in the overall worldwide production and marketing system, a mineral's vulner-

TABLE 2.1. *Percent commodity share in country total export by value**

Country	Product	Percent	Year (other than 1965)
Algeria	Petroleum (oil)	51.1	
Burundi	Coffee	73.9	
CAR†	Diamonds	53.8	
Congo (B)‡	Diamonds	42.7	30.1% (1968) registered
	Wood	38.9	50.1% (1968) exports
Ethiopia	Coffee	66.5	
Ghana	Cocoa	61.0	(1970)
Guinea	Bauxite	45.7	(1964)
Ivory Coast	Coffee	37.8	
Kenya	Coffee	22.3	(1970)
	Tea	12.7	(1970)
Liberia	Iron ore	72.5	(1964)
Libya	Petroleum (oil)	99.4	
Malagasy	Coffee	31.5	
Mauritania	Iron ore	95.1	
Nigeria	Petroleum (oil)	57.1	(1970)
	Cocoa	15.0	(1970)
Rwanda	Coffee	50.5	
Senegal	Peanuts	37.3	
	Wood	27.0	
Sierra Leone	Diamonds	60.0	(1970)
Sudan	Cotton	46.5	
UAR§	Cotton	44.5	
Uganda	Coffee	59.0	(1970)
Zaire	Copper	60.0	(1968)
Zambia	Copper	97.0	(1970)

*Given currency fluctuations and other variables, these figures are, of course, approximations.
†Central African Republic.
‡Congo (Brazzaville).
§United Arab Republic as of 1965

SOURCES: E/CN.14/401, table 15, 150-51 and table 4, 79. *Standard Bank Reviews,* 1970-1972. *Area Handbooks.* International Monetary Fund. *Surveys.*

ability to competition from substitutes, quality, cost, and availability of skilled labor and proficient supervisory personnel — all shape the relationship between one individual state and the outside world. Mining interests in Zambia, the former Belgian Congo, Gabon, and Botswana, at varying times and to varying degrees are known to have operated outside the sphere of public control, in effect constituting rival governments.

One of the most important aspects of the relationship of mining to the power and influence structure within individual states is that until recently mineral development in Africa took place in response to world demand and not as a result of the industrialization of African countries. The bulk of the output was exported, and only an insignificant portion was used internally. Rising output, therefore, had no appreciable effect on the several host economies and did not measurably raise the African standard of living. Typically, mining industries formed foreign enclaves interested primarily in increasing output to further the interests of mineral processors overseas. As a result, the African countries within which the deposits are located did not receive the benefit of valued added by processing. It is only very recently that oil refineries have been established on African soil.

Changes in the mining sector can therefore have profound impact. The effect of redirection of mining output from external to internal application could be similar to the effect of a switch of output from a generator, directing the flow of electric power to serve internal rather than external appliances. Here, iron, tin, copper, and bauxite should have a more profound social impact than gold, which cannot be utilized in socially significant quantities in the surrounding economy. Cobalt also may just as well remain within an enclave. Critical in this respect are the secondary and tertiary effects of production — that is, the nature and economic value of industries services — and of other industrial, commercial, financial, and social ramifications of mining.

A source of special frustration and diplomatic ambivalence has been the unfortunate dependence that certain mining operations in the new states have on Western armament efforts. As is well known, even the price of cocoa was affected by the Korean war. In general, the level of agricultural as well as mining output in Africa has been, and to an extent still is, largely determined by the level of world industrial production. In Africa's case this means dependence primarily on the West. Whether one calls the condition neocolonialism or another name, the colonial roots of today's nominally independent economics run deep. The export-import pattern dramatically reflects that condition.

Kindleberger summarizes the situation as follows:

> [Moreover], investment and government expenditure are linked through some sort of accelerator model. In government expenditure there are two connections. Increased exports give rise to the demand for increased government expenditures to improve ports, transports, and marketing facilities associated with sales abroad. In addition, they bring in revenue through export taxes and, somewhat more slowly, through their general income-multiplier effect. Lacking a developed capital market, government must delay its expenditure — unless it is prepared to undertake purely inflationary finance through bank credit — until it has the funds in hand.

Kindleberger then notes the effect on government policy options of the high propensity to import, an inevitable consequence of an inability to produce consumer goods locally; monetary policy is further circumscribed.

Monetary expansion in many instances inevitably leads to increased consumer demands, hence increased imports, loss in foreign exchange reserves, and so on.

A key element in monetary policy is the provision for lean years when the one or two principal export crops fail to bring in anticipated revenue. All previous increases in income, usually the result of booms on the world market due to factors wholly or principally outside the control of the African government or economy, must be laid aside to cover import requirements later on, during a world recession, for instance. Kindleberger points out that this saving means "anti-cyclical measures of some considerable proportions."[11]

The caption of this particular section in Kindleberger's book is significant: "The Limit of Independent Monetary Policy." To cope with the cyclical developments that flow from world market conditions, governments attempt to maximize their options, thus improving the degree of independence, by several fiscal and monetary defense measures such as rationing of foreign exchange to assure critical imports and insistence on pay-as-you-go, living off the collection of exchange proceeds from exports. Still the degree of independence gained is more apparent than real. The kind of incentives as well as the administrative skills required to sustain such policies, be they voluntary or compulsory, simply are not yet part of the African experience.

The true center of gravity on the continent then must be located somewhere within the socioeconomic complex that includes the former colonial mother countries as well as their wards. Increasingly it encompasses the world of the centrally controlled economies in the East. The universe of time and space within which that center may be found extends over decades and over whatever geographic areas are economically relevant. This suggests that the international position of the new states has a reality of its own. That reality cannot be understood or appreciated if one component — for example, the economic — is conceptually or analytically detached from others. Of course, it will not be understood if subjected to economic analysis alone.

In the circumstances, attempts to draw distinctions between colonialism and neocolonialism may be misleading. There may be none of any consequence. The argument has been advanced that one differs from the other in that colonial governments used to intervene directly; they were the government overseas as well as at home. Now, under neocolonialism, they are said to govern indirectly. Such distinction falls away, however, if the relationship is viewed on a different plane. In the context of socioeconomic power and influence, distinctions between governmental and nongovernmental and between public and private domains tend to evaporate; at best they become socially inconsequential.

Some Analytical Implications

Political analysis has treated the new states as single or individualized systems. With an occasional bow to economics, a passing reference to the dual economy — the European-African juxtapositions — single system analysis has flowered unabated. But if money and wealth are substituted for vaguely conceived political power resources, a substantially different picture emerges.

To the degree that wealth in its diverse forms attracts, it is clear that in the European-African juxtaposition Europe disposes of more attractive power than does Africa. The same is true if the system is seen as divided between a modern and a traditional sector. If one visualizes three poles of attraction — foreign, African national, and African local — it should be obvious that groups and individuals will be attracted differently by the several poles with different results.

TRIPLE ECONOMY CONCEPT

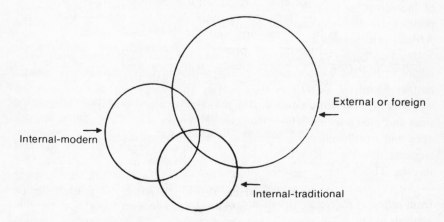

In the opinion of one experienced observer, "at its present stage of development, economic activity in African countries cannot be reduced significantly to a single system or complex."[12] Leaders in the new states — that is, the elite elements — may actually divide their attention between several systems, deriving benefits, hence power and influence, from all. They may derive strength from the internal-modern and the foreign sectors, seeking gains in both, hence favoring development of both, their value judgments being shaped by their personal investment interests and opportunities.

As soon as the realities of development economies have demonstrated the futility of nationally concentrated development, the focal points of the power struggle will shift to the modern sector exclusively. Then as the feebleness of the domestic sector impresses itself more dramatically, contenders for power may retreat to the foreign sector, leaving aside proforma local commitments and skirmishes. This cycle appears to have been the experience in Latin America.

Social analysis should benefit considerably from calculation of the consequences of production patterns in the developing countries. Once it is accepted that in the power and influence calculus the foreign economic sector may outweigh all others, an event such as a slowdown in the demand for African cotton, an increase in the foreign consumption of metals, a reduction in the demand for chocolate, or the development of a synthetic substitute for sisal would deserve, among factors on which social analysis should be based, a priority higher than it has received so far.

Foreign investment, it is more and more realized, exercises its own influence and shapes social institutions far more decisively than nationalist rhetoric would indicate. Prominent in any socially meaningful analysis should be the mere fact that foreign capital or non-African owned domestic capital may in the final analysis constitute the life blood that courses through both the modern and the traditional sector.

A resounding testimony on premature generalizations about development, modernization, independence, nation-building, and the like is offered in the following projection of trade balances in Africa.

> By 1975, the sub-region will still be importing large quantities of consumer goods — particularly food — and capital goods. The trade deficit is considerably larger in 1975 than in 1963, and this is a natural consequence of rapid development based largely on imported equipment and the fact that investment is always made a few years before output compensates for the foreign exchange loss. In fact, only when the economic development slows substantially, will the trade deficit disappear. This trade deficit also reflects the fact that agricultural output is seldom susceptible to such accelerated growth plans as industry because of the reluctance of farmers to change farm technique.[13]

Given the importance of foreign exchange in the economies, hence social systems and subsystems of the developing societies, the trade deficit phenomenon, evidently an inescapable impediment for years to come — perhaps a permanent one for some of the states — will generate a degree of dependence on outside capital that will overshadow by far any other causal factors of social and human behavior. To undervalue, or even ignore, these considerations is to attempt to solve a mathematical problem without considering all of the components: $3 \times 3 + (2 \times 5)$ cannot be solved by looking only at the first half of the mathematical sentence. A partial analysis would be even more disastrously wrong if it turns out that 2 × 5, in the special circumstances prevailing, really should be written as 2 × − 5.

The full extent of the feebleness of African economies is brought out in an assessment of the value to these economies of certain remedies designed by international agencies — for example, the "special drawing rights" allocated to them on the International Monetary Fund (drawing rights designed mainly to help overcome the consequences of unfavorable balance of trade and foreign exchange losses). The Economic Commission for Africa noted that a deterioration in the terms of trade of less than 1 percent would wipe out the increase in the African countries' reserves arising from these drawing rights.[14]

The generalization seems to be warranted that it is not possible to conduct an anatomy of the power and influence systems on the developing states without careful assessment of the ties between the several economic sectors, without adequate assessment of the feebleness of the African sectors, without full regard to the international distribution of control points. The image of the lunar profile produced by the computer, referred to above, may still be a more helpful guide to conceptualization of African independence than any scheme or profile produced by social scientists so far.

3

Political-Economic Profiles

At first glance the political map of Africa of 1972 (figure 3.1), indicates the existence of 41 independent states and several territories still under colonial domination. Actually, as noted in the preceding chapters, the best one can say is that there are degrees of independence. Likewise, the internal structure of the new states is not necessarily what it seems. The combined effect of continued dependence on foreign power and internal imbalances, stresses, and strains produces socio or political-economic profiles that differ substantially from those of the developed nation-states we know.

Considered in terms of economic dependency or orientation, the critical factors in our scheme of analysis, one can identify these major clusters: 18 of the nominally independent states, again as of 1972, were still essentially part of the French or franc sphere of influence, although to varying degrees; 14 were developing degrees of independence within the British sphere, or the sterling bloc; the rest, leaving aside territories not yet independent, were either positioned somewhere between East and West, as Algeria and Libya, or were captives of the Republic of South Africa or, like Zaire (the former Belgian Congo), were veering toward the United States. The emergence of a stronger European Economic Community, potentially encompassing virtually all of Western Europe, including Great Britain, injected an additional factor but only gradually.

Considering the broad implications of the international relationships just discussed, and concentrating in particular on the political-economic consequences of these relationships within the two largest blocs — the French and British influenced groupings — this chapter examines in greater detail the more prominent political-economic features of Senegal and the Ivory Coast, both part of the French associated group, Ghana and Nigeria, the two strongest states in former British West Africa, and

Zambia, and Kenya, the strongest and potentially most viable black-ruled states in what once were British East and Central Africa, respectively.

French-Influenced

Relying momentarily on a form of quantification, one might express the essence of French hegemony over most of French-speaking Africa during

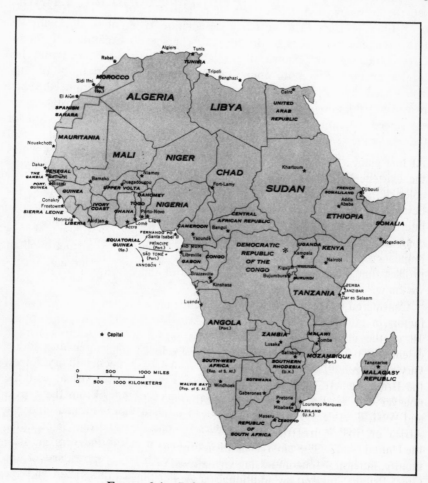

FIGURE 3.1 *Political Divisions of Africa*

*Zaire

NOTE: Boundary Representation is not necessarily authoritative
NOTE: Most illustrations in this book are drawn from Senegal, The Ivory Coast, Ghana, Nigeria, Zambia, and Kenya.
SOURCE: U.S. Department of the Army, *A Bibliographic Survey, Africa: Problems and Prospects,* DA • PAM 550-5, Appendix F, 189.

the independence period and immediately thereafter by the following formula (as of August 10, 1969).

$$1 \text{ CFA} = 1/50\text{th of 1 French } franc \text{ or}$$
$$1 \text{ U.S. } \$ = \text{CFA } 277.710 = \text{French } franc \text{ 4.937}[1]$$

This formula translates as follows: The Central Bank of France as of 1969 stood ready in transactions with banks throughout the zone to buy and sell the currency used in the zone at a fixed rate of 1 CFA for 1/50th of 1 French franc. (The currency designation CFA originates with the term Colonies Francaises d'Afrique later changed to Communauté Finan- cière Africaine.) Of course, the relationship between France and her former territories is more complicated. Still, the convertability of cur- rency used locally, and actually worth far less than its guaranteed value, provides a floor for currency that would otherwise in many instances be suspended precariously over a bottomless pit, mainly because few of these countries produce enough goods and services to generate local backing for their currencies. The arrangement ties most of the new states in the zone securely to the financial apronstrings of the treasury in Paris.

To be sure, new perspectives are forming in French decision- and policy-making circles. To an extent, these perspectives reflect the arrival on the scene — in some instances by invitation from hard-pressed French bankers — of well-financed competitors, including United States banks and corporations already deeply involved in the economy of metropolitan France. In part they reflect enlightenment in financial circles and recog- nition that benefits sought formerly by force can now be secured more cheaply by more sophisticated means.

SENEGAL

The history of Senegal is shaped by three major developments: severe repression accompanying conquest of the area by French military forces, emergence of Dakar as a hub for all of French West Africa, and the collapse of that system during the independence decade. From the arrival of French military columns in the area to modern times, French influence has made itself felt primarily in a narrow coastal strip from Saint Louis to Dakar. The remainder of what became known as the independent state of Senegal has unchangingly been little more than an appendage of the central control point, power politically a dependency of Dakar and the French forces that support the capital.

From that point on, Senegal is more usefully pictured as consisting of an enormously oversized head, a dwarfed body, and an extended umbilical cord sprouting from the top of the head and terminating at the treasury in Paris. An experienced diplomat, answering a question about run-of- the-mill social science literature on such topics as the one-party state in Senegal, offered this comment:

   If the entire Senegalese system were to collapse tomorrow, the majority of
the people would not notice it. The concept of Senegal does not mean
anything to them: is has no substance. To view the country, the party,
the social system, the traditional way of life as one unit each, or together,
is to consider significantly separate and distinct, and unequal entities as
equal and united, if not uniform. But to consider them even approximately
equal in social and economic respects would be a grave mistake.[2]

Aside from the special position occupied by Dakar and consequences
flowing from that, Senegal's profile is characterized by three additional
factors: (1) extreme dependence on one crop, the peanut; (2) consequent
dependence on outside assistance; (3) need for military stabilization, which
for the first decade of independence was furnished by French armed
forces based on either Senegalese soil or ready to intervene from nearby
bases in southern France.

In so many ways Senegal's profile in its general outline is typical of
that of most other underdeveloped countries: for years to come, whoever
rules Senegal is compelled to come to terms with the main commodity,
the peanut. To attempt to ignore the economic and social demands flowing
from its production, collection, and distribution and sale is to invite
economic, hence political, disaster. That condition allows little elbow
room for imaginative government; the continuous downward trend of world
prices for agricultural commodities, of course, does not help.

Dependence on the peanut brings in its wake predictable imbalances in
the distribution of wealth. Typically, even though the greatest share of
the country's wealth is derived from peanut production, the sector that
dominates Gross Domestic Production computation is commerce, and
that, again predictably, is mainly in foreign hands. The resultant spatial
pattern of income distribution strongly suggests that caution is indicated
before one speaks of cohesive and integrated national systems in Africa.
In this case, nearly half of the territory is occupied by a little less than
10 percent of the population with a density of slightly below 5 square
kilometers.[3] The prevailing distribution of political power resources mili-
tates in favor of Dakar, the national capital, and against the vast hinterland. Low per capita income in the rural sector is further compounded
by higher retail prices — driven up by distance from port facilities — and
by a lower per capita share of school population, physicians, hospital
beds, students enrolled, inadequate means of communication, and rickety
transportation.[4] By any meaningful measure of power potential, about nine-
tenths of Senegal's population must be regarded as too feeble to play an
active role in national policy matters.

The critical gravitational mass in the power field is located, as noted,
in Dakar, and aside from the numerically small foreign elite and its
indigenous partners consists of a typically inflated administrative class.
Because of its size, its high geographic concentration, and the resources

it consumes coupled with an exceedingly low economic productivity, the power political impact of this class overshadows by far such traditional contenders for leadership as the political party, the trade union, or the ideological movement.

In a manner of speaking, the oversized cranium — the coastal Dakar-based complex — functions as a parasite growth, draining the already depleted and dwarfed body of whatever sustenance it may produce. National development plans, brave new worlds of African national renais-

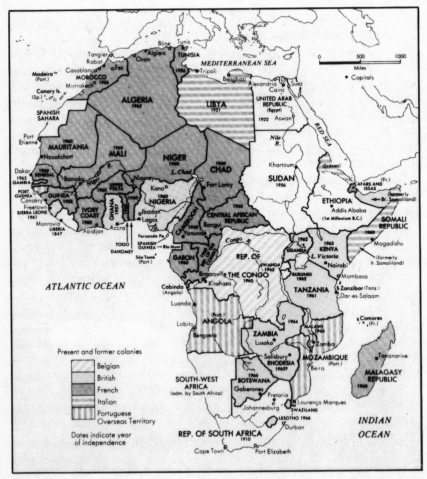

FIGURE 3.2.   *Africa: Foreign Sovereignty and Dates of Independence.*

SOURCE: Gann and Duignan, *Africa and the World*, xvi. Copyright© 1972 by Chandler Publishing Company.

sance, schemes to achieve equalization of wealth or to drive out the foreigners vanish in the quicksands of Senegal's voracious *salariat*.[5] As one observer put it, the Senegalese budget more and more becomes an "état des soldes," or a statement of pay.[6] Of course, the French presence could be terminated in a moment of blind passion, but such a drastic step would solve not one of Senegal's fundamental problems.

IVORY COAST

What we have noted about Senegal applies in many respects also to the Ivory Coast; more or less it applies to all of French-influenced Africa. What appears as a uniformly colored area on the political map — or is described in the literary universe as one cohesive national system — if subjected to close analysis emerges as something quite different. Significant internal distinctions become noticeable, and most if not all generalizations demand reconsideration. As in Senegal, an expansive, flexible, but extended umbilical cord links an oversized cranium to the source of what we might call auxiliary or supportive wealth, namely France.

There are, of course, differences, some worth special attention. The position of the head, Abidjan, relative to the rest of the country is earned and not, as is Dakar's, a reflection of past glories or of pressure emanating from an unproductive but demanding sector. This is in part a reflection of a somewhat different mode of production. Cocoa and coffee and a comparatively more diversified economy call for different forms of finance and different investment and production patterns and consequently create different patterns of income distribution.

As in Senegal, understandable fascination with nation-oriented concepts must not be allowed to obscure the equally if not more important international aspects of Ivorienne existence.

A realistic assessment of the Ivory Coast's position in the wider European-African context requires appreciation of at least four major problem areas: (1) the involvement and participation of French metropolitan groups in the local economy, especially in cocoa, coffee, palm oil, and peanut production coupled with extensive two-way transactions that link France to the Ivory Coast in one financial network; (2) the role of French nationals and groups stationed in the Ivory Coast; (3) the predominant position of Abidjan in the Ivory Coast; and (4) the dominant position of the Ivory Coast in relation to neighboring former French colonies such as Upper Volta and Niger.

As military power grows out of the barrel of a gun, socioeconomic power in the Ivory Coast grows out of cocoa and coffee plantations, shipping and transport enterprises, some manufacturing and processing, and, of course, investment and banking. As an economic organism — as distinct from the political one — the Ivory Coast is rooted in banking and commercial circles in Lyons, Marsailles, and Paris and in the administra-

tive arrangements made by France to endow the arrangement with an air
of legitimacy.

British-Influenced

In comparative studies of the French and British spheres, much is made
of such matters as quantitative and qualitative differences in education,
where French-speaking Africans are given the edge. Though important in
some respects, it is doubtful whether these and other derivative or secondary cultural differences and distinctions convert to significant advantage
for black subjects in either area. Far more important probably are distribution of wealth among the major races, black and white, of economic
opportunities, and of prime levers of subsistence control.

A point frequently raised relates to the number of non-African, mainly
European, hands through which French- or British-controlled financial resources will flow before they become available to black hands in one form
or another. Both systems feature white settlers, traders, plantation owners,
managers, bankers, industrialists, and technicians. The argument runs that
the relatively more pervasive, if not ubiquitous, French presence throughout French-speaking Africa generates social consequences of major import.
This is doubtful. It is likely that the proximity of large numbers of French-
men, even in remote areas, considerably raises the level of skill and efficiency as against comparably located sections in British Africa. Black
cocoa producers in the Ivory Coast, for example, may enjoy an advantage
over their next-door competitors in Ghana, who must operate in comparative isolation from their principal sources of capital and ultimate customers.

But strongest in the councils that matter are those whose hands hold the
reins on currency value, export-import, and foreign exchange. Increasingly
Africans knowledgeable in such matters shift their attention to these
strategic points in state and society. Increasingly they discover that cultural
assimilation or not, and regardless of the number of foreigners their
countries may harbor, the commanding heights in the life-controlling and
supporting economic system are occupied by outsiders, in crucial respects
in about the same proportion in both French and British systems.

The British pound sterling has dominated public and private life within its immediate range of effectiveness as thoroughly as has the French
franc. In the French sphere the governing principle associated all satellitic,
or dependent, economies with the treasury in Paris, while the British
variant allowed degrees of budgetary autonomy, but within limits. In both
areas basic pacesetting economic activities, strategic control points, the
principal arteries of commerce and industry — the economic jugular veins,
so to speak — were securely within the grasp of foreign financial control
centers. The value of money itself was foreign controlled.

In both systems the economic fruits of African production were funneled through European-controlled marketing and distribution facilities,

resulting in a net loss of capital resources that could and should have been applied to development locally. As one comment puts it, when demanding control over the proceeds from the sale of their resources, the new African states were made to feel that they were like children demanding access to their savings. Actually, both systems practiced a form of diversion of African resources to support development abroad, usually in their own back yards. Again, for illustrative purposes we examine a few representative political-economic profiles.

GHANA

The image of one cohesive, sovereign, and absolutely independent Ghana also requires modification if tested against socioeconomic reality. This argument may be difficult to accept at first glance. Under the forceful leadership of Nkrumah in the fifties and sixties, Ghana came to be synonymous with vigorous self-assertion and increasing national potency. Unlike Senegal, Ivory Coast, and most of the other satellitic states on the continent, Ghana *appeared* to have developed the capability of warding off further inroads by predatory foreign interests. Yet the inventory of Ghana's ailing economy, taken after Nkrumah's fall in 1966, rather dramatically illuminated the wide gap between independence rhetoric and degree of self-determination actually enjoyed. It emerged that Ghana had in fact not succeeded in removing the parasitic growth that also afflicts her neighbors.

Ghana's actual freedom of economic movement is determined largely by the amounts of foreign exchange available for disposal by the government. Unlike those of her French-supported neighbors, Ghana's foreign exchange requirements will not be met automatically by inflows from overseas reservoirs. Furthermore, overdependence on a crop subject to wide price fluctuations and other unpredictables makes it most difficult to forecast the financial resources likely to be available when the next budget becomes due. This condition, described as a form of dependence on external movements of prices and incomes (the incomes are those of the potential consumers of cocoa abroad), was severely exacerbated when under Nkrumah the economy was allowed to become critically indebted. Eventually portions of the external debt were repudiated with predictable internal repercussions such as at least one additional coup, but the core problem remained. Ghana did not shake off the impediment of seasonal fluctuations, nor did it learn to cope with the machinations of unscrupulous foreigners ready to exploit desperate situations.

In Ghana freedom is escape from dependence on cocoa. Any form of government or ideological orientation or any formula for social and economic reform must relate to cocoa if it is to be relevant and if it is to succeed. Over the decades, especially since nominal independence in 1957, this golden goose has been plucked to the point of ruination. Excessive taxes, levies, withholdings, and other burdens, though providing governments with revenue, demoralized the farmers. On several occasions the deteriorating situation surrounding cocoa spawned severe political crises. Support can be found for the thesis that cocoa first brought Nkrumah to power and then caused his downfall.[7]

One-third of Ghana's Gross National Product derives from agriculture. Cocoa dominates that sector, accounting for about 55 percent of total exports by value and supporting one-third of the population in one way or another. The cyclical movements accompanying the production of cocoa cause annual shock waves that reverberate through all sectors. Fluctuations of the world market price can affect earnings so drastically as to unbalance not only current budgets but also development plans for years to come.

Financial transactions related to cocoa govern the behavior of individuals and groups. As the money supply of banks contracts — to finance purchase of the cocoa crop — pressure on scarce foreign exchange resources increases to sustain non-cocoa-related investment needs. Soon after cash reaches the hands of cocoa farmers, business activity accelerates throughout the country. Then cash balances in banks soon increase once again.

We speak of the power of governments but do not adequately investigate what resources that power is based on. Under severe pressure caused by a very ambitious program of economic diversification and expansion, the Nkrumah regime created its own independent sources by making use of its power to borrow money. This use of power interposes yet another barrier between government and people, for in the real world few people understand, let alone are in a position to interfere in matters of high finance. In practice a zone of indifference is created between the government and the people it is supposed to represent, thereby adding a special reservoir of power hidden from public view. In Ghana during the 1966-67 fiscal year, internal borrowing accounted for more than half of all government receipts.[8]

In economically weak countries one of the most pernicious and debilitating social forces arising from indiscriminate and excessive borrowing — excessive in terms of the country's ability to support this activity over an extended period of time through productivity, for instance — is the accumulated public debt. Reminiscent of the sorcerer's apprentice, it demands to be served, year after year, decade after decade lest the credit standing of the entire economy be brought into total disrepute. Since the 1960s this force has had a strangling effect on the material potential of Ghana to cope with pressing social and economic problems.

All the time, and regardless of the steps taken to ameliorate the situation, the inexorable pressures emanating from increased expenditures in the as-yet unproductive non-agricultural sectors of society create or exacerbate what has been called the scissors effect. Mounting government spending on public services, on patronage, on experimental development of pioneering industries, and so on, creates a corresponding increase in pressure to import consumer goods as yet not produced locally in sufficient quantities. To conserve scarce foreign exchange reserves, government moves to curb imports, which in turn drives up prices, while the import restrictions reduce supplies of critical materials and create other dislocations and stoppages, with an inevitable rise in unemployment. To be sure, in theory all this can be avoided or at least kept within bounds. In practice it cannot for reasons we shall consider throughout this book.

Ghanaian social and political behavior also may be explained to a considerable extent by the mode of production of cocoa. Unlike the peanut, cocoa does not require a climatic condition that dictates cultivation through a narrow window in time. Although up to 3 years may be required for the cocoa tree to blossom, up to ten years may be required for it to bear fruit. From that point, however, and barring disease (several kinds constantly threaten the crop), a tree may produce wealth for its owner for up to 25 years.[9]

Cocoa should not be allowed to altogether obscure gold as a major source of influence. Ghana is the world's sixth largest producer of that precious commodity. Unlike the at-times wildly fluctuating agricultural commodities, gold enjoys relative price and production stability. In a tight foreign exchange situation those who are at the helm in that sector can generate considerably more potential for themselves than can the aggregate group of cocoa producers. This advantage appears to have been so toward the end of Nkrumah's rule. The position of gold in the interest and influence context differs from that of cocoa for yet another fundamental reason. Once the mining concessions have been awarded, the African side is effectively eliminated from production control.

Until the new economic policies of the 1960s, income distribution in Ghana had not been much unlike that in neighboring Ivory Coast. Principal sources of wealth had been controlled mainly by expatriate interests. Indigenous groups participated in the distribution of benefits from commerce and finance only to a limited, rather modest extent. With relatively minor differences in land use and other social conditions affecting production and use of wealth, the Ghanaian cocoa farmer and owner occupied a position very similar to that enjoyed by his counterpart in the Ivory Coast in relation to other income strata. He was important, but mainly as a milk cow.

The significance of this position was diminished somewhat when under the Nkrumah regime different emphases were placed on the social uses of that wealth — for example, a shift in development emphasis from the cocoa region to the coastal sector and from consumer satisfaction, where cocoa farmers would have had more influence, to industrialization. Indicative of that change was what has been referred to as the "strong nodal attraction of the Accra-Tema region" (a port-industrial complex), which resulted in part from the creation of the Volta River Project and in part from the plan to develop an alternate modern port for Ghana.[10] Even so, the substantive earning capacity of the cocoa growers remained unchanged, being covered only temporarily by the blanket of Nkrumah's development program. The cocoa trees remained where they were, and productivity continued essentially unimpeded by ideological designs.

As in all other African states, the socioeconomic profile reveals pronounced regional disparities in income, which progressively widen with the distance from the capital and socioeconomic hub. Within the urban region, especially Accra, the income disparity between public servants and the rest of the population is not so wide as in Dakar. Unlike the relationship in Abidjan, Africans as a group do not visibly suffer income disparities as compared to Europeans.

NIGERIA

In spite of the size of her population — estimated as above 60 million — and in spite of the federal structure, it can be argued that Nigeria's political-economic profile does not differ significantly from that of her smaller neighbors in fundamental respects. For some time to come the overwhelming majority of the population will be unable to attain levels of education and social organization needed to participate significantly in the distribution of sources of power. The federal structure facilitated accommodation to the point that the interests of the ruling elements in the major divisions contended for control of the country as a whole. On the surface, for public consumption, that accommodation appeared to be achieved between independence and the 1966 coup via the parliamentary system centered on Lagos, the coastal capital of the Federation. Actually, the attempt failed to accommodate the vital interests of the rulers, the socioeconomic control groups in the relatively underdeveloped hinterland, and the groups that controlled the strategic height of the economy at the federal center. The idea of a fair and equitable distribution of power among the Northern, Western, Middle, and Eastern Regions collided with the necessities of international trade and finance and economic development. The constitutional federal grid did not match the socioeconomic power and influence grid.[11]

The much discussed confrontations within and among Northern, Western, and Eastern tribal units may be described more accurately as confrontations of pressure and interest groups known the world over. Clearly present are aspects of class warfare. Examination of key documents on tribal or ethnic conflicts reveals economic survival fears as the core problem. Even those cannot necessarily be classified along tribal lines. Analysis in depth shows that within these so-called tribal groups classic divisions of economic interest suggest yet different groupings and confrontations.[12]

It is said that Nigeria differs from other African economies in degree of diversification, market potential, and an inherently sounder foreign exchange base. Superficially viewed, this cannot be denied. There is room for doubt, however, whether these characteristics are substantive enough and permanent enough to translate into power potential internationally or only for the benefit of key producing or consuming areas internally. It is by no means clear whether these structural characteristics are indeed as perceived. There are as yet no reliable indicators to show that one solid market actually awaits the manufacturer or that economic conditions are substantially the same throughout the country. It has been noted that export and import tend to play a more decisive role in small nations than in large ones. But what if profitable economic activities in the large nation are confined to a small zone, probably near the coast or principal port facility? What if interior transportation and other infrastructural facilities are inadequate a few hundred or even less miles from the principal port? In such conditions the large unit breaks down into several smaller socioeconomic ones: the principal and dominant one where the bulk of modern economic activity takes place, or at least where it is centered, and the others in the interior where weaker versions of the central economy are interspersed with traditional economies. In these circumstances export and import still may dominate the scene very much as in the smaller countries.

Externally Nigeria will not be able to capitalize on size of population until interior means of transportation are more fully developed. There is reason to believe that with respect to economic strength the large African nation is the equal of smaller ones as long as it cannot match the smaller nation's advantage of lower transportation cost, the result of shorter distances between agricultural production and collection points and the ports.[13]

Economic diversity affects internal distribution of power only if control over the several segments of the economy also is diversified. However, many of Nigeria's production sectors, aside from groundnuts and palm oil products, may be too feeble to generate interest group pressure or even competitive bases of power.

Like Ghana, Nigeria benefited initially from the colonial policy of accumulation of marketing board surpluses. As in Ghana, the cornucopia dried up soon after independence, even though Nigeria was not subjected to the exhausting spending policies characteristic of Nkrumaist Ghana. As everywhere else on the continent, power gravitated toward the poles of export and import, dependence on world market prices became accentuated, and the search for alternate sources of internal revenue was redoubled, with predictable consequences for the distribution of wealth and sources of production of wealth. Truly critical and therefore inevitably expensive components of development plans had to be laid aside. Soon, and notwithstanding the elaborate federal structure, Nigeria's socioeconomic profile began to suggest a ballooning policy center in and around Lagos to which was attached a shrinking body that comprised the vast geographic expanse of the rest of the country. Theses on modernization, socialization, or generally on all mass-phenomena must reflect the existing and pronounced inequities, disparities, and imbalances if they are to be taken seriously. For some time to come Nigeria viewed as a whole will continue to hover on the threshold of modernization. A decade after independence the truly modern sector was very small indeed and concentrated within a few square miles.

The form that future federations may take has only limited significance. The administrative reorganization, begun in May 1966 following the collapse of the independence federation, produced 12 states in place of the former 4 regions. This was little more than a paper exercise. Unless an economic deus ex machina materialized it, too, would collapse, or at best atrophy slowly. Several of the new creations simply lacked the means of contending successfully for a proportionate share of the nation's wealth to augment their own inadequate resources. (The old federation collapsed mainly because no generally acceptable way was found to divide the unequally distributed resources equitably among the major contenders for power.)

It is possible, though not probable, that the deus ex machina has already sprung from the oil wells in the Southern Region. The prospects of an oil-based economy certainly encouraged leaders in the former Eastern Region to attempt secession, which led to the civil war between 1967 and 1970. (This even though most of the oil-bearing sections were situated outside the Ibo region.)

If continued at the rate achieved by 1970, oil output promised to yield an annual net foreign exchange inflow of over 75 million, about 3 times the value of the foreign exchange inflow before the beginning of the civil war — a substantial change indeed. The prediction at that point was a 2 million barrels per day output by 1975, which would place Nigeria among the 10 major oil producers in the world.[14] Unlike the rhetoric of ideology, this development contained truly revolutionary potential.

Oil revenue is produced in a relatively narrow strip along and off the coast. Most likely it will therefore be distributed principally, if not exclusively, through federal or central government channels. This should further strengthen Lagos, the civil service control group there, and whatever civilian regime emerges eventually. If military controls prevail, the pattern will, of course, strengthen the armed forces. Ramifications surrounding production, distribution, and sale of this particular resource inevitably alter the relationship between national and foreign interests as it has done elsewhere in the world.

In some respects Nigeria may begin to resemble Zambia more than Ghana, because its revenue base will shift toward extractive industry. Assumed they are so inclined, federal policymakers could apply the new resource in their hands — that is, the revenue portion of the new value —

to pursuit of national development goals regardless of local preferences. If they are so inclined. The same deus, however, could also exacerbate existing weaknesses, widen and magnify corruption because larger sums of money will be concentrated in fewer hands, and introduce new sources of tension because the stakes will be higher. In any case, before the infusion of oil into the national subeconomies will make a material difference a great deal of modernization will have to take place.

The sharp imbalances that characterize Nigeria's social profile in education, literacy, social values and ethics, and resources of necessity will convert oil-based revenue differently from section to section. Wide variations in population density and quality of infrastructure and vulnerability to rains and floods, disruptions from other causes, and disease and even starvation will continue to shape patterns of influence and social potential in general. Investors will continue to concentrate their resources near ports, near centers of administration, and generally near the principal sinews of commerce, industry, and transportation.

Barring truly radical developments, the position of the foreign sector within the Nigerian economy and the potential of outside interests as influences on internal policy decisions will remain formidable for some time to come. In the words of one of Nigeria's leading economists, "there appears to be little doubt that both the choice of policy techniques (in the realm of development) and the effectiveness of their execution are still constrained by the powerful influence the foreign sector exerts on the national economy, out of proportion to its simple statistical magnitude."[15] It remains to be seen whether the policy of Africanization of foreign-owned private enterprise — energetically pursued by the military government as soon as oil revenue began to provide a cushion for that potentially costly operation — will tip the balance in that respect.

ZAMBIA

Somewhat like Senegal, Zambia's basic problems stem from an act of separation depriving the newly independent unit of vital trade and supply routes, outlets, sources of critical materials, and ready access to investment capital. There the similarity ends. Unlike Senegal, Zambia is landlocked, disposes of one of the world's richest copper deposits (third largest producer in the world), and soon after independence embarked on a state of undeclared warfare against her original parent, Southern Rhodesia. Moreover, half of Zambia's border abuts European-dominated territories.

Like Northern Rhodesia, Zambia was an integral, in fact subordinate, component of the former Federation of Rhodesia and Nyasaland. Under British tutelage and control, the northern area was designated as the principal supplier of raw material — copper — while Nyasaland (now Malawi) was assigned the role of principal supplier of labor. Southern Rhodesia, of course, was the center of control and principal economic beneficiary of the arrangement. Located in the southern portion were the key financial, administrative, technical, and physical — military control — terminals. Southern Rhodesia controlled export and import from and to the northern region and the principal sources of fuel and power without which the copper mines could not operate. Most of the secondary industries that produced some of the manufactured goods required by the population in and around the copper-bearing areas were located in the south as were sources of supply of capital goods. Of all levers in the hands of the European control group in the south, the one enabling them to choke off transport to and from the north appeared to be the most formidable when independence was granted to that region under the name of Zambia. In short, the new black rulers presided over an economy in foreign hands, not unlike their counterparts to the north in the Congo, (now Zaire) when that huge colony was cut adrift by Belgium in 1960. They were little more than puppets and were painfully aware of it.[16] They knew that for decades to come they would be haunted by the material consequences of the arrangements made by the British-Southern Rhodesian architects of their new status.

In violation of the old constitution, the lion's share of the federation's revenue had been used ingeniously to serve mainly the advancement of European interests in the south, leaving the black majorities elsewhere far behind educationally, technically, and economically. Even non-African agriculture, mainly white, was subtly advanced at the expense of African agriculture. Tariff policies had been designed to attract more capital and skills to the already industrialized sections, further accentuating the northern region's dependence on copper mining and export. The carefully engineered educational deficiencies had left the new state virtually stripped of critical administrative and technical skills. The freedom of the new state to develop as its leaders saw fit was further circumscribed by inherited arrangements that accorded to foreign-owned corporations proprietary rights and privileges over lands and resources, in some instances in perpetuity. Confidence in the effectiveness of the control system in 1964 persuaded the European rulers of Southern Rhodesia to unilaterally declare themselves independent from Great Britain, setting off severe repercussions for Zambia and beyond.

"It is a peculiar economy, the economy of Zambia." With these words the Seers Report — for years a definitive document — introduces the subject of copper, noting that in 1961 copper accounted for over half the total value of all goods and services produced in the country and sold for cash. By 1970 this ratio was reduced somewhat, but not by much. Copper revenues still provided nearly two-thirds of all government income and more than 90 percent of all export earnings.

This peculiar position of one mineral spawned a foreign-dominated enclave, an economy within an economy. In 1961 profits and royalties after taxes accounted for one-third of all values of exports. Because most of the capital employed in the industry was held abroad, most of the value from export flowed out of Zambia in the form of remittances, debt services, and interest. An additional drain on capital resources was caused by a sizeable bill for imports, including electricity, which was generated at the Southern Rhodesia-controlled Kariba Dam. Even the high salaries paid to the Europeans, without whose active and direct participation copper could not have been mined at the time, eventually accrued to economies other than Zambia, for the earnings were remitted abroad either at once or later on retirement.[17]

Zambia is not unique in its imbalance between urban and rural sectors. It is unique in the heavy concentration of economic activity and related social and economic infrastructure along the line of rail. In addition to serving the mining and manufacturing industries, that line also has attracted most other modern economic activities; it has become a core area very much like the coastal strips of the West African countries or the highlands of Kenya. (The line of rail runs from Mufulira in the north, near the border with Zaire, to Livingstone in the south, near the Victoria Falls and the Zambia-Rhodesia border. In the 1970s another line will link Kapiri Mposhi and Dar es Salaam in Tanzania.)

Another cleavage exists within the rural sector itself. Highly capitalized and efficient, hence highly productive, agriculture is carried on by approximately 700 European farmers concentrated in a very limited area. The mass of the rural population numbers about 450,000 families and is spread over the rest of Zambia with levels of production not even remotely comparable.

TABLE 3.1. *Value of agricultural sales in million £.*

1964	European Farmers	African Farmers
Total value of sales	7.7	3.2
Tobacco	3.0	0.2
Maize	2.5	1.0
Cattle	0.8	0.8
Other crops and livestock	1.4	1.2
Acreage	182,000	(app.) 5,000,000

SOURCE: Central Statistical Office, published in Zambia, *First National Development Plan 1966-70,* 2, table 1.

The ethnic composition of the country is fairly balanced; no one tribe dominates.[18]

The lower portion of the social pyramid is, as everywhere else on the continent, black; in the middle are the Asians, mainly Indians, and at the top the Europeans. The Asians and Europeans were represented most heavily in the mining, commercial, and service sectors.[19] Zambia differs from the previously discussed countries in yet another respect. Over 25 percent of her population is in urban areas.[20]

To escape dependence on Rhodesia and on the sources beyond that regime, several alternate routes of access and egress were considered. New oil supply lines, routes of evacuation of copper, and alternate internal sources of coal supply were developed in part with the assistance of foreign governments and in part with foreign private capital. Some of these measures initially were quite costly to Zambia and imposed severe hardships on large portions of the population. (Zambian coal deposits had been neglected during the colonial period, while the Wankie collieries in Southern Rhodesia were developed as the principal source of fuel for copper mines and smelters in what is now Zambia.)

National income patterns, Gross National Production, and revenue data reveal the high degree of imbalance and dependence on the mineral industries. For instance, recurrent revenue as projected into the sixties offers the profile in Table 3-2.

TABLE 3-2. *In million £*

Income tax	
Copper companies	131.4
Personal and other comp.	58.8
Customs and excise	65.9
Mineral royalties and export tax	193.9
Other	74.8
Total	524.8

SOURCE: *First National Development Plan*, 14, table 5.

The bane of African rulers and development planners — the at-times wildly fluctuating world market price of their principal export commodity — plagues Zambia as well. (In 1965 the price of cash wire bars had closed at 567 per ton, then rose to 700 per ton in March 1966, to 787 in April, and then dropped catastrophically to 430 in December of the same year.[21]) It is quite clear that this factor will haunt Zambia for some time to come. National pressures to reduce dependence on outside forces will mount, but so will internal pressures demanding redress of economic imbalances and costly improvements of living standards. The viability of the total economy will be subjected to severe strains and stresses as governments attempt to reconcile what at first glance may appear to be irreconcilables, for reduction of the satellitic status inevitably weakens African economies before internal sources of strength can be developed and profitably so.

The seminal position of the copper industry in Zambia's economy endows the labor force with greater potential than is characteristic for labor in most other parts of the continent. Of the total force employed in 1964, 96.17 percent were employed at the large mines alone, which adds an element of concentration of substantial social implications for the country as a whole.[22] Predictably, problems, tensions, and conflicts, as well as grievances and demands pertaining to that force, play a prominent part in the support politics in the country. In addition, the consumption capacity of a force estimated around 50,000 in 1970, relatively highly paid and geographically concentrated by itself, constitutes one of the prime motors of Zambia's economy.

To cope with the satellite syndrome, the leadership of Zambia moved in 1968 (the Mulungushi reforms) to dismantle the network of foreign controls. A series of limited nationalization measures culminated eventually in the takeover of the copper mines. Rights over mining areas held in perpetuity by foreign interests were terminated. Legislation concerning taxation, licensing, and remittances of earnings abroad were tightened to further reduce openings for foreign influence. As a result, certainly on paper, the powers of Zambian decision makers to regulate and supervise the copper industry, in particular the rate of exploration and production for long a special bone of contention, were augmented considerably. Crucial for development, these measures were expected to enhance the Zambian government's ability to direct resources away from copper toward other pressing tasks.[23]

KENYA

Three major problem areas characterize Kenya's socioeconomic profile: (1) special commercial, financial, hence political, ties with Uganda and Tanzania, the surviving links of a close association formed when all three territories were part of an integrated British East Africa; (2) European settler control in significant sectors of the economy, a problem further complicated by the preemption of middle class positions by an immigrant population from Asia; (3) a high level of dependence on agriculture.

The postindependence East African association has taken several forms. Whatever the form and whatever the name, Kenya's dominant position has been a source of tension. Kenya has dominated the relationship mainly because under British rule European settlers concentrated in the Kenya region, in particular the highlands, developed there a strong economy, including a capital surplus that created a favorable climate for further investment, and attracted modest industrialization. Administrative headquarters of government and private enterprise, including commercial and financial houses doing business throughout the East African region, were naturally located in Nairobi, the capital of Kenya. But unlike Dakar, Nairobi was not wholly dependent on survival of the original regional organization.

The multiracial power structure is the direct result of two deliberate colonial policies: the encouragement of large-scale immigration of Europeans, mainly British, into economic control positions, and of an even larger immigration of Asians, mainly Indians (Pakistanis) and Goans, first to provide labor for the construction of a railway from the coast to Uganda and then to fill the middle class positions and provide skilled and semi-skilled labor to sustain an essentially European standard of living. Asians also dominate retail trade and certain salaried occupations. Large tracts of land were reserved for European settlers, and beyond that their economic positions were securely sandbagged by appropriate legislation to the detriment of the indigenous African population.

Thus, what appears at first glance as a multiracial system emerges on closer inspection as a race-oriented class structure. Of course, with time the boundaries that separate the races become blurred. In any event Kenya's economy, somewhat like that of the Ivory Coast, still is split; the greater part of the value of agricultural and manufacturing products is derived from non-African farms, plantations, and manufacturing enterprises.[24] In general, racial tensions center on land distribution, wealth and income equity, and employment opportunities in the as-yet weak nonagricultural sectors.

A modern geographer has expressed the geographic dimension of Kenya's position as follows:

> The contemporary spatial patterns of modernization in Kenya are largely the products of the attitudes and objectives of the former colonial power and the resident (European) minority. It will take many years before these patterns cease to reflect the functions and requirements of a colonial territory and become restructured to serve independent African government attempting to construct a cohesive national community within its territorial boundaries.[25]

The situation can be expressed in the formula: fertile central highlands + agriculture + European control = European-dominated power and influence structure. If one adds to this, first, the vital component of capital needed to develop, expand, and modernize the principal resource complex — agriculture — and, second, the unlikelihood that needed capital can be generated in Kenya alone, the country's true position emerges quite clearly.

A key to the land question is the frequency of rainfall. Scarcity of rainfall renders only 25 million acres out of a total of 140 million suitable for raising livestock and for intensive crop production, even though of the 1.5 million families in Kenya in 1965 no more than 400,000 derived their livelihood mainly from sources outside agriculture. It was agreed generally that there seemed to be no real way to alter this pattern without substantial infusion of capital from abroad.

Thus the effective sources of power and influence are concentrated within relatively narrow areas in and around the highlands and in spots along the coast but decidedly not in the vast but barren expanse of the northern region, along the southern boundary with Tanzania, and in the remainder of the coast area away from Mombasa and Malindi. Although the game parks contribute a substantial share of revenue from tourism, they cannot be regarded as significant generators of power and influence.

Kenya's agriculture is more diversified than that of most of the other

African states, thanks to direct European participation at the production end, but it still yields only a narrow range of products, most of which are vulnerable to influences outside the control of Kenya's economic planners.

For instance, the rainfall factor combined with the high cost of irrigation raises havoc with economic planning. Likewise, since coffee, maize, tea, sisal, and wheat account for the bulk of agricultural production — most being raised for export — the extreme sensitivity of these products to world price fluctuations adds yet another set of unpredictable inputs to economic planning which, to be successful, depends heavily on a steady revenue flow from that sector.

A degree of stability and predictability is provided by production and export of Kenya's pedigreed livestock and high quality dairy products, both of which account for another large share of domestic production. Indeed, the diversification in the agricultural sector as well as the high quality so many of Kenya's products have attained have undeniably been furthered by the rather controversial policies of past governments by which the best lands were reserved for European use and by legislation that protected European positions in the economy thereafter. Secure in their holdings, European farmers accepted the risks inherent in experimentation, which is essential to diversification, and vigorously exploited the special marketing privileges granted them by the British home government.

The dual economy aspect warrants special attention. The patterns and modes of production tend to have a distorting effect on Kenya's overall socioeconomic profile. The high share of national income that goes to the expatriate community, as in the Ivory Coast but to a lesser degree, creates an illusion of economic progress. Over the period from 1964 to 1968 the most rapidly growing sectors were building, construction, transport, and to a slightly lesser extent banking; mining and quarrying declined during that same period, and livestock production slowed down.[26]

An inevitable consequence of this pattern is a growing differentiation in income between the urban and rural sectors, especially between the fortunate few and the black masses employed or unemployed, the peasant farmers, and black small holders. Also inevitable is a continuing reliance on foreign capital and skills, which has predictable consequences for the distribution of power and influence in state and society and for the degree of independence Kenya can expect to enjoy in the coming decades. The development plans of 1966-70 and 1970-74 clearly indicate that Kenya's planners did not expect significant changes during the plan periods or possibly beyond.[27]

Kenya's economy will continue to depend heavily on foreign trade — in particular, trade with Western consumers of her primary products.[28] Principal export markets are the sterling area, the European Economic Community, and North America.[29] Barring drastic steps, such as debt repudiation, Kenya remains firmly lodged in the financial-economic web generally known as the sterling bloc — the British Commonwealth or its eventual equivalent should the Commonwealth be formally dissolved some day. Foreign exchange holdings for some time to come will remain barely above the waterline.

In the circumstances, and increasingly so, ever larger circles of black Africans will develop a vested interest in the retention of these ties, albeit in terms progressively more favorable to Kenyan interests. Coffee production interests Kenya in international agreements that for a long time to come will reflect principally the tastes and desires of consumers in the richer countries. This applies also to tea, sisal, and pyrethrum.[30] The 20 or so statutory boards, positioned at critical junctions in the economy, continue to direct their attention to prime and, what is most important, relatively stable and reliable markets. So do the increasing numbers of agricultural cooperatives.[31] Besides, as everywhere else in Africa, development expenditures remain dead figures without substantial foreign assistance — about one-half to two-thirds for Kenya, depending on the method of programming and accounting.[32]

The role of tribal aspects in Kenya's politics often is exaggerated. At first glance tribalism appears to affect if not pervade every major conflict situation. Certainly the conflicts of interests between white Asians and Europeans and black Africans loom large. However, beneath what appear to be tribal conflicts, as we will note below, lie some rather basic socioeconomic conflicts that invariably seem to cut across tribal and racial lines. In any case, caution is indicated whenever the tribalism generalization is invoked.

Most explosive is the Asian question. In mid-1965 Asians accounted for no more than 1.98 percent of the total population, but Asians comprised 32 percent of the population of Nairobi. In 1962, 93.4 percent of all Asians but only 5.3 percent of black Africans resided in urban centers. Asians comprised 26.8 percent of all professional and top management personnel, 41.5 percent of skilled office workers and middle and lower income management, and 35 percent of the modern skilled manual workers.[33]

The potentially incendiary nature of these distribution patterns is all too clear. Although the events accompanying the Mau Mau activities in the 1950s may have conveyed a picture of stark and grim racial confrontation between blacks and whites in the country, the reduction of visible controls by Kenya whites and the substitution of invisible (power and influence) instrumentalities for visible and provocative ones — land alienation, land waste through enclosure policies designed to protect such privileges as fox hunting and luxurious residential arrangements — may have defused this particular source of conflict, at least relative to other momentarily more pressing issues.

III

Sources and Uses of Power: International

Two-thirds of the world's people live in the developing nations, and by the year 2000, this ratio is expected to rise to about five-sixths. The political outlook for these countries and their relations with the developed world depend heavily on economics. For the political issues of development are mainly economic issues. Income growth is the developing world's political imperative, affecting the fate of its political leaders, bringing about changed trade and financial flows, and dominating diplomacy between rich and poor countries.

MALMGREN
"COMING TRADE WARS?"

4

One's Weakness Is Another's Strength

A wide gap separates the form from the substance of international relations everywhere. The language of diplomacy is notorious for its reliance on euphemisms. States are said to have joined together in alliances without either the means or the intent to carry out the terms agreed on; many of the world's alliances, pacts, and international or regional organizations are little more than formalized gestures, vague expressions of intent defined in the vaguest possible terms. The deficiencies that beset African states underscore the need for special assumptions about their international capabilities, the feasibility of all regional and certainly all continental organizations, and — perhaps most important — the chances that African states will develop on an essentially independent basis.

In this chapter we consider, in greater depth than before, the more basic, power politically more salient sources of strength — as distinct from uses — from which foreign influences over African affairs largely derive. Chapter 5 highlights the more pervasive, hard-core aspects of applied power as a determinant of relations between the developed or advanced countries and the African states. Chapter 6 attempts to draw a balance of African assets and liabilities in the context of international as well as inter-African relations.

Geographic Impediments

More than a dozen of the new states are severely handicapped by geographic location alone. Independence interposed international boundaries that separated economies from ports, markets, sources of supply, and rail terminals to which they had been linked under colonial administration. For understandable reasons colonial rule had concentrated first on securing trade and shipping terminals along the coast. Areas farther inland were ignored, or if something of value was discovered there or a threat to colonial security seemed to materialize from that direction a modicum of remedial effort was applied after a punitive expedition. Whatever the contribution, it was usually negligible and administered in a perfunctory manner.

Since even seemingly favored coastal territories suffered neglect and emerged into independence burdened with debt, poverty their destiny and chronic instability the rule, it seems obvious that the economies in the interior must be even weaker. As we have seen, even relatively wealthy Zambia has to struggle in order to overcome the disadvantages of geographic isolation. Mali, Upper Volta, Niger, Chad, the Central African

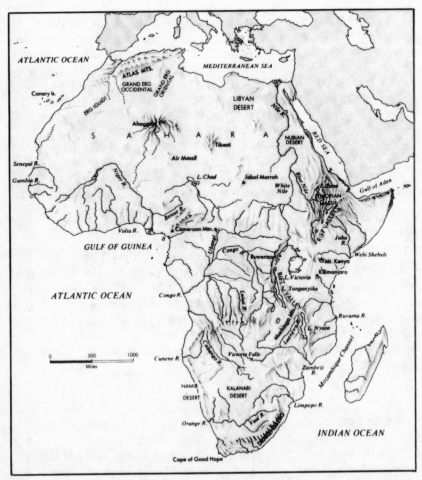

FIGURE 4.1 *Physiography of Africa: Mountains and Rivers*

SOURCE: Gann and Duignan, Africa and the World, 14. Copyright ©
1972 by Chandler Publishing Company.

Republic, Rwanda and Burundi, Uganda, and Malawi face overwhelming odds in their struggle to survive without substantial outside aid. Rhodesia could find herself in similar circumstances should her economy be cut off from the port of Beira in neighboring Mozambique, should Botswana to the southwest turn hostile, and, equally unlikely, if the Republic of South Africa ceases to serve as a support base. Botswana, Lesotho, and Swaziland are wholly dependent on the Republic of South Africa. One can describe them as captives.

The problems of landlocked states are actually staggering; where no or little inherent economic strength has been developed, the consequences could be beyond repair. In a highly competitive world, a producer of agricultural products saddled with long lines of transportation or without modern transportation of its own does not have much of a chance. He has no prospects of overcoming the competitive advantages of coastal states, such as close proximity to ports and rail terminals, nor does he have the capacity to develop alternate sources of income as long as investors are attracted to the already existing, relatively more developed and hence more promising opportunities elsewhere.

International as well as internal trade are governed to a controlling degree by cost-gain considerations. Commodities of marginal value — those vulnerable to substitution, for instance — are especially sensitive to high-cost transportation. Moreover, and regardless of the cost factor, African road and weather conditions make access to rail facilities often a matter of economic life or death, and the economic fortunes, hence the diplomatic political potential, of many a state on the continent are governed by this factor. Whatever the past ties, present alignments, or future aspirations of a state may be, a certain dependency relationship based on shared means of transportation will dictate international relations on the continent for some time. The list of such actual or potential relationships is impressive:

> Dakar-Bamako
> Abidjan-Ougadougou
> Lagos-Fort Lamy (incomplete)
> Lagos-Niamey
> Douala-Fort Archambault (planned)
> Douala-Yaoundé, Bangui (planned)
> Lobito-(Benguela)-Lusaka (copperbelt)
> Beira-copperbelt-Zaire-Blantyre
> Beira-Rhodesia
> Dar es Salaam-Lusaka (copperbelt, underway)
> Dar es Salaam-Bujumbura
> Mombasa-Kampala
> Djibouti-Ethiopia
> Lourenco Marques-Rhodesia-Djibouti-Zaire-Zambia-Swaziland[1]

As in all such situations there are, of course, alternatives theoretically. As the former French Soudan, now Mali, has shown, an interior state can avoid isolation by merging with the state at the end of the line of rail — Senegal in this instance. But as evidenced by the swift 1960 breakup of the ensuing Mali Federation — the former Soudan and Senegal — such mergers have the quality and durability of shotgun weddings.[2] There is considerably more to mergers than the placing of two sections of a railway under one constitutional umbrella.

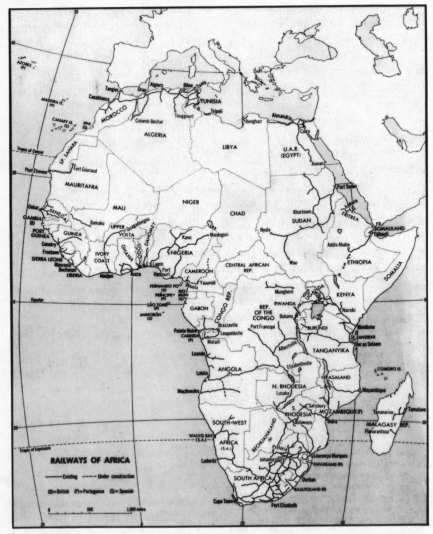

FIGURE 4.2   *Railways of Africa*

SOURCE: William A. Hance, *The Geography of Africa*, 36. Copyright © 1964 Columbia University Press.

In view of the transportation network of the entire southern portion of the continent, and on the assumption of what at this point in time seems very unlikely — namely, a peaceful resolution of the black-white conflict over race — enormous developmental potential could be generated if all the major arteries of commerce could be brought within one integrated system. The gigantic economy, by African standards, of white-ruled South Africa, reinforced by that of Rhodesia and by Mozambique's potential, could create an economically desirable mix of transportation, markets, and sources of supply that would lift participating states, possibly including Zambia, Malawi, and Botswana, far above their currently projected levels of existence.[3]

To an extent, but only to an extent, the decision to proceed with the Tanzania-Zambia railway may foreclose such a solution altogether, since it lessens Zambia's motivation to come to terms with the Republic of South Africa, even if South Africa should modify its racist stance. Much depends on who or what force is ultimately installed at the end of that line, at Dar es Salaam, or, alternatively, whether Zambia, Tanzania, and other black states in the region can combine their resources in an effective regional organizational framework such as the Eastern African Economic Community or its successor.

States with their own ports and in control of their own export and import also cannot shake off the restraints of weakness. When in the 1960s Kenyan circles thought of prohibiting any ship or plane from entering her jurisdiction if it also served proscribed South Africa, cooler minds quickly noted that Kenya was likely to suffer more than the intended target. Alarmed shipping interests convinced the government that South Africa was "much more significant in the business world than Kenya, and under such stringent regulations, it would be East Africa not South Africa, that would be boycotted."[4]

While the Suez Canal is closed, East Africa is separated from traditional sources of supply and markets by a long line stretching from Western Europe and the United States, around the Cape of Good Hope to Dar es Salaam, Mombasa, Mogadishu, and Berbera to Djibouti. When the canal is open, Red Sea ports and those below still are subject to comparatively high freight rates because of the canal dues. In any event Indian Ocean ports from Mombasa south, unlike ports elsewhere — in West Africa, for example — must strive to keep their freight rates low if they and the economies they serve want to remain competitive, mainly because they have no practical way of substituting markets nearby for those halfway around the world unless they tie into a developing South African-Rhodesian-Mozambican system. Recognition of this problem led Israel to invite East African states to avail themselves of the Israeli-controlled landbridge connecting the Mediterranean and the Red Sea.[5]

West Africa, of course, cannot afford to allow freight costs to rise too high. It is likely that the competitive position of products from the Ivory Coast, Ghana, and Nigeria will drop below acceptable levels unless this factor is controlled. The competitive position of Nigeria's oil, for example, could be affected vis-a-vis producers closer to Europe, the main oil importing region.

The direction of trade in the interior by the shortest possible route from the source to the port has created in some areas anomalies and conditions of progressive economic obsolescence that may be beyond repair unless supported by wholly improbable massive aid and assistance programs. Attempts to compensate by bringing together in one form or another several of the unbalanced and ailing economies have proven most difficult for reasons summarized in a United Nations report:

> The distance separating, for example, the Addis Ababa-Asmara economic center of Ethiopia from the East African Community industrial centers of Kampala and Jinja (in Uganda), Nairobi-Mombasa, Arusha-Dar es Salaam are very significant. And the rich "Livingston-Copperbelt" region of Zambia is widely separated from Eastern African markets. Furthermore, the bordering areas tend to be economically inactive. For instance, the northern and northeastern parts of Kenya, bordering Ethiopia and Somalia, are among the least developed areas in Kenya. The same is true for the Tanzania-Zambia border and the Tanzania-Rwanda-Burundi borders.[6]

Material Deficiencies

In more advanced countries energy production is not by itself a significant source of influence. It usually is little more than a matter of trading energy for cash. In Africa possession of sources of energy comes close to monopoly position. Two of the major hydroelectric power sources — the Kariba and Cabora Bassa dams — either are or will be located on European-dominated territory. The Kariba, serving Zambia and Rhodesia, is situated on the Rhodesian side of the Zambesi River, at that point the boundary between the two hostile states. If guerilla action or other pressures do not prevent its construction, the Cabora Bassa Dam will be strategically located on Portuguese-dominated territory in the northwestern corner of Mozambique. Kariba could also become a target for guerilla action from Zambian bases should Zambia's growing industries be supported from alternate sources of energy — unless, of course, the new sources are vulnerable to white retaliatory strikes. In any event, unless the black states create alternate sources of energy for their own use they must of necessity deal with the Europeans across the black-white divide.

Dislike and distrust of a neighboring owner of a major dam, incidentally, motivated Ivory Coast and the associated states of Togo, Dahomey, and Upper Volta to decline a Ghanaian offer of energy from the Volta River Dam while Nkrumah was president. The leaders of these states saw hidden in this offer and in the resultant ties the possibilities of political blackmail.[7]

Whatever the paper provisions may say about Malawi's independence, a major proportion of that country's labor force has no alternative but to seek employment in South Africa and eventually in Mozambique and Southern Rhodesia. Prospects for development of adequate employment opportunities within Malawi are extremely poor. This creates special opportunities for South African diplomacy. South Africa gains badly needed export outlets, and Malawi remains aloof from black Africa's opposition to apartheid. Cut off from Southern Rhodesia by her own choice, Zambia must secure new outlets for her copper, somewhere around £350 per ton at a minimum as of 1966. If that level is not reached, a greater share of Zambia's development program will have to be supported from abroad, with predictable consequences for Zambia's real independence.[8]

South Africa's leading position in world diamond output, backed by ready access to world centers of finance and commerce, provides openings for South African diplomacy in at-times unexpected places. So does her ability to furnish such special supplies as mining equipment at prices below those of competitors from outside the continent. Capital resources originating in South Africa are widely employed, knowingly or unknowingly, throughout black Africa. (For a period even the Soviet Union appears to have accepted South Africa's controlling position in the diamond market; both shared an interest in price stability.)[9]

Lack of finance capital looms ever larger as a prime weakness; if it should occur that African investment opportunities should lose ground to more lucrative, more stable, possibly more sympathetic investment opportunities elsewhere in the world, pressures on African governments to adjust their policies and postures may become irresistible. Increasing signs indicate that all but the most venturesome investors are becoming discouraged. The principal exception seems to be the mining investor who is still prepared to accept high risks and cope with social unrest, corruption, and inefficiency. One spur clearly is the promise of a high rate of recovery of the investment in a relatively short period of time, usually made possible by tax moratoriums ranging up to five years in some cases.

Until the competitive position of African states begins to match that of foreign interests, at least in the more critical and more sensitive sectors of state and society, the more lucrative, sometimes glittering, economic prospects on the continent will continue to be open to the reckless and irresponsible hit-and-run operator along with the dependable investor who is sincerely committed to advancement of African interests along with his own. One prime source of vulnerability to exploitation lies within the information ambit.

The relatively small, weak, and isolated African user of international finance capital, public or private, has few means of accurately and reliably informing himself on money matters, including matters relating to his own capital invested abroad.[10] Foreign interests are in a position to buy information to acquire African trade secrets, so to speak. Of course, where local skills are not adequate to cope with requirements foreign firms will be called on routinely to provide the know-how — for example, in cotton ginning, peanut shelling, and coffee cleaning. If African independence is to mean anything at all, however, African governments must have at their exclusive disposal confidential and, of course, competent sources of advice and information.

In some respects African economies, or at least certain sectors, are in the position of the drug addict in relation to his supplier. Whether foreign money is introduced through official aid or through private channels, the habit-forming propensities of one-way flows of economic benefits invariably make themselves felt. This is aptly reflected in the following observation, made with reference to foreign subsidy of African trade unions, incidentally.

> By a kind of Say's law (production creates not only the supply of goods but also demand for them) of international aid, the supply of foreign money creates new demands for its use. While this has many facets, the most important is that western financial aid to one faction in a country leads to (or follows) communist (or Ghanaian) aid to a rival faction. The result is that externally provided resources are absorbed in factional dispute.[11]

There are more subtle forms of addiction. Some of the economic narcotics are surreptitiously introduced into the African economy, though with the full knowledge of whoever negotiates these arrangements. Eventually they are like hooks in the bodies economic and politic, difficult to extract short of major surgery. Experiences with supplier credits in Ghana and Nigeria are cases in point. Because it is difficult, at times impossible, to obtain conventional loans, governments hard pressed to undertake certain projects (although opportunity to realize some graft is also known to have been the motivation) turn to alternate, predictably more expensive, sources of financing. Under the arrangement the supplier of skilled manpower and material, the contractor, also acts as the financier. While the project progresses, a credit line is opened for the contracting state; then interest accumulates at a rate considerably higher than would have been called for had a conventional loan been secured. The resultant spiraling of debts is reminiscent of the terrors experienced by the sorcerer's apprentice.

Foreign Exchange Shortages*

Looking at copper-rich Zambia some time ago, a group of experts

*The term refers to currency and other negotiables that a country earns for its exports or obtains otherwise and that are convertible. In the African context foreign exchange is most valuable if it can be used to purchase vitally needed goods and services. Because these currencies are backed by a high level of productivity, the dollar, the pound, the mark, and the other West European currencies are among the most sought after; e.g. More can be bought for U.S. dollars than for Spanish pesos.

optimistically concluded that the country's prospects for development were good.

> [The] basic problem of an underdeveloped country is always foreign exchange. It may have other serious problems, such as too few factories and insufficient tractors. It may face an acute shortage of professionally and technically trained personnel. But if enough foreign exchange is flowing in, the things people needed can in the end be bought or hired. At the heart of any strategy of economic development lies the maximization of the earnings of foreign exchange and their careful use.[12]

In time, a more sombre view has prevailed. More recently, Kamarck noted that

> [The] economic and financial dependence of the African economies on the rest of the world is so great that they would have to possess relatively enormous foreign-exchange reserves to gain much latitude in pursuing an independent monetary and credit policy.[13]

Given the crucial role of money and credit in all states and economies, one can generalize that lack of sufficient foreign exchange reserves will cramp the style of any government in any conceivable external and in many internal respects. Given, furthermore, the ever-expanding needs that face the governments of Africa, it is not difficult to see that it is quite easy for a country to exhaust its foreign exchange reserves on a relatively minor effort. The International Monetary Fund offers convincing statistics on this point. At one particular time, during the fourth quarter of 1968, foreign exchange reserves of all of Africa except the Republic of South Africa and the United Arab Republic did not exceed the reserves of little Denmark. South Africa, alone at that point, counted a reserve of U.S. $1,471 million compared to that of the rest of the continent, excluding the two exceptions, of U.S. $2,130 million![14] It should be small wonder if in especially critical and financially strained conditions certain international financiers or other private influentials with access to sources of foreign exchange are accorded highest priority and receive red-carpet treatment ahead of accredited ambassadors.

The amount of foreign exchange earned and kept in reserve must be considered along with foreign debts. The capacity of most of the states to cover such debts is exceedingly low. The resultant pressures on the economies can be deadly. Economists are in disagreement on what constitutes a reasonable or manageable level of foreign indebtedness for an underendowed economy. A crucial factor is a country's ability to earn and save foreign exchange over and above immediate requirements such as consumer satisfaction, law-and-order expenses, and other minimum demands on the treasury such as maintenance of current sources of income

— that is, preventing their decay — and including servicing of all existing debts as payments become due. Mounting debts increase the premium on individual or corporate ability to obtain relief for the hard-pressed African government. Any foreigner who can demonstrate an ability to secure adjustments in the interest payment schedule, to soften terms, to secure credits on bearable terms, or to persuade foreign creditors to suspend interest payments altogether may rise to impressive heights of power.

In conditions normal for Africa, legal transfers of power from European to African hands do not always accomplish what is intended. Steps empowering African governments to regulate the outflow of foreign exchange — steps that have routinely followed independence in all of the former British colonies — generally have not been effective. For a variety of reasons scarce foreign exchange continues to pour out through myriads of small as well as some very large and clearly visible openings. More important, the expected freedom of discretion on purely internal monetary matters, such as allocation of foreign exchange to domestic projects, does not materialize with the establishment of statutory controls. As long as foreign assistance is required, veiled references to such intangibles as investor's confidence, fiscal stability, investment climate, and the like will continue to give pause even to the most determined African leader who wants to embark on measures intended to widen his range of freedom in monetary matters.

As long as large numbers of foreign hands remain in control of entire links in the chain of production, distribution, and sale of prime sources of foreign exchange, and as long as these same hands, or financially related ones, remain in control of the chain of production, distribution, and sale of imports to African countries, foreign exchange controls remain ineffectual. Financially the African hare continues to experience the trials and tribulations of his exhausted counterpart in the fable who, attempting to race the tortoise, always found one of an identical pair already waiting for him at each end of the racecourse.

Manpower and Skill Deficiencies

For decades to come, the new states will be in need of a continuous supply of foreign experts, technicians, administrators, and teachers.[15] Most likely, in many areas a mass exodus or complete stoppage of supply of expatriate experts could bring the modern economy to a temporary halt. As yet relatively few Africans command high-level skills to permit rapid Africanization of key positions envisaged by many of the black leaders at the time of independence. The roots of that problem are obvious and well known. Colonialism militated against the development of skills and of knowledge generally among the subject people to ensure foreign domination and control. Today, for better or for worse, the European-dominated hierarchy, which many black leaders are pledged to dismantle, actually has been consolidated and reinforced. French Africa leads in that respect, leaving aside the openly white dominated redoubt in southern Africa.

The most sensitive aspect of this problem is that most shortages are in key positions. Exceedingly few Africans were trained in high finance (let alone modern economics), in banking, as business executives, as top-command soldiers, or as high-level police officers. In some states no Africans with skills of any note existed at independence. Enormous influence opportunities for foreign interests in positions to provide required skills opened up with the postindependence expansion of social, economic, diplomatic, and technical activity.

Under colonial rule black leaders had been kept in virtual ignorance of the real world. With independence, torrents of demands broke on the new government centers, triggered in part by the substantial increases in government revenue, in part by the opening to new outside influences of what theretofore had been closed societies. Positions and related skills not even dreamed of suddenly became vitally necessary and had to be filled.

The seeds for future troubles had been sown when lack of vision or motivation had deprived Africa's more gifted children of access to educational opportunities in keeping with future requirements. Now the irrelevance, in terms of African needs, of much European planned and directed education at all levels became dramatically clear.[16] A time lag problem had been created, and its remedy was beyond the material and technical capabilities of both the former colonial powers and their African dependencies. The exodus of foreigners had to begin, although a reverse movement got under way temporarily in parts of French Africa. It is not an exaggeration to say that none of the states in the black regions have among their own nationals sufficient high-level manpower skills to execute development programs now on the drawing boards, let alone complete those already started.

Aside from material advantages, Europeans have been able to draw on additional sources of influence, mainly in cultural and sociopsychological respects. Although shorn of formal authority, Europeans continued to benefit from the habits of thought and custom that survived among Africans from colonial days. This residue has enabled them to recapture or maintain vestiges of their former power in some areas. Independence brought to the national level internal tensions commonly referred to as tribal which previously had been overshadowed and contained by the controlling European presence. A demand for neutral arbitrators to assist in the control and eventual resolution of the more pressing internal conflicts created special positions for nationals from the former colonial powers.

Continuous identification, especially among the elite (sometimes, and perhaps unfairly, referred to as Euro-Africans) with Western habits of thought, ways, and customs also played a part. So did the failure of attempts to substitute continental African languages for English and French. Retention of European languages, while assuring continued contact between developing Africa and the technologically more advanced parts of the world, also allowed the Europeans to retain the keys to a vital section of the communications system. (The suggestion has been advanced that compulsive use of European languages may in fact, be a source of an inferiority complex among Africans.)[17] There is evidence that determined efforts in certain countries — Tanzania and Libya, for example — to eliminate this source of alien influence have been less successful than the reformers had hoped.[18]

At a different level, European, generally Western, modes of living, tastes, and consumption habits have become accepted throughout Africa — mainly of course, in the urban areas. This acceptance, as is well known among students of merchandising in developed countries, can also have the effect of a drug. The conditioned reflexes, accustomed to certain types of goods, for instance, or certain imported foodstuffs or textiles, provide influence opportunities for whoever is in a position to satisfy demand.[19] Conversely, inability to compete effectively for consumer support has so far disadvantaged Soviet Russia and Communist China, even where, as in Nkrumaist Ghana, the public was exhorted to shift its consumption habits.[20]

Postindependence, anti-Western rhetoric if accepted at face value would suggest that the socialist countries, socialist thought, and socialist culture started with an advantage over the heavily compromised Western culture once anticolonial forces were in control. This does not appear to have been so. On the whole, the socialist countries have lacked the experience to overcome deeply rooted and well-entrenched European positions. Actually, it should not be difficult for Soviet theoreticians to identify the sources of their problems. The Polish economist Oscar Lange recalls that for decades Chinese revolutionary forces were unable to dislodge the ruling groups at home because of the necessity of preserving the state-operated irrigation works.[21] Unable to offer alternate, more efficient, and more economical production methods, alternate sources of income, alternate outlets or markets, the socialist countries have not penetrated far beyond a very limited and restricted circle of ideologically kindred spirits. Whatever the extent of penetration, there is much room for doubt whether significant breakthroughs have occurred, whether socialist thought and practice have become sufficiently accepted to forecast shifts in social behavior, or better, have actually led to adoption of new values, norms, and modes of living.

The uncertainty surrounding the efficacy of non-African socialist thought applies also to religion. Christian and Muslim missionaries and practitioners claim conversions; there is much room for doubt about the effect of such conversions on social behavior. It is possible that identification with

Islam conditions an individual to follow more or less irresistibly the instructions from members of the same faith. But it is also possible that what really motivates a Muslim follower in Eritrea to rebel against Christian rule, in Northern Nigeria to resist domination by the south, or in Chad to resist black rule are essentially socioeconomic interests that happen to coincide with religious divisions or are traceable to such division, but only in part. It is too early to draw definitive conclusions on this subject, especially in view of the history of Arab-black relations in Africa.

5

Applied Power

Economic Power

The literary Right credits the colonial powers and their associates with virtually anything that has developed on the continent since the bow and arrow; if anything is of value it must of necessity have been imported, most likely from the benevolent and wholly altruistic West. From that perspective the East or the centrally controlled economies of the Soviet Union, Communist China, and their associates cannot possibly contribute to Africa anything but instability and tension, probably bloody revolution, and eventually chaos.[1]

The literary Left is no better. By its reading of history, colonial, imperialist, and subsequently neocolonialist predators have been ravaging the continent at will, to no ascertainable purpose other than their own selfish advantage, for profit most likely. Anything the West can do, the East can do better and always and consistently to the advantage of the oppressed peoples of Africa.[2]

These portrayals, typically formulated in extremes, are, of course, caricatures. The history of Africa's relations with the outside world reveals shades of gray. While not all acts of commission or omission by Western interests are innocent, not all are methodically diabolical, either. The Left seems inclined, almost as a reflex action, it appears, to regard as imperialist methods wholly unintended consequences of economic activity. Perhaps some of these consequences over the years have become methodical; they need not be deliberate, however.

Since Africa is at or near the bottom of the international economic opportunity shopping list of all major and most middle powers, what some observers view as evidence of clear exploitation may, in fact, turn out to be an unavoidable consequence of relationships initiated by Africans in response to at-times desperate internal economic pressures. Foreign investors are said to invariably exploit African labor. Actually, for-

68

eign investors do enter less developed economies in part because wages there are low. For that reason foreign investments tend to act as brakes on wage increases, but there is difference between a side effect and deliberate action. Exploitation may, in fact, be too harsh a term where both the investor and the less developed country benefit — that is, both are better off than they would have been had things remained as they were. It may be going too far to say that the less developed country always benefits from investment, but it may also be unwarranted to regard as deliberate method what actually may be only a consequence.

Colonial interests are blamed for what is referred to as the Balkanization of the continent. The argument is that an otherwise whole and undivided continent has been parceled up primarily by Western interests to facilitate economic exploitation. When confronted by a determined African independence movement, these interests proceeded to assure dominance of the continent in perpetuity by encouraging the establishment of several dozen prospects for satellite status. This view is far too simplistic.

There never was a whole, undivided unit called Africa except in the vaguest possible sense. If many of the new states are feeble and dependent, the position is a consequence, not a purpose, of several hundred years of rather chaotic and unsystematic Western presence. The following discussion is restricted to bring out those aspects of international behavior that clearly and unmistakably reflect intent and may therefore legitimately be regarded as direct means or methods employed by foreign interests to achieve ascertainable and specific ends.

Foreign Aid and Assistance

Evidence is mounting that Western aid to developing countries has resulted in a net drain of capital from the economies aided. It is entirely possible that a final evaluation of all aid given by capitalist countries to the poorer nations will show that aid generally is designed primarily to serve the needs of the rich. For example, aid administered to Latin America under the Alliance for Progress appears to have achieved little more than to enable clients of the United States to meet interest payments for a few years. Other charges — for example, that the real end purpose of economic aid is long-range influence or even permanent control — are more debatable. Aid does indeed facilitate influence, but it is not a prime candidate for the role of imperialist or neocolonialist villain assigned to it by some commentators.[3]

Aid invariably is an extension of national policy on the part of the donor country. Unavoidably, the wealthier donors take on the dimensions of Goliaths in African eyes. Much of what is related to such awesome presence can be frightening if not terrifying, regardless of its actual influence potentialities or intents. Examined more closely, however, aid offered by the pluralist industrial powers more likely than not is multi-directional, multipurpose, at times substantially uncoordinated if not at odds with other contrary, national objectives. Aid materializes only after having gone through the purgatory of aid bureaucracy and red tape. In fact, it may prove impossible for even the shrewdest imperialist mani-pulator, intent on subverting aid to serve his purposes, to find his way through the bureaucratic jungle in his home country or abroad.[4] Inciden-tally, imperialism to serve nefarious purposes, if that should be the intent, should be far easier to harness, design, and package in the centrally con-trolled and planned economies of the Soviet group.

Many aid features regarded as objectionable are in all probability un-avoidable if substantial amounts of aid are to be made available for the developing states. Certainly it may prove most difficult to dissuade financial and commercial interests, and military interests also, in the donor states from seeking some quid pro quo such as investment opportunities, export outlets, trade concessions, or bases. If these aims are not sought, minimum expectations may suggest a degree of diplomatic neutrality and uncom-mitment in respect to major strategic issues. None of these conditions or expectations need to be formally expressed; yet expressed or implied, they are not infrequently described as strings or ties.

One must concede that it may be difficult for observers in the receiving countries not to regard these conditions as clear manifestations of ex-ploitative intent. Whether some conditions attached to offers of aid actually are intended to serve power drives or whether they are innocent side effects may at times be impossible to tell. Conditions governing re-payment of loans, terms controlling the convertability of currency in which loans are to be repaid, precise stipulations concerning the amounts of local currency to be set aside to match foreign aid — the so-called counterpart funds — and similar facets of aid are difficult for proud people to accept. Commonly, governments of borrowing countries are required to guarantee all official loans. Thus, future borrowing capacity is limited commensurable with existing obligations, and future projects must be accommodated within these limits. Even such obvious side effects as the costs of servicing equip-ment received free of charge or the unavoidable consequence of going back to the donor for spare parts and replacements can at times be irritating to the independent-minded beneficiary. (A high rate of attrition of equipment, characteristic of developing, hence inexperienced, countries, especially in the tropics, maximizes this source of irritation.)

Some consequences of aid may, in fact, have been invited by the recip-ient. At times under extreme financial pressure some African countries have mortgaged all or part of their entire agricultural output for years in advance. Subsequently, they have found themselves hamstrung economically and unable to take advantage of improved world market conditions or changes in production alternatives at home. Most difficult to accept, of course, are express or implicit prohibitions that prevent aid recipients from experimenting with temporarily uneconomic, hence costly, projects during the lifetime of a major grant. None of these features, however, can really be treated as sources of power in a direct sense. They provide opportunities for direct influence over policy decisions, but the relationship between aid policy and accompanying terms and effect on the policy alternatives open to the recipient country are tenuous and indirect as a rule.

Confusion also arises over negative effects of aid on the structure of receiving economies; there is suspicion that certain economically debilitating, disorganizing, or disquieting consequences of aid were intended to undercut and eventually ruin African economies. We have already referred to the addictive qualities of aid. Although some of the narcotics were requested by the receiving country, imported freely and eagerly as a matter of record when the at-times ravaging consequences of a poorly designed or inadequately thought-out project become noticeable, a hue and cry is heard that foreign interests are out to destroy the embryonic economy to their advantage. The evident inconsistency in this statement does not appear to prevent the argument from being made.

Turnkey projects have indeed many of the characteristics of a narcotic. The recipient is enticed or persuaded or tricked to accept a project that promises construction of a plant in its entirety by foreign interest. The project is financed through loans made available either by the contractor or by his government. The result may be impressive, but the consequences often are painful if not disastrous. The loans invariably are of short duration, interest and prices for equipment are excessively high, and management and marketing arrangements for the output of the ready plant usually are left unresolved. The full measure of the effect of this type of arrangement emerges from an examination of the total end cost to Ghana for projects of that sort.[5] Is the financial drain a mere accidental by-product of otherwise sound financial offers? There can be no doubt whatever that the invidious nature of projects of that type is fully known to all concerned. One reason, of course, that few whistles are blown is that a fair share of such loans never is applied to the projects but finds its way independently into bank accounts abroad.[6]

In many ways outside aid is unavoidably a corrupting influence. Aid lessens pressure for mobilization of internal resources. (In that respect, too, it acts as a drug.) Its social costs are high in other respects. Invariably those who have, receive more.

Clearly, aid applied in excess of the recipient's digestive capabilities produces disastrous results. Few states can constructively absorb all aid offered. A substantial share of all inflows must therefore find its way into unproductive channels. Yet the flow is not curbed on that account either, partly for fear that denial will be interpreted as an unfriendly act.

This does not deter some applicants from charging donors with malicious intent.

Some African planners have discovered that "availability of aid does not always mean that it is economically wise to use it." Kenyan planners have offered this cautionary note.

> It is natural that (these) governments and their agencies would want to be in a position to defend at home the uses to which their aid has been put. Unfortunately this need implies that aid sources will have a bias in favor of clearly defined projects that are imposing in design and structure. This preference for glamorous projects means that many elements of a plan will go unaided destroying the integrated pattern of development in favour of disorderly advance.

Again, hard-pressed governments have accepted such superfluous projects, then promptly made them the butt of complaints.[7]

One of the major sources of frustration and irritation arises from prevailing world conditions that reduce the value of aid with every passing year, mainly because of inflation. Consequently, as one observer puts it, "much of the discussion on aid ... sounds like a medieval theological disputation."[8] While it is being discussed and fought over, the object turns out to be an illusion. In addition, a relatively minor shift in the world market price of the primary export commodity in some cases is sufficient to negate the entire annual aid contribution. Though difficult if not impossible to attribute to donor countries alone, this form of attrition and its practical consequences also are identified as neocolonialist conspiracies against the sovereignty and independence of African states.

Conspiratorial or not, French aid to her former colonies has been and to a considerable extent still is an integral part of the entire armory of French power and influence. Because of the stigma attached to acceptance of substantial amounts of aid, recipients of French aid have been reluctant to reveal the full extent of their indebtedness. Perhaps it would be more accurate to say that the full measure of French aid in its various forms is concealed, which poses certain difficulties in research. But it is not impossible to assess the basic characteristics and identify the major categories of this particular variant of economic power.

Aid and trade are at times difficult to separate. In the context of French-African relations the two activities are integrally related, really part of the same system of benefit and control. French aid and trade are conducted through elaborate subsidy arrangements that virtually tie the African economy to French capitalization, consumer practices, and policies. When in 1964 most direct subsidies were overtly terminated, the rest of the control machinery remained intact, and France retained the ability to manipulate production, distribution, and sale very much as before. Perhaps most important in this regard is the preferential treatment of French client states within the French market system. This benefit, in turn, is parried by quota provisions that protect French exporters to Africa from competition from outside the preferential zone. French-originated measures have compelled alteration of segments of locally devised development plans. As a United Nations analysis views it, "[Quantitative restrictions on African imports] are predetermined measures, directed more toward consistency with objectives of France's commercial and financial policies than they are towards alleviating their own problems of trade imbalance."[9]

Vital foreign exchange holdings of the West African client states are controlled by a skimming-off process in Paris, where external reserves of client states are held in an operations account at the French treasury. In fact, a direct line connects the treasury in Paris to the African treasuries, which, in turn, "act as government fiscal agents and as bankers for the public sector," which, in turn, places the central treasury in Paris in an obviously controlling position.[10] We have already referred to the important factor centering on the ready and unrestricted convertibility of currency used in French-speaking areas for French francs at a fixed rate.

French control over national as well as group and individual means of subsistence in Africa is sufficient at this point in time to enable French interests to influence policy decisions without direct and obvious activation of the instruments of control everywhere and at all times. A few examples seem to be sufficient. French support was totally withdrawn from Guinea in 1958 in direct retaliation for Guinea's failure, or refusal, to accept the DeGaulle Constitution — that is, accept continuous French dominance. Mali also experienced the repercussions of resistance to France as did others such as Dahomey, but to a lesser extent. When Mauritania in 1970 proposed to make Hassanic Arabic the national language, replacing French, French aid to Mauritania was reduced by exclusion of the compensation for franc devaluation that was being paid to other, more compliant, states.[11]

British official aid is obligated to advance donor interests. Yet, aside from seeking to serve British private enterprise and, of course, British settlers in such places as Kenya and Rhodesia, British aid has been comparatively unobtrusive. However, intended or not, determined anticolonialists have portrayed some manifestations of British aid as aggressive and imperialist, tantamount to direct interference in the internal affairs of the new states.

Kenya provides one such case. At independence, a major task confronting the newly formed black government centered on satisfaction of a widespread and vigorously advanced African demand for transfer of large areas of desirable land that previously had been reserved for use by Europeans. The demand was pressed by thousands of African farmer aspirants, many of whom had fought for their rights in or with the Mau Mau resistance. Success in the land transfer and, most important, profitable use of lands transferred as well as lands continuously worked by remaining Europeans hinged on availability of funds. To acquire European reserved areas without adequate compensation paid to the owners would have produced severe repercussions for the economy, for much of the government revenue would still have come from European enterprise. Only British funds were available for such a purpose. Inevitably this situation became a source of embarrassment, for a major policy task confronting a nominally independent African government now had to be externally financed.[12]

Soviet Russian and Communist Chinese aid and associated programs offered by Soviet satellites have not escaped being perceived as forms of imposition and intervention. As one may expect, Western interests, which enjoyed monopoly positions for so long, were quick to point accusing fingers at the interlopers. However, aid offered by countries that have no other economic roots on the continent is difficult to equate with aid from powers already well entrenched economically and culturally. Whatever one may discover about aid from the socialist, centrally controlled economies, it does not appear to be their intent to develop enclaves, carve out property rights, or otherwise secure economic controls in black receiving countries. Of course, if for one reason or another they should acquire monopoly positions unintentionally, the situation could be different. In any case, some similarities exist between the aid and assistance programs of the so-called Communist powers and those of the West.

The matter of currency convertibility is one such instance. Since the Soviet ruble cannot be readily converted into, say, dollars, all purchases made under agreements with the Soviet Union must be consummated in the donor country or in countries associated with it. This condition has several adverse consequences for the recipient while adding to the donor's influence leverage. The loan recipient is prevented from freely shopping around to secure competitive prices, thereby enabling the donor to set any prices he finds power politically practical as well as economically necessary. If aid is given as a loan, loan repayment also will have to be made in that country through sale of sufficient goods, usually at less than world prices. At times, valuable foreign exchange reserves must be tapped to repay loans made in currency of marginal economic value.[13]

At first glance, terms of Soviet loans may appear to be more generous than terms set by Western donors. There are many flies in that ointment, though. It has not escaped attention that prices of equipment supplied under Russian loan agreements are sometimes 20 to 30 percent above the prices of similar equipment purchased in the West, and that Russian manpower is substantially more numerous and more expensive in the aggregate than equivalent American manpower would be — all of which makes the low interest charged on the Russian loans look quite different and rather high.[14] Similarly, Communist Chinese practices include provision for purchase of Chinese goods in repayment of loans such as the one granted to construct the Tanzania-Zambia railway. These loans are said to be interest free, but since they lock the recipient to nonconvertible Communist Chinese currency and purchase of a rather narrow range of Chinese goods, in the People's Republic, the donor needs only raise the price of these goods, all state controlled, to recapture his lost interest.[15]

Numerous opportunities to influence and control arise also from semi-official and private aid in one form or another, but whatever the form, or outer garment, the grinding poverty characteristic of so many aspects of African life today automatically increases the influence potential of any given unit of money. Foreign subsidies are common as prime sources of revenue for certain trade unions. For example, the American-based United Automobile Workers, the United Steel Workers of America, and several lesser unions have injected considerable funds into African trade unions throughout the continent; the best-known instances are Kenya, Nigeria, and Liberia.[16] Almost certainly, African trade unions, including unions that support guerilla action against Europeans in Portuguese Africa, have received financial support through front organizations that were supported, in turn, by the United States Central Intelligence Agency. The Soviet Union, of course, has availed itself of the same opportunities, frequently channeling funds through associated states such as East Germany, and so has the Chinese People's Republic.[17]

All euphemisms aside, the aims of the superpowers appear to be identical in fundamental respects, though different, of course, with respect to specific strategic targets. To use the favorite Soviet Russian phrase, the intent is to bolster "fraternal working-class organizations." In some respects subsidies paid by American labor to African counterparts are more directly related to legitimate trade union goals; often the intent is to influence wage and working conditions in Africa in order to support similar demands at home.[18]

Other forms of foreign influence, if not control, result when foreign owners or managers of outside capital participate directly in industrial, commercial, and financial activities in the African economy. To conceal this participation various stratagems are employed, such as substitution of black African faces in front offices or increased African participation, though frequently in a wholly subsidiary role, on boards of directors.

Even where African interests have secured majority rights, usually through public ownership, foreign control is not necessarily ruled out. Possession of expertise, access to additional investment capital and ready markets, and all of the other paraphernalia of international finance and commerce combine to favor the foreign side. Even wholly African, state-owned enterprises are known to have been harnessed to foreign interests and have been milked to foreign advantage in the process. Inevitably this condition has allowed outsiders to shape essentially internal policies. The interesting argument has been advanced that nationalization of foreign enterprises, a favorite step these days, may actually invite foreign exploitation rather than prevent it; it may lend itself to exploitation "worse than colonialism."[19]

The extracting industries create special opportunities for direct participatory control. In Gabon, for instance, the French Atomic Energy Commission together with private French interests retains capital ownership, and all production of uranium is exported to France.[20] Oil and copper create similar influence opportunities; simply stated, the mineral extractors who enjoy a monopoly or near-monopoly position have their hands at the throat of the producing country; they dictate or manipulate production volume, distribution (which they also control), marketing, and royalty payments. The principal and most critical technique employed in this case relates to pricing. To break that stranglehold, African governments must accept the risk of substantial losses. The arm twisting that results is rarely reported but represents a major portion of local power politics, nevertheless.

The desire of African governments to attract increasingly scarce foreign capital at times creates conditions in which foreign investors, or, as a Nigerian source has called them, "machine peddlers," are handed the controls over a major segment of the economy. This situation becomes especially critical when the development of entire industries is turned over to foreign investors. The problem starts with the African government's assumption of investment guaranty, mainly, of course, to assuage suspicions of planned takeover or fears of civil disturbance and insurrection. Such guaranties are also required to assure regular repayment of loans and interest whenever payments fall due. Should the new and invariably inexperienced company, or group of companies, fail to meet obligations internally, the government guarantees satisfaction of creditors. In return, the foreign group undertakes all tasks required to get the enterprise or industry under way. In the process, however, it may overcharge, say, the Nigerian economy by posting higher prices for its own product, imported from its own home base, and exact higher management fees than would ordinarily be indicated on a free market. If the company is unsuccessful in what may well be an uneconomic venture, it simply falls back on the original guaranty.[21]

Expert and Referent Power

For better or for worse, colonial rule secured for Europeans high social status and prestige throughout the continent; many achieved positions they could not have secured at home. In some areas these positions were carved out and defended by force or threat of force, principally in the Belgian Congo, for a time in East and portions of South Africa, and in most of the African portion of the French empire. Elsewhere, Europeans achieved high social status simply because the skilled are admired by the unskilled, or the affluent by the unenlightened poor. It is now known that the notion that light skin is a mark of superiority over black was propagated, and accepted, by means of the power of suggestion. This and similar myths were continuously strengthened by false and misleading accounts of European and African history, false and scientifically unfounded generalizations concerning the black race. All this is not saying that prestige and eminence were not truly earned by many Europeans. It is drawing attention merely to the historic bases on which the myth of white superiority was founded. Independence changed the relationship between the races, but not so drastically nor so rapidly as many Africans desired. Much remains to be done.

To be sure, transfer of legal authority reduced the white minority's aggregate political power and narrowed the legal and cultural bases for further propagation of superiority myths. At the same time powerful impetus was given to the advancement of black culture, black identity, and black power. The ability to deport whites for even minor infractions of the new code of public conduct alone constituted a persuasive deterrent against racial arrogance.

As member states of the European Economic Community, the United Nations, and other international bodies have entered former British and French Africa, British, French, and Belgian referent power has been reduced as Africans have come to see that knowledge, technological proficiency, and skills are the monopoly of no one. Still, it will be a long time before British and French and generally Western cultural roots are replaced by older or new influences from other parts of the world, or before the continent develops its own identity and cultural momentum. (There is no need, in this context, to enter into the discussion of Africa's historic past and its implications for the present and the future.)

For some time to come, British, French, and U.S. nationals, including diplomats, technical advisers or expatriates, civil servants, businessmen, or teachers, will draw on the support, directly or indirectly, overtly or covertly, of far-flung financial, commercial, and cultural foundations laid out in colonial days. The new rulers cannot easily forget, and if they forget they are quickly reminded, that the still-substantial aid and assistance supplied from sources in Paris or London or from the United States really are not free.

The French community, backed by French authorities at home and abroad, controls the economic racetrack in nearly all of the client states. They determine the conditions in which economic projects are to be launched. They set the rules for competition and reserve the right to place obstacles in the paths of their nearest competitors, both African and non-African. In 1969 an American businessman in the Ivory Coast complained: "Every time we offer to investigate an industrial project, a French group makes a counter offer within 24 hours. This could only mean that French businessmen have direct access to confidential government negotiations."[22] And access they have indeed; French technicians are behind every minister. The condition that produces this anomaly is characteristic of all of French Africa, with one or two exceptions. It was brought on with the systematic prevention of the growth of an adequate corps of African civil servants.

In colonial days much of public policy planning and everyday decision making by the French rulers was conducted in an atmosphere of leisure, very much "by the seat of their pants." (A French banker used this term in an interview describing decision making by French economists in Senegal.) That mode of operation obviated, or at least so it seemed, the need for development of African experts and of a body of statistics compiled locally and available to the African public for study inspection and, if necessary, self-education. Absence of such a publicly accessible body of information also shielded the preserve from unwelcome prying eyes. French banks, trading houses, and metropolitan government departments jealously guarded their trade secrets even after independence, when such information should have been made the property of the new states. Moreover, French technical experts in the public sector and their counterparts in the private sector managed to keep their African trainees and eventual successors from learning too much. They even attempted to prevent African students at home and abroad from acquiring expertise in modern subjects such as econometrics.[23]

In many sectors African competition does not even begin to match the accumulated skill and experience of foreigners. The inequality enables even marginal non-Africans to secure and maintain an advantage. One of the best studies on this subject suggests that Asian dominance in the retail trade throughout eastern and southern Africa is, in part at least, the product of an underdeveloped sense of economics among Africans who seek to capture a share of the trade.

> [The African] does not know prices or where to buy stock advantageously . . . . the African shopkeeper [does not] know in detail what each item costs him and he doesn't bother to figure out a fixed mark-up, item by item. For this reason he often sells at a loss without realizing what he is doing. Furthermore, he typically makes no distinction between capital and income. When business has been brisk, and he finds himself with an unusual amount of money, he is under the impression that he is rich. He does not fully realize that the larger proportion of what he has in his hand is capital, not profit, and that it must be re-invested if he is to stay in business.[24]

It is far too early to offer definitive judgments on the impact of non-Western experts and technicians on the legitimacy and referent power of a regime prone to rely if not depend on foreigners, especially on light-skinned or, worse, European and imperialist nationals. Ideally, interests that seek to infiltrate and eventually dominate a weak African state might prefer placement of a large number of their own nationals in key positions.

Yet African leaders who depend on such support too obviously and too openly tend thereby to reduce their internal acceptability. At least it appears to be that way. Anticipation of such difficulties with leaders whom they want to support has caused some foreign powers to cut back the number of their nationals in front offices and to curb their enthusiasm for public expression of their feelings or of their ideological or cultural preferences. Soviets and Communist Chinese, French and British, Belgians, and certainly nationals of lesser states have retreated to less visible positions. In the Ivory Coast, for instance, where the *présence francaise* still is most pervasive, it is often impossible for the uninitiated to locate the French advisers who actually run a given ministry department or office.

Military Pressure

Power is said to abhor a vacuum, and since most of sub-Saharan Africa is devoid of internationally effective military power one might expect interested parties, certainly the major contestants for world supremacy, to be unable to resist temptation in this region. So far, nothing truly dramatic has occurred. Instead, during the first independence decade military and military-related activity by the super and former colonial powers was confined to four types, all of relatively modest dimensions:

1. Direct but temporary intervention by French and British forces — by the French far more than by the British — to protect French and British interests or shore up or in some cases reinstate preferred regimes.
2. Application of the force-in-being concept through stationing of forces on African soil or at convenient nearby bases.
3. Provision of training facilities for the regular armed forces and police, either on African soil or abroad, of training personnel and related financial support, and of hardware and logistic support where and when needed. The last was directed more toward preservation of internal stability — the law-and-order mission — and defense against incursion across the long, unprotected, and often disputed boundaries.
4. Provision of training personnel, training facilities, and equipment in support of guerilla activity, mainly against European dominated regimes presumed to be pro-Western.

All four types brought in their wake such concessions as permission to use naval bases and airports, overflight privileges for military aircraft, and permission to emplace special military or space-tracking equipment.

Following an initial flurry of direct interventions between 1960 and 1964, a shift occurred "from force to power."[25] It had become apparent that overt intervention to prop up weak, even unpopular regimes invariably turned into a source of acute embarrassment for all concerned, including the regime so aided. The consequences did not seem worth the effort. More discrete use of military power appeared to be called for in normal conditions; emergencies could always be dealt with thanks to rapidly improving logistic support possibilities. French and British as well as Belgian and Portuguese interests were served and protected to an extent through the naval and air arms of the North Atlantic Treaty Organization should more serious and more critical threats develop. (This protection was, of course, not explicitly a responsibility of NATO, but no one could doubt the standby commitment in the event the principal NATO target, the Soviet Union, should attempt massive military intervention in Africa.)

Provision of materiel and personnel support for Africa's growing armies and police forces becomes more urgent as the new states are increasingly subjected to internal stresses and strains, to instability, and occasionally to riot, insurrection, and secession. The boundaries of most of the new states are extremely vulnerable to incursion by hostile forces.

Senegal and the Ivory Coast view with justified misgivings their borders with the Republic of Guinea. Chad is wide open to interference from the north and northwest. Without strong outside support the former Congo (Zaire) may be a prime candidate for incursions from several directions. Ethiopia has severe problems along her disputed boundary with Somalia and over Eritrea as well as with the Sudan. Uganda is similarly vulnerable. The civil wars in the Sudan and in Chad alone constitute direct threats to weak neighbors increasingly subjected to internal pressures as well. The entire Arab-Black juxtaposition cannot be separated from the Arab-Israeli conflict. The black-white divide to the south is a fuse that leads to a powder keg; it poses direct military threats to both sides. All this opens wide the doors to military pressures applied not necessarily only by men in uniform but also, perhaps predominantly, by diplomats carrying supply and military and police training contracts in their briefcases.

Foreign influence possibilities arise primarily from the nexus between arms and equipment in use and replacement sources and from habits developed by African officers trained in European or United States military ways and traditions. It is highly probable that several military coups — perhaps one Ghanaian and one Ugandan, possibly also the first in Mali — were triggered when sensitivities on these points among Western-trained officers reached the critical stage. The matter has been put rather bluntly by one observer who notes that military hardware is far more expensive than a dozen limousines driven by corrupt politicians.[26] The capacity of African economies to assure continuous and increasing satisfaction of the appetite of the developing military forces is extremely limited; in some cases it is virtually nil.[27]

Both superpowers and many other suppliers of military and police support prefer to conceal at least a portion of their contributions. Not even key Senate committees are able to untangle the web of United States aid to determine with finality how much is military and how much civilian aid and assistance.[28] The Soviet Union is known to have shipped military equipment in crates marked as Red Cross gifts. The fall of the Nkrumah regime and of the Obote regime in Uganda brought to light several of these deceptive techniques. Whether actually used or merely held in readiness, overt or covert, the control potential of arms aid and related supports must be rated high in view of the increasingly prominent role played by the military in the new states. A reaction of sorts has started, and offers of military aid may be refused if the donor poses unacceptable conditions. Competition among the principal suppliers of military support, foremost the United States and the Soviet Union, will make this refusal increasingly possible.

The law-and-order rationale cited by Western suppliers and the defense-of-people's-republics argument offered by the centrally controlled economies suggests a special relationship between the supply of military equipment and military and police instructors and the flow of influence. Much of United States military support is said to be earmarked for security or public safety, while Soviet and Communist Chinese arms support is said to be offered to ward off capitalist, imperialist, or neocolonialist designs on the former colonies or to assist national liberation movements. Significantly, Soviet Russian publications are reticent on the subject of arms aid. Mainland China, on the other hand, does not conceal its increasing support of guerilla forces along the black-white divide.[29] The rhetoric is revealing. Western observers are wont to refer to military and police support as "a first line of defense against subversion and terrorism."[30] In part this is certainly justified, but only in part. A French source charmingly avers that France "will not intervene against the popular movements."[31] Or to justify intervention in Gabon in order to counter a military coup in 1964: "The intervention . . . was the result of an appeal made by the legitimate authorities for help against a handful of armed putschists."[32] The question arises: Who are the subversives, who the terrorists or the popular movements, and what is a legitimate authority in a former colony? In the United States dictionary, normally all social revolutionary forces are subversive; in many instances the term is applied also to forces that favor only social change. "Terrorists" are not only guerillas schooled in spreading fear and alarm among civilian populations but unfortunately also what in World War II would have been called heroes of the resistance had they been on the correct side.

Who are the popular movements if not the forces that oppose the regimes to whose support French troops have been flown on several occasions? Intervention was directed precisely against popular movements in Gabon, Dahomey, Cameroon, and Chad, as well as in Algeria, of course. Military support that the United States granted to Zaire or Ethiopia or Liberia was not so much directed at insurgents who threatened from outside as against internal opposition. Through the semantic gap that separates legitimate opposition and subversion, resistance and terrorism flow large sums, much military equipment, and much influence.

What of intra-African military pressure? Threats of military action usually have had reference to African unity issues, especially the race confrontation in the Southern region. While Nkrumah was at the helm, Ghana hinted military deployment against Rhodesia and, of course, did train guerillas for deployment in several black as well as European-dominated states.[33] For some time guerilla units equipped with arms supplied by the Soviet Union and China have infiltrated Portuguese territories and Rhodesia from Zambia and Zaire bases, with approval and some modest support from member states of the OAU.

Individual Egyptian pilots appear to have participated in action in the Sudan and during the Nigerian civil war. Nigeria offered military support to Guinea to defend that country against further Portuguese led or inspired incursions in 1970. When a socialist-oriented junta replaced a conciliatory regime in Somalia in 1969, word was spread that the new regime favored a kind of holy war by all Somalis in Kenya and Ethiopia, together with other "oppressed peoples," such as the Galla of Ethiopia, toward creation of a Greater Somalia.[34] (Serious or not, this rumor tended to enhance influence opportunities for the Soviet Union, which shortly thereafter assumed total responsibility for the development of Somalia's armed forces.)

The influence potential of Africa's armed forces is easily exaggerated. The arithmetic of military power in black Africa for some time to come would suggest that 2 times 2 does not necessarily total 4; 40 airplane pilots plus 40 MIG's does not necessarily mean that a single MIG can be airborne or deployed against a hostile force unless foreigners fly them, as they apparently did during the civil war in Nigeria.[35]

Organized International Influences

With the fading ability or willingness of major powers to assist the new states — ability in terms of funds set aside for assistance purposes — agencies such as the International Monetary Fund and the International Bank for Reconstruction and Development (IMF and IBRD, respectively), agencies of the European Economic Community, and other lesser sources of international support must step into the breach. This changeover creates new influence and control opportunities.

Ghana is a striking illustration. Hard pressed in 1964, partly because his government had overextended the economic and financial resources available, Nkrumah called on the IMF to consider an application for support. Although none of the IMF advisers sought to apply pressure directly, many of their recommendations inevitably looked to suspicious Ghanaian officials like direct foreign intervention in the internal affairs of a sovereign

African state.[36] These suspicions were reinforced after Nkrumah's fall in 1966 when the same IMF, called on again to help bail out an even weaker economy, insisted on measures that tended to weaken that economy still further. One United States observer who had been quite critical of Nkrumah's economic policies actually suggested that "some of the independence gained under Nkrumah was now being lost" to international agencies, in particular to the IMF.[37]

At issue were differences of opinion on matters of priority. In the eyes of IMF officials, current balance of payment requirements overrode long-range balance of payment considerations. As a result of overcommitment under Nkrumah, Ghana had incurred a staggering debt. Servicing of that debt became *the* prime preoccupation for the successor regime. Since some of the debts had been contracted through wholly unfeasible, even reckless ventures priced far above the going rate for projects of the same type elsewhere in the developing world, thought was given to repudiation of the least defensible debts. The IMF signaled its opposition to *any* financing of the remaining debt unless *all*, even the most predatory, commitments were met. This position ignored the interrelationship of debts, debt servicing, the tendency of the servicing to spiral to astronomic proportions in very short periods of time, and economic growth and development generally. Yet, in the absence of viable alternatives IMF or IBRD strictures must weigh most heavily indeed.

Guided by considerations common among bankers everywhere, IMF, IBRD, and other international sources of capital think conservative and big. Though perhaps vital to weak economies seeking to reorient themselves, many project applications are turned down because they are too small, too impractical by prevailing financial standards; some are turned down because net gains are uncertain and too far into the future. In line with such perspectives, projects stand a better chance if they promise immediate or short-range yields, which invariably means retention of existing economic activities and patterns laid down under colonial rule. It is obvious that this position clashes with social revolutionary insistence on radical economic reform.

In light of the established record, it is difficult to allay suspicions among independent-minded African leaders that the IMF and the IBRD, already candidates for the role of stalking horses for United States capitalists (the United States does dominate voting in both agencies), are not also devices to entangle Africa in a web that is little more than a novel form of colonialism, this time with an international face. To be sure, allegations that international conspiracies have been directed against specific regimes, such as Nkrumah's, solely in response to perceived ideological threats cannot be taken seriously. Even if the Nkrumahs, the Tourés, or the Nassers occasionally do get under the skins of United States, British, or French owners or managers of capital, it is improbable that these interests are prepared to place in jeopardy other, in the aggregate far more important, financial interests elsewhere merely to bring down one relatively inconsequential African leader. Competition among Western interests alone tends to discount broad international conspiracy theories. More plausible are speculations to the effect that consumers of Africa's primary products may combine to protect their interests and to prevent formation of an effective collective bargaining front among producers.

Shortly before his fall, Nkrumah had charged that United States and British refusal to lower tariff barriers in favor of cocoa products was inspired mainly by a desire to ruin the Ghanaian economy, thus hastening the removal of a prime antagonist of imperialism and neocolonialism. Lowering of tariff barriers, he argued, would have increased the flow of products and offset the then-depressed cocoa price by increasing total consumption. He also charged the consuming countries with deliberate stockpiling of cocoa to depress the price in the first place, with denial of investment funds and credit guaranties to encourage potential investors, with placing increased pressure on investors and sources of credit to reduce their contributions to the Ghanaian economy, and with sabotage of Ghanaian loan requests in diverse Western capitals as well as in the IMF and the IBRD.[38]

As do so many simplistic analyses of complex matters, this one misses some rather basic points. Cocoa consumers or users, for example, are not independent agents. Manufacturers of chocolate products, for instance, must seek stable, even predictable, sources of supply and will bargain toward those objectives. Theirs is a competitive industry dependent on consumer purchasing power, preferences, and tastes. At the same time these same interests also seek to stabilize the price in order to protect producers from the ravages of at-times wild fluctuations. Both objectives require the setting of production quotas, which can be burdensome. They can freeze an entire economic sector by enjoining a country from increasing production to take advantage of higher prices, for instance. Although hardly in the category of conspiracy, the consequences of such measures often seem deliberate to those at the receiving end.

6

African Defenses: A Balance Sheet

Ironically, one of the prime sources of strength for many of the new states is their weakness. The Soviet Union will go to any length to maintain control over Czechoslovakia but will quietly accept ejection of Soviet citizens or ambassadors from Guinea or Kenya, arrest of Soviet seamen in Ghanaian territorial waters, or sharp attacks on Soviet foreign policy by African heads of state. The United States will not accept expulsion from areas in the world deemed vital to the national interest but will not offer much resistance if denied access to some African state. Most of Africa simply is not sufficiently important to the world's major or middle powers to induce them to enter into serious disputes or even struggles. In most instances the costs of all-out efforts to deter the new leaders from a given course of action will not be justified by the best possible outcome. Operating under this umbrella of indifference, the diplomacy of even the weakest state can realize some concrete bargaining opportunities and some net gains.

The bargaining position of some states is enhanced by nature; certain natural resources found on the continent are vital to some or all of the world's powers. Even if the latter should not themselves require the resources, it may be in their best interest at least to deny them to adversaries. More than 50 percent of the minerals critical to the military or industrial needs of the superpowers are located on the continent. Rhodesia and South Africa are, of course, in the lead in this respect, but oil, copper, cobalt, chrome, and uranium are found elsewhere as well. Nigeria, Libya, and Algeria have grown considerably in international stature because of oil. The Congo (Kinshasa), now Zaire, and Gabon have risen on the strength of uranium. Morocco, the Congo, and Zambia found cobalt a potent bargaining weapon.[1]

Even after taxes and royalties paid to the African government, profits on investments still are quite high as compared to opportunities in the developed economies. In some cases investors are reported to have been able to recover their entire input within the short span of four to five years. United States monopolies are said to enjoy a profit margin of no more than 8-12 percent in their own country as compared to 22-30 percent in some of the former colonies.[2] Furthermore, the former French, British, and Belgian colonies still provide considerable amounts of foreign exchange for the benefit of the metropolitan centers. The African members of the franc zone contribute to French currency reserves as a result of a trade surplus with nonzone trading partners.[3]

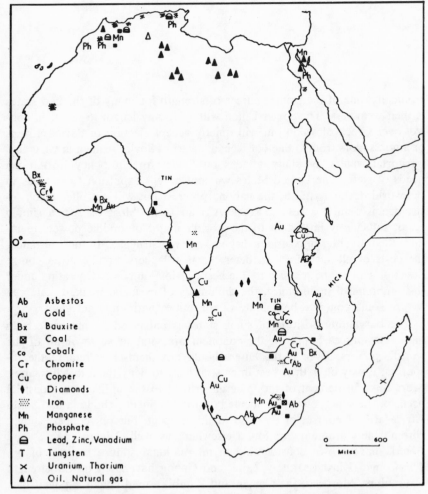

Ab	Asbestos
Au	Gold
Bx	Bauxite
⊠	Coal
co	Cobalt
Cr	Chromite
Cu	Copper
◆	Diamonds
⠿	Iron
Mn	Manganese
Ph	Phosphate
⊟	Lead, Zinc, Vanadium
T	Tungsten
×	Uranium, Thorium
▲ ▵	Oil. Natural gas

FIGURE 6.1   *Mining in Africa in the Early 1960's*

SOURCE: Mountjoy and Embleton, *Africa: A New Geographical Survey,* 148. © by A. B. Mountjoy and C. Embleton, 1966, 1967.

African regimes have been able to extract concessions from seemingly invulnerable international financial colossuses. Africans were added to top policymaking boards; corporations were compelled to open their books to African or African-employed inspectors; investment and exploitation policies of major corporations were redirected to conform more to local requirements. Depreciation schedules were altered on African insistence, and in some instances exploitation of major resources was slowed down for a period to allow the producing country to develop its own absorptive capacity.[4] To create the requisite preconditions for increased pressure, foreign corporations have been forced to register locally and to transfer their headquarters for African operations to the host country.[5]

The Most Effective Weapons

After overcoming tenacious French resistance, several of the former colonies have created openings for competitors from outside, either by lowering tariff barriers or by directly inviting non-French banks or investors. Some have shifted their trade eastward, either toward Japan or to the Soviet Union or Communist China. Although still relatively insignificant, the trend is discernible and does provide new bargaining opportunities. Certainly the ability to convince British and American negotiators that alternate developers of Zambia's copper resources — mainly from Italy and Japan but possibly also from the Soviet Union — were waiting in the wings broke the ice and enabled Zambia to proceed with nationalization of the mines on terms relatively favorable to her economy. Ghana achieved a breakthrough with regard to the Volta River scheme as soon as the Soviet alternative materialized on the scene; Soviet offers to construct lesser dams rekindled United States interests in the major project.

The nationalization option is the most formidable, but it is not so readily available as it might seem if cost-benefit considerations are allowed to bear on the decision. The experiences and the plans of oil-producing states to maximize their options, possibly by takeover of foreign owned and operated concessions, illustrate the position of the nationalizing state.

First, however large the share of revenue from oil, other sources of foreign exchange remain to be considered. No matter how sanguine the expectations of future gains from oil might be, Nigeria for some time to come will not be able to escape a certain dependence on agriculture. During the initial exploration period, oil revenue tends to be inadequate to support current governmental requirements. Nigeria's development planners readily conceded in 1970 that to assure modest fulfillment of plan goals agricultural production still would have to be improved, while at the same time still some 20 percent of the net public sector program would have to be financed by external aid.[6] As we have seen, external aid turns quite sluggish in the face of nationalization.

Short of taking that extreme step, oil-producing states have additional options. They may establish national corporate bodies to compete in the mining industry from exploration to refining, thus forcing foreign interests to raise the quality of their performance. They may improve their intelligence capabilities to reduce the ability of foreign firms alone to determine costs and prices and rig output figures and otherwise deceive the host government. "Control without technology is a joke," one high Nigerian civil servant commented with an eye to the oil industry.[7]

The professionals among African policymakers are not oblivious to the high costs of oil marketing and refining, as they are not unaware of similar problems in other production processes. Caution seems to be the rule before governments take over major sources of foreign exchange that they know they cannot operate. Granted, few enterprises or industries will come to a complete stop if nationalized. There will always be, and increasingly so, a reservoir of talent, unencumbered by colonial traditions, that can be hired from alternate countries if necessary. But the markets overseas and in many cases the international financial supports will not remain at the disposal of a stubbornly recalcitrant regime.

In the circumstances, the nationalization weapon may have to be placed in cold storage in many countries unless the world market situation changes radically, favoring even the weakest or weaker producers. In 1971 Nigeria moved to take advantage of gains negotiated by the stronger oil producers in North Africa and the Middle East.[8] In anticipation of rising demands, pressure on oil companies was increased, and Nigeria proceeded to strengthen her capabilities for more effective supervision and control with the allocation in the 1970-71 budget of £N 200,000 for reorganization of the colonial-rooted Mines and Power Administration.[9] In 1971 the establishment of a £N 900,000 Petroleum Training Institute was announced; this move was followed logically by creation of a National Mining Corporation to offer some competition for foreigners. (Nigeria stood to benefit from two special advantages: while the Suez Canal remained closed, Nigerian oil was closer to Europe, the main importing region, than was oil from the Persian Gulf area; and its low sulphur content made Nigerian oil especially attractive to pollution-conscious consumers.)[10]

The Balance Sheet

Many of the options seemingly open to the African states — at first attractive and feasible — turn out to be quite burdensome in their consequences and quite impractical after the decision to seize a given opportunity has been made. Even if it is too late for the incautious country, the lessons will not go unnoticed nearby. Nationalization often seems quite unattractive if measured against the losses likely to be incurred. Why, ask some African leaders who are urged to proceed precipitously against foreigners, expend funds and manpower, risk losses and investments, and incur animosities by acquiring something you already have? There is another catch. International investment circles, it emerges, have a rating scale somewhat like chambers of commerce have in the United States. By that scale countries with minimum Africanization in key executive and technical positions rate higher than do those where the majority of key posts in commerce, industry, and government, especially in the technically most sensitive sectors, are staffed by relatively untrained Africans. In other words, leaving key industries in the hands of foreign managers may be financially rewarding, even though it may be hazardous in terms of domestic politics.

Takeover, or nationalization, in any case is not what it appears to be. The actual arrangements made following spectacular nationalization of banks, insurance companies, or oil companies, and in Zambia the accommodations negotiated with regard to the copper mines, differ markedly from what nationalistic rhetoric leads the public to expect. Nationalization of foreign banks, for instance, may mean transfer of the meat of banking back to the bank's home grounds, while only the shell of banking is taken over or is given a local coloring. Moreover, funds withdrawn — in Senegal, for instance — find their way back into the nationalizing economy through expatriate export and import houses, which generate as much influence as before.

The chips on the African side have a way of disappearing, or at least diminishing quite suddenly and unexpectedly. Shortly after the copper mines were nationalized — only to the extent of 51 percent, incidentally — Zambia experienced the aforementioned catastrophic loss when the largest mine, Mufulira, caved in.[11] Also in the back of the minds of Zambia's leaders was the warning issued by mining experts: "although Zambia has 25 percent of the world's copper reserves, there is a danger that much of it will never be mined because of the cost definition; it is not ore but waste."[12]

Two major alternative sources of possible strength for the African side are frequently cited — international organizations, including regional ones, and African unity. Although we have touched on these sources previously, it is useful to summarize their overall value to Africa at this point.

In concrete terms the United Nations has not been able to generate the potential that the new arrivals from the Third World expected from it in the first blush of their coveted membership. In respects truly critical to African interests, the organization has not proceeded far beyond production of general statements of intent. The Organization of African Unity also is far from achieving the capabilities ascribed to it by its more enthusiastic devotees. African unity is converted into strength only through action, either militarily or economically. Even combined, which is a rather remote possibility, the 40 or so African states do not realistically dispose of the material means to sustain military operations against such determined antagonists as Portugal and the Union of South Africa. It has crossed the minds of black leaders that continued reduction of trade with white-dominated regimes may create conditions in which those regimes might no longer have reason to avoid military incursions of their own in retaliation against black-supported guerilla operations.[13]

Strength through economic unity is no more promising. Efforts to improve Africa's position through association with diverse worldwide producers' associations have not yet borne fruit. Haltingly but inexorably, the new states wherever possible are creating their own economic opportunities quite unrelated to the demands of continental or regional unity. As individual industrialization programs are started everywhere, rivalries and competition that have troubled Europe for so long will sweep aside the entreaties by African unity proponents. Occasionally some successes may be scored. An individual corporation, bank, or even a country may be dissuaded under the combined pressure from black regimes to abandon or to withdraw support for a project in a white-ruled area. Zambian insistence that interests eager to enter the Zambian economy, such as Italy, withdraw support from the Portuguese-controlled Cabora Bassa Dam appears to have been successful, at least in some instances.[14] But most of the demands based on assumed African unity seem to be quite unrealistic. Nkrumah was particularly euphoric in his assessments of continental strength. Advocating "reversal of the flow of wealth," he predicted that Africa would soon be placed "among the most modernized continents of the world *without recourse to outside sources.*"[15] We have seen how unrealistic such an assessment of Africa's future is.

Always remaining at the end of the unity rainbow are the stark realities of self-interest, fanned as it is, and constantly so, by resourceful interests from outside. The situation has been aptly summarized by the president of Malawi, Dr. Banda, with reference to a resolution passed by the Organization of African Unity calling for withdrawal of African bank balances from Britain in retaliation for Britain's refusal to take decisive steps against Southern Rhodesia when that colony unilaterally declared itself independent: "Are they to withdraw their overdrafts?" he asked.[16]

Inveterate optimists point to the International Monetary Fund and the World Bank as the last lines of defense. Undoubtedly these agencies contain to some degree the germ of effective support for the development of African unity, but no more than the germ. Unless and until the resources behind the Fund and the Bank are augmented to begin to match Africa's needs, they can do little more than furnish band-aids. The staggering requirement posed by the needs for economic diversification on top of current needs to keep the economies above water are entirely outside the range of both agencies as presently constituted and governed.

IV

Sources and Uses of Power:
National-Internal

The *Rainmaker* is Daba, the chief in a desperately poor, primitive and atavistic rural Zulu community. . . .He is powerful partly through his hereditary ability to produce rain — or more accurately, gauge when it is likely to come so that he can *appear* to have produced it — and partly for the weightier economic reason that he possesses all the cattle.

JACK COPE
BOOK REVIEW OF *The Rainmaker*

7

Legitimate Economic
Resources and Allocations

Financial resources form a major nucleus of power at the national level, as they do internationally. Constitutional authority to raise funds, statutory authority to spend them, and even authority to apply physical force to secure control over all public and private affairs in the final analysis depend for implementation on financial resources *actually available*. A full understanding of the nature and flow of social power therefore requires an understanding of the processes by which these resources are generated, materialize, and are applied to implement public policy decisions.

Prevailing economic conditions in Africa necessitate forms and patterns of public authority and government that differ significantly from typical textbook descriptions. The economics of poverty, or where riches of some proportion exist, the economics of imbalance or maldistribution, quickly and inexorably erode even the most carefully constructed constitutional or statutory defenses against arbitrary rule. Barriers set up to protect private interests against public tyranny are likely to be swept aside where public financial resources dominate the economy. Central or national governmental power, for example, follows in the wake of financial grants to local government units, because public power flows inevitably into the private sector through openings created by private subsistence interests.

This power gives modern African governments the edge over the as-yet anemic African private domain; local and traditional interests do not have a chance in the crunch against the comparatively overwhelming financial steamrollers operated by central governments. This disadvantage may be modified where financial resources at the disposal of central authority prove inadequate for current public needs. In such conditions, foreign and at times even indigenous capital resources can and frequently do create a reverse flow of power, eventually replacing public with private authority. This phenomenon is increasingly recognized in the developed systems where the power of giant private corporations begins to rival public authority. Such shifts of power usually remain concealed from public view.

It is not our intent to deprecate or belittle constitutional or statutory allocations of public power. Formal arrangements do, of course, play a significant part in the management of power, if for no other reasons than as terms of reference and means of legitimization. What must be appreciated is that in Africa the form and the substance of government perform distinctly different functions. Parliaments, elections, and constituent assemblies serve mainly as facades whose basic purpose is retention of the loyalty of the masses, while the socioeconomic substance — money, finance, wealth, and economic opportunities — serves as the infrastructure of effective government.

A president of the United States is reported to have said of his successor: "Poor Ike, he is going to sit behind this desk and say, 'Do this, do that,' and find that nothing is going to be done. It will be quite frustrating." African leaders, who enjoy considerably less material and administrative support, must experience a far greater sense of frustration. It is not unusual for public officials to discover that the means at their disposal do not match the authority granted to them under a constitution or under statutes that established their offices. Increasingly, African leaders who feel unnecessarily constrained by constitutions they believe were imposed from outside, or by parliaments they are convinced are a luxury their country cannot afford, tend to dispense with both. When total abolition proves unfeasible, constitutions and parliaments have been vitiated to the point of insignificance. But even unlimited authority turns out to be a paper weapon against the reality of poverty.

To be sure, rulers may employ physical force, even terror, to compel acceptance of their dictates. Incompetence, corruption, and mismanagement may be concealed by various means, and badly depleted financial resources may be stretched by sheer bravado. Governments may rob Peter to pay Paul — that is, they may pay bills by juggling accounts — but few such measures will actually move the ship of state far from the precarious position it was left in by the colonial regime. So far, no methods have been discovered to work miracles, to extract water from rocks or blood from turnips.

Prime Sources: An Overview

Realistically, the economic component of governmental power derives, first, from funds actually realized and available for application. Wellsprings of these funds are not public oratory or political party resolutions but net gain from aggregate economic productivity, public and private. Second, governmental power draws on the ability to dispense or control means of subsistence, ranging from lucrative contracts — a major form of political patronage — to employment opportunities for individuals.

To an extent, the public side of this power is revealed in the national budget, but only to an extent. African budgets and other published statements on the financial resources on which these are based do not lend themselves to firm conclusions about how public funds are managed in reality. Even in budgetary respects things are not always what they seem to be; caution is always in order before cold print on government finance and related affairs is accepted as a basis for sociopolitical analysis. (It is worth noting that few textbook accounts of public finance even hint at irregularities or procedural lacunae in African budgetary and fiscal management.)

Full assessment of the operational value of financial means as instruments of power must, as we have shown, take into account the element of foreign control. It would be quite meaningless to interpret any budget without regard to where the money is coming from. In Zambia in 1969 over 60 percent of all government revenue was generated by one commodity in one way or another — namely, copper. Cocoa, groundnuts, and other commodities, almost exclusively traded abroad, provide the largest single bloc of revenue for most of the new states. The implications are clear: the budget contains the seeds of foreign control, a fact of life unmistakably revealed in the foreign exchange and receipts from abroad components of national budgets. Obviously, as long as French interests predominate in such countries as Senegal, Ivory Coast, or Gabon, the national budgets there cannot be taken seriously without careful and extensive interpolation of data pertaining to French financial and commercial transactions, public and private, within the African systems and with the mother country.[1]

Budgetary freedom to effect reforms or to initiate social revolutionary changes is limited also by the unhappy circumstance of dependence on agriculture. As long as agriculture dominates the economy, the social institutions and processes spawned by agricultural modes of production and distribution will set the pace and determine what can and what cannot be done. Furthermore, the at-times wildly gyrating world market conditions tend to raise havoc with any long-range planning and persistently undercut any attempts to develop sources of revenue relatively free from foreign control. It seems that whenever success appears to be in sight and diversification of sources of revenue appears to be within reach a sharp drop in the world price of the principal export commodity wipes out the modest surplus, and with that go the means without which new industries or other new, untried, hence relatively costly, ventures cannot be launched. Even in optimal conditions the prospects of successful escape from these forms of bondage are poor.

Nigeria became a prime example after high-quality mineral oil was found there in commercial quantities. Oil differs substantially from other modes of production as a source of social power. Located under the ground near or offshore, it yields income mainly for the government before leaving the economy in barrels to be sold for the benefit of foreign corporations. For that reason alone the impact of revenue from oil on the relative position of the central government vis-a-vis the subunits or states (the federal structure in Nigeria) could be profound. Between 1965 and 1971 the oil share of total revenue rose from 7 to 47 percent. So explosive a rate of growth in one sector could affect a federal system of distribution of powers more profoundly than could any change of government, including revolutionary overthrow.

In practice the impact of oil on the economy will be delayed. Other sources of income have supported the system for more than half a century and have shaped it in the process. Institutional and procedural blocs created by traditional modes of production and grown to formidable size over that period will deflect the new input for some time to come. Of course, in ideal conditions — for instance, an incorruptible, efficient, and dedicated military cum civil service regime — skillful application of the new revenue could turn Nigeria around. It is unlikely, however, that the major share of that revenue will soon be available for development and, if it were, that it would be applied as planned and would not be dissipated in the usual ways. In the main, oil yields initially less revenue for the African government because substantial amounts earned by producers must be diverted to cover the high cost of exploration and early production in addition to profits and other charges.

The new resource differs from traditional ones in yet other respects. Oil generates few secondary industries; to be economical, those that are oil related — for example, petrochemical — must be located near refineries, which must, in turn, be situated near port facilities, since local consumption still is in its infancy. Agriculture, on the other hand, does support secondary, mainly processing industries that may prove profitable even if located in the interior. This means fairer distribution of sources of revenue, more equitable distribution of income, greater financial viability for local government units far from the capital — all of which is of fundamental importance to a country the size of Nigeria. Absence of such an equalizing force or, conversely, further and unhindered growth of central government financial power could so debilitate and demoralize the vast hinterland as to render illusory all prospects of nationwide development.

Oil also differs from other sources of public finance in that oil revenue is processed by hands distinctly different from those that handle cultural income or revenue derived from most industrial activities. Oil revenue accrues directly to the national government; thus, in theory at least, fewer opportunities should exist for sticky fingers to interfere with the lawful application of funds. There should be fewer opportunities, too, for local interests to enrich themselves through inefficiency that generates patronage and other unproductive methods. Then again, old ways could survive, but on a more lavish scale. Corruption could mushroom, reaching gigantic proportions.

Government controls over indigenous corporate and individual means of subsistence are of far greater weight in the scales of power in Africa than is commonly realized. The virtual absence of meaningful alternatives to dealing with public agencies and to working with public funds, the absence of alternatives to political patronage compel all but the most indispensable foreign and all African or local entrepreneurs to enter into dealings with public officials on a basis more urgent than is necessary in more highly diversified, decentralized, and developed systems. Constitutional provisions and statutory regulations are commonly believed to be adequate to curb the ability of public officials to direct the flow of public funds as they desire. For run-of-mill contracts and routine allocations this is true enough. It is not true, however, where the stakes are really high.

Statutory curbs, even constitutional restraints, are eviscerated where no effective independent inquiry into the allocation of public funds may be conducted. In the absence of a truly independent press, without an independent and vigilant body of educated citizens, and without an independent authority of the caliber of a House of Commons or a Congress, those who want to obtain access to the cornucopia of public finance must deal with public officials. In the circumstances, covert and illicit use of public funds becomes an integral part of government operation. Already under colonial rule a special relationship had tied private corporate interests to government and vice versa. Then government officials often acted as representatives of corporate interests, mainly European, enabling those interests to extract values far in excess of what might be considered their fair share of public wealth. As can be expected, private beneficiaries of such arrangements responded in kind to favors granted.

In return for concessions, licenses, and permits, large corporations as well as more substantial individual entrepreneurs were permitted, in effect, to bend the systems to their will. In turn, private interests eager to partake of lucrative ventures displayed great vulnerability to blackmail or coercion on the part of key officials and political leaders; after all, such costs could always be written off as business expense. Where legal restraints have been all but abolished, public officials in position to exploit this particular mine find it difficult to resist temptation.[2] Because this set of sources of power, working in both directions from public to private and from private to public authority, is illegitimate if not illegal, the price exacted by either side for services rendered or benefits bestowed is typically not part of the public record. It is, however, as integral a part of the machinery of government as are demands of ordinary taxpayers or pressure and interest groups known and operating entirely in the open.

OPERATIONAL DIMENSIONS OF THE ALLOCATIVE FUNCTION

The key to an appreciation of what can and cannot be done lies then in the financial resources actually available and in the machinery appropriate for their effective use actually in existence and functioning. Given the precarious base of public finance, the role of foreign owners or managers of capital must be regarded as an integral component of government. Public power cannot be meaningfully separated from private power as a rule. If it is separated conceptually, the firm and unabiding linkages should in no circumstances be overlooked or left out of account.

In practice, the constitutional machinery functions only as a vast umbrella, a very flexible one at that, spread out over state and society to provide legitimizing cover. Equally important, powers formally assigned to government may turn out to be illusory and may not be at all implemental, or government may by choice or by necessity elect not to exercise powers as prescribed by constitution or by law. These discretionary prerogatives should be regarded as crucial variables in the allocation of funds everywhere; in the typical African systems, characterized by scarcity, the importance of these variables cannot easily be exaggerated.

The element of selectivity in the use of resources and in the use of powers injects a complicating factor into all calculations of government operation over and above the unpredictables and intangibles that arise from the rationality-irrationality syndrome. Even where greed, avarice, and, more generally, corruption are not at the root of public policy decisions, subterfuge and deception are unavoidable consequences where oratory and hard financial data simply will not match. This situation creates a source of dissension and bitterness. Though artificial, it nevertheless tends to create instability, and of course, it creates special problems for the social analyst.

Applied Power: The Budget

In developed areas budgets are subject to some juggling, but in the main the final document does accurately reflect the fiscal situation. African national budgets are not that dependable. Dependence on outside resources and the deleterious effects of internal fiscal and administrative weaknesses allow those at the spigot of public finance to manipulate the allocative machinery often as they please. In most of French-influenced Africa in the 1960 and early 1970s, for instance, the national budgets were playgrounds for foreign as well as domestic manipulation. The provision of separate budgets for primarily outside supported development did not alter this freedom in any way.

Since the bottom may drop out of any budget at any time, the allocative propensities must be regarded as quite unpredictable. Thus, universally understood budget categories, or lines, do not mean the same thing in all of Africa. Public debt charges, ever on the increase, may be concealed effectively or may, as in most of French-speaking Africa, simply not be recorded; small wonder if the same budgets differ substantially in their French and African documentary incarnations.

Still, a very large share of the GNP flows through the public sector, and budgets remain useful indexes to allocative decisions and practices, always provided they are viewed with caution. Typically, the public sector and the export sector combine to direct the flow of money and all that this flow entails. Since the government generally is the largest employer, especially of labor forces concentrated in and around the capitals, the total wage and salary bill alone is the equivalent of entire blocs of constitutionally authorized power, and budgets provide a clear view of that.

Means are influenced by ends, and allocative policies continue to be shaped by the fact that the gravitational centers of African economies still are located somewhere between the foreign wellsprings of capital and overseas markets on the one hand and African production centers on the other. This distributive pattern shapes the instrumentalities of government, even though these may remain unchanged in their outer, formal appearance. Whatever the social purposes and intents, allocation of resources and wealth will not be as taught in schools.

African governments more often than not must operate under immense financial pressure, which profoundly affects their intent as well as their style. Are those at the public spigot inclined to use the potential of public money to advance the economy as a whole on a broad front, or do they elect to employ resources at their disposal to patch holes, obtain spot support wherever it can be found, and generally seek to keep barely ahead of the wolf of financial insolvency and the rival contenders of power?

The Marketing Boards

Hammers have been used to build and they have been used to murder. The interesting aspect of instrumentalities of power everywhere is that they lend themselves to diverse, even contradictory, purposes. Failure to take this aspect into account has generated a great deal of confusion in and about Africa. The stories of the marketing boards in British-influenced Africa and their equivalents in the French regions dramatically illustrate this point.

Originally, under the colonial regimes recognition of the cyclical and erratic price movements for prime commodities on the international markets had led to the creation of instruments of economic stabilization. Briefly, it was the purpose of these boards to facilitate collection and eventually sale of agricultural commodities and then siphon off from the net sales price enough to provide a cushion for years when government revenue would be reduced as a result of adverse world trade conditions. (Pierre Moussa has captioned this chapter in the history of colonial exploitation of Africa's resources "La Politique Josephienne" in honor of the young Israelite who, interpreting the dream of the seven fat and seven meager cows, had recommended that provision be made for the expected seven lean years.)[3] To an extent, the stated ends were served and served well, but aside from the rather substantial diversion of funds collected by the boards in the sale of African commodities abroad to support the British effort in World War II and to cope with the aftermath, the stabilizing functions were only part of the story.

Soon after certain decision-making functions had been transferred to African rulers, the still considerable reserves accumulated by the boards (there was one board for nearly every major and some minor commodities) and the power associated with their use attracted the eye of political leaders intent on building their own personal machines. Their objectives were facilitated by certain ambiguities in the terms of reference under which the boards were to function. Nominally semipublic but in reality under the thumb of whoever controlled the public sector, they could at one and the same time be used as extensions of public power and be considered not public.

Promptly under various guises funds were diverted to noneconomic and even nonpublic purposes. Pretending that the intent was to reduce foreign influence through promotion of African enterprise, funds were funneled into private hands, all too frequently not in the interest of either stabilization or development. For instance, greatly indebted African producers were said to be protected against further exploitation by imperialists through loans and other contributions drawn from the reserves accumulated in the boards' coffers. As is so frequently true, devices brought into being to protect someone soon turn into devices to exploit him or someone else.

Warning voices were not heeded. The argument that African funds had to be available to achieve African ends was irresistible and incontrovertible in the sphere of public debate. All that had to be said was that the funds were being used for development.

Increasingly, beneficiaries of munificence tapped from marketing board funds turned out to be supporters of the dominant political machine. Under the pretense of "preventing the complete domination of the economy by expatriate interests," millions in badly needed funds were diverted into economically unproductive channels in the power and influence structure. Frequently this diversion was done through investments in banks or various commercial and industrial enterprises that promised high yield to the investor but low benefits for the economy as a whole.

The power politically seminal position of most of such investment opportunities is especially worth noting. Instead of assisting, as was claimed, "the growth of well-established indigenous banking institutions so that they might be able, if placed in a strong financial position, to assist in the private sector of the country's industrial and commercial activities," the banks, real estate enterprises, and the like frequently turned out to be captive

golden geese to assure continued support for the respective ruling machines. (It is noteworthy that observers who ascribed to the boards beneficial contributions to development as a rule did so on the basis of data
that covered the period up to but not after independence.)[4] Investigations,
tribunals, and commissions of inquiry throughout British Africa — no
such practice seems to exist in French Africa (!) — uniformly show this
form of abuse. At best the funds collected were used to "socialize savings,"
at worst to build private fortunes. In between, millions were placed at the
disposal of manipulators of public resources for a variety of ends, few of
which reflected the stated purpose of the boards when first created.

The disease affects all statutory corporations for identical reasons. It
should, of course, surprise no one if large sums made available to inexperienced hands on very short notice — millions of pounds actually changed
hands within days — were misapplied or disappeared from public view.
Given the already overtaxed personnel structure in all relevant administrative areas, ranging from accounting and supervision to detection and
prosecution, and considering the widespread complicity of potential en-
forcers of the law, whatever existed in the way of control machinery simply
could not creak into action.

Efforts to close the doors to that variant of misuse of public funds
foundered on many rocks; a major problem was naiveté in the perception
of political reality on the part of commissioners entrusted with the investigations, for it prevented discovery of effective remedies — assuming that
discovery of effective remedies was the intent. Typically, the recommendation was that legal or administrative barriers be devised to keep politicians
out of policymaking positions in statutory corporations or agencies.[5] A
charming example of a substantial misperception of the relationship between
public money, officialdom, and power politics is offered in the following
recommendation by a commission of inquiry into the then badly misman-
aged affairs of the Nigerian Railway Corporation.

XIII.15. Board Members should be carefully selected. They must be nonpartisan and be endowed with talent and broad outlook, of high integrity
and unimpeachable public and private life. *They must be completely disassociated from politics and political control and should be men of enterprise and of proven business success.* The field from which Board members
may be chosen is very wide indeed but the immediately related field in
which to look for them is as follows:
transportation
finance
business organization
trade unions
Chamber of Commerce or Business Houses
rail users
eminent citizens
top management in the Nigerian Railway Corporation.[6]

While there is little room for debate on the first and second sentences, the third one reflects a total lack of understanding of reality or an unwillingness to acknowledge it. Only an exceedingly narrow concept of human motivation and behavior could support the belief that "men of enterprise and proven business success" can completely disassociate themselves from politics and political control. Statutory corporations are, of course, used by governments for political purposes. A railway corporation, for instance, may decide, or the appropriate agency of the government may decide through that medium, as did the Nigerian Railway Corporation in the Bornu railway extension in Northern Nigeria, to benefit a particular section or a particular group.[7] All too frequently, as in the highly developed and industrialized countries, the respected head of a commission turns out to be the partisan of a particular social philosophy or ideology, either of which he may diligently espouse while in office. Perhaps more relevant, no commission chairman in the United States can actually disassociate himself from the political world in which he lives and acts. The setting up of statutory corporations to manage portions of a country's wealth is by definition a political act, and the exercise of the prerogatives requisite to such purposes is politics. Collection of produce, payment, even weighing of cocoa or coffee bags, quality control, and all else associated with government in business is political, cannot be disassociated from politics, and perhaps should not be, for if it were, it would surely be out of this world.

Other Regulatory Powers

A common understanding of the essence of governments' power to regulate public and private affairs seems to assume an overriding concern with the public interest on the part of public officials. According to that view, regulatory powers are exercised to assure peaceful resolution of conflicts and maintenance of law and order and minimum standards of public health and welfare. To an extent, such an understanding is correct. However, since pressure is a key factor in public policy decisionmaking, regulatory powers are likely to be brought into play in direct proportion to the force commanded by interests that are to be regulated or that seek to have regulations imposed on others. In practice, at the top of priority lists are income regulation, regulation of ways and means governing access to sources of wealth or production of wealth for the benefit of those already well situated, and regulation of access by the masses to basic means of subsistence. As in so many other respects, social ritual and euphemisms obscure the large volume of transactions along these lines, but it does not require too great an effort to lay bare the essence of applied regulatory power in the modern state, developed or underdeveloped.

The limits of power to regulate are in part set by public awareness of what is being done and why. But the ways of political economic regulations are devious and complex; fiscal regulations, openings to enormous opportunities for the informed and the alert, are beyond the comprehension of the vast majority of people in the new states. Few indeed are in a position to penetrate to the inner circles of decision making in this relatively complicated sphere. Those actively engaged in bending regulatory machinery to purposes not in accord with the public interest as a rule need not fear exposure; the sole exception is a falling-out of benefactors and beneficiaries, usually as a result of a major political upheaval. Even then it is interesting to note how little actually is exposed.

The concept of regulatory power over economic affairs was inherited from colonial days, but as was true of so many other facets of colonial rule it was only a vestige of that power that actually was transferred. Except where large reserves had accumulated, as in Ghana, the financial situation that faced the incoming African regimes left them very little to regulate unless they turned to the principal producers of wealth within their reach — the peasants and farmers, who have been sources of revenue for rulers since the beginning of recorded history.

To the extent that they have entered the cash economy, Africa's peasants and farmers, or, more exactly, their income, constitute the largest single target for regulatory activity. Estimates vary in regard to what share of that income is subject to manipulation by anyone or by combinations of government agencies, but it becomes apparent from any set of national production statistics that unless agricultural income is tapped and channeled into nonagricultural sectors the modern economy, hence state and society, would quickly collapse.

A formulation by the International Bank for Reconstruction and Development expresses the crux of the government-agricultural producer relationship when it states that minimum producers' prices are scheduled for all major agricultural commodities at the beginning of each crop year based on world market prices and on "internal political considerations."[8] Behind that seemingly innocuous phrase lies the thralldom of Africa's masses; the phrase is a euphemism for redistribution of income from the many for the benefit of the few. To attain its objective, government relies on a wide variety of instrumentalities, ranging from tax collection through price setting for seeds, fertilizer, and agricultural implements, grants of small loans between harvests, and compensation of farm labor.

Often disguised as regulatory activity to serve the public interest, loans policies turn out to be prime instruments of pressure and control. Few of the applicants for government loans have resources of their own. Savings are extremely rare; hence recipients of loans can offer no resistance to power plays by dispensers and regulators of working capital. In the circumstances, individuals and groups who depend on government finance for survival provide the nucleus of political support for those in power in most of Africa.

A clue to an understanding of African politics is hidden in the maze of bureaucratic controls; it is difficult to locate because signs displayed along the way usually are misleading. For example, "financing production and trade" should read "distribution of income to ensure political support"; "regulation of farm income" should read "extraction of surplus to provide a margin for political patronage."

A leading authority on business and lending in Nigeria found that a varying component of any cost calculation of loans to business in developing areas must be political manipulation or bad debt losses from politically inspired loans.[9] The loans he had in mind were those approved by government officials who instead of conscientiously assessing "prospective commercial viability" of a given venture granted loans on political grounds, usually to ensure support for a given faction or personality.

In scarcity settings, then, the central theme running through any realistic discussion of regulatory powers is subsistence interest. Power to regulate economic activity under prevailing conditions is power over economic, hence social, life and death. From this command position flow veritable streams of control and influence.

For the lower strata the power to license access to means of subsistence is, of course, basic. French, Belgian, Portuguese, and white South African and Rhodesian power over the black masses was, and in great measure still is, based on leverage obtained by this means. In fact, licensing of work opportunity has been the keystone of colonial power and still is the keystone of the South African control system. (The legal titles used by the apartheid regime in South Africa to conceal this rather basic and raw power often are ingenious.) The colonial practice of issuing certificates or agricultural permits has survived in places like Senegal.[10] So has the practice introduced by European settlers to secure land for themselves by regulation of acreage and production quotas.

The machinery of financial support control, usually disguised as an instrument to secure social justice or to regulate the few in the interest of the many, represents one of the most potent tools in the hands of Africa's rulers and lesser government officials. Labor unions, for instance, and even the vaunted single-party systems, have their financial resources regulated quite conclusively by those at the controls. The power to register or deregister trade unions, assumed by more and more African governments, provides the government with an enormous stick.[11] Simply stated, government reserves for itself the right to withhold operating funds without which groups in Africa simply cannot function effectively.

Throughout the world the option open to government to enforce or not enforce a given regulation is a prime source of political leverage. In the African setting discretionary use of the power to tax — to collect revenue — combined with the power to prosecute known violations is one of the most pernicious instruments in the hands of public authority. The effects of this particular usage are felt in their rawest, often most brutal form, at the rural receiving end where the power to increase or reduce taxes by administrative or quasi-administrative fiat has turned many a local official into a tyrant.

Predictably, the efficacy of this particular instrument increases in direct proportion to growth in *per capita* income. Herein lies one of the ironic twists of fate for Africa's masses. Under colonial rule few had entered the cash economy; hence few were of interest to government regulators or manipulators. Improvement in the income position, one result expected by Africa's masses with independence, unavoidably changes the individual's social status from relative independence to that of a subject for government regulation, hence control. The index of control can be read from any income tax table, especially from the changing ratio of direct to indirect taxation. In one case the ratio changes as follows:[12]

Income	Percent Direct-Indirect Taxation
Under $80	20:80
$81 to $199	27:73
Over $200	40:60

The power to regulate income is the crux of relations between central and local government. The extreme poverty of the typical local government unit reduces it to putty in the hands of whoever controls disbursements.[13] This dimension is easily overlooked if one relies on official documentation. Close examination of the total package, which consists of all financial allocations from central to local governments, may reveal as a general development that although grants may increase, allocations for local recruitment of competent staff may decrease, accompanied by cutbacks in operational allowances. The net result is reduction of local government capacity to resist central authority. From that point on what may appear as harmless and routine regulatory powers may, in fact, amount to supreme and total control. The true nature of this relationship emerges from an analysis of total allocation of financial resources on a per capita basis. In those terms the contradiction between public rhetoric, which seems to favor devolution of powers downward and toward the interior, and reality becomes apparent. In spite of accelerating rural migration to the cities, local government allocations fail to keep pace with population increases.

Ever since colonial authority first intervened in the affairs of traditional government, chiefs have been subject to central government recognition. Since most of the cash revenue base for traditional rule evaporates unless rulers are recognized by dispensers of financial support and licensers of tax collection authority, bureaucratic controls and regulatory powers flowing from the top are tantamount to subsistence control; as such they strike at the root of traditional rule.

Educational underdevelopment, another characteristic of colonial rule, places a premium on the value of government scholarships, typically the sole means of higher or advanced education for African youths. Even superficial examination of colonial government grants reveals the political edge of this benefit. Independence has carried the practice forward.[14] It is still used to reward friends and punish enemies.

In the Eastern Region of Nigeria the regional government "effectively limited the proceedings of the Whitley Councils by an artful administration of trade union scholarships."[15] Government scholarships in the Ivory Coast were reduced sharply after students demonstrated against the regime.[16] On the other hand, but underscoring the potency of this particular instrumentality, after disturbances at the University of Dakar in 1969 the government opted against withdrawal of scholarships because of an awareness that in Senegal not only did the students depend on the grants but the scholarships also provided income for the recipient's entire, probably extended, family.[17]

The low level of living conditions that afflicts most of Africa makes provision of basic amenities one of the central themes of life. Consequently, demands for roads, housing, water, electricity, schools, and medical dispensaries creates vast new opportunities for accrual of power to those who dispense these blessings.

All-weather roads are the sine qua non for farm income production throughout the continent. The speed with which a unit of government rushes to the aid of an area isolated by the perennial floods can be a very revealing index of social control. Railroads are used for the same purpose at a higher level. Rail links, a form of capital amenity like major roads, have been extended into some areas as a reward while being denied to others as punishment.[18] Good roads leading up to a friendly village are followed by impassable roads to the village beyond.

The cost of modern housing is beyond reach of all but a handful in most of Africa. The price of a low-to-medium-priced house typically represents about eight years of income as against three to four years in the United States.[19] To increasing numbers unwilling to spend their lives in houses built of mud or other primeval materials, access to a modern house becomes an imperative of subsistence. As government payrolls swell and incomes increase, housing becomes a fulcrum for regulatory power. The situation is expected to become more critical with every passing year as the gap between demand and supply widens. Demand for housing generates the greatest influence opportunities for dispensers of this amenity in urban areas where between 25 and 50 percent of dwellers are reported to live in conditions considered unsuitable for human habitation by official standards on housing in the developed world.[20] Inevitably, housing scandals characterize much of African urban politics.[21]

In prevailing conditions patronage — the bestowal of favors on supporters or potential supporters — becomes a prime source of power, and the regulatory dimension of government becomes a form of income control with predictable consequences for social relations. It took a simple member of Parliament in Kenya to articulate the unvarnished truth:

> If there was no money, we would never have come [to Parliament] because we were paid with money. Mr. Speaker, Sir, this is why I say whatever we say about money and the control, the techniques which are embodies in this [document on African Socialism] as political democracy or the political equality which we are talking about, is a mere daydream.[22]

Banking, or the Financial Management of Power

It is curious how otherwise perceptive analysts have failed to note the social power potential of banks and bankers in capital-starved Africa. Historians have long been aware of the influence of banking houses like the Fuggers and the Rothschilds over Europe's monarchs, but the dependence of Africa's new rulers on the Rothschilds' modern counterparts seems to have escaped attention of all but a handful (probably Marxist-trained) of observers. At best it is only vaguely hinted at.

Kindleberger comments on the revival of banking influence in underdeveloped countries following loss of power and *authority* in developed areas with the creation of free capital or stock markets. His formulation is significant. Speaking of banking in the United States, and referring in particular to the struggle of such giants as Henry Ford to "free themselves from dependence on banks" he notes that only "in particular industries, such as motion pictures, *where profits are insecure,* do banks exercise great authority."[23] Insecurity of profits being a characteristic of African economies, one can expect banks to attain similar levels of authority.

Kindleberger shows awareness of this potential but fails to draw the obvious inferences from his comment that "in underdeveloped countries, there is a revival of industrial banking partly for the sake of decision-making in the allocation of investment, partly to seek out credit-worthy private enterprise and get it going."[24] Actually, it is banking generally, not just the industrial variety, that has been revived, for capital also is required to finance agricultural production, for instance. In any case, what Kindleberger really is saying is that in underdeveloped countries bankers may vie with public officials and political leaders for primacy in allocation of resources vital to key elements in state and society. As brokers of authority bankers may turn out to be as important as the principal bureaucrats commonly regarded as central decision makers. Assuming always a rational approach to social and economic problems, authority without financial substance is a dead letter; authority is a dead letter indeed in much of Africa unless the inflow of capital into the economy is assured over and above what is currently consumed. (If economically hollow authority is kept alive by sheer force, which can be done for unexpectedly extended periods in certain conditions, one can surely no longer speak of economically rational decision making.)

Though formally hemmed in, supervised quite strictly, and assumed to be controlled by whole sets of public agencies and commissions, the larger banks in the United States have manifested an unabiding capability to wield influence over public policy and, of course, over private policy. This influence is accomplished through multiple channels, often by combinations of means such as interlocking directorates control — voting power — over large blocks of stocks, and informal relationships such as use of the same law firms, membership in the same clubs, old school ties, or intermarriage.[25] In Africa the means as well as the ends are the same in all essential respects.

During the colonial era only non-African banks operated on the continent. Their control of key strategic arteries in commerce, finance, and public policy in general was not noted because banks traditionally do not operate in the open, their files are not open to public inspection, and in any case their business is too complex to be understood by the uninitiated. Gradually the veil is being removed. (By far the most illuminating treatment of this subject also is offered under the heading "physionomie de l' oligarchie financière" in Suret-Canale's *L' Ère Coloniale*.[26])

The web of foreign economic controls, considered in preceding sections, provides an ideal framework for survival of banking power in nominally independent states. This control has been developed into a fine art in French-influenced areas. Even if the privileged position of French banks should gradually be eclipsed by new arrivals from the United States, Italy, or other capital exporting countries, the system used is worth noting as a classic example of the marriage of political and financial authority and power.

The system reminds one of blood transfusion. The owner or manager of capital, situated in France, controls the input very much as the physician does. It is he who decides, in cooperation with public and other private sources, how much capital shall be made available for development and support of specific projects and precisely to whom. The political edge of such decision-making power is concealed by such terms as feasibility, efficiency, or profitability. The blanket of influences that can be thrown over a given African economy, by these means is revealed in all its magnitude in the following passage from a summary of transactions and trends in the administration of the Caisse Centrale, principal French government outlet for development capital for Africa.

> In the interest of efficiency the [Caisse] also endeavours to coordinate the credits it grants with those of other banking or financial institutions which may contribute to the development of the country in which it is acting.[27]

The "other banking and financial institutions" are, of course, mainly French. But foreign groups also controlled over 80 percent of all banking in Nigeria in 1965.[28]

In practice, "development" of the African economy from the banking point of view means preference for non-African users of capital, for European ways of doing things, for projects likely to assure continued foreign dominance. It means retention of traditional economic pursuits and of modes of production, which ensure continued economic opportunities for foreign capital.[29] Even locally generated capital — for example, accumulations by traditional rulers — has been and still is channeled by foreign and domestic banks away from activities that might offer competition to foreign investors and into apartments, internal transportation, and other power politically harmless services.[30] As a result, a type of African businessman was created, a system of financial dependency devised that today characterizes the economic politics on much of the continent.

The high-risk nature of small business and agricultural production restricts such operations to a very small segment of the population — the most venturesome, courageous, and skilled. Of those, Africa still has exceedingly few. Consequently, the local partners of foreign banks and also of domestic banks are foreigners, nationals of the former colonial powers, Lebanese, Syrians, or, as in East and South Africa, Asians.[31] Judged by their investment postures in Africa, foreign bankers for understandable reasons uniformly turn out to be more conservative abroad than at home. In view of the concrete impact of banking decisions on the bases from which the new African polities arise, such conservatism is of seminal importance to the Africa of tomorrow.

The ability of private banks to help solve personal needs of rulers and lesser influentials has traditionally provided openings for bankers to gain access to public policy decision making. There is reason to believe that to be drawn abroad many a loan granted to African influentials had as its sole collateral some right or privilege granted to the creditor. Though, of course, they will not publicly discuss such transactions, banking circles privately point to specific examples in which rulers came to regard foreign banks as limitless sources for personal income. In fact, it was partly the desire to spread this particular burden that led French banking circles to allow United States banks to enter their preserve.

Abuses by foreign banks and the investors they support provided the rationale for creation of indigenous houses; eventually central banks were established everywhere to facilitate transfer of banking, money management, and investment control from Europe to the new states. Another powerful incentive for substitution of African banks sprang from the realization on the part of the more astute among Africa's new leaders that bank deposits were readily convertible into political muscle.

Nnamdi Azikiwe of Nigeria was first to recognize the political potential of banking; he also was first to feel the wrath of his European competitors when he succeeded in establishing his own bank and extracting from it funds to support non-economic operations. In a spectacular inquiry, a quasi-public trial, he was found guilty of misuse of funds entrusted to a bank he had organized. What had been the nature of that misuse? It turns out that what he had done had been, in effect, normal acceptable procedure for European-owned banks; he had used bank loans to finance enterprises that he owned and that, in turn, supported in various ways the activities of a political party headed by himself. His defense was entirely plausible. A calculated consequence of loan policies followed by British banks had been the prevention of the growth of a truly indigenous, independent Nigerian entrepreneurial class. At the same time, these same banks had funneled Nigerian wealth — earned by devious and certainly political means — into projects furthering British — colonial — interests, again a purely political objective. In setting up what the British inquisitors termed front corporations, he had merely emulated colonial practice to serve the interest of Nigeria. Public response to his condemnation by the British established and directed tribunal of inquiry indicated that regardless of the legal status of his transactions under British colonial law, the Nigerian public was prepared to enthusiastically legitimize what he had done.[32]

A few years later Azikiwe's contemporary, Chief Awolowo, and his principal lieutenants were to face similar charges, this time formulated and prosecuted by a Nigerian federal government. The charges were that the hapless group again had set up front corporations to receive loans from banks established by the principal corporation owners or their representatives. It was alleged furthermore that they had contrived to deposit substantial sums from marketing boards under their control in the same banks, creating a system that permitted tapping of public funds in support of political parties. Guilty or not — though a tribunal once again found the practices illegal — it would be difficult not to recognize in these schemes practices that have been part and parcel of political practice in Great Britain and in the United States for more than a century. There the dividing lines between private banking and political objectives are at times impossible to determine. Have not the banks in these countries consistently favored the already rich and powerful? Was it in the circumstances a crime for Nigerian Leaders to attempt to correct the imbalance of channeling the fruits of Nigerian labor back into Nigerian hands? Whatever the legality or legitimacy of these transactions, in due course the newly independent states proceeded to seize the reigns in these respects, at least in part.

A major source of concern to the new fiscal managers was the ability of private commercial banks to add to the total volume of money in the system by creation of credits and loans. Private commercial banks also enjoyed strategic advantages over the new governments in that the vital foreign exchange flowed through their channels. Accordingly, central banks were created to assume overall supervision, if not control, of the management of the state's monetary system and related activities; eventually some states went further and nationalized all banks, or at least created national banks to offer competition. Foreign banks also were compelled, as far as practical, to incorporate in the countries within which they were licensed to operate.

Universally, the purposes of central banks among other objectives are to regulate the power of private banks to stretch and contract the supply of money as they please, to assist these banks as a backup reservoir of cash, and to act as the banking outlet for the government in its transactions. Most critical for Africa, however, was the interdiction of foreign manipulative transactions and the freeing of the national economies from foreign financial bondage. This was more easily legislated than done. Legalistic arguments to the effect that these banks were autonomous, hence beyond political control or interference, can safely be dismissed.[33]

Nominally, central banks were empowered to regulate the flow of money and volume of credit and through direct contributions to reinforce development plans and priorities. Most critical, they were made sole custodians of vital foreign exchange reserves.[34] The new powers were employed to meet special crisis contingencies, such as rescuing a crop — financing of crops when no alternative supports were in view — shoring up indigenous manufacturing, and supporting other embryonic enterprises.[35]

The new powers also were used to increase government ability to control the economy in line with indigenous political and economic precepts. Foremost, central banks were brought into play in support of development projects that would never have qualified for support by conventional banking standards.[36] Naturally, the resources at the disposal of central banks were mobilized to cope with major crises such as the 1967-70 Nigerian civil war.

Whatever the new states may do to protect their interests, the true disposition of economic resources, markets, and international trade and finance in general leaves many an influence avenue open to foreign banks and their private counterparts. Commercial banks continue to draw on overseas resources that far exceed those at the disposal of central banks for loan purposes in most of the new states. Availability of free funds is not the only advantage enjoyed by foreign banks and by bankers in general. Demands on central banks are staggering, and increasingly African entrepreneurs, few as these are, turn to private sources. Moreover, inefficiency and waste and corruption compel public officials to protect private banks, for these may be the only remaining institutions that in order to operate properly cannot afford to be corrupt, in the usual sense of that term. In any case, central banks must continue to relate to financial authorities and developments elsewhere, and cannot ignore the ties between their own and the economies whence their country's exports are heading; therefore their establishment cannot be interpreted as completely closing the door to the influence of bankers.[37] In French Africa — in Senegal, for instance — it would be most unrealistic to consider the central bank as separate and independent from the financial directorate in the French banking system in the metropole.

Foreign interests continue to dominate the domestic money market and the financial system in general. African depositors, the new African bourgeoisie as well as their colonial-rooted predecessors, continue to entrust their capital to foreign banks, in contravention of legal prohibitions if necessary.

There has developed an anomalous situation in which native African capital is transferred to circulate abroad, there to assist in further development, while foreign capital, although reluctant to provide needed assistance in critical areas, is allowed nevertheless to influence government decisions in the new states.

8

Coercion and Suasion

Not many words need to be expended to demonstrate that the power of the gun made Africa safe for colonial rule and sealed the continent's fate for centuries. Astonishingly modest expenditures in money, men, and material were required to maintain control over so vast an area. In the typical colony law and order was maintained by a mere regiment or two, either soldiers or police or both. In some instances the same regiment was responsible for the peace in a whole cluster of colonial territories. The occasional rebellion or insurrection was put down swiftly and effectively by a punitive expedition or by what the French euphemistically called "pacification of rebellious tribes."[1] Most of the time the mere presence of a handful of European-commanded soldiers in a colony was sufficient to deter potential challengers of European authority.

With such exceptions as the Belgian Congo, Algeria, and the Republic of Guinea, the colonial pacification or coercion apparatus was transferred to the new African rulers virtually intact. In most instances European military and civilian officers and officials remained in key security control positions. Also transferred in tact were the crucial special or secret services. Run by Europeans in many cases, or by combinations of Europeans and Africans, these services initially provided effective protection for the new regimes, ensuring a certain degree of impartiality, nonpartisanship, and secrecy, while keeping internal security costs low. Also taken over by the new regimes was the concept of government monopoly of arms.

Eventually the cost of security began to rise as Europeans were phased out of the armed services, the special services, and the police. They rose even more sharply where severe internal repression became necessary or where, as in Kenya, Ethiopia, and the Sudan, border incursions, major rebellions, or insurrections were under way.[2]

113

Examination of estimates and budgets shows that initially most of the new leaders failed to make adequate provision for their own and their regime's security. The assumption seemed to be that since colonial rulers had not required large contingents of bodyguards, outlays for that purpose were luxuries the hard-pressed African treasuries could ill-afford. Ghana under Nkrumah pursued a different course, while Nigeria, much larger and far less stable prior to the first 1966 coup, followed the general pattern of benign neglect of the security function. It is significant that both strategies failed to prevent overthrows of the respective regimes.

There can be no doubt that the personal security of the ruler or rulers is paramount in any system, whatever its philosophy, ideology, or structure. Perhaps equally important is protection of all key or strategic command positions elsewhere in the country. Yet it emerges that the same scarcity syndrome that interfered so devastatingly with government financial and economic powers, both nationally and internationally, also prevented or discouraged effective measures on the internal security front. Shortly before the principal leaders were murdered, for fiscal year 1964-65 the federal Nigerian government increased allocation for "Cabinet Security" to £85,000, an increase of a mere £25,000.[3] — this at a time when an entire region was bordering on a state of insurrection, powerful oppositional forces were maneuvering for positions of power, and rumors of impending coups were abundant.[4] Instead, expenditures for the armed forces were increased by more than £1 million.[5] In the end, on January 14, 1966, it was the army that furnished the contingents that executed federal and regional leaders, overthrew the regime, and ended the first republic. One may speculate what the outcome might have been had expenditures for the armed forces been reduced or had they been kept at then current levels and expenditures for cabinet security been increased.

President Nkrumah, on the other hand, expended far more on personal security.[6] Yet he could not prevent his overthrow, and the substantial amounts expended on bodyguards and a vast array of other intelligence and security measures were of no use to him whatever when the critical moment came.[7] The 1971 overthrow of President Milton Obote in Uganda teaches a similar lesson.

Between 1957, the year of independence, and 1964, expenditures on the armed forces and the police very nearly doubled in Ghana.[8] The army overthrew Nkrumah shortly before his personal security apparatus threatened to become effective. In Nigeria, as tensions mounted from about 1962 on, law-and-order expenditures rose sharply. The pattern of military and police construction outlays indicated an intent to disperse the forces to strategic points throughout the federation. By 1965, on the eve of action by Eastern forces, the resource allocation pattern reflected an intent to strengthen the police in the Islamic North, to provide added security support there, and to strengthen the army's presence throughout the country.[9]

In light of the eventual outcome and in the absence of other stabilizing factors, it would seem that the security payoff of such resource allocation policies is virtually nil; it may actually hasten a military takeover.[10]

Always to be considered are the high costs of independence. As fiscal controls, including responsibilities of accounting and inspection, pass from the hands of relatively neutral foreigners, many a military construction project remains on paper, for the resources allocated either will be diverted to other uses or at best will be applied to the intended purposes only in part. Corruption and bribery, previously kept within bounds, now get out of control. Deteriorating social conditions, tensions, unrest, and strife do the rest. Inevitably the armed forces are drawn into the arena of public controversy and become identified with partisan positions. From there to military intervention and the coup is but a very small step.[11]

In the circumstances, it would seem financially sound and politically judicious if the new regimes continued to rely, at least for a time, on the European military contingents and on European services generally. This has been the decision in most of French-influenced Africa. The governments of Kenya, Zambia, and Malawi, while pressing forward with Africanization of command positions in the armed forces and the police, continued for years to rely on Europeans in key positions.[12] In the long run this dependence will, of course, not be possible, for the demand for complete withdrawal of whites from all public positions is constantly mounting.

Yet another alternative to increased expenditures on and expansion of military forces, all of which tend to court takeovers, is reliance on forces from other African states. While Siaka Stevens, the prime minister of Sierra Leone, was in danger of being replaced by yet another coup in his country, he invited a small force from the neighboring Republic of Guinea, a move made possible by a defense agreement signed shortly before.[13]

It is possible that the security function must, as in the Soviet Union, be separated from the regular armed forces and police. Of course, this approach, as any other relating to physical force, is fraught with danger. But security services by themselves do not seem to stage coups. Guinea and Tanzania seem to minimize reliance on regular armed forces for national security (excepting the Sierra Leone mission, which is a different matter). Undependable and unreliable as they are, by and large Africa's armed forces invite some kind of watchdog supervision and independent control, assuming always that civilian rule is to be preferred to military rule, itself a matter of debate. The Egyptian formula under Nasser relied on sets of diversified, competitive intelligence services. Guinea and Zanzibar relied on militia. Who watches the watchdogs? Usually a personal bodyguard, uniformed or civilian beneficiaries of the regime, or clients of the same ethnic background as the principal ruler.[14]

The discipline governing the conduct of European troops seems to have been reserved mainly for European benefits, especially in areas where

European forces or forces commanded by Europeans have run amok, as in the Belgian Congo and certain French pacification campaigns. In more recent times British forces, especially in West and East Africa, attained high levels of public responsibility and civility toward the African populations. For the first decade or so this civility also characterized the new African forces, both military and police.

Soon the lack of tradition and breakdown of inherited controls loosened the reigns. The result was illegitimate and unauthorized use of force or threat of force. Invocation of a legitimate right to use force in support of illegitimate objectives in certain conditions becomes a permanent feature of rule. Regions far removed from the national control centers began to see lesser functionaries or lesser officers and noncommissioned officers under military rule, exploiting what authority they could command for personal gain. The value of such currency increased in direct proportion to the severity of measures taken by the regime to ensure its own survival. Abuses under the Ghana Preventive Detention Act, instituted to protect the Nkrumah regime, were legion, provided the base for personal power exercised by lesser functionaries, and made a mockery of formal constitutional safeguards for individual rights.[15]

Suasion

Man is said to be susceptible to the power of suasion. Communications are believed by many to be the key, or a key, to an understanding of social processes and behavior.[16] Certainly, impressionable minds, especially those that lack intellectual resources of their own, are vulnerable to the spoken or written word or to dramatic graphic representation. Illiteracy, poverty, and poor health further reduce individual defenses. Whatever may be the precise value of communications as an instrument of power and influence or social control, the absence of *effective* competition enables those in control of modern means of communication to establish and maintain with relative ease a virtual monopoly of information.

Many of the mass media in circulation in Africa are foreign owned and managed, but few African rulers need to entertain any fears on that score. British, French, and other non-African owners and managers of mass circulation papers, interested in the main in profits from advertising, are quite sensitive to the fact that their license to publish is always subject to revocation, their expatriate staff subject to deportation on very short notice, and their indigenous staff never far from jail. Understandably they have uniformly adopted an extremely cautious stance. Foreign broadcasts are received by a small minority and in any case pose no real threat.

The power to license publications and impose import controls — initiated, incidentally, by the colonial regimes to protect their captive markets and preserve foreign exchange — place the ruling groups securely astride the power-politically most important channels of communication. Secure in their monopoly positions and dealing with a relatively placid audience, the "holders of effective power . . . can interpret the essentially ambiguous rules of legitimacy [and] can rationalize almost any power structure they prefer."[17] Does it make any difference? Are the power positions of the effective rulers threatened if the public is infected with the virus of doubt, regarding the government's legitimacy, for instance? We do not really know the answer.

Cartwright reminds us of the elementary truth that if an "agent of power" is to persuade a subject it is necessary for him to get his message across to that subject.[18] Aside from Doob's work on *Communications in Africa,* not much has been produced in the way of concrete evidence that would show that informational suasive efforts, or messages, actually are received and are received as intended.[19] To the contrary, one is led to believe that an extremely wide gap separates intent to influence from ability to influence through communications.

The principal problem arises because the language symbols most likely employed fail to strike responsive chords; more likely than not they are alien to Africa. Commonly, the symbols and the thoughts and ideas behind them are drawn from European, North American, or Soviet Russian language banks. Kwame Nkrumah's writings, or those attributed to him, the revolutionary rhetoric of Guinea's Sékou Touré or the Algerian leaders, the learned dissertations on material dialectics from the pens of distinguished Soviet academicians and published in African newspapers are classic illustrations of this form of social irrelevance. All exhortations addressed to the African "proletariat," for instance, to rise and to overthrow the bourgeois power structure will be in vain, since by all indication an African proletariat has yet to materialize.[20] One may also doubt whether Chinese Communist rhetoric addressed to the African peasantry is germane to African conditions.[21]

If suddenly and unexpectedly the rhetoric of African independence were converted into reality, few if any of the states could avoid total bankruptcy. If, for example, promises of social equality, fair distribution of income or wealth, employment for all, Africanization of all key posts in government, business, or industry, and elimination of all foreign control in the economy were to be brought even close to realization, all modern economic activities would be brought to a standstill. Mercifully, means of communication and messages transmitted are so ineffective that conversion of rhetoric into reality is improbable, even if leaders mean to do what they say. Verbal formulations will not lead to concrete accomplishments, but neither will they give the public, and especially regime opponents, anything to focus on. Coincidentally, continuous expansion of the communications network and proliferation of outlets will simply increase opportunities for graft and patronage — that is, it will further dilute the effectiveness of public funds, since means of monitoring communications output are less well developed than are means of checking on other, more concrete forms of production.[22]

More to the point in Africa is the language of tradition. To the extent that that language and the appropriate channels of communication are at the disposal of modern rulers, some influence and some control can no doubt be achieved by such a route. Access to the well-organized and well-established channels of Islam, for instance, has been for more than a decade an important instrument in the arsenal of the Senghor regime in Senegal. There the animateurs, traditional religious equivalents of agitprop agents in the Soviet Union, served as paid links between central government and rural masses. Few of these communicators were literate. Their main stock in trade were time-honored props employed in ancient systems — talismans, jujus, prayers, and incantations. They served the established regime well. Given the existing language barriers, widespread illiteracy, and prevalence of superstition, such instrumentalities of influence as the often intimidating ways of secret societies, cults, and similar relics of the past appealed to modern would-be manipulators of human minds in Africa as they have done without interruption in the technologically more advanced societies of the West.[23] The clearest case for suasion as an effective instrument of power over the mind of man, hence of social control power, can be made with reference to its confusion and neutralization value. Given the multiplicity of available channels of communication and therefore of public opinion formation, opportunities for rulers to obfuscate and fudge on issues are virtually limitless. The public can be indefinitely bombarded and saturated with torrents of plausible-sounding ideological propositions.

Covert Uses

Favoritism and Patronage

The African political landscape invites abuse of power. An independent press is a rarity. National judiciaries all too often, and increasingly so, are being subverted; many must be regarded as outright captives of ruling groups or personal political machines. It cannot be denied that judiciaries the world over are vulnerable to nonlegal outside influences. However, the involvement of many African courts in substantially extralegal concerns goes far beyond, let us say, the federal judiciary in the United States. Increasingly, African courts are reduced to the role of mere handmaidens of principal control groups in their respective countries.[1] Moreover, organized opposition to government either is eliminated outright or is rendered ineffective by one means or another. This state of affairs creates veritable oceans of troubled waters for all manner of nefarious fishing operations.

In these murky waters distinctions between public and private property, public and private interests, legality and illegality, and legitimacy and its opposites tend to become obliterated. Values and norms governing individual and group conduct are shaken up in kaleidoscopic fashion as the colonial standards dissolve before alternate standards become operational at the national levels. This is not denying the historic fact that Africa and Africans have indeed developed their own high standards of behavior. It is merely noting that these standards have not yet been codified nor are they sufficiently entrenched or established to serve as guidelines or clear reference points for evaluation of public and private behavior. During such periods of transition almost any set of standards of ethics, of propriety, and the like can gain currency, at least for a while.

One consequence is that personal support machines have been built with relative ease by combinations of public funds legally and legitimately disbursed and funds diverted or procured by illegal, at best illicit, means. Evidence on this manipulation is so overwhelming that one must wonder why so little has found its way into social science literature.[2]

Perceptive students of the use — as distinct from theory — of federal executive power in the United States should encounter no difficulty in recognizing patterns of abuse of executive power in Africa. Most common are selective enforcement of the law — tax laws in particular — selective prosecution for smuggling and other violations, and the combination of award of lucrative government contracts and failure to enforce standards or insist on performance as stipulated in the contract.[3] The prerogative to institute or not institute inquiries and legal proceedings against persons and groups known to have violated existing laws is especially potent as a means of covering up illegal acts where modern legal concepts and traditions are not yet deeply rooted. Colonial regimes employed this particular device, or at least attempted to employ it until persuaded that exposure of embezzlement, even necessarily of outright and open diversion of funds, for illicit purposes did not adversely affect the target of such actions.[4]

The power of patronage has been wielded at times without restraint. Yet caution is indicated before embarking on simplistic explanations. To say that payrolls are padded or funds diverted to advance political goals is to be insensitive to the social imperative for African socioeconomic development. As a rule, alternate financial sources to recruit support for an idea or an objective are few; there may be none. Thus, recourse to public funds may be unavoidable if a given African cause is to be advanced against well-financed foreign interests.

Nkrumah appears to have intended initially to divert funds earmarked for one purpose to serve substantially different ends, mainly to create additional economic breathing space. That example was emulated throughout Africa.[5]

Unfortunate for the feeble economies, what had started out as a legitimate course of action to augment African campaign chests for the struggle against colonial rule and its liquidation soon became a major reservoir for drafts of illicit power to stage assaults on the rights of majorities in some cases and on embryonic democracies in others. In many instances the end was clearly personal.

Richard Sklar offers a list of devices that the Nigerian ins used to keep power and the outs used to seize power through exposure of what the ins were doing — that is, squandering of public funds through liberal allowances and expense accounts for regional ministers and legislators, victimizing of party political opponents, again by economic means, and using such means as taxation, school fees, and levels of price support of cocoa.[6] Milking of investment companies, banks, and statutory corporations for party political and/or personal political gain, as noted earlier, has been and still is a common occurrence in African politics. On one occasion, according to the recorded minutes of a top-level party meeting, the president of a major Nigerian party, Chief Awolowo of the Action Group, is alleged to have stated outright that his party was not alone in appreciating the "invaluable benefits" to be derived from existence and successful operation of investment companies; the rival parties — the NPC in the north and the NCNC in the east — were known to have sponsored similar ventures.[7]

Again the critical difference between such uses of economic means in Africa and, let us say, the United States lies in the absence of effective checks and controls in most of Africa. It appears from evidence presented in the Coker Report, which looked into certain practices in the former Western Region of Nigeria, that millions of pounds could actually evaporate without any trace whatever.[8]

It should not be difficult to identify dubious uses of economic resources at either end of the legality or legitimacy spectrum. Wholly legal or legitimate uses need not be concealed or obscured. If they are obscured, the diligent analyst should have no difficulty in penetrating the screen. Wholly illegal or wholly legitimate uses are brought to light from time to time by judicial proceedings, tribunals of inquiry, or exposure following a coup or other major change of government.

It is the twilight zone between legality and illegality, or between legitimacy and illegitimacy, that proves analytically most elusive. It is in that zone that the shrewd manipulator can operate most successfully, always moving along the thin edge that separates the proper from the improper. African economies are not yet rigidly structured, and resources, cash as well as credit, flow quite freely, without too many restraints, at all levels. It is all too easy for the skilled to establish himself at a leakage point, a faucet so to speak, or to create his own opportunities and drain off whatever he requires. In the typical African setting, but perhaps everywhere in the world, those who operate in the open may be praised, those who operate in clear violation of the law may be prosecuted, while those in the penumbra between legality and illegality may be the most successful. They may be the principal beneficiaries of the best of both worlds.

Comparisons between the more highly developed and less developed economies with regard to relative importance of covert uses of financial resources must not lose sight of major differences. In an otherwise very perceptive article, one writer clearly fails to note obvious distinctions between United States, British, and developing systems. His principal error stems from his failure to realize the quantitative factor of differential distribution of fiscal responsibility between central and local government units in the United States and those in the less developed areas of the world. Also overlooked is the role of private investment funds in support of political machines in, let us say, the major cities of the United States and the virtual absence of such funds in comparable African settings. In American cities, machine bosses who want to meet public demands for amenities or to pursue naked power are known to have marshaled private funds. The African counterparts of the Hagues, Daleys, and Tweeds in the African urban centers must tap public resources if they are to approximate what they have promised. What spells the difference really is the relative importance of government finance in the total economy, especially as compared to private finance available for consumer satisfaction as well as for various forms of patronage.[9]

The Matter of Corruption

Much Western criticism directed at African examples of corruption and bribery is hypocritical. Westerners whose countries have grown rich and powerful partly by corrupt means, an integral part of any way of life, prefer to point out the mote in Africa's eye instead of extracting the beam from their own. As in so many other debates, the outcome hinges on definitions. It may turn out that what a European or an American may describe as thrift, foresight, enterprise, shrewd business acumen, or even ruthless ambition is corruption or bribery or some other disreputable trait by just another name. Still, even though by Western standards it is only a mote, corruption in the new states takes a toll larger in relative terms than does corruption, let us say, in the United States.

It is a time-honored tradition in the United States to use public funds to win friends and influence people. Although attempts are continuously made to identify and eventually control what is commonly referred to as conflict of interest, in practice the job proves most difficult. The best that can be hoped for in a highly developed and comparatively well-organized society is reduction of the problem and elimination of the more blatant violations of the rule. The situation is different in a less developed, less organized society.

Comparisons break down on one count alone, namely the scope and volume of corrupt money involved in public policy decision-making processes. It is not very meaningful to observe that corruption is universal.[10] More important to political analysis is the extent to which public affairs are afflicted or permeated by corruption. The political machine of an urban boss in the United States, for example, must contend against competing machines in other urban centers in the same state, with the machine of the boss at the state or even national level, as well as with the well-financed machinery at the disposal of independent private enterprise, including powerful lobbies and the banks.

To compare, as one literary critic did, United States Congressman Adam Clayton Powell and Kwame Nkrumah is to ignore the substantially different setting in which each man operated, leaving aside numerous other, for present purposes less relevant, distinctions and differences.[11] In one fiscal year, Nkrumah had at his disposal £2 million, a so-called contingency vote. This constituted, at the time, about 3 percent of the total budget expenditure of Ghana. The vote was at his sole discretion to be used as he saw fit.[12] With that kind of money he could cut across various levels of power and influence and intervene almost at will in the affairs of the entire country.

At another level, defense of corruption in Africa is offered with reference to what one might call a theory of beneficial corruption. Geoffrey Bing, formerly attorney general under Dr. Nkrumah in Ghana, thought that what really matters is the social end objective a corrupt official has in mind. Examining the charge that a certain official had harmed the pre-independence economy by using loans for political purposes, he asks:

> ... who did the more harm to the Ghana economy — the officials of the [British controlled] Agricultural Loans Board who scrupulously refrained from outside business activities and yet never examined the problem which confronted them and in consequence could never make up their minds to grant any loans, or Mr. Djin who was responsible for setting up an organization which tackled the problem.[13]

This raises an important point. It offers a yardstick with which to measure the social value of corruption. If, as was so here, agricultural productivity is the test, and if politically tainted loans bring about or even coincide with a substantial increase in productivity in the sector that benefits most, Bing's argument can be accepted, given the deep-rooted nature of corruption in less developed areas. If, however — and this was true in the Ghana cocoa sector — no conclusive proof can be produced to show that political loans increased productivity, the thesis must await further investigation and validation.

A constructive approach to the problem can be developed from the British Doctrine of Repugnancy, which guided colonial lawyers, judges, and administrators in most of British Africa. Under that doctrine, application of indigenous laws, concepts of justice, customs, and traditions was limited on principles of "natural justice, equity, and good conscience." If a British official was tempted to take advantage of his public office to secure private gain, he was expected to follow British concepts of legality and ethics. His African counterpart, though could feel free to take advantage of the opportunity because such action was very much in the African tradition, which, one must add, did not really distinguish very much, if at all, between public and private gain. Whatever the perspective or prescription, it may well be that at this point in time not much can be done to minimize either corruption or bribery in Africa. A sudden shutoff may have traumatic effects analogous to a sudden cutoff of blood circulation. In most of Africa corruption is part of life, which is precisely one major reason, as we shall note again, that reform programs cannot be taken too seriously. Sudden termination of all corrupt uses of money would, in effect, destroy most if not all local government and local authority structures.

Corrupt practices are at the very root of power and influence, a consequence of a combination of past practices and current modernization, development, and growth. It is often very difficult to distinguish between gifts customarily received — by traditional functionaries, for instance — and bribe in the modern sense.[14]

For our purposes most important, the high incidence of corruption in Africa and especially the pervasiveness of the disease provide alternatives for the wealthy or the influential to by-pass established legal and legitimate channels at all levels. The susceptability of traditional rulers to mild forms of bribery conditioned them to be receptive to more remunerative approaches in the modern setting. National authorities avail themselves of the same means to influence local officials, and eventually foreigners find here the keys to the political kingdom that independence was to have granted to the Africans. Some Africans, of course, are merely returning to the scene where they had engaged in similar practices under the protective umbrella of colonial rule.

The machinery of African politics is powered largely by public funds, which have greater influence value than the same amounts would have in the more highly developed countries, for alternate sources of influence — from the private sector, for example — are few and far between. In Northern Nigeria millions are spent annually by predominantly illiterate-led native authorities. During one period prior to 1966, 71 such authorities spent £12.13 million annually, while 150 spent a mere 10 million in the Western region, and 110 spent £5 million in the Eastern region.[15] This spending must be viewed against the background described by an observer who happened to be profoundly sympathetic to Northern Nigeria. "A grave state of maladministration and financial irresponsibility exists throughout the whole fabric of the Native Authority." The situation elsewhere must be similar, for the circumstances and conditions are similar throughout the continent.[16]

It has been said correctly that to identify instances of corruption in Africa is child's play. Simply stated, the absolute power that colonial rulers enjoyed over their subjects corrupted that system absolutely if it had not already been thoroughly corrupted in its European cradle. Where executive branches of government are not separated properly or at all from the legislative or the judicial, where law enforcement is not separated from lawmaking or law interpretation, where public and private interests are indistinguishable all doors are open to bribery, graft, and corruption.[17] Europeans controlled the definitions. As they were gathered by Europeans, ill-gotten gains were profits earned. But woe to the African who followed in his master's footsteps. Whether he turned a profit of a few shillings or operated on a larger scale, if he was caught up in the net the law was interpreted against him.[18]

Small wonder that as soon as the air was clear — the apparatus of law enforcement was in African hands, or at least subject to African influence — public treasuries were raided almost at will in some instances. At first genuinely, or as a subterfuge, public funds were siphoned into coffers of political parties, into bank accounts of African nationalist enterprises, or into private bank accounts purportedly to reinforce the independence struggles.[19]

In some instances prior to independence but routinely thereafter, the rapidly fading boundaries that separate legality from illegality, legitimacy from illegitimacy, propriety from impropriety began to vanish altogether for those powerful, influential, or unscrupulous enough to take advantage of the multitude of opportunities. Still, since European ways and particularly European economic controls prevailed, some leaders caught in the act offered the seemingly plausible defense that their sole intent was to further African independence. Even outright misappropriation of public funds or other more blatant abuses could be defended on those grounds, and one could dismiss out of hand the argument that stealth and deception were mandatory where all legitimate and legal channels for acquisition of wealth were controlled by foreigners.[20]

Whatever the rationale, the flow of money into decision- and policy-making channels from public treasuries as well as from private sources, foreign and domestic, and with that the contamination if not decay of the last remaining bastions of public service integrity, accelerated until corruption permeated both the traditional and the modern sectors. It is significant that while no evidence has yet been offered to show that corrupt money was indeed applied to advance African political causes in the manner claimed by defendants in the several public inquiries throughout West Africa, evidence abounds that, in fact, the typical end effect if not purpose was personal enrichment.[21] Again, it can always be argued that even creation of a millionaire by such means is a step closer to African independence, but neither were such side effects claimed nor can they be regarded as proper use of public funds or private funds obtained through public office.

One must appreciate some of the causes. Dismantling of colonial administration produced acute shortages of supervisory and accountancy personnel.[22] At the same time, the remaining Europeans — or, as in East Africa, Asians — who might have been in a position to assist in the preservation of minimum standards of ethics either felt themselves intimidated and looked the other way or joined the parade.[23]

Fudging of distinctions between public and private interest brought Africa back to precolonial days. So did erasure of separation of power, however tenuous it may have been under colonial influence. It had always been part of the African tradition not to insist on separation of powers. In Northern Nigeria, for instance — and this is fairly typical of Africa — native authority, including native law enforcement, native law interpretation or adjudication, state, society, economy, religion, ethics, ideology, political party platforms, even family ties are indistinguishable from one another in practice. The trend now was in that direction once again.[24]

Some outstanding illustrations were brought into the open as a direct consequence of upheavals in Nigeria, Ghana, and Sierra Leone. The overthrow of the Awolowo regime in the former Western Region of Nigeria in 1962 produced the voluminous *Coker Commission Report* plus appended materials, a detailed chronicle and account of uses and abuses of money in politics.

Following the military coup against Nkrumah in Ghana, entire series of inquiries were instituted partly to discredit the previous regime, partly to create a more favorable climate for a more truly democratic form of government. Reports by the several commissions of inquiry are, of course, not objective but do contain irrefutable data on the role of money in Ghanaian politics during the Nkrumah years. A similar turn of events in Sierra Leone produced the Foster Commission report, which reveals that that small country also had a seamier side to its politics.

All inquiries reveal a common pattern of misconduct. Office holders, long impressed by the power that money manifestly brought to the European strangers in their midst, availed themselves of the earliest opportunity to harness that same power to their causes. Under one pretext or another, sums ranging from petty cash to millions of pounds were diverted from public use to directly serve the immediate tactical or strategic goals of political parties, factions, cliques, or individuals. Political war chests were filled by establishment of contingency funds, as mentioned, up to £2 million in Ghana, and establishment of investment companies, banks, or other institutional receptacles. Substantial funds were extracted from private entrepreneurs, especially Europeans, Syrians, and Lebanese, through assessments, kickbacks from contracts, donations, or outright deposits in foreign bank accounts.[25]

Large sums were diverted to private companies set up either by or for office holders or members of their families, or to companies willing to include official African benefactors or members of their families on their boards of directors.[26]

Evidence submitted in Ghana and Nigeria indicates use of private banks, public boards, such as marketing boards, or private or semiprivate companies or corporations as depositories for a kind of revolving fund for the group in power. One prominent Western Nigerian leader regularly deposited unreceipted sums in a safe that he kept at a bank. Payments from that source went to individuals of special interest to the leadership of a particular political party in power, to "allied parties," and in support of "various activities of the Party leaders for which they require funds."[27]

Some of these "requirements," it turned out, were purely private, including those of the principal depositor himself. It seems, according to the testimony offered before the Coker Commission, that he acquired 15 landed properties while in charge of the operation.[28] The same report asserts that the principal leader of the party in question donated funds obtained by these various means to supporters or to persons whose support he was soliciting. There was an element of blackmail in all this, because persons who wanted to partake of the cornucopia had only to signal their intent to join an opposing party or faction to qualify for a share of the war chest.[29]

Testimony was offered to show that the party leadership was not incautious. Moneys withdrawn from the depository were paid out at first as loans to be converted later into outright grants if recipients performed as required.[30] Since the donors frequently also had control of executive as well as legislative powers, they often were in position to dispossess beneficiaries who refused to perform as contracted. At the petty cash or small bribe level, leaders distributed more modest monetary gifts, cars, jewelry, free trips on government aircraft or ships, or accommodations abroad, again to make political friends and influence people.[31]

The informality of African politics, together with the peculiarities of law interpretation, law enforcement, and adjudication characteristic of Africa, in effect suspended all processes of investigation and virtually prevented exposure even of flagrant violations of conflict of interest unless and until the power of the perpetrators was broken in a coup or similar radical upheaval. In that climate, regional and federal ministers could amass fortunes through manipulation of public funds in several capacities. As government officials they could establish depositories, as chairmen of boards in control of these very creations they could dispense the same funds and authorize or refuse to authorize loans, grants, licenses, permits, or contracts.[32] Inquiry into the assets of ministers, political party functionaries and other persons associated with the former regime of Nkrumah reveals that the practice of charging commissions on contracts became a vast loophole through which numerous persons were able to enrich themselves. An attempt was made to legitimize the practice by a directive that moneys collected in that manner should be used to finance the party. Actually, most of the funds were applied to entirely different purposes.[33]

The underdeveloped state of African private enterprise assigns an overpowering role to government in business, industry, and trade, making it doubly difficult to distinguish corrupt practices from economic uses of money, or money in politics from money in economics. The point has been made by one economist whose view is worth quoting.

> The explanation for the rash of "machinery-sale public investment" projects is political: prestigious capital-intensive projects can be achieved quickly, they provide well-paid directorships for politicians as well as jobs for the unemployed, they are an important source of party finance via the "kickback" and they do not require any money down — they are financed on

the basis of supplier credit. The drawbacks of this type of public investments are the extensive promotion of political and personal corruption,
inflated capital costs (by 100% or more) serious external debt-servicing
problems, and money losing investments. The reasons for this last and
economically most damning fault are (i) that both the selection of the
industry and its location are based upon political grounds and can seldom
pass the test of economic viability, and (ii) the machinery merchants'
method for providing managerial staff to the projects they commission is
inadequate to ensure efficient operation.[34]

One may debate whether the explanation for such practices is political
or economic. The nature of the transactions described would suggest that
the motives are purely economic and that the benefits obtained accrue to
individuals rather than to abstract institutions. There is some danger in
attempting to distinguish between personal and political corruption, because
the result may be a mistaken diagnosis of the social ailment and may make
a cure impossible.

FOREIGN-INDUCED CORRUPTION

An inevitable by-product of the internationalist character of postcolonial
economies is the extensive and deep involvement of foreigners in corrupt
practices at all levels. Corruption thrives on economic pursuits unre-
strained by moral or ethical commitment. What can be less committed in
these respects than a non-African investor who seeks quick profits in an
alien African environment? Moreover, the most lucrative opportunities
for quick and substantial gain by corrupt means do arise mainly from
foreign investment, since bribes can be offered and paid outside the legal
jurisdiction of the African state. Also, the juiciest contracts are let to
foreign firms, because few African contractors as yet possess the capacity
to bid for multimillion dollar projects.

Shortly before independence and at an accelerated pace thereafter, the
level of intensity surrounding the flow of money into channels of power
and influence increased sharply with the commencement of major construction projects to take up the slack inherited from colonial days. Larger
sums of money suddenly were injected in a more concentrated fashion.
In Nigeria, for instance, each of the major regions competed with the
others for leadership, each seeking to outbuild the others. This competition
attracted to the African scene the heavyweights among European, North
American, Japanese, and Israeli investors and contractors.

In the at-times fierce competition, and given the extremely soft defenses
each regional government would offer against bribes, an entirely new ethos
emerged. Whereas under colonial rule British bidders for contracts in the
colonial territories were subject at least to British legal and ethical rules
of conduct, all of these safeguards evaporated in some instances; only
some were lost sight of in others. Now major, even multimillion dollar

contracts were let in highly irregular fashion. It was not necessarily the lowest bidder who would be victorious but the least scrupulous. Enormous sums became available for illicit purposes as bids were routinely driven up to accommodate multiple claimants for payoffs.[35]

The ability of foreigners to provide new and extremely lucrative opportunities encouraged, as noted, a peculiarly uneconomic if not wasteful approach to public construction. African leaders who had authorized superfluous or wasteful projects, and especially those who were benefiting personally from the accompanying largesse, were now subject to blackmail by their foreign partners in crime. Foreign influence was reasonably secure as long as these partners remained in office; as a result, corruption, foreign influence, and domestic politics became hopelessly entangled. There is reason to believe that some African governments selected even foreign aid projects with a view to creating new opportunities for graft.[36]

French-influenced Africa does not publish the results of inquiries in the few instances where such actually are conducted. Instead, investigations are held *in camera*. However, a United States ambassador provided a rare glimpse of reality in his book dealing with his experiences in Gabon.

> It was not simply that there was graft. The evil was deeper than that. The state at the time of which I am writing was corrupt, and the principal agents of its corruption were the first large forestry interests and other French businesses which had long been the main support of the regime. In 1965 they gave a convincing demonstration of their power. Private French interests were discovered buying up land along the route of the big iron-ore railroad that had just been traced by Foley Brothers. The Director of the National Planning Office in the Ministry of National Economy drafted a decree making the land along the right of way government property: the President refused to sign the decree and cashiered the Director.[37]

The same source raises another rather crucial point when he reports the French ambassador as saying: "This is Africa; you cannot apply the same moral standards here as in Paris or New York."[38] Since moral standards in Paris or New York are, of course, actually not higher than standards in Africa — they are only subject to different, possibly more constraining counterforces — the absence of adequate restraints in Africa inevitably, perhaps inexorably, results in dilution of all moral values there to a level mainly determined by foreign corrupting interests. Those African officials who still remain motivated to maintain or even improve existing levels of public morality and professional ethics will find such efforts increasingly difficult and frustrating.

REMEDIES

As in so many other human pursuits, in this one also the road to hell is paved with good intentions. For all major and many minor infractions in the handling of public funds there are several sets of remedial prescriptions. Alas, few of these contain the promise of success.

Colonial legislatures did not compile a distinguished record for themselves in their anticorruption efforts. It was all too apparent that their zeal, if any, was directed exclusively to embarrass African competitors.[39] Post-independence anticorruption officers had authority to institute investigations or inquiries only if authorized to do so by the most likely suspects — the cabinet collectively or the prime minister individually.[40] In any case, as noted elsewhere, their detection devices were carefully tuned to avoid setting off the more explosive charges.[41] But the problem did not arise solely from lack of authority or lack of determination. It was and still is often a matter of perception or understanding of what is and what is not possible or practical in real life.

A post-Nkrumah commission in Ghana sought to devise methods whereby "dishonest" persons could be prevented from qualifying as members of parliament. They arrived at a curious definition. A dishonest person was one whom a commission of enquiry found to be dishonest.[42] The report fails to reflect any awareness whatever on the part of the commissioners of the ambiguity of their definitions. The evils that the commission sought to eradicate are, of course, referred to as dishonesty by whoever sits in judgment; businessmen call them business opportunity when they involve members of parliament, and parliament members call them legitimate outside income. Members of parliament who are lawyers, landing lucrative contracts for their clients or for firms with which they are or will be associated simply remove themselves from the beneficiary by a step or two; in fact, it is the failure to recognize the indefinite variety of opportunities to obfuscate or becloud the issues, to conceal true conflict of interest, to circumvent ambiguously drafted legislation that relegates most such preventive measures to impotence. It is significant that although a deterrent against indiscriminate and unscrupulous amassing of wealth by members of parliament was written into the post-Nkrumah constitution of Ghana, several years later the majority of MP's still refused to reveal their private assets, a requirement also written into the same constitution.[43] Small wonder if Ghanaian students became disenchanted with what they perceived as double standards — standards applied to the Nkrumah regime by its successors and those applied to the successors themselves.[44]

A measure of the effectiveness of anticorruption steps taken by succeeding regimes is given by the number of public officials found guilty of stealing public funds *after* commissions of inquiry into similar or identical offenses made public their recommendations. Following the January 1966 coup in Nigeria, 12 regional ministers and 7 other officials were found guilty of theft of over £62,000. This after repeated inquiries into the very same activities and in spite of sets of reform recommendations produced over more than a decade.[45] It is entirely possible that one of the reasons that the first military regime in Nigeria was replaced by another was the first regime's decree empowering the national military government to seize ill-gotten wealth "acquired by corruption and abuse of office." This pointed directly at the power elite in the Northern Region, since the first coup itself had revealed antinorthern tendencies. The July 28-29, 1966, mutiny which followed the January coup, may well have been instigated by northern politicians fearful that the decree might be allowed to take effect against them while the southerners guilty of similar infractions were left free to enjoy their gains.[46]

10

Internal-Regional

Under modern conditions, governments may still ignore or virtually ignore substantial portions of their populations, even entire regions, but such postures are increasingly fraught with danger. Even in the least developed country prudence calls for some degree of involvement of all people, preferably some form of popular participation. Broad-scale involvement and popular participation in turn mean extension of central government power and influence through all levels down to the village. For a variety of practical reasons some kind of devolution or decentralization of power accompanies this extension. No central administration can provide all basic public services throughout the state, keep law and order, and generally supervise everybody everywhere. At the same time, personnel shortages, especially in skilled categories, inappropriate administrative patterns and divisions, and the imperative of relatively rapid economic development — for whatever social ends and regardless of its philosophic direction — pose serious obstacles to an orderly, systematic approach to the problem. Whatever the policy preferences or the civic goals, the matter comes down to a question of means and ends, principally of financial means and social ends.

Early Approaches and Plans

Under colonial rule distribution of power between the central administrative center and the remainder of the territory was simply a matter of expediency where all doubts were resolved against the remainder. Eventually two major considerations compelled the postindependence regimes to decentralize and begin to share some of their powers with lesser units in the interior. First and most crucial, the need for increased revenue suggested transfer of a degree of self-government to the interior as a quid pro quo for increased production and stepped-up revenue collection. Second, the masses, who had been virtually ignored under colonial rule, could not indefinitely be denied at least some of the fruits of independence promised to them during the independence campaign. Also, the more far-sighted among the leaders thought it advantageous to construct personal power bases for future use in one section of the country, usually their own home ground.

Schemes to achieve a more equitable distribution of power took various forms; most for obvious reasons reflected European precepts and habits of thought. Federal schemes were introduced, for example, in Nigeria and the Congo (Kinshasa), modified regional-provincial administrative arrangements or quasi-federal schemes prevailed in Uganda, and unitary schemes modified only by faint gestures toward the hinterland were adopted in most countries. Whatever the form, resources available for implementation of paper plans failed to measure up to requirements. Consequently, key features of independence constitutions remained dead letters. Overall patterns of distribution of wealth and of sources of power remained essentially as they had been during colonial days.

Colonial rule had failed to prepare the ground for easy adaptation of such imports as federalism — extremely costly, actually, if they were to bring any concrete benefits to the masses. In other words, colonial rule had failed to create the resource base for meaningful self-government. No amount of determination on the part of the new rulers could compensate for that neglect. Financial dependence of interior units of government on the comparatively rich central treasuries was near total if measured in terms of minimal revenue requirements to secure material resources, skills, and equipment to satisfy minimal consumer demands for basic amenities, public services, and other fundamental human needs.[1]

In these circumstances, schemes incorporated in the independence constitutions, including revenue-sharing plans and equitable distribution of police and taxation powers, could not be fully implemented. Features incorporated in development plans to alleviate geographic imbalances were not likely to fare better.

Proposals to eliminate internal regional disparities between the more highly developed and the wholly neglected areas reflected the same air of unreality as did the independence constitutions. Equalization of income throughout the states was, of course, a practical impossibility; it may well be argued that this idea would have been wholly counterproductive in terms of development needs. The best that could be hoped for was a modest narrowing of the internal development gaps, especially between urban and rural areas.

But redress of imbalances required drastic departures from previous policy approaches and incisive shifts in priorities. Development of theretofore neglected areas called for radical redesign or relocation of existing economic infrastructures, most of all transport and communication. To that end, local government units had to be allowed to retain a greater share of income from local production, and foreign exchange reserves had to be allocated on a different basis. Development projects would have to be located to reflect local interior needs; development planners would have to lessen their customary economic costs arising from initially low productivity.[2]

In some cases overthrow of too highly centralized or authoritarian regimes generated a desire to compensate for past excesses as well as forestall a repetition of administrative encroachment on local and regional autonomy.[3] Here again the reality of actual distribution of wealth and power interfered with plans to redress imbalances.

The Reality

The principal stumbling bloc to equalization of economic opportunity, hence fairer distribution of the means to secure power and influence, is the existence of the urban goliath among the rural economic pygmies. Starving goliath to feed the pygmies is a sure invitation to civil unrest if not economic disaster. The full dimension of the problem emerges if one begins to recognize that concentrations such as Dakar, Abidjan, Lagos, Kinshasa and Lubumbashi, and Nairobi, to cite but a few examples, may well possess more of the essential characteristics of nationhood than do any of the economically feeble ethnic units in the surrounding country. Shades of the early history of France may be recognized in the Ivory Coast where by 1975 the population of the capital, Abidjan, is expected to increase to 813,000, from 1,400 in 1912. By 1975 Abidjan's position vis-a-vis the rest of the Ivory Coast may indeed be similar to the position the Paris region enjoys with regard to the rest of France. Percent of total population alone — 18.5 percent in the Ivory Coast — does not reveal the full measure of the relationship.[4] Increasingly income earned by urban breadwinners serves to sustain extended rural families, while at the same time, it exercises a magnetic pull to encourage ever larger migrations toward the glittering attractions.

One major cause of internal imbalance is the high capital-intensive nature of the typical African economy, modern sector. The new states depend on constant injections of foreign capital, yet cannot very well invite foreign investors to sink their funds into substantially or wholly unproductive regions far from the support structure without which investment cannot flourish. Thus there is, in effect, a built-in incentive to retain existing imbalances, at least for a few more decades.

There are, of course, internal imbalances aside from the urban-rural juxtaposition. In every state one or more regions contribute more to national income than most or all of the rest. In the Ivory Coast, the *Centre* department, for example, produces nearly half of all coffee.[5] In 1963-64 Kano Province in Northern Nigeria accounted for nearly half of all ground-nut (peanut) purchases by the government, portents of Kano's relative power position when it became one of six states carved out of the Northern Region following the upheavals of 1966. Katsina and Bornu together accounted for over 70 percent of the total of Nigeria's prime export, leaving out mineral oil. In 1969-70 the Midwest State (formerly the Midwest Region), also in Nigeria, had dramatically doubled its expected revenue from one year to the next because of commercial quantities of oil that had not even been suspected to be there when the region was carved out of the then Western Region. Obviously this differential capability to produce income must affect plans to redistribute legal, administrative authority.[6]

Other examples could be cited at random to demonstrate the iron law of unequal distribution of wealth in Africa. The principal conclusion to be drawn from this disparity is that the distribution of power among competing rural or interior sections is much more a function of the nature of the commodity produced than of legal-constitutional arrangements. If power shifts occur they are more likely the consequence of world price fluctuations or discovery of new sources of wealth than of administrative fiat.

We have discussed the socioeconomic dimensions of oil. They are worth considering again in this different context. What exactly is the impact of mineral oil production on the internal-regional distribution of wealth and power? Revenue from that source, coming mainly from coastal and off-shore areas, most likely under central government or joint central government-state jurisdiction, does not generate secondary industries in the same manner and to the same extent as do other traditional sources of revenue. A federation supported largely from oil revenue will differ in significant respects from one founded on revenue from agricultural production where locally situated processing and canning industries are feasible. In Nigeria, following cessation of the 1967-70 civil war, the impact of oil revenue probably was far greater on internal-regional distribution of power in either or both of the contending sections than would have been so had the secession been successful, for the secessionists had lost control of the oil-bearing region early in the conflict. As it was, by rejoining the federation the former rebel area could legitimately share in the benefits from oil. Put differently, ideological or ethnic factors are of scant value unless backed by massive production of wealth.[7]

Conversely, straightforward injection of available surpluses — from oil, for example — does not necessarily improve conditions in the less developed interior.[8] If no foundations exist to facilitate smooth absorption of a bonanza from oil revenue, the abrupt infusion of raw funds could cause a hemorrage or even kill the patient.

The sociological implications of input from oil revenue alone are most interesting. It is quite possible that lessons learned from the study of the social impact of cocoa, groundnuts, cotton, coffee, or tea, possibly also iron ore, diamonds, or gold, may not apply to mineral oil. Entirely different hands are engaged in its production; a substantially different relationship exists between the end product, the land from which it is produced, and the form of production. Most likely a class will be created that will be different from any class seen before in Africa. But as before, this new class will be concentrated at the fleshpots of urban Africa. The more recent Nigerian experience in attempting to arrive at a generally acceptable and workable formula for peaceful accommodation of conflicts among disparate subdivisions reveals the outlines of yet another dilemma.

Both the civilian federal regime and its military successors, aware of the enormous problem posed by the relatively backward north, attempted to improve the situation through various forms of revenue allocation and through the several regulatory and legislative instruments at their disposal. This was opposed by the northern rulers who were determined not to allow alterations in the disposition of power skewed by the colonial regime to favor traditional-religious interests. Consequently, financial contributions by the federal government intended to advance federalism in Nigeria more likely than not were diverted into relatively unproductive channels, and much of the design to achieve a modicum of regional balance was frustrated. Following the military coup, another approach led to the substitution of 12 states for the original 4.

At first glance this was a sensible approach, for the old Northern Region had clearly enjoyed an unfair advantage over the Southern tier. However, the new dispensation simply was not auspicious once one examines its financial bases. Most of the new states showed deficits in their first sets of estimates before development budgets are considered. The size of the deficit depended largely on the capability of the new state administrations to collect taxes. Most of the six new states of the north were notoriously weak in that respect. The full measure of dependence on federal supports was reflected in the share of federal aid or refunding or other contributions, based either on oil-pooling formulas or other arrangements, that each state required to meet basic and pressing obligations.

The actual power disposition within the new structure was candidly reflected in the following statement found in the estimates of Kwara State; it is typical of similar statements in the estimates of all of the other states of the north except Kano.

> [The projected deficit] in effect means that in the absence of external financial aids or assistance, the State will continue to find it extremely difficult to embark on the prosecution of vital development projects. The financial survival of the State therefore depends on what individuals will be prepared to offer in the way of personal sacrifices and honest devotion to duty.[9]

Chances were that even optimal response to the concluding appeal would not materially improve the situation.

The question of what share each region, later each state, was to receive from oil revenue was predictably subject to heated and protracted debates.[10] One is tempted to translate allocation of revenue into development capacity and beyond that into power and influence within the system. Actually, whatever the formula — whether a given state, regardless of direct contribution to oil production, receives 50 percent of all earnings or less — only a few states had the capacity to digest whatever share was injected into their fiscal systems. Millions of pounds were simply consigned to waste because of a formula that ignored the crucial aspect of digestive capacity and set aside a more substantial distributive pool out of which all states were to receive a share in addition to extra shares for the federal government and for the producing states.

On the assumption that the federal government alone can make proper use of the sharply increased revenue from oil — from the profits tax, for instance — as well as from its share of the distributive pool, it might be argued that actual improvement of the disparities between states required reduction rather than increase of the share going to each. Certainly, even if the states had been well established, tried and proven in fiscal adminis-tratiion, they were not prepared for massive windfalls and other counts. Most likely such additions would ruin whatever digestive capacity each possesses through intensification of corruption and related malpractices, for example. A further measure of the problem emerges from examination of central government and state expenditures on internal security. Actually none of the states of Africa seems to put its money where its mouth is as far as internal distribution of police and other security expenditures are concerned. In fact, as we shall note in the section on local government, inconsistency seems to be the watchword in all matters relating to correction of regional inequity.[11]

Other factors intervene to frustrate and defeat plans to correct internal imbalances. Disparities in educational respects — literacy, for instance — realistically cannot be overcome by means of revenue allocation alone. In many parts of Africa the rate of population increase alone is such as to negate all efforts to upgrade education. Indications are that Nigerian educational programs, for example, "have not begun to alter the tidal wave of illiteracy that threatens to inundate the far northern states."[12] Elsewhere on the continent, education statistics, shortages of funds if related to population increase, and shortages of amenities that might attract competent teachers as well as administrators indicate regression rather than progress. In such conditions equalization of power and influence within states might actually amplify the voice of the growing illiterate portion of the population or most likely that of their self-appointed spokesman, in public policy determination. Anticipation of an acceleration of this trend seems to have been one of the factors contributing to the events of 1966 in Nigeria. It is possible that to an extent education, more basically literacy, may determine the rate at which truly representative government may become feasible on the continent.

All governments encounter resistance when attempting to assign skilled, high-level personnel such as administrators, teachers, or other professionals to what the assignees perceive to be hardship posts. Predictably, in the typical African situation assignment to the severely underendowed bush are likely to be even less well received. Like investors of capital, highly trained and educated persons are disinclined to waste their resources and opportunities on what they regard as hopeless enterprises.

As a result, a vicious cycle ensues. Backward conditions repel social and administrative personnel without whom the root causes of backwardness cannot be attacked. Of critical importance in that connection is the demonstrable link between level of education, level of public health, and general standards. Low performance at these levels translates into few schools and hospitals, no electrification, and poor communications and transportation.[13]

The Dilemma

Correction of internal-regional imbalances runs into a basic conflict between initially irreconcilable requirements. Whether the objective is mere narrowing of the development gap or whether something more is envisaged, industrial and commercial and financial equalization must be sought at an early stage. This equalization clashes with basic economic requirements, regardless of the dominant social philosophy of ideology. Whether foreign investor or African development planner, whether pragmatic socialist or capitalist, basic considerations of profitability, relative costs, marginal benefit, and the like are of overriding importance during the initial phases.

Throughout Africa, partly to compensate for the imbalance created by the nearly universal colonial policy of concentrating on straight interior-coastal product evacuation routes, lines of rail, and ports, development planners have entertained proposals to place certain industries in the interior. Certainly, the cost for interior consumers should be reduced considerably if such a shift could be brought about. Alas, interests along the established and favored transportation routes or at the favored administrative or production centers, ready to do battle to protect their positions, will have no difficulty at all in persuading policymakers of the initial high cost, for a decade or so, of such redistribution of functions. In most instances location of even modest industries in the underendowed and neglected interior, experimental of necessity, would call for prohibitive expenditures.

A pioneering study of Tanzania draws our attention to a fascinating phenomenon. It seems that in nearly a hundred years the geographic pattern of modernization in Tanzania appears not to have changed significantly. The author speculates that this may be the predictable consequence of variance in receptivity to modernization among different regions within the country, reinforced by consequent low-priority assignments on the part of policymakers.[14]

Actually, there is no doubt that if resources are concentrated on one area or one sector localized modernization can be achieved. Sector by sector modernization, however, usually brings chaos. In any case, the less modernized sector cannot compete against relatively more affluent ones in bringing pressure to bear on central government, hence the vicious cycle effect noted in Tanzania. The tendency to further neglect already neglected areas will persist. Allocation formulas will continue to favor the wheels that squeak loudest, as perceived by central development planners. Reliance on "existing poles" of production, tried and proven infrastructural benefits, familiar modes of transportation, customary amenities, and so on will remain the principal sources of policy inspiration.[15] Cries for social justice, expressed through diverse forms of regional representation, continue to fall on deaf ears. Perhaps the formulation offered by the Kenya government depicts the possibilities most accurately and realistically. Discussing "Income Distribution and Regional Development," the Kenya Development Plan, 1966-70 concedes:

> It is not possible to have uniform development in all areas of the country — if only because of differences in natural resource endowment. Moreover many of the less developed areas are also very sparsely populated, and the costs of basic investments in roads, water supplies, power and telecommunications in these areas would be very high in themselves and excessively high in relation to the population to be served. Even for countries far richer than Kenya it is a long-term task to create the necessary infrastructure for the development of all regions and all remote corners of the country.[16]

It seemed that not even periodic starvation in the poorest region compelled a different stance.

Whatever the policy, it is clear that unless states want to "solve" the problem by a rob-Peter-to-pay-Paul formula, which would be like generating wealth through taking in each other's laundry, they must leave the actual resolution of the problem to outside financial assistance. This again must be provided by foreign governments, because private investors find little of interest in regional equalization projects.

In the interim, development strategy as distinct from development rhetoric requires that scarce resources be put to work where they promise the greatest yield in the shortest period of time. This means concentration on already highly developed regions such as the Kenya Highlands, the Kampala-Jinja-Mbale triangle in Uganda, the Accra-Tema-Koforidua triangle in Ghana, the Arusha-Moshi region in Tanzania, the Lagos-

Apapa area in Nigeria, and the line of rail in Zambia. The capital investment in a city like Nairobi alone makes it mandatory for any regime in
Kenya to favor it over the barren, unproductive north or the coastal strip.[17]

The anatomy of power can be read without much difficulty from the
economic development map. The relative power position of highly developed internal regions vis-à-vis less developed ones attracts continued,
possibly increasing, resource support accompanied by progressively greater
relative neglect of the back areas. As economic velocity increases with
population density, costs of consumer goods drop the closer one comes to
ports, administrative headquarters, or lines of rail. Industries follow earning — buying — capacity, which is increased, in turn, by employment and
wages. Some compensating factors are associated with economic backwardness, but none of these suffice to compensate for the widening power
gap within the states of Africa.

Local, Traditional,
and Religious Power

The vast majority of Africans in all probability know only their immediate local, traditional, or religious rulers and governing councils. National, most likely also regional and provincial, government and economics probably are far beyond the ken of the individual, who usually is an agriculturalist eking out a bare existence in a rural area far removed from the din and excitement of national politics from which headlines are made or political theories spun. It is appropriate, therefore, that any analysis of Africa should dwell at some length on these immediate and vital realms.

Local Government

Since funds without which local government cannot operate are funneled downward from the center and from the regional and provincial levels, the low man on the totem pole, local government, cannot expect much, however clearly earmarked local government supports might be. All too often local government effectiveness is measured in terms of constitutional divisions of power, statutory allocations of responsibility and revenue, and the usual rhetoric born of wishful thinking. Similarly, manuals and handbooks prepared by bureaucrats or consultants who often seem to be out of touch with reality are all too regularly accepted on face value.

Another view holds that since central power dominates the national scene, national and local politics must of necessity be closely linked. Again reality appears to be sharply at variance with perception. Links between the national centers and local government units are quite tenuous, and communications are characteristically sporadic and unreliable. In any event, local government affairs are to the national centers what sideshows are to the big tent. There is much confusion on this point.

In an attempt to revive local government in Ghana after the coup of 1966, one commission of inquiry fell back on John Stuart Mill's treatise on "Considerations on Representative Government."

> The ideally best form of Government is that in which sovereignty or supreme controlling power in the last resort is vested in the entire aggregate of the community; every citizen not only having a voice in the exercise of that ultimate sovereignty, but being at least occasionally called on to take an actual part in the government, by the personal discharge of some public function, local or general.[1]

Mill, of course, was addressing himself to supreme, not subordinate, power, to essential, not peripheral, activity. In the context in which he wrote and thought, local power was local only. Considering the vital question of economic development alone — a question that surely is central to citizen concern in neglected parts of the world — Mill has nothing to offer, for in economic development matters the typical African is but an innocent bystander. Perhaps in the aggregate mass public opinion and mass pressure may stir a faint echo or response among those who order national priorities, but even that premise is doubtful. Always under pressure, and increasingly so, national decision makers cannot wait for the ponderous processes of opinion formation characteristic of the vast expanses and poor communications in Africa.

Throughout the world local government units find themselves hopelessly bogged down. Financially, hence operationally, they have great difficulty in keeping their collective heads above the waters of bankruptcy. After salaries and wages have been paid out, and after all of the more demanding palms have been greased, resources remaining in the local treasury usually are insufficient to cope with such pressing tasks as education, roads, sanitation and public health generally, market and water supplies and other concerns vital to the existence if not survival of local communities. Examination of actual expenditures in Ghana, Nigeria, Kenya, and Zambia reveals that by far the smaller share of all resources is applied to feeble efforts to meet the most urgent tasks, while two-thirds or more are regularly consumed merely to maintain local councils and their affiliates. One of the few candid inquiries into the financial support bases for local government (in Ghana) concluded that local government there was an organizational feature in the final stages of decay.[2] One reason this decay often goes unnoticed is that national governmental officials and some social analysts outside government are all too prone to surrender to what one source terms "financial make-belief."

Budgets generally are processed far too slowly to be of practical use to local government authorities. When they are approved it is on the dubious assumption that revenue collection will be 100 percent successful. Such assumption is fanciful. Local government potential is further inhibited by severe shortages in skills. The typical local government official even in advanced industrial countries is relatively inexperienced, frequently serving on a part-time basis only. In underendowed systems, levels of experience — in the modern administrative, not traditional sense — and levels of skill are likely to be far lower. There may be only one medical officer available to serve tens or even hundreds of thousands, one engineer usually of very limited experience to survey local requirements for an area the extent of which may stagger the imagination.

For these and other reasons, what there is of *management* of local government — again in the modern sense of the word — is handled at the national center far from the scene. "Even minor decisions are passed up a long hierarchical line to be taken by some anonymous and unaccountable authority far removed from the job or the local consequences" of decisions made.[3] This detachment produces what may be called the stretch effect of institutional growth. Proliferation of local and generally inland agencies and institutions to serve local needs beyond available and prospective manpower resources dilutes effectiveness per budget allocation unit in direct proportion to distance from the nearest urban and relatively well-endowed administrative center. In most instances throughout the continent, that center happens to be the national capital; for the typical resident in the interior that center may well be on the moon, or beyond.

What frequently is described as excessive centralization may well be an inevitable, practically unavoidable accompaniment of public affairs management in underendowed societies. This sort of management may be obvious, but the implications for any attempt to actually vest effective power at local levels and assure effective exercise of this power in the local context and in the local public interest may not be generally realized.

Because local government is so weak, political leaders have been unable to resist the temptation to harness these potentially valuable sources of patronage to their chariots. Local government even in the developed countries is an appendage of political or personal machines, as the case may be.[4] Nkrumah, Obote, Tubman, Houphouet-Boigny, and Touré are outstanding examples of the successful manipulator of this particular type of power resource. Significantly, it is an extension downward of power wielded at the top instead of the other way around.

Proposals have been offered to minimize partisan political patronage at the local and regional levels by substitution of nonpartisan civil servants for political hacks.[5] This idea misses a basic point. Whether civil servant or hack, unless funds are allocated and delivered to local treasuries, dependence on the central dispensers of bread and amenities will sap local energies and will sooner or later either corrupt the nonpartisan emissary of the central government or motivate him to return as quickly as possible to the fleshpots of the capital. If he remains in the bush he surely ceases to be nonpartisan vis-à-vis the fund-dispensing ruling group or faction, whatever its label, be it a political party, a cabal, or a junta.

In actuality, central governments carry the lion's share of local expenditures. In Tanzania (Tanganyika) at the time of independence, central government bore 85 percent of the financial responsibility for general education, 82 percent for health, and 86 percent for water supply. In Somalia and Ethiopia in the early part of the 1960s, local government was practically non-existent; the entirety of public resources was collected and spent by central government. In other areas expenditure by local and provincial governments was higher, ranging up to 50 percent of total public sector expenditure in such countries as Kenya and Uganda.[6]

Data on local government are, of course, of very low reliability. Whatever the local share, we are aware of leakages and waste that is likely to increase with distance from relatively competent, sharp-eyed, and impartial central government accountants. Local government power or, conversely, the question of central government preponderance over local units must be viewed in the context of resource allocation. Unless and until central government directors are persuaded that resources allocated to local authorities will generate wealth, no substantial changes will occur. As we noted earlier, if local conditions do not improve substantially, competent civil servants cannot be persuaded to go to the bush in sufficient numbers to make an impact. This is the dilemma that local government faces throughout Africa, and no amount of quibbling about local face-lifting, creation of cooperatives, self-help schemes, or "harambee" projects in Kenya will alter the problem. Continued predominance of central government-controlled funds at local levels assures continuation of central government influence. The language of money is more persuasive than the language of self-government or self-determination advocates.

With the dawn of fiscal responsibility, as the euphoria of self-government wore off, central government proceeded to assume whatever local revenue-raising powers had been left over from colonial rule. The grant system, familiar as a control device to students of state and local government in the developed countries, was employed to keep local units in line. In Nigeria, and at one time in Kenya, regional and local (municipal) units actually had the power to raise funds abroad. For obvious reasons they were shorn of these prerogatives as soon as was practical.[7] Throughout Africa as pressures on central governments mounted, the relative lack of competence at the local level to cope with routine requirements and services, let alone disasters such as floods or droughts, became ever more apparent. In the circumstances, the notion that local units should raise funds abroad in competition with central government in an already tight and progressively tighter money market eventually became unacceptable. The blight that struck local units of government in the richer parts of the world predictably strangled and virtually gutted local units in Africa.

In many respects proposals to strengthen local units by grants or by permitting them to raise limited taxes or rates are analogous to advising a legless man to run faster. In parts of Nigeria, the north in particular, regional authorities allowed local units to raise revenue to a greater extent than is common throughout the rest of the continent. Ostensibly this freedom was permitted in order to "reduce" the dependence of local units — emirates and towns, for instance — on regional government. Actually this generosity must be viewed in light of the equally important policy objective, typical of regional authorities in feudal or semifeudal areas, that seeks to ensure maintenance of the developmental status quo as a social control device. In any case, whatever revenue is raised and used locally must be assessed on a per capita as well as per capita need basis. This is to say that a very backward area such as the Nigerian north simply requires more revenue than the comparatively more advanced southern regions, unless a decision is made to leave the neglected areas relatively poor. Allowing local units to raise taxes or rates and to use them locally, then, is a form of economic narcotic, or water treading. It leads nowhere in the long or short run.

Tradition and Religion

It is not always clear whether qualities or potentialities attributed to tradition and religion should not perhaps be traced to other sources. Is influence wielded by an Islamic functionary, for example, the product of religious processes, strictly speaking, or is it due to other factors? Similarly, considered in isolation from the socioeconomic processes that gave birth to them, the institutions of priest and chief and the religious and traditional powers associated with these positions are formidable. Evaluated in the context of the modernizing society, they lose significance. According to Balandier, traditional rulers were endowed with certain powers in response to communal survival needs. The surrounding system of chiefly power reflected the group need for order and defense, the desire of the weak to be protected from the strong, the poor's fear of the rich. The system evolved from the authority enjoyed by the head of the family, the lineage group, or clan; it was ceremonial, conventional, customary, ritual, and religious. Addressing himself to the conflict between tradition and modernity, Balandier ascribes certain innate resilience, a capacity to resist change, to traditional power to the point where he seems convinced that traditional institutions and relationships may actually survive the onslaught of modern economic forces.[8] He is in excellent company in his perception.

Balandier equates *political* with *power,* a common error, as we have noted throughout. "Dans les sociétés en voie de modernisation, la preponderance du politique reste accentué."[9] Actually, it is economic rather than political power that must be the mainstay of traditional and religious rule if either institution is to survive in conditions of modern competition. The noneconomic facets of chiefly and priestly power are rapidly turning into anachronisms.

Traditional rulers are not without value to secular rulers. Most certainly under colonial rule and thereafter they have served as pacifiers of potentially troublesome masses. The lieutenants and captains among them have served as conveyors of secular power, while the higher officers managed to convert that same power to personal or group advantage.

As their utility as keepers of the peace waned, alternative sources of power came into view for the more skillful and the shrewd. For many, new opportunities developed as colonial interest focused more clearly on the economic potential of conquered territories. At that point chiefly power with regard to resource allocation, principally land use, proved invaluable. Chiefly and in many parts priestly power to compel collection of rubber, as in the Congo, of groundnuts or peanuts, as throughout West Africa, emerged as the pivotal point around which evolved a special and mutually beneficial relationship that tied local functionaries to the territorial and eventually national centers. From modest beginnings, including, of course, the lucrative slave trade, there arose the new African class — the businessman-chief.

The role of peacemaker commends the traditional ruler and priest to the modern African government as well. Even in the copper mines of Zambia or the tin mines of Nigeria tribal elders are known to have served as direct instruments of central government authority, charged with responsibility for increased production.[10]

Although by no means typical of such forms of rule, the system established by the Senegalese Mourides offers useful illustrations of points made so far. The apparent base of rule in that sect is religion, Islam to be exact. For our purposes the critical ingredient is a solemn commitment on the part of believers to honor mutual obligations that center, in the main, on production of wealth. The strictly religious dimensions of whatever power is generated for the benefit of the religious functionaries, the marabouts, seem to be ceremonial and propagandistic in character. The real value of the social position that accrues to the Mouride leaders seems to be economic.[11]

Within the group precincts the marabouts exercise some control over group members through the medium of religious loyalty. On balance and over time, that control alone is not worth much. The ability of the more skillful to convert religious loyalty into economic resources at the local level also does not weigh too heavily in the scales of power. To be of political survival value, both religious fealty and economic acumen and its fruits must be of demonstrable value to the secular national leaders. Thus, in Senegal the true strength of the marabouts is a function of their role as supporters of the national leadership. The wealthier among these leaders use their income, derived from direct levies, gifts, and contributions in kind, to maintain clienteles, which in turn serve as support troops for the marabouts' allies in Dakar.[12] Incidentally, although these same support troops can in theory be thrown into battle against the national power center, in practice, when all the chips are down, the national forces have proved superior time and again.

Another source of power for local rulers and functionaries relates to the workings of subsistence economies. At the point where the subsistence economy comes into contact with the modern money economy, certain functions of the traditional ruler become critical to the individual farmer.[13] As cash becomes available to the farmer he crosses what has been termed the "security threshold";[14] at this point the subsistence economy begins to fade in his range of perception, and he is at the level of existence "above which forethought and effort is possible and below which resignation and fecklessness set in."[15] It is clear that even a modest monetary increment above that threshold must have a profound effect on the individual's life. The hand that holds the controls over that increment, however small and insignificant it may be in general economic terms, must be ranked high in the subsistence, hence social control, hierarchy at the local level. In a way, the traditional and religious rulers together with their immediate supporting functionaries — the tax collector, for example — stand astride the security threshold of the vast majority of Africans, at least during the very extended period of transition.

While considering Islam as a source of power, it is appropriate to note that the mere incidence of quantitative expansion of Islam southward across the Sahara should not be mistaken for evidence on substantive social behavior changes among the people nominally affected. Hidden within religious complexes are at times overpowering nonreligious drives that are known to have caused believers to line up on opposite sides in certain conflict situations. In any case, attempts to encompass within one set of generalizations the Arab rebellion in the Chad, the bitter conflict between Muslim and non-Muslim groups in the Sudan, conflicts between northern and southern Nigerians, and the events in East Africa, in particular Somalia and Zanzibar, collapse of their own weight.

TRADITION - RELIGION - EDUCATION

The tendency of Islam to restrict education in the general mass of its adherents reveals a great deal about its internal power structure. A glance at Northern Nigeria at independence offers ample support for a hypothesis that there might indeed be a strong correlation between Ismalic beliefs and practices and a near void in formal modern education.[16] But the fault should not be sought in the mosques. Exclusion of the masses from all modernizing influences is an imperative common to all feudal and semi-feudal elites. The aim seems to be preservation of a social order convenient and profitable to the upper levels. In that respect religions through time have served as facades or as handmaidens for the powerful.

By the same token the relatively advanced educational status character-istic of groups in areas penetrated by Christian missionaries cannot nec-essarily be attributed to the tenets of Christianity. More likely the accident of teaching religion through literature, the Bible mostly, invited establish-ment of schools, bringing literacy and a kind of education to millions.

Whatever the psychological or sociological explanations, there is a close statistical correlation between religion, in particular Christian reli-gions, and the general level of education among the proselytized. All other things being equal, Kenyans of Christian upbringing were likely to be better educated than Kenyans of different religious backgrounds.

Uneducated males aged 15 and over

	Among All	Among Christians	Among Others
Kenya	60.3%	42.3%	83.9%

SOURCE: Kenya Population Census 1962, Vol. III, Table VII, 48.

There is nothing inherently regressive about Islam as there is nothing inherently progressive about Christianity. Poor and ignorant masses can be oppressed and exploited by a minute few under either system. At the same time, both systems have demonstrated that substantial differences in educational achievement can be attained once the bars have been removed. Furthermore, certain differences are recorded within each religious com-plex, as, for example, in Kenya. Census data there show that the propor-tion of Christians without schooling is larger in central and northern Nyanza, among the Luo, than among the average Christians throughout the country.[17] Whatever the relationships or explanation, in the veritable ocean of illiteracy the person who can read a book, be it the Koran, the Bible, or a Sears-Roebuck catalog, has an edge on the one who cannot. Beyond that the ability of the few on top to lead and exploit the many rests to a considerable extent on educational differential.

Yet another important facet to traditional African life is the role of occult powers and beliefs. Again, it is difficult at times to detect where the boundary lies between the occult and religion as these terms are under-stood in the Western world. In any case, evidence abounds that the occult serves as a source of power and influence in the traditional as well as the modern sector. It is not likely that witchcraft, juju, or magic substantially affect the outcome of high-level public policy decisions, although in known instances this may have been the case.[18]

Occult and related beliefs and practices do play a central part in the lives of Africa's masses and must therefore be regarded as integrally re-lated to social institutions and processes in general. Incidentally, and not irrelevant to the subject of power in society, witchcraft, juju, and magic are important elements in physical and mental health care in traditional society. Whatever the form, the social power potential of occult matters arises mainly from the belief "that such means are used and that they can be effective.[19] The power of suggestion that occult forces are or might be at work or might be brought into play against someone — for example, to discourage practices or activities deemed undesirable by the ruling group — might well be sufficient to act as a deterrent. Statutory provisions prohibiting oathing, drumming, and other traditional practices in conjunction with voting or other constitutional processes are a gauge of official awareness of the problem.[20]

Potentially one of the most dangerous consequences of recourse to occult beliefs relates to the practice of oathing. This practice involves swearing of an oath coupled with the adjurer's firm belief in the supernatural efficacy of the oath or coupled with the enforcement of oath-contracted obligations by terror and physical punishment. The momentum of the Mau Mau revolt in Kenya in the late forties and early fifties somewhat was maintained by such means. Subsequently, similar practices were reported to have been employed by persons who supported opponents of Jomo Kenyatta, then president of Kenya, and Kenneth Kaunda, then president of Zambia.[21] In the absence of adequate alternative means of communication, modern rulers and administrators as well as party political leaders and revolutionaries do rely on traditional channels and the language and symbols of traditional beliefs. They are aware, however, that this is a dangerous gamble for such forces; once revived or released, they can be turned against the user.[22]

Tribe and Ethnicity

One of the most misused and abused terms encountered in the study of Africa is *tribe*. One must suspect that frequently its use reflects a mindless addiction to labels. It may also reflect a desire by Western observers — a desire founded on ethnocentric perspectives — to make invidious distinctions in favor of their own culture. Many, possibly all, of Africa's tribes may well be figments of non-African imagination. They certainly seem to have more substance in the eyes of outsiders than they do among indigenes. They are, in the main, products of definitional efforts not only by non-African anthropologists, sociologists, and linguists but also by colonial administrators whose perception of ethnic identity appears to have been governed by administrative considerations. One consequence of this effort is that new tribes are continuously being discovered. For instance, as one report puts it in discussing Kenya, the "Kalenjin tribal cluster, comprising a population of almost 1 million people, is *a new entity* based on recent recognition of existing linguistic and cultural relationships." That same report noted that the "discovery" of new clusters "suggests the possibility that beneath existing clusters and language groups there may in fact be others, as yet unrecognized, segments of which are scattered, by historical accident or by colonial design, or by the workings of modern economics."[23]

The 1960 census in Ghana defines *tribe*, with Ralph Linton (*The Study of Man*), as follows: "A group of people occupying contiguous (sic) territory and having a feeling of unity deriving from numerous similarities in culture, frequently friendly contacts and a certain community of interests."[24] Significantly, agreement proved impossible during preliminary discussions among authorities on the subject in an attempt to arrive at a universally acceptable definition of tribe suitable for census taking. Predictably, once a questionnaire was applied in the field, respondents differed in their perception of their own tribal affiliation. In part the difficulties stemmed from varying functional attributes that the designers attached to the rubric of tribal affiliation, such as linguistic variations, the meaning of geographic propinquity, or group self-identification.[25] The Ghana census, but also other sources, shows that breakdowns into units or categories smaller than tribe become mandatory whenever analysis focuses on behavioral particulars or on specific functional group characteristics such as proclivity to urbanization.[26] The Ga-Adangbe in Ghana as a whole may be urbanized to the extent of 40.3 percent, but the percent of urbanization within that grouping may range as low as 5.5 percent among the Adangbe and as high as 76.6 percent among the Ga. The Ghana census notes that to use the overall percentage for the larger or wider grouping would skew the data and adversely affect the study of group tendency to migrate to or live in urban centers.[27] Actually, indiscriminate use of the term *tribe* can skew any study and has had that effect.[28]

There are ample grounds to suspect that if African respondents were to be asked, first, questions related to their socioeconomic status and interests and only last questions related to their perception of tribal affiliation or identity a substantially different profile of contemporary Africa would emerge. During Nigeria's civil war, when it was outright hazardous to be identified as an Ibo, people who prior to the conflict had been believed to be Ibo now identified themselves as Ngwa, a small, relatively insignificant, but distinct language group.[29] Thus, if we continue using that term for want of a better one it is with profound reservations and misgivings.

In any case, we are concerned here with group characteristics that might be regarded as significant sources of power and influence. Among these are elite status, language, literacy and education, and mode of production coupled with the group's share of responsibility for the principal sources of wealth in the wider state or society. Also relevant is the value of the group to the national rulers in the context of social stabilization, or mobilization, or in whatever context seems appropriate to the rulers to ensure survival of the established order.

Commonly, tribes are ranked on the basis of sheer numerical strength.

There is no reason to believe that such ranking has any other but purely quantitative significance. The relative position that a group or members of a group enjoy in the wider area in which they normally reside depends on numerous variables, only some of which may be associated with numerical strength. A minute group may rise to eminence simply because it has produced the country's principal leader or president, and because that person happens to prefer the staffing of more sensitive offices with members of his own group. Nkrumah was partial to Nzima, a small and marginal group whose language is scarcely, if at all, used outside the group's geographic limits. His successors preferred Ga or Akan. Often a clan or other sub-group, possibly based on a town, rises to prominence for similar reasons — for example — the Bende "mafia," which clustered around leaders of the former Eastern Region in Nigeria, or the Wolof or Lebou of Senegal.

A tribe may dominate because it happens to be situated near or literally on top of riches such as copper or oil. The Bemba of Zambia, located where Zambia's wealth, copper, is produced, were exposed relatively early to outside influences, skills, and values.[30] Nigeria's Ibos profited from proximity to the coast; Kenya's Kikuyu owned or claimed to have owned the principal source of wealth in Kenya for decades — namely, some of Kenya's most fertile land. Nigeria's Fulani, already dominant in the north for centuries, found themselves in control of some of Nigeria's principal sources of wealth and revenue as the economy developed.

Some tribal groupings, again because of the accident of geographic location along the invasion or penetration routes, came to gain a relatively early cultural edge, including advanced skills. Thus, the Ga-Adangbe of Ghana predominate among white-collar workers;[31] so did the Ibo of Nigeria until the events of 1966. The Ewe of Togo and Ghana dominate in certain sections of the public service, the Kru of Liberia in sectors of transport and portage. Yoruba and Hausa predominate among traders throughout West Africa. Do African politicians seek to convert tribal loyalties, attachments, or emotions to personal or factional advantage at the regional or national levels? Judging by the frequency with which such charges are voiced in African politics, it would appear that way.[32] One could gain the impression that the tribe indeed constitutes a firm base for individual and factional assaults on established, constitutional, national regimes. Actually, close examination of the substance behind the common allegation of tribal politics reveals that it is the exception rather than the rule that tribal characteristics in the strictest sense of that term play an important part in national, higher level politics. More likely than not, what we are witnessing is none other than age-old patronage politics or group favoritism.

When Simon Kapwebwe, a rival for power in Zambia, was accused of mobilizing his tribe, the Bemba, against the allegedly nontribal national regime led by Kenneth Kaunda, he did not seek to convert tribalism as such into political ammunition but into social discontent among a numerically strong group with substantial claims to the wealth of the country. Discontent typically is based on the belief that one is entitled to a greater share of the national wealth than the economy seems prepared to yield or the privileged group is prepared to part with. This is at the root of the Luo-Kikuyu conflict in Kenya, the Ga-Ewe or Ga-Akan rivalry in Ghana, the Ibibio-Efik, and Itsikirri-Urhobo confrontations in southern Nigeria, or the Tiv-Hausa-Fulani tensions in the Nigerian north. Often it is quite simply a question of the outs seeking to replace the ins.[33] Tribalism serves as a foil; it is not the heart of the matter.

Because non-Africans chose to classify the peoples on the continent in that manner, language, again as understood or perceived by strangers, was taken to be the core of what was rather arbitrarily termed the tribe. Whatever the nexus among language, customs, and traditions, or ethnic distinctions, there is a correlation between language and the ability of its users to improve their social standing. As the 1962 Ghana *Census Report* formulates it, the "proportion of persons literate in the language(s) of any given tribe other than their own is of particular importance . . . such a proportion could perhaps be taken as an indication that a particular language has attained a greater degree of diffusion and the language itself, therefore, could become a medium of communication, education, and information."[34]

Quite obviously, language has been one of the sources of success for the colonial regimes: the Europeans made their own language, hence their own intellectual skills and ways of life, the principal means of social control within territories under their jurisdiction. Next to the near-monopoly the European languages enjoyed, certain indigenous languages conveyed varying degrees of power and influence to their users. In Ghana, Asante-Twi, a language in the Akan group, appears to be a key to success along with Akwapem-Twi and Fante; these language groups form the most widely diffused Ghanaian communication systems.[35]

From the foregoing flows a secondary, derivative source. Any other group able to speak the primary group's language may thereby plug into the primary group's potential. Certain minor and some major groups have demonstrated that facility, being perhaps more adaptable or having attained higher levels of education.[36]

Education generally converts readily into social group power, mainly through economic opportunity; certainly the combination of language facility and social adaptability generates economic opportunities. A large teacher-student contingent associated with a given tribe has historically been the key to political success in the colonies and shortly after independence. A social castelike hierarchy emerged everywhere: the region around and including the capital generated more opportunity, hence power and influence, than did the other urban centers, urban centers more than rural areas, and certain tribes more than others. In Ghana, for instance, the

Akan, Ga-Adangbe, and Ewe excel. Greater Accra, the capital region, and Ashanti, the center of cocoa production, clearly dominate the scene and together account for nearly half of the total national secondary school population.[37]

In the eyes of tribal leaders the time lag between education received and power and influence generated by education at critical points in state and society places a premium on group members with education who at the same time are eligible for deployment in the economy. In this respect the coastal groups or, in Kenya and Zambia, the groups that by other means attained high educational levels early have a built-in advantage over the rest. Even though all governments are pledged to extend the benefits of education to the less advantaged regions in their respective countries, it will be most difficult for the disadvantaged to close the enormous gap between themselves and the more highly developed groups. In Ghana about half of all persons over 25 with school experience in 1960 were of Akan origin or identified themselves with that group. Conversely, the Mole-Dagbani in the northern parts could claim no more than 2.3 percent of all persons over 25 with school experience.[38]

The relationship between tribal and religious identification also is of some consequence. In Ghana the Nzima, ranking highest in terms of percentage of Christians in their group, also had garnered more high-level manpower and managerial posts than their overall share of the population would have warranted. Even though Nkrumah's personal preferences benefited them, it still would not have been possible for him to place a substantial number of that group in high positions unless they had possessed commensurate skills.[39]

The tensil strength of tribal units, or even clusters, is a function in part of ethnic homogeneity, the degree of geographic concentration or density, the degree to which each unit is confined to a specific location or area, the incidence of internal and external mobility, foreign and domestic migration, or adaptability to modern influences, especially to new modes of production.[40] Group mobility, for example, enables one unit to leave relatively unproductive grounds in search of more rewarding opportunities, while lack of mobility may condemn another to stagnation. The Bemba of Zambia, though advantaged by relatively close proximity to some of the world's richest copper deposits, could still have failed to benefit had it not been for an innate ability to seek economic opportunity beyond the traditional tribal limits.

All of the foregoing characteristics may not suffice to lift a given tribal group to social dominance and sustain it at that level. Considerable economic substance is required. The key to an analytically meaningful assessment of tribal power may well be the wealth accumulated by group members and, perhaps more important, the portion of such wealth that is available for group development. Even though a tribe may be responsible for production of a major share of the wealth of an entire country, this responsibility will not convert into group power unless the propensity to save has been sufficiently developed to accumulate resources and unless these are indeed utilized for the improvement of the group's living standards and conditions.[41]

It is one of the consequences of colonial rule that few African tribal groups have been able to accumulate sufficient wealth to fend off socioeconomic forces competing for the loyalty of group members; tribal resources usually will not match those brought into the field by trade unions or farm cooperatives, to mention but two of the strongest rivals. Tribes also have not devised ways to capture and hold the loyalty of their wealthier sons as have the Ismaelis or the Mourides.

At a different, principally local level, tribes do still generate a measure of power, mainly in relation to basic survival needs and expectations among increasingly insecure group members. With modernization, individual welfare requirements loom ever larger. Especially sensitive are death and burial and notification of the next of kin. Though taken for granted on the home grounds, the group member who migrates to the town or lives in a mining camp finds that the cost of death and burial exceed his resources.[42]

The ranking of a given tribe also may be influenced by what one may term its crisis value. For instance, the events of 1966 caused a major shift in the relative power positions of the principal Nigerian tribes, mainly the Ibo, Yoruba, and Hausa-Fulani, especially vis-a-vis certain minority groups. As the regions formerly dominated by Ibo, Yoruba, and Hausa-Fulani gave way to smaller states, groups such as the Tiv, Efiks, Ogoja Edo, and Urhobo were able to play a more prominent role in national affairs. The large number of Tiv in the military was believed to have materially augmented the bargaining power of that group, mainly because the ruling military group needed to secure allies against the now-dissatisfied majorities.

Land and Land Use

"It is not easy for those who know only the industrialized countries of the Western world, to realize the significance of the position occupied by the land in the eyes of most peoples of Africa." With these words, Lord Hailey opens the chapter on "Land" in his comprehensive *African Survey*.[43] Still, perhaps because he is basically committed to colonial rule, he fails to penetrate to the core of the problem — namely, the use of land as a means of social control, of social power. In fact, two of the mainstays of colonial rule were: (1) alienation of vast acreages of land, especially the most productive land, from traditional users; and (2) establishment of the principle of chiefly control over land and land use and incorporation of that principle in the socioeconomic code of colonial rule.[44]

Land alienation accrued mainly to the benefit of European settlers in northern, eastern, and southern Africa. Eventually, possession of the best land in predominantly agricultural economies provided British, Portuguese, and Afrikaaner elements with the leverage needed to assure total control, leaving aside force of arms and other instrumentalities of colonial rule. Since traditional rule also was based in part on land use, exploitation of land in many areas was conducted by colonial and traditional rulers working in tandem to mutual advantage.

Because the overwhelming majority of Africa's peoples are engaged in subsistence agriculture, the magnitude of land control as an instrument of power is self-evident. The mutually satisfactory arrangement is worth emphasizing. Diverse forms of land ownership, predominantly communal in law or in fact, but more important, land use allocation facilitated the development of ever smaller plots, progressively less efficient and less and less productive.[45] This division assured a wide margin of economic advantage to the ruling groups, such as settler elements in Kenya or large African landowners elsewhere. Colonial rule and traditional feudal rule, as in Ethiopia, protected landlords' privileges and advantages against their clients. In return, settlers or African landlords served "as pillars of the power structure."[46]

In its postcolonial form, the arrangement sees the central government in the role of what Potekhin calls "feudal landowners." The instrument of state ownership is the tax levied on agricultural production.[47] As the peasant is concerned, this line of analysis suggests that it makes little difference whether the state owns the land or the owner is a private or tribal landholder. The combination of effective state ownership by one means or another, traditional feudal patterns, and fragmentation of land at the bottom of the pyramid is the key to appreciation of the value of traditional-religious power in the modern African state.[48]

Deserts and other vast stretches of wholly unproductive or even marginally productive lands are of no consequence in the present context. Critically important are lands in or near the centers of administration, principally the capital, and land of high wealth production potential, such as mining areas, cocoa-bearing regions, and the heartlands of coffee, tea, and groundnut cultivation. We find that gradually and in total disregard of traditional concepts of land use changes were effected that figuratively, and eventually literally, removed the ground from beneath the feet of the peasantry, wiping out what little power they once had over traditional rulers and setting them up for a final assault by the new but wholly impersonal state landlord.[49] Land value was converted to money value, and traditional society was rendered vulnerable to money-related power plays.[50]

Colonial rule and what is euphemistically called reform of land tenure went hand in hand.[51] But as do so many other legal formulations, this statement, too, actually diverts attention from the role of land as an instrument of social control. Whatever the legal form of land tenure may be, the economic value of land makes the critical social difference in the final analysis. What matters is whose money or capital dominates production, distribution, supplies (e.g., seeds, fertilizer, where appropriate), purchasing, transport, processing, and eventually marketing and sale of the product gained from land. The prevailing winds indicate progressive pauperization of the African masses. Whatever else the law may say about land ownership, only the state — that is, the ruling elites, the bureaucracies, and the support troops, mainly the bourgeoisie — will remain in the competition for effective utilization of Africa's lands.

Nationalization of land, viewed as a panacea by many, will effectively alter the power and influence function of land only if material benefits from it are distributed in accordance with democratic procedures. Actually, nationalization would require rural-based participatory democracy, a most remote possibility given the rate of change in that direction, especially in rural Africa, as evidenced by the record of the first development decade. Experience with the marketing boards following "democratization" of government shows the likely outcome of nationalization of land, an approach favored by Soviet theorists.[52] Short of nationalization, revival and modernization of collectives, communal ownership, and even private ownership have been recommended as correctives. Wistfully, Soviet academician Potekhin recorded that "[e]ven the International Bank mission [to Tanganyika in 1959-60] does not conceal that the transition to private landownership raises the risk of excessive indebtedness, eventual concentration of ownership of land in the hands of those who have money to lend, and the creation of a destitute landless class."[53]

Communal ownership, increasingly favored, still cannot escape the pervasive presence of the traditional rulers or ruling class. Too often, in order to secure stability even enlightened modern rulers allow communal ownership to be undermined and reduced to where it is "nothing but a screen for the semi-feudal exploitation of the peasants."[54]

Rule by the Islamic emirs of Northern Nigeria, the Baganda mailo chiefs in Uganda, or the marabouts of Senegal could be sustained only if supported by control over land use. Religious features have reinforced and augmented socioeconomic holds over the masses.[55] More likely than not, attempts to modernize and reform these relationships remain dead letters.

In spite of legal-constitutional control provisions, for all practical purposes traditional rulers have continued to operate in a limbo somewhere between modern legality and traditional legitimacy, as they have been able to do ever since colonial rule was first extended to their areas. This, always provided, of course, that they do not violate any of the fundamental assumptions on which central government recognition of their offices depends.[56] The power of money seems to penetrate seemingly impervious barriers. The basic issues to be considered and socially resolved relate to the direction in which land-generated money will flow and in what proportion it will be distributed, through what channels and by whom.

For Africa's masses, land remains the source of subsistence control. Efforts are under way throughout the continent, though only rhetorical in many cases, to assure a modicum of democratic control over the usufruct of land use. Marxist prescriptions are the most drastic, insisting that nationalization of large private or semiprivate holdings and elimination of "intermediary rent collectors" is mandatory if feudalism is to be overcome.[57] This view demands attention, for it appeals to ever widening circles from Libya to Zambia, from Senegal to Kenya.

It can be stated more broadly that the core problem affecting any reform in Africa for decades to come remains what has been described as the murkiness and ambiguity of land law.[58] Beyond law there is widespread murkiness and ambiguity in rural Africa generally. For some time to come, sufficiently large loopholes will remain, or new ones will open up, to permit outside interests to avail themselves of the power potential inherent in land and land use. Foremost among these will be the bureaucratic controllers of revenue and, where permitted to operate, the owners of capital, the banks, the lenders. Legal murkiness also will continue to facilitate traditional rulers' control over native law and the courts. While such measures as land registration will bring some order into an otherwise chaotic situation, conveying to increasing numbers of African farmers a greater sense of social stability, many of these same measures will also set up new targets for predatory interests.[59] In Sierra Leone and Liberia, increasingly in Ghana, Western Nigeria, Kenya, and probably throughout the continent, choice lands are brought up by the moneyed classes situated usually in the nation's capital and sometimes by foreigners, by proxy.[60]

Attempts to curb or regulate the exploitation of land and land use for personal or group advantage at the expense of the peasant or farmer frequently are made without regard to reality. In Ghana, for instance, chiefs as custodians of stool lands had the power to allocate lands within their jurisdiction. To assure "proper use" and to curb abuse through chiefly prerogatives, it was proposed to subject the passing on of "any interest in or right over any stool land" to approval by a lands commission.[61] In practice, of course, this proposal means creation of a new coalition: traditional ruler and commission members joined to any other interests in a position to control the commission's decisions. In prevailing conditions, recognition of the rights of such traditional landlords as the Nigerian obas, the tendana priests, the Ashanti hierarchy and others in Ghana, and the marabouts in Senegal merely sets the stage for the emergence of a new class of real estate operators in traditional garb.[62]

Aside from prolonging traditional prerogatives and potentials accruing to chiefs, modernization of land tenure, registration, and the like has caused a shift from individually (family) operated farms to plantations frequently owned by expatriates or strangers from other parts of the country, more likely than not from the capital. Plantations, in turn, mainly in the Ivory Coast, Ghana, and in parts of Nigeria, introduced large numbers of migrant workers, many of whom come from other African states. Where this is the case, the local population, including former owners, live off the proceeds of the arrangement "without work and without inducement to work."[63]

One of the several dilemmas confronting African policymakers in connection with land as a source of social power arises from development needs. There is no longer any doubt that existing systems of land tenure, land use, and related practices constitute effective blocs to economic growth.[64] Sharp reductions in revenue are inevitable where agriculture is the prime or one of the prime sources of revenue, as in Kenya, and especially where European-owned and operated plantations or large cattle ranches provide the bulk of that revenue, nationalization, cutting up of large estates, or other major incisions or changes. Again, in Kenya under the continuing impact of the pressure built up before and during the days of the Mau Mau rebellion, there was an increasing need for settlement of ever larger numbers of black claimants to land.[65] The comparatively rich plantations in French-influenced areas also attract the attention of Africanization enthusiasts, understandably.

In Kenya the government machine effectively curbed the European farm bloc as a land-based power group. What was the actual effect of this restraint? The African farmer, in effect, was a mere tool in the transfer of power from European to African politicians' hands. African farmers lacked experience and capital, were burdened by debilitating family ties and dependencies, and tended in any case to regard ownership of land as an invitation to leisure after the example of the departed European landed aristocracy.

Virtually helpless, the new users of the former "scheduled" or alienated lands joined the queue of Africans petitioners for government assistance, becoming political fodder in the process.[66] Vast new channels for power and influence were created as a result. Government corporations took over where European private capital had worked before. Increasingly, the government supervision and control that inevitably follows financial support became a feature of Kenya agriculture. When African farmers were given the option to purchase shares in cooperative farms, because they lacked the funds they took on shadow partners who shared in the profits.[67]

V

Rulers and Governors

. . . political power is that power which every man having in
the state of Nature has given up into the hands of the society,
and therein to the governors whom the society hath set over
itself, with this express or tacit trust, that it shall be employed
for their good and the preservation of their property.

JOHN LOCKE
TRUE END OF CIVIL GOVERNMENT

12

The Code of Power

No clear and precise lines separate political from economic affairs, one level of government from another, or one group of rulers from another group within the same system below, above, or adjacent. One can only identify types and categories of agents of power, types and categories of groups and of resources, the commanding heights and the valleys. One can also identify the strategic crossroads and positions, always mindful that none are permanent and what appears to be a commanding position today may tomorrow be a mere peripheral outpost. In the sections following we shall attempt some identifications, but the multiplicity of resources and the changing circumstances that surround their use alone suggests extreme caution.

If there is a pattern to the analytical system we employ, it is discernible not so much from the categories of agents or groups but from the relationship of one to the other and of each to the power resources at their disposal. All are related to the circuits or markets wherein power flows, is exchanged, and consumed, and from which new sources arise.

Although the groups we analyze in this and the succeeding parts are not meant to be clearly delineated one from the other, they are substantive, socially live, and assertive; they are themselves instrumentalities of power, capable of merger with others or of partial metamorphosis. Today's pressure group concentrating on one issue may split into several new groups tomorrow, each pursuing different, even entirely new goals. Whatever their orientation or their composition, they demonstrate by their own performance what is likely to be the record of performance of most other groupings of similar or even different coloring. It is not the name of a given ruler, his office, or title, nor is it the name or formal organizational shape a group may assume that matters or is of lasting significance. In the final analysis it is the overall impression, the aggregate record of behavior of individual rulers or groups that spells the long-range significance of the system and its parts.

In professional literature and in political lore, legality and authority have acquired power attributes all their own; they have come to evoke the same awe and respect as power itself. Actually, both are little more than elaborate but shallow myths maintained by use or threat of use of force. To the perceptive student of politics and power, both terms are more shadow than substance. Penetrating beyond the curtain of social myth in search of legality and authority, one encounters all too often merely a clever manipulator, perhaps a naked emperor. Yet because both concepts are firmly embedded in the formal arrangements behind which power is wielded, a few general comments on legality and authority as mainstays of the code of power are in order.

There can be little doubt that constitutions, statutes, and other formalized procedural instruments leave their imprints on distribution of power and influence in state and society. Still, one cannot afford to ignore that human hands manipulate these instruments, make the arrangements, and exploit them to individual and group advantage. Similarly, one cannot afford to become hypnotized by artificial boundaries that separate formal states from one another and from the international universe generally. If certain perquisites of sovereignty are shared, as we have shown, across national boundaries, if it is at times impractical to attempt distinctions between national and international sources or uses of power, then legality and authority also are shared. Internally, legal authority does not extend uniformly to all parts, and constitutional provisions are not uniformly relevant throughout a legal system. It is probable that the effectiveness of law and authority in the typical African state decreases with distance from the source of the authority-giving center; wholly or substantially extralegal, even unconstitutional norms may govern in the hinterland.

Legal arrangements and dispositions are quite ineffectual if they are utterly devoid of legitimacy or social relevance. As commonly understood, legitimacy derives from proven, verified, popular acceptance of the basic principles of government, of the broad outlines of a constitution, and of the principal personages associated with their implementation. The only known reliable test of popularity or representativeness is free and secret election of government officials by a reasonably enlightened and informed electorate. At the end of the first development decade it would be difficult to find instances of truly free, truly secret, reasonably universal elections anywhere in Africa.

Thus, in all cases under review legitimacy is more a matter of assumed or given acceptance — a form of social fiction subscribed to by Africans and Europeans alike in the interest of peaceful transfer and subsequent retention of certain facets of power. The importance of this acceptance must be kept in view as the challenges to that assumed legitimacy mount throughout the region and throughout the universe of the less developed countries.

The social relevance of constitutions tends to be obscured by ritual and rhetoric. The 1970 debate in the United States over the nomination of Supreme Court justices illustrates the point. While the Chief Executive pursued foreign policy objectives, and possibly domestic policy objectives also, whose constitutionality was highly debatable, he insisted on strict constitutional constructionism in other respects and selectively cited constitutional prerogatives of the Executive in defense of his position. The tactic is universal.

African practice replicates the Western example. In June 1969 the government of Zambia staged a referendum to end all referenda. The move cleared the way for amendment of the constitution by a simple two-thirds majority; in effect, it attacked constitutionality at its base, since the legislature at the time was effectively controlled by the government.[1] Nkrumah resorted to similar tactics to endow an entire series of unconstitutional measures with an aura of constitutionality.[2] It is noteworthy that at the time he went through the formalities of a referendum he already possessed and, in fact, already had used the powers to achieve his goal — namely, to eliminate the opposition and establish firm control over the judiciary.

The few African leaders who were still under an illusion on this point soon discovered that independence was basically a paper transaction. The resources without which independence was meaningless were still in foreign hands. In part the illusion of substantive progress toward effective self-determination stemmed from a misinterpretation of the nature of the term *political* — misinterpretation carefully nurtured and propagated by colonial theorists and practitioners. Nkrumah's classic admonition to his followers: "Take ye first the political kingdom and all other things will be added to you afterwards," illustrated the mistake. Under colonial rule economic, social, and military power had been welded into one solid bloc of firm if not absolute controls over the subject people. The African claimants then were conditioned to believe that something termed *political* could be separated from that bloc, transferred into their hands, and converted eventually into full and unrestricted self-determination.

The fallacy was accepted even by observers who should have known better. The Seers Commission, examining Zambia's condition at independence, reported that a problem had arisen because "economic and social power [had] been abruptly divorced from political power.[3] Actually, the problem had arisen because only an illusion had been transferred: political power cannot, in fact, be separated from economic power. Where it is separated it is meaningless. Zambian independence in the beginning was meaningless because the economic bases of all power had been retained in one disguise or another by the colonial power itself or by the European-controlled regime in the former center of the federation, Southern Rhodesia.

Foreign economic controls are a key factor and may materially affect the power political cutting edge of specific legal-constitutional provisions. Provisions of special operational value to foreign investors, such as clauses regulating acquisition and use of private property, may be live and meaningful, while much of the remainder may be of interest only to constitutional historians, legal scholars, and public information officers.

The gap between appearance and substance is especially striking in French-speaking Africa. Although on face value the elegantly formulated independence constitutions seemed to have been designed to serve Africans first, a careful analysis of the actual state of affairs from Senegal to Madagascar shows that the real intent of the Paris designers had been to assure continued French presence and control in the former colonies. The Westminster model, an important British export to the Commonwealth, attempted to do the same for British interests in Africa, as did the Belgian counterpart prepared for the Congo and the constitutions written for Spanish territories.

In French-speaking Africa the designation "federation" to describe west and equatorial possessions actually was a misnomer, since the essential ingredients of federal power, military, police, and fiscal, had at no time been conveyed to the federations but had been retained by France for a number of years. Even after the federal design gave way to separate entities, a central reservoir of power remained essentially undisturbed and under French control and influence.[4]

The most critical ingredient of live legal-constitutional provisions and arrangements may well be finance. Neither military force nor political will, neither ideological dictate nor administrative skill or shrewdness can for long overcome lack of finance. Only to the extent that sustaining financial support can be secured and effectively applied do legal arrangements survive the vagaries of social conflict. An elaborate federal structure whose parts do not equally and uniformly attract and use financial sources or do not equally generate such support will be under severe strain unless compensatory forces can be mobilized.[5] No national party will get off the ground if in terms of financial support no nation but only a few scattered urban centers exist. No elaborate court system, no equalization of urban and rural, developed or undeveloped regions will be effectuated without commensurate financial backing.

Talk of "legal separation of power" among the several branches of government is unrealistic when the material sources of power are not also separated. Although one can appreciate the problems facing the civilian regime in Ghana following the quasi-dictatorship of Nkrumah and the succeeding military regime, efforts to incorporate in the new constitution firm guaranties against recurrence of personal rule were quixotic.

The following remark, made by then Justice later President Akufo-Addo, exemplifies this point. "The sure way to avoid the abuse of power by government agencies is to divide the political power and vest it in the hands of diverse persons so that there is effective check on power by power."[6] The justice cited Woodrow Wilson as his source. The key word in that formulation is, of course, *diverse*. Wilson meant by that word not just different persons but persons actually and effectively independent from one another, each protected from the other by superior force, each secure in his position. In a developing society such diversity is hard to come by.

The deliberations in African constituent assemblies reflect a desire to escape the past without actually coming to grips with the present or the future. This may be a universal characteristic. The socioeconomic interest that happens to be dominant at the time will attempt to place its stamp on the document and so arrange affairs as to secure its dominance for as long as possible. The situation turns critical, even explosive, when pressures for social reform assume social revolutionary proportions. Throughout Africa social revolutionary forces are on the ascendancy, but designers of constitutions continue to pretend otherwise.

In post-Nkrumah Ghana the incoming ruling coalition of middle class professionals, traders, businessmen, army and police officers, judges, intellectuals, wealthy farmers, and civil servants did not begin to represent the broad social movement on whose crest Nkrumah had risen to power. One perceptive, reform-minded member of the Constituent Assembly complained: "We have been in a way following the British system of parliamentary democracy, and it may be very difficult to disentangle ourselves from that, and I do not want to propose to fight, what is obviously a losing battle."[7]

A colleague of this member inadvertently exposed the raw nerve of constitutional government when he argued in favor of flexibility in the constitutional amendment process to obviate "the need for our gallant soldiers to take up arms to effect changes in our social fabric."[8] Granted, intervention-minded military in Middle Africa have evidenced little concern with social change, and the fears expressed in that regard were misplaced; but as a pretext for military takeover, the social irrelevance of African constitutions well serves military conspirators. If the member sought to stave off another round of military interventions on those grounds, his was a lost cause, for few of his colleagues in the Constituent Assembly and none of the leaders then in power were prepared to allow the new document to accurately reflect the rising social if not revolutionary discontent or ferment. Consequently, efforts to cope with conflict of interest involving public servants, judges, and members of parliament, and beyond that with the control of power, were reminiscent of the council of mice considering ways of belling the cat.

Rarely is the question of conflict of interest properly formulated: interest in what? Invariably the interests said to be conflicting are interests in self-advancement; they are said to be conflicting with interests of a *public* nature. But no interests are purely and wholly public. All interests reflect personal or group aims. Conflicts arise between sets of personal or group interests.

The task before designers of constitutional provisions intended to regulate such conflicts, then, must be a more realistic identification of interests and of the mechanisms by which they are brought to bear on decision-making processes. Some of these interests relate to the heart of the matter; the distribution of wealth, or to related positions of power and influence; others relate to purely marginal or peripheral issues. In Africa a state of affairs that sees some constitutional doors opened to accommodate the powerful and the influential while all doors are firmly closed to conflict of interest of a lesser kind involving the middle and lower groups or classes is, in effect, an invitation to intervention by the "gallant soldiers."

One of the more basic flaws in the formal structure of government in the new states is failure to accurately reflect the impotence of the masses on whose shoulders the entire structure is said to rest. While lip service is paid to "the people," Staley's observation still seems to be correct. "Democratic forms in a country where most of the people are illiterate, politically unsophisticated, fearful of those in accustomed authority, and at the same time easy prey to demagogues, may merely camouflage continued control by a small segment of society."[9]

If one adds to this cupidity, corruptibility, vanity, greed, and other human frailties, and considering the high probability that personal rule tends to be the outcome of the power struggle in most underdeveloped countries, the warnings of Sir Arthur Lewis, friend and confidant of many African leaders, must be taken seriously. Firm restraints must be devised to control rapacity, and no one person should be trusted with the public till. (Sir Arthur should have relied on his skill as an economist, for the prescription he offers — a multiparty system — cannot be expected to work in Africa for a long time to come; the prevailing economic distribution of power and means of power will continue to militate against such a solution.)[10]

Sir Arthur cannot be faulted, however, for his insistence that one-man rule be repudiated as an alternative to democracy. Although personal rule appears to be inevitable, it need not necessarily be sanctioned, given legitimacy, and enshrined in constitutions. Nor should constitutional provisions leave the door open to personal rule by neglecting imposition of *effective* blocks. Those blocs, however, must be based on the firm grounds of actual, as distinct from presumed or perceived, distribution of power in state and society.

Certain students of Africa brought to Tanzania an understandable enthusiasm — especially those students, who, coming from Nkrumaist Ghana, now saw an opportunity to influence another, seemingly more rational leader to avoid Nkrumah's mistakes. Yet what may appear to some as

President Nyerere's greatest contribution to the science of statecraft may in the final analysis be an invitation to disaster. His seemingly modest, low-key, measured approach to development still is predicated on concentration of power at the center, in fact even if not in constitutional terms.

Tanganyika has a long history of overconcentration of power at the center. Though not intent on maximizing the opportunities provided by this power to his personal advantage or to that of his fellow rulers, Nyerere inadvertently accelerated the move toward absolute power and the inevitable consequences. Since neither his personal characteristics nor his person are immutable or immortal, he may have created a monster to be manipulated eventually by less scrupulous successors. All this may be unavoidable in actual life. It would still be a mistake, certainly an analytical error, if these likely consequences were to be ignored in a rash of what has been dubbed the fever of Tanzanphilia.

The legal minds who tend to predominate in constitutional councils either do not understand these facts of life or prefer not to work them into formal institutional and procedural arrangements. Business interests, financial interests, and related concerns clearly stand to benefit if their deep involvement is omitted from consideration by constitutional assemblies. Social science analysis that fails to come to grips with the same reality becomes the handmaiden of these interests and is abdicating one of its proper functions, social criticism. A phase in this abdication is the emphasis on relative trivia, such as drawing boundaries for local government, constructing designs for regional and provincial government, making electoral laws or the obverse, and emphasizing equally unreal if not irrelevant arrangements at the international level — all without due regard to the essentials without which all such forms of social organization remain dead letters.

The heart of the social power structure is not difficult to discover. Its outlines, shape, and location may be inferred from a study of actual resource allocation: from the who gets what, when, and how of politics.

13

The High Command

Of Rulers and Elites

Webster defines elite as "a minority group or stratum that exerts influence, authority, or decision power." Robert Dahl stresses the vagueness of elite studies, theories, and models. He shows that many hypotheses simply cannot be tested for lack of precision on scope of power, on the universe within which elite prerogatives are exercised. He also notes that even theses on elite status, adequately and convincingly formulated, have rarely been subjected to empirical tests.[1] Finally, Dahl questions "how anyone can suppose that he has established the dominance of a specific group in a community or a nation, without basing his analysis on careful examination of a series of concrete decisions."[2] But a major flaw in elite analysis is demonstrated in the work of Dahl himself. Like most other political scientists, Dahl does not break through to the core of the problem. To him, those who own or control the means of production of wealth are not "political"; they do not "govern." We know differently.

It is not our intent to *establish* dominance of any group in the sense in which Dahl uses that term; instead, it is our intent to show the preeminence of economic, in particular financial, means among those likely to generate decisive social power.

Taking that position is not being deterministic; it is merely a matter of repairing the damages done by abstraction of political phenomena from their economic and physical substance. To return elite study to that more complete analytical framework should be a first step. Careful examination of concrete decisions, the test recommended by Dahl, will then be more meaningful, for the decisions identified by that method should be more significant than those deemed critical by reference to political criteria alone.[3] Elite analysis that focuses on wealth and the ability to convert wealth into power and influence should prove far more fruitful than analysis that relies on ephemera or mythology. Though by no means foolproof, this approach minimizes the chance that puppets are mistaken for manipulators or shadow is mistaken for substance.

Overly meticulous attempts to classify or categorize elites in developing societies may be an idle exercise. Too many forces are at work obliterating neat classifications as soon as they have been recorded. Moreover, concentration of power in the hands of exceedingly few tends to further reduce the value of differentiation.[4] Within such a restricted setting individual elite elements or factions may easily move or shift from one category to another without significant changes in their behavior or their public utterances.

The capabilities of the few can, of course, also be exaggerated. Frantz Fanon has questioned the capacity of Africa's new elite to take full advantage of opportunities. To the extent that education and training are critical, Fanon may be correct. It is quite apparent that colonial planners of African independence have banked on their ability to take advantage of deficiencies among the new rulers in these respects. Expectations of early failure, if not disaster, on the part of their appointees appears to have motivated the Belgians to work with Lumumba, the British with Nkrumah and Nyerere, the French first with Touré and then with Keita, to cite but a few examples.

Certainly, the high incidence of financial and generally economic dependence on outside sources, is a crucial variable. There may be ample justification for viewing most of the African elites as integrally related to a broader international class, a view shared by most if not all social revolutionary analysts in and outside of Africa.[5] (Epithets such as imperialist stooges, puppets, or worse, the Maoist term "running dogs of imperialism" are commonly used to describe the first-generation African leaders.) In these respects many of today's African leaders resemble their Latin-American counterparts of the forties and fifties. In both instances the keys to the political kingdom were not where Nkrumah thought they were — in the hands of the new nominal rulers — but in the vaults of banks and corporations in Europe and the United States.

There is, of course, no empirical basis for the belief that Africa's elites on the whole are less intelligent than any other, or that unlike elites elsewhere they do not know where their opportunities for self-advancement lie. As a rule African leaders show awareness of the fundamental economic facts of life, and as a rule they behave accordingly.[6] Exceedingly few of Africa's top elite echelon appear to have cut themselves off from the wellsprings of capitalist munificence. Indeed, what is referred to as generational conflict among and within African elite groups may instead be more a conflict reflecting different socioeconomic preferences and commitments. Cleavages along these lines, then, separate those intent on developing purely

African bases of power from those committed to work within a Euro-African, or United States-African framework; such cleavages demonstrably do not reflect age differential, except in rhetoric.

An immediate effect of nominal independence has been an alteration in the complexion of the Euro-component among the colonial elite. Colonial officials were replaced by chairmen of the board or by managers of the dominant corporations or by their ambassadors. Major banks, construction firms, trading houses that enjoyed a monopoly (or something close to it), or mining combines now assumed the roles of former administrative departments. (This change went generally unnoticed by the first postindependence analysts, who continued to be hypnotized by the faint traces of long-corroded power of colonial offices.) Significant changes also occurred within the European civilian component as managers of capital elbowed owners of capital into subsidiary positions. Perhaps most ominous for African independence, the economic means at the disposal of the commercial, financial, and mining giants, who now flocked into the former colonies, exceeded by far the influence potential of European traders and financiers of former days.

The African component also underwent a metamorphosis. At first, traditional rulers were replaced or pushed into the background by the colonial administrators or their proxies. A new African trading class, promoted by and dependent on colonial interests, was replaced, in turn, by an African administrative class. Both traditional and modern African leaders had to come to terms with their European counterparts or their own indigenous replacements until two new forces arrived on the scene: international capitalism and social revolutionary movements, the first originating in the West, the second gathering mainly in the East though rooted intellectually also in the West. Somewhere along the way, Africa's traditional elites, the chiefs and their supporters, were edged out. The fortunate ones were allowed to enjoy some vestiges of their former eminence under the tutelage and watchful supervision of colonial and successor regimes.

Contrary impressions, such as those formed by David Apter in his study of the Baganda elite in Uganda, stemmed from overestimation of traditional power and underestimation of basic economic forces. The totality of the economic resources at the disposal of the Baganda elite simply was no match for the resources available to their secular antagonists. Ascription of influence potential to the Baganda elite was an inevitable consequence of acceptance of abstract theories on traditional rule unseasoned by social and economic theory on power and influence. The true disposition of power potential within the larger Uganda system would have become clearer had a distinction been drawn between the raw but unwieldy, power politically marginal agricultural wealth produced by thousands of small farmers and the socially refined wealth at the disposal of the national government. Each of the small farmers produced only limited wealth, all subject to controls wholly outside the ken of traditional rulers.

Increasingly, African systems of government have succumbed to personal rule. This is, of course, nothing new in the history of mankind. The administration of cities in the United States has been in the hands of political bosses primarily because superior economic forces were disinterested in contending for power locally. Many of the new states of Africa have had similar experiences for identical reasons. "For forms of government let fools contend . . ." has been the motto of many of the new leaders as well as the foreign manipulators of the economies. Into the vacuum stepped the ruler who fashioned a personal machine based on a patron-client relationship of his own making, sustained by regular raids on the public till, supplemented by generous contributions extorted or enticed from the private sector, and backed by police power and a personally directed secret intelligence apparatus.

Not all such machines relied on all and everyone of these support elements or sources. Some operated relatively honestly and without undue demands on the private sector. In any case, among the best known personal machines are those operated by Nkrumah, Touré (Guinea), Keita (Mali), Houphouet-Boigny (Ivory Coast), Senghor (Senegal), Sir Albert Margai (Sierra Leone), Tubman (Liberia), Mobuto (Congo-Kinshasa or Zaire), Banda (Malawi), Bokassa (Central African Republic), and Obote (Uganda); the Emperor of Ethiopia also operates such a machine.[6]

Personal power is not unlimited. Where poverty or exceedingly precarious economic conditions are the norm, personal rule is severely circumscribed as it impinges on or interferes with production of wealth. This limitation is generally not appreciated. An otherwise very perspicacious observer missed the point entirely when he wrote: "In a society in which the power of the central leader is paramount and absolute, the economic organization and economic legislation of the society is designed, at least ideally, to serve the self-oriented purposes of this leader."[7] Actually, no economic organization is so designed, ideally or practically. Personal rule only exploits or feeds on the economy; the overall design of the economy is left to the discretion of entirely different elements and reflects entirely different considerations. If, as was so in Ghana under Nkrumah, an attempt is made to impose personal idiosyncracies of the ruler on major sectors of the economy, economic reality quickly asserts itself. Nkrumah of Ghana, Keita of Mali, Lumumba of the Congo, Olympio of Togo, and Obote of Uganda all had to bow eventually to that reality.

The position of the personal ruler and his machine is radically different where countervailing economic forces, foreign and domestic, have either been brought under control or have been eliminated altogether as an independent factor. This condition is difficult to achieve. It could conceivably be accomplished in thoroughly socialist systems, but then only if these systems have attained a level of substantial self-sufficiency. No African state has reached that point. Ghana, Zambia, the United Arab Republic, and Tanzania, possibly the Sudan and Algeria, have come close. In general, the personal machines, the cliques, cabals, or juntas are allowed to operate relatively freely outside the preserves of international and national finance capital; few will survive should they be so rash as to attempt to interfere and challenge either. (It is worth noting that Nkrumah, for example, in all of his rabid anti-imperialist, anticolonialist attacks on international capitalism, carefully omitted from his publications the names of international capitalists with whom he collaborated closely in Ghana.)

The question "who rules?" is asked usually on the mistaken premise that only one governmental system is in existence in any one country, and only one ruling hierarchy can be accommodated in each system. It is highly probable that the multidimensionality of international-national and local economic relationships suggests collusion among contenders for power from diverse backgrounds and pursuing diverse interests. Under the resultant dispensation, God and Caesar are not the only two contenders for loyalty; there are at least two Caesars. One may be permitted to milk the treasury to buy personal support and dabble in internal and external affairs of minor consequence while the other lords over the economic realm in more basic and essential respects. To the first Caesar is left the privilege of radical rhetoric, to the other the business of economic management.

The Political Elite

Traditionally this component of the wider social elite is treated as though it were separate and distinct from all others. This is a reflex action: as the term *political* comes to mind, certain public positions and roles and certain names or titles immediately suggest themselves. Usually an entire hierarchy takes shape. We have considered the roots of this conceptual aberration in the earlier sections. In recent years attempts have been made to endow the concept with a greater degree of scientific accuracy by adding *behavior*. But *political behavior,* we find, is no more precise, and no more helpful in social analysis of the real world as *political* was before it was embellished or camouflaged.

One might inquire whether the most prominent of all modern African leaders, the source of "Take ye first the political kingdom and all other things will be added onto you," Dr. Kwame Nkrumah, can accurately be described as a member of Africa's political elite? At first glance this view might be supported. He was instrumental in organizing and leading to a series of electoral victories a political party. He was appointed by the colonial regime to head the first black government of his country. Did all this make him a member of a political elite, the equal of such elites elsewhere, or did party and government leadership of and by itself in a small African state at that point in time not really amount to little more than window dressing? Did the roots of his status not lie elsewhere?

Behind his title, first as leader of her majesty's government business, then as prime minister, eventually as president of a republic, loomed very large — actually overpoweringly so — these hard facts of life: continued financial, administrative, military, and police as well as foreign diplomatic support by Great Britain; and continued financial, including credit, support by other foreign governments, substantial private investors, and the World Bank, the International Monetary Fund. Last, but certainly not least, his status at home and abroad was the direct consequence of access to a substantial portion of the reserves accumulated over the years by the preceding colonial administration from the sale of cocoa and built up to sizable proportion through the windfall of rising prices during the initial phases of his tenure.

It seems that economic and military force assisted mightily in Nkrumah's rise, in maintaining him in power, and in extending his rule, at times against overwhelming odds. His elite status, in other words, and that of others similarly situated cannot conceptually be pried out of its socioeconomic setting. Without the highly diversified support systems, largely international, Nkrumah's elite status would have been confined to a motley circle of inconsequential admirers and hangers-on. Without the accident of Britain's desperate need for exports and for dollars earned from the sale of cocoa to the United States, among other things, without the cold war hysteria then guiding foreign policymakers in the United States, and without the corresponding moves by the Soviet leadership, Nkrumah could not have survived. Preoccupation with the so-called political side of his career tends to obscure his derivative elite status and diverts attention from the more important roots of leadership in Africa.

Nkrumah's friend and admirer, Patrice Lumumba, after his installation as premier of an independent Congo in 1960, attempted to base his rule and his opposition to machinations by the former colonial power, Belgium, on the same myth of a polity that he believed to be separate and distinct from the financial, industrial, and commercial universe then still under the firm control of Belgian and associated foreign interests. In the process he lost not only his feeble political kingdom but also his life. He died probably still not knowing the full extent of his error and the nature of his impotence.[8]

To be sure, all elites derive their strength and their sustenance from a variety of sources. What can be said of the so-called political elite can also be said of economic, military, cultural, and all other elites. The main point to be considered relates to the rank order of the political elite. Are the political elites, then, as seems to be asserted by so many students of politics, the principal elite group? Do they dominate on grounds of something that is less economic than political, or less a matter of social psychology than of something called political? Is their behavior, individually as well as collectively more political than economic? Do their prime motivations, which may serve to explain their rise or their personal drive to positions of leadership, relate more to acquisition of political power than to economic wealth?

To cite one example, if the desire, said to be common among African leaders, to free the people from colonial rule is the prime spur of the personal drive to achieve elite status and to maintain it, what relative value should one attach to that desire as compared to the desire to achieve personal security? Which of the several motivational sources, in other words, most satisfactorily explains the drive and the resultant status? The desire to free one's people is shared by hundreds, if not thousands, and not all of them achieve elite status. What, then, produces success in that respect? Are not the most critical, perhaps, the strictly financial means by which socioeconomic forces are harnessed, controlled, and directed? For how long can a purely political — that is, substantially noneconomic, nonmilitary — elite maintain its status in the real world?

In the human as well as in the animal kingdom elites, of course, range from the top of the hierarchies of power and influence to the very bottom. There is an elite among the lions as there is an elite among the ants, and there are elites all the way up and down the evolutionary ladder. To validate the thesis of a political elite, claims have been advanced that by sheer assertiveness have elbowed aside rather self-evident proof to the contrary. But this particular emperor has no clothes either. As we have seen, office-holding in Africa is subject to controls from a wide range of forces, some of which are local, but the weight of influence seems to be foreign. Office-holding elites, prime ministers, cabinet officers, political party leaders, and so on, always have the option to burn down their houses. In that respect they are wholly sovereign and independent. But by that token a group of children playing with matches must be regarded as a social elite also. To maintain or even to build a house, to expand and modernize and develop it requires skills and material resources that simply do not flow from what traditionally are thought of as political resources. Neither elections nor mass demonstrations, neither rhetoric nor quiet diplomacy can alone begin to provide the means of support for Africa's exceedingly feeble office-holding elites.

To an extent, the political office-holding elite are the kept mistresses of foreign capital and/or domestic military force. If now and then an individual leader succeeds in extracting another concession from the foreign supporters, it merely proves the point. On a power and influence scale ranging from 100 to 0, the office-holding elite clearly is not near the 100 mark; it must be ranked below the elite of money and guns. How far below depends on many factors, obviously different from country to country, and on the prevailing disposition of economic and military forces. It is entirely possible that the closer an African office-holding elite moves to the 100 mark, the more it must lean on sources of support essentially outside the mythical political kingdom, and the weaker and the more feeble the kingdom becomes.

What of the area characterized by a more visible confluence of office-holding and economic status, the so-called bush in the interior? Bienen reports that in Tanzania's "regional and district headquarters the elite of power (the political elite) is almost synonymous with the elite of wealth and status. Where there has been little indigenous private ownership of the means of production, wealth and status are derived from holding political or civil service office."[9] The total amount of wealth generated from that source or sources is minimal. Its potential can be measured rather accurately, for few are the opportunities to translate economic productivity at the local level into sources of power and influence. At best, the local "elite of power" is a petty elite and its power marginal.

Public Sector Elites

Although lines of demarcation between the public and private sectors are not so clear as social theory suggests, one can identify a domain based on publicly owned financial resources and concerned, at least outwardly, with the public interest. Within the limits set by the other domain, which we have identified as international in essential respects, one can speak of a public sector civilian elite. It would, of course, be a mistake to view that elite in isolation from its principal sources of sustenance.

Superficially viewed, military and all police look 10 feet tall in a typical developing country. But guns, ammunition, and equipment must be bought, and the men who use them must be hired. (Though limited supplies of men and material can be obtained by other means — through gifts, for instance — the sustained effectiveness of means of coercion so obtained is quite limited.) In the public domain these powers actually do not play much of a role as a rule, but the power of the purse does. Most impressive in the councils that matter is the voice of whoever fills that purse and keeps it full.

In his critique of the ruling elite model, Dahl commits one fundamental error when he suggests that the model, any such model, leads to ultimate regression: he argues that there will then always be another power elite behind any elite identified. If measured in terms of the power of the purse, there is in the production of wealth and of fiscal power a point where that process begins. Dahl's basic problem stems from his inability to consider clearly what he means by "political"; the old bugaboo of political scientists. Or, to put it differently, Dahl refused to consider the economic dimensions.[10] Only in the nebulous universe of political power can a regression theory have a deterrent effect on analysis. In economics it has less relevance. Money does not, in fact, grow on trees. If the principal source of wealth available for use as an instrument of rule is produced in the African state (say, groundnuts in Senegal), the point of departure for elite analysis clearly does not lie somewhere among the farmers. The process of wealth production begins at the point where the crop is exchanged for money or credit — in other words, where negotiable value is added. That is where the roots of the public sector elite, for example, must be sought.

Apart from rigorously socialist systems — and none has emerged in Africa so far — the public sector elite must be evaluated in all its aspects, in its entirety: public face as well as private or semiprivate roots. Popularly, the process of public elite formation is believed to begin at the point where public funds materialize, somewhere around or near the public treasury. Actually, in terms of the sequence of production of wealth the process begins much earlier; it commences at the point where an influential sets his sights on public office, on a particular policy matter, or on a particular decision. It is only because it has been viewed as a separate, effectively autonomous, even independent group that the public sector elite has come to be treated, in literature mainly, as a kind of order of knights of the public interest. Actually, and especially given the precarious economic conditions that govern public and private affairs in Africa, the vaunted public sector elite is in the uncomfortable position of a mouse within reach of the cat. Only as the cat will allow may the civil servants, party political bosses, and other office holders play.

Although publics everywhere seem to be dimly aware of the truth, the veil hiding it usually is too thick. As we have noted earlier, pertinent data are revealed on relatively few occasions. Only in the rare instance when elites fall out among themselves, and only if the quarrel is over fundamental issues, will the public be permitted to catch a fleeting glimpse of reality at high levels of government. The inquiries already cited — for example, the Nigerian Coker Commission, the numerous post-Nkrumah inquiries, and the Foster-Sutton and the Foster inquiries — reveal that exceedingly few persons who hold high public office draw exclusively on public funds. With notable exceptions, the higher echelons of the public service have increasingly become involved in financial manipulations, real estate, and other business transactions, not excluding graft, bribery, and corruption generally; in the process, the line separating the public and the private sectors is continuously being crossed.

For a few among the higher echelons, the payoff from rule or from public office below the level of rule may be satisfaction of lust for power; for the majority, the payoff is personal wealth or economic security or both. Satisfaction of lust for power without substantial material benefit accruing to the powerful is an improbability in the real world. The public service elite can therefore not be considered separately from the owners of capital who have specific and highly desirable benefits to bestow or deny.

One reason that the intimate connections between holders of public office, higher civil servants, and private wealth are not more widely perceived and are not better documented is familiar to the student of public law; laws of libel, secrecy surrounding bank transactions, the intricacy of international finance — all interpose series of formidable obstacles virtually impossible to surmount. In any case, the smoke generated by the aforementioned commission reports strongly intimates that there is fire indeed.

To be analytically meaningful, *rule* must then be interpreted to encompass the covert and clandestine dimensions of public policy and decision making along with the more familiar overt and public ones. It is appropriate to recall a point made earlier. Even the most disciplined and rigorous social scientist permits himself the privilege to speculate, induce, or deduce from fragmentary evidence. Although still fragmentary, circumstantial evidence that in the public sector all is not as traditionally depicted is rather persuasive now that at least the virtually impenetrable colonial veil has been drawn aside.

More widely interpreted, then, rule in the French zone includes the owners and managers of the banks in Marseilles, Lyons, and Paris; elsewhere on the continent it must include interests in London, Brussels, and New York. The Banque de l'Afrique Occidentale Francaise (BAO) or Barclay's Bank, then, is as much a part of the ruling elite in Ouagadougou or Nairobi as is the pennyless leader who may barely have assumed office. The owners and managers of the United Africa Company and its affiliates and subsidiaries, of Ashanti goldfields or of Lonrho, of Anglo-American Selection Trust — in other words, the controlling interests in the respective economic systems — must be treated as full-fledged partners in the enterprise of rule whether they are physically located on the continent or operate from bases overseas.

The pattern is mirrored in the structure and reflected in the behavior of the supporting bureaucracies. The much touted neutrality allegedly governing the conduct of public servants, especially in British-influenced areas, applies only to lesser officials who either have no options or lack the skill to create some. Again, there are, of course, exceptions, but the ethos of public service is changing and quite rapidly.

Few of the first-generation African leaders possessed the skills, though many possessed the intelligence, to understand let alone manage and direct complex ministries in the crucial sectors of finance, foreign and domestic trade, industry, the central banks, and the sensitive areas of telecommunication. The potential of high-level civil servants increased in direct proportion to the lack of experience, know-how, and expertise of the African political heads of ministries.

Nkrumah certainly would have been justified on ideological grounds had he dispensed with the services of certain expatriate and many British-trained African civil servants in high and sensitive offices. He appears to have entertained doubts about their loyalty from the moment he assumed office. Yet he continued to tolerate even those whom he suspected of directly opposing him. Although Ghana, like Nigeria, had been fortunate to develop a corps of skilled public servants larger than those in the East African colonies of Britain, for example, government and administration were still plagued by critical shortages of men capable of running rapidly expanding ministries and departments. Ideologically acceptable or not, a principal secretary holding together the strings of diverse and diverging components of the internal security apparatus, or keeping tabs on the vital foreign exchange situation, or maintaining a vestige of order in the tangled web of export and import licenses could count on being retained. Someone able to conduct negotiations with wily and infinitely more experienced foreign firms was worth his weight in gold whatever his nationality, race, or ideological disposition. Technically untrained leaders know instinctively that disaster is likely to result from dismissal of a half-dozen or so of the principal civil servants in the more vital sectors.

For identical reasons, high-level public servants who had loyally supported Nkrumah were retained by his successors with astonishingly few exceptions. Dismissals affected mainly lesser public servants.

Do 17 men, mostly foreigners, run Tanzania?[11] Do a handful of top-level civil servants "keep Nigeria going?" There can be little doubt indeed that the linchpins of African government are the trained administrators in a few select offices: the cabinet offices, the principal statutory corporations (electricity, railway, shipping, telecommunication), the security affairs offices, and the revenue-collecting agencies.[12] However, to speak grandiosely and indiscriminately of a bureaucratic elite may be pleasing to some, but it would be a false image that would be created.

The Military-Police Elites

Power, someone said, grows out of the barrel of a gun. Though meant to be symbolic, this statement is too simplistic. More accurately, power grows out of many barrels skillfully deployed and sufficient in number to counter all weapons in the hands of one's opponents. Initially, colonial penetration was made possible by superior force of arms. It was maintained, in part, by monopoly of arms. It should surprise no one if those who inherit that monopoly, and that tradition thereby acquire the means to slip into positions of power and control. Still, it is possible to speculate on the reasons the military have taken over the governments of some states while loyally serving civilian rulers in others.

One explanation for the epidemic of coups relies on the ubiquitous politicization argument, which we have already encountered elsewhere. Military takeovers, it is argued, occur where soldiers are used by civilian rulers to serve political ends. For example, whatever scruples Nigerian officers may have had on the subject of intervention are said to have been set aside when they were asked to intervene on the side of the federal government against the civilian regime in the then Western Region.[13] This may well be so. More likely, many African military officers and occasionally noncommissioned officers intervene because they are not prepared, or conditioned, to accept forever the life of self-denial and austerity that they were taught to accept and that traditionally has been the lot of the British and French military and police. As soon as control over public resource allocation has been transferred from the relatively remote European-colonial to the more familiar and accessible African hands, the problem becomes acute. Officers and ranks see an opportunity to improve their economic position and proceed to seize it when convinced that regular channels, constitutional ones, will not do the job.[14]

The civilian office holder's authority over the military tends to evaporate as the rather thin veneer of loyalty (a carryover from colonial days that convinces no one to the core) wears off. Civilian rulers, it turns out, have neither the arms required to prevent military takeover nor the skills required to neutralize and fend off the threat. Their sole defense lies in an alliance with either external or internal military forces. Samuel P. Huntington makes the astonishing observation that "military explanations do not explain military interventions."[15] Of course, no single factor can cover every aspect of such an event. But there can surely be no room for doubt that to intervene one must dispose of superior force that, in each and every instance has been and will continue to be military in nature.

Whatever the explanation for the rash of coups, the true character of the African military has been obscured by other, at times simplistic, categorizations. Many of these are transfers from literary sources dealing with the military in the older Western countries where military officers as well as leaders in the professions, the police, the universities, and the civil service are depicted as nonpolitical by definition. When these leaders, the military in this case, do intervene in what by definition is outside their normal sphere, one is tempted to explain the event by reference to "the general politicization of social forces and institutions." As Huntington sees it, the problem — the task of keeping presumed nonpolitical elites out of politics — is compounded by the ability in the developing countries of "all sorts of social forces and groups (to become) directly engaged in general politics."[16] One must conclude that by "general politics" Huntington means all social affairs. What else could it be?

All societies since time immemorial have been permeated by general politics. If the distinction between military and political elites relates to formal and public participation on the officers' part in formal organizations such as political parties, it is meaningless for Africa. If, however, it relates to involvement in the machinery of power and influence in state and society, only the perfectly naive can accept the thesis of neutrality, or abstention, on the part of the military. If it has any meaning at all, politics does relate to pay and promotion, to procurement of arms and equipment, to social position.

Position does not mean colorful medals or elegant uniforms so much as firm and secure economic status. Top military leaders everywhere in the world, are deeply and intimately concerned with production and distribution of economic resources. They may not understand exactly how resources are produced, but they are concerned. When resources show signs of drying up, passive but interested concern turns into aggressive desire to intervene. Thus, the best that can be said of the politicization of the military argument is that what at the point of intervention is but a passive, possibly dormant interest is suddenly activated.

The belief in the nonpolitical character of the military and the police elite corps lives on in Africa. Seeking to close the door to abuses that had characterized the Nkrumah regime, possibly also to prevent a coup against the civilian successor regime, one of the Ghanaian Commissions charged with responsibility for correcting past faults solemnly proposed that "the Police Service as a disciplined service and an instrument for the maintenance of law and order (be) effectively insulated from political control . . ."[17] How was this insulation to be accomplished? Instead of being appointed directly by a partisan political official, the head of the police was to be appointed by the presumably nonpolitical president acting on advice of the prime minister! It was unlikely indeed that the prime minister would relinquish control.

A similar misconception is reflected in the following plea by a member of Ghana's Constituent Assembly: "I submit that military power should always be subordinated to civilian power and in pursuance to clause 151 subsection (1) the Commander-in-Chief should move the Army only with the approval of Parliament."[18] If this arrangement did not work in the United States or in Britain, how could it work in Ghana? In any case, military power cannot be subordinated to constitutional provisions that are demonstrably inoperative against far weaker contenders. It can certainly not be subordinated to provisions that rest on the assumption that African states have parliaments potent enough to resist a commander-in-chief intent on moving the armed forces wherever he pleases, whenever he pleases.

Similar provisions were proposed with regard to the military. Of course, in the setting characteristic of the less developed countries where all power is concentrated in a relatively narrow sphere, no service and no person can be "effectively insulated from political control," for political control is whatever control is operative in the system, including provision of economic support for the service and its individual components. The only way by which the military and the police could conceivably be insulated from what is termed political control is to assure them independent economic supply lines. This, of course, is highly impractical and improbable.

If by political control is meant control by the political party leaders outside the effective ruling elite — that is, outside the sources of funding, equipment, and supply — no fears need be entertained. These lesser leaders, purely patronage-oriented, are far too weak to enter into contests with those who actually control the supply lines to the services.

Events in Togo, in Ghana, and in a number of other countries indicate that to enter the ranks of national power elite a military leader need not only control enough men and arms to overcome whatever defense force happens to be between him and the ruler or rulers at a given moment. Overthrow of the nominal ruler, and the office holders is, however, only part of the task. Control of the remainder of the effective elite — those who control the resources required to sustain the armed forces — must be secured. It would seem that since few if any military leaders possess the requisite skills and resources to sustain the effort, they as much as the civilian elite group they overthrew remain dependent in the first instance on the good will and support of whoever controls the production and distribution of wealth.

The military elite, and the police elite to a lesser extent, are of value to whoever rules, overtly or covertly, mainly on three counts: the continuing need to bolster the prestige of the new African regime, and the internal security requirements. The measure of that value is expressed in budget allocations and beyond those in privileges and perquisites extended to these forces. Except in semifeudal settings such as have characterized the Ethiopian armies for the last century, it is obvious that the lower the level of support of the forces as a whole, the lower will be the position of the respective uniformed elites.

Expenditures on the military and the police in Kenya, Nigeria, Ghana, and the Ivory Coast indicate that the rise of the uniformed elite was a result primarily of internal security requirements, except for Kenya where both forces were engaged in a protracted conflict with internal as well as external dimensions.[19] Eventually the situation changed drastically in Ghana and Nigeria for reasons we have referred to — Nkrumah's personal security requirements and the Nigerian civil war.

Military expenditures are, of course, difficult to analyze with precision. Security requirements forbid full disclosure of details or end use of budget allocations. Either to deceive their own public or their enemies or potential enemies, governments at times conceal totals. Under Nkrumah, but also elsewhere, though there more carefully camouflaged, funds nominally not part of the defense complex, such as the contingency fund, may be diverted for military or police purposes.[20] Or budget allocations intended for the armed forces are diverted to clandestine, personal security purposes, such as bodyguards, in the guise of defense expenditures.[21]

A matter of considerable consequence for the relative standing of the military elite in several countries has been the transfer of internal security intelligence from the army to either the regular police or to several non-military agencies. In Nazi Germany, this transfer gave rise to the most determined opposition to Hitler among army officers. In the Soviet Union it appears to have affected relations between the Party and the officers corps almost from the beginning. In Africa the best-known examples are the United Arab Republic under Nasser and Sadat, Ghana under Nkrumah, and Guinea under Touré.[22] Transfer of the security intelligence function, if successful, severely limits the vision of potential conspirators among army officers; in Ghana this condition eventually provided the rationale for an alliance between officers of the regular armed forces and the special police.

As could be expected, allocations to the armed forces rise sharply following a military coup.[23] As a matter of course the military elite, joined in Ghana by the police, move to the forefront, their leaders seizing the top command positions. What is less obvious is the relationship, or ratio, between allocations for personal emoluments and outlays for military and police hardware. Analysis of that relationship strongly suggests that social rather than military considerations govern policies in these respects.

Before the civil war, patterns of expenditure in Nigeria reflected the struggle between the northern and southern components in the civilian government, the north seeking to redress the imbalance in favor of the more highly developed south, a pattern bequeathed by the colonial rulers. Beginning in 1962 and accelerating sharply by 1964, plans were under way to strengthen the army's presence in key areas around the country. Accordingly, the armed forces and the police forces were expanded. But from the northern perspective the expansion did not benefit the north, and from that point on the energies of northern leaders were directed to assure that appropriations, in particular construction and training programs, financed from federal funds were to be diverted as far as possible to northern advantage.[24]

The link between appropriations for military and police purposes and growth of the uniformed elite, or elites, is in the personnel section of defense and security appropriations. It is highly significant that as the years went on a wide gap opened between expenditure on personal emoluments and those on military hardware. That expenditures were rather high on the salary side reflected a rapid expansion in numbers of both forces without development of an adequate officers corps.[25]

The confrontation over the Somali-Shifta problem caused the government of Kenya to reinforce law-and-order contingents there, beginning with the 1964-65 fiscal year.[26] This expenditure was more an external than an internal defense commitment, even though part of the undeclared war was being fought in the Northern Province of Kenya. That it was primarily an external matter, however, profoundly altered the nature of the Kenya military and police elite. Unlike Ghana where both were intended primarily for internal security purposes, recruitment for the Kenya military and police was more with a view to professional competence than to partisan loyalty or complicity. This is not saying that the officers corps in Ghana, or elsewhere for that matter, did not contain professionally competent men. The effect of partisan considerations becomes manifest mainly at the top command levels; in an environment that places a premium on personal loyalty to the national leadership, or leader, the fully trained field officer tends to be eclipsed by the opportunist.

French-influenced Africa, of course, followed a different route. By *présence francaise* was meant also presence in the former colonies of French troops. This, coupled with French domination of the economy and, not least important, control of the several secret intelligence and security services by French officials and operatives, tended to stunt development of an effective corps of African officers and noncommissioned officers. In the Belgian Congo a similar state of affairs had consigned the newly independent country to virtual chaos.[37]

The growth of an indigenous military and police elite and the ability of such an elite to participate meaningfully and effectively in major policy and decision-making processes is directly affected by the size and intensity of foreign military presence. In Senegal, the physical presence of a substantial French military force, inhibited for decades all opportunities for Senegalese officers to play an active role in state and society. As long as the external and internal security responsibilities remain essentially in French hands, it is virtually impossible for Senegalese officers to play a role other than that of clients of the ruling civilian group; that group, in turn, also exists in a twilight zone between Dakar and Paris. Nominally, in French-speaking Africa all portfolios of key importance, in particular *sureté* (secret service), are assumed by the presidents. With one or two exceptions, the offices of the president are honeycombed with French personnel.[28]

Personal supervision and control of the military by the presidents of Ghana and Mali, Upper Volta and Dahomey, Togo and Somalia did not prevent conspiracies against the civilian regimes from getting under way and did not stave off the eventual coup. It may well be that the only way in which the emergence of an independently powerful uniformed elite can be prevented or controlled is by disestablishment of the military. Nkrumah planned precisely such a step 5 minutes before 12. Touré and Nyerere have moved in that direction. It seems that disestablishment of the Guinean regular army, relegating it to the fringes of the republic, probably spared the Touré regime the experience of a coup when other socialist leaders fell. But this policy exacts a steep price. In Guinea it enabled a small band of foreign troops to operate virtually unhindered in the streets of Conakry in December 1970.[29]

Leaving aside the overriding importance of intelligence and basic economic and financial control over the leadership in both forces, three additional status and influence factors must be considered: identification with force superior to all others in the state as a rule, identification with a dominant tribal group, and social class identification.

By training and by profession, military and police leaders possess technical knowledge and skills superior to any other group of comparable size. It is significant, for instance, that while African civilian trainees in British universities and institutes and their counterparts in British-run African universities found their training high on classics, literature, and philosophy and low on technically and socioeconomically relevant knowledge. The trainees at Sandhurst and St. Cyr, the French equivalent, graduated as equals of their European colleagues. At least, there were no basic differences or disparities in quality of training for the British and French officers candidates and that accorded the African trainees, few as those were.[30] Uniformed officers are experienced in teamwork, in the coordination of large numbers of personnel, and in effective use of modern means of transportation and communication. They enjoy international contacts, mainly with their fellow graduates from British, French, and, more recently, American, German, and soon Socialist, mainly Soviet Russian, training institutions.[31]

The tribal input into military elite formation stems directly from colonial practices. Frequently, troops were recruited from among certain tribes, mainly from those proven to be docile, adaptable to military discipline, and relatively uneducated if not illiterate. Also considered were physical stamina — that is, ability to withstand the rigors of service in the field — and willingness to obey commands as well as understand them. In some instances, such as in the Belgian Congo, ferocity and even the capacity to proceed with brutality appear to have been criteria for recruitment. Kenya relied on Kamba, Nigeria on Tiv and Hausa, Ghana on the northern territories, the Belgian Congo on a mix of Ba-ngwala, Western Baluba, and Ba-kongo.[32]

Naturally, command positions were filled mainly by personnel from more highly developed, more educated tribes. In Nigeria southerners, and among those the Ibo, dominated until the Civil War.[33] In the Ivory Coast Bete, and in Ghana, Ga, Fante, and Ewe furnished material for command positions.[34]

When Nigeria became independent nearly 40 percent of inspectors and constables in the police force were Ibos, 14 percent Yoruba from the west, and about 15 percent Yoruba from the north. The remainder, divided among 10 different groups, also came from the south.[35]

The African officer resembles his European prototype or model more closely than the African civilian leader resembles his. He is typically better educated; most likely he started his career from a better vantage point, because normally only the well-to-do families could raise the funds required for a better than average education. He is, in other words, a natural candidate for elite status.[36]

The higher military officer is linked to the civilian elite, foreign and domestic, for several reasons. Because the armed forces lack the means of producing the wealth required to provide for them, their leaders are of necessity compelled to forge dependable ties with industrial and commercial suppliers, sources of finance, arms, and equipment. Marxist-oriented observers implicitly recognize this need. More cognizant of the nexus among social status, power, influence, and mode of production, they invariably are led to inquire into the economic bases of the military elite and usually end by associating military officers with class, most likely the capital-owning one.[37] By that token, since they require less military hardware, few or no aircraft (though helicopters now), and few or no ships, the police force and its leadership usually rank below the army leadership corps. Among the armed forces, because of the relatively high dependence on equipment the navy and air force may find themselves pressing hard to reach the top of the procurement, hence influence, hence status or class, ladder. This seems to be chronically true in Latin America.

Salary and pay requirements of the troops alone tend to orient military leaders toward whoever disburses funds and beyond. Top officers cannot ignore that problem in view of the many pay rebellions, or revolts, that have occurred or are known to have been brewing in Africa. Because the rank and file do have the means of reinforcing their demands for higher pay and greater privileges, and many have done so throughout the continent, military leaders can be expected to be more sensitive on such matters than are their civilian counterparts who are being pressured by relatively harmless civil servants, employees, and wage earners.

The inate search for hardware, adequate pay for officers and men, and similar material supports tend to shape the ideological posture of the command echelons in the armed forces. An exception might be where the question of financial support has been solved, as it has been to an extent in the centrally controlled economies, usually following nationalization of whatever modest industrial sources of supply are available locally. A possibly warranted generalization is that ideological orientation of military command echelons is governed by their perception of how best to assure unimpeded continuous flow of resources into their sector. Like the officers who staged the Libyan revolt, those who are persuaded that their objectives can best be attained by nationalization will favor Socialist policies; those who foresee a drying up of ready funds and a withering of supports if foreign investment is discouraged, curtailed, or cut off altogether will tend to espouse opposite social philosophy.

Whatever may have motivated military rebellion, on the morning after the coup the debts must still be paid, bills must be met, and the means by which the necessary funds are generated loom larger than ever. The skills possessed by the military, adequate to command and administer military forces and obviously adequate, but barely so, to accomplish a coup, now prove to be quite insufficient to run a country in all of its complex ramifications. The care and feeding of the goose that lays the golden eggs is not taught at military academies. In all critical respects, the military postcoup elite is very much like the civilian elite. Both depend for survival on the sources of wealth; both are continuously face to face with the nemesis of African government, foreign exchange shortage.

All appearances aside, the African officer basically, is sui generis; our image of him may, in fact, be badly distorted by our own cultural predispositions. Although similar to his European counterpart — he was in all probability trained by the European — the typical African officer differs from his intended prototype in several fundamental respects and should therefore be evaluated with an eye to his own characteristics and on his own merits.

African cultures, though certainly not devoid of military traditions (who does not know of the Ashanti and Zulu wars and of the Ethiopian defeat of the Italians), do nevertheless lack the pervasive, if not infectuous, militaristic atmosphere and the traditions associated with Germany and Japan and, to lesser extent, the softer British, French, American, and Russian variants. Where strong military traditions are part of the culture, as in Ashanti (Ghana) or among the Fulani in northern Nigeria, or the Yoruba for that matter, it is doubtful that anything but the most superficial linkage can be established between ancient tribal traditions and the requirements for membership in the elite of the modern, technologically sophisticated force. In terms of social role and mission alone, the traditional African warrior and his modern counterpart are, of course, worlds apart.

As in so many other respects, things are changing in the military sector. Demands for rapid Africanization of command positions have produced a sharp break with past promotional systems. A new generation of African officers is on the rise, ready to replace the older products of the colonial experience. The Nigerian civil war provided the spur for a sharp departure from past practices partly in response to the immediate staff requirements of a rapidly and suddenly expanding army, partly in response to reflections on the role of southern, in particular Ibo, officers in the outbreak of hostilities and the events preceding.[38]

Fascination with the power of the gun all too often causes analysts of coups to regard the successful officers as a self-contained group capable of achieving their nonmilitary goals — social and economic reforms, for instance — without assistance from the civilian sector. Nothing could be more erroneous. Without advice and assistance from the civil service, the African and perhaps most military leaders are like fish on land. The internal and external financial aspects of their rule are definitely not within their professional ken; without an adequate corps of civilian experts, their own wells of expertise run dry within days.

To an extent, African civilian leaders are not much better prepared for the tasks of governance. But usually the civilian ruling elite does include a fair share of individuals highly trained technically and professionally proficient. The near-total lack of expertise on the part of some civilian leaders, heads of political parties, trade union leaders, and the like does not, therefore, constitute so severe a handicap for the ruling group as would be so should army officers attempt to rule alone. Again, because the immediate constituency on which military rule normally rests — the lower officers corps and the ranks — is likely to be more insistent on reaping material rewards than are the civilian support groups of civilian rule, the need for technical expertise may be greater after a coup than before.

The position of the successful coup leader is more delicate for yet another reason. In all probability his own actions or those with which he is identified have contributed to a breakdown of loyalty and discipline, especially where violence accompanied the takeover. The Nigerian precedent of murder of superior officers inevitably placed an added strain on their successors. For these and the other reasons cited, coup leaders may be more dependent on rapid economic progress than were their predecessors. The tolerance threshold of dissidents within the military is most likely lowered considerably as the tight preindependence discipline crumbles.

Advisers

Are foreign or domestic advisers to the principal policy and decision makers fully qualified members of the power and influence structure, and are they members of the elite of a given African state? The answer must be an unqualified yes. If a flood threatens to inundate the countryside, the dike engineer ranks above the landscape artist. If the national treasury is depleted, the financier is more welcome than the designer of new projects. If foreign exchange reserves are critically low, the red carpet is out for whoever is in the position to replenish the coffers, while experts on how to spend foreign exchange may not at that moment command much respect. In other words, in certain conditions an ounce of advice may be worth more than a ton of legal authority. In certain circumstances a foreign chairman of the board of a country's principal source of foreign exchange — a gold or diamond mining corporation, for example — can in a 30-minute conference with the head of government cancel out the combined recommendations, counsel, or expertise of the entire national cabinet plus the entire leadership of the dominant political party.

The point can be carried further. The person in a position to provide critical advice that may help to solve, or solve, a major financial crisis need not be a citizen of the country concerned, need not be elected or appointed formally, need not even leave a trace on the appointment calendar of the head of government to fully qualify as a quasi-member of the national policy- and decision-making elite. Thanks to modern means of communication, he need not even leave his office in London, Paris, or Brussels.

Foreign advisers for obvious reasons tend to overshadow indigenous ones. They have been part of the African scene since the inception of colonial rule as they were fixtures before at the courts of China, Japan, and Russia.[39] Most likely, though, foreign advisers to contemporary African rulers may be comparatively far more influential than were their counterparts in the 18 and 19 centuries. Unlike the adviser to the emperors of Japan or China, the expatriate in Africa today brings to his task a relatively far more advanced technology and relies on a far greater accumulation of expertise. The gaps between techniques in fiscal, commercial, and social management at the disposal of experts from the developed areas and techniques at the disposal of Africa's rulers is alone far greater than was the case a hundred years ago.[40] The relative value of advice drawing on advanced technology should be correspondingly greater.

A hundred years ago financial advisers drew on resource bases that were relatively limited, probably restricted to those of a single company or corporation. The emergence of the multinational corporation, the international combine or conglomerate, the multinational organization adds a new dimension to traffic in advice. Membership in the globe-girdling fraternities or brotherhoods built on banking, investment, shipping, trade, construction, or industry should certainly endow advisers drawing on resources of that magnitude with overpowering potential vis-a-vis the new African elites caught up in progressive pauperization.

International or not, the African economies' high degree of dependence on outside resources suggest acceptance of foreign advice and advisers as prima facie decision making in the local national context. This independence is reinforced by the personal dependence of individual rulers on foreign-based economic and physical support. There is reason to believe that the personal fortunes of some African rulers respose in the hands of foreign trustees, formally or informally. Advice from these trustees is likely to be heeded, apparently more in French-speaking Africa than in other areas.

The effectiveness of an adviser is a function of his ability to sense and to respond appropriately to the ideological predispositions and inclinations of the advisee. In a manner of speaking, to be effective the adviser's appliances must be wired to accommodate the local current. Failure in this respect appears to be a prime source of difficulty encountered by advisers from the socialist countries even in socialist states such as Nkrumaist Ghana, Guinea, or Tanzania. Needless to say, language also must be taken into account in this connection. It is difficult to give advice across impenetrable language barriers. Still interpreters are available, and increasingly African leaders are able to use English and French. How does one bridge the ideological schisms that separate African socialists and Western capitalists? In many cases they are simply not bridged, and potential investors turn elsewhere. The norm, however, appears to be that the investor either disregards, discounts, or ignores what he perhaps deems inconsequential and irrelevant to his pursuits, or he strikes a pose acceptable to local ideologues. Businessmen and industrialists have managed to cope with the problem and have, in effect, become part of the decision- and policymaking elite in countries whose leaders were engaged at the same time in rabid anti-imperialist, anticapitalist rhetoric. Perhaps, money tends to neutralize ideology.

A decade after independence foreign advisers and technicians occupied high-level positions in state and society throughout the continent. They still hold key positions in the armed forces, the police, and the secret services. Foreign advisers still carried the brunt of the more complex and more demanding tasks facing the new governments, though increasingly assisted and reinforced by progressively more highly trained, more sophisticated Africans.

French *assistants techniques* dominate entire departments and sections. In 1969 in the Ivory Coast, of a total of 2,188 such *assistants* (a euphemism for advisers in many instances) 1,710 were teachers or were otherwise engaged in nonpolicymaking pursuits. Several hundred, however, occupied key positions; 68 in economic and financial affairs, 25 in justice, 21 in interior, 22 in public functions, 59 in agriculture, 37 in transport and public works, 109 in public health. The total of French advisers in key positions relating to defense and internal security was not reported.[41]

In countries burdened with the special consequences of direct European rule, where virtually no Africans were available to staff high-level positions at independence, foreign advisers were, of course, indispensable. In 1966 Zambia reported 4,668 expatriates in the civil service.[42] The resulting dilemma is reflected in the following statement issued by the Zambian Public Service Commission following a thorough review of the chances of Zambianization of the service.

> The attainment of *political* independence and the pressing desire to develop the state *politically,* economically and socially, have brought in their wake new and unfamiliar administrative problems. ... The Commission has had to meet this challenge by recruiting from external sources men with skills which are essential for the many specialist fields in the service but which could not be obtained or found locally only in insufficient numbers.[43]

The references to political development, and to political independence in the statement are of special significance. Too much pressure on expatriates to leave would, in the opinion of Zambia's rulers at that time and in the view of the commission, bring in its wake severe setbacks in the most critical economic sectors, would inject factional and tribe-based disputes into the working of government, and would in all probability reduce rather than increase the degree of Zambia's independence. It is clear that in those conditions foreign advisers could be regarded as integral parts of the local elite.

Kenya's experience was similar, but not for identical reasons. Well into the period of independence, to the dismay of militant proponents of more extensive Kenyanization, foreigners (noncitizens) dominated all key positions. From the cabinet level on down, the speaker of the House of Parliament, the higher ranks of the defense force and police, executive positions in finance, business, industry, and agriculture, Europeans occupied the top positions, followed by Asians. Unavoidably, experts, technicians, and general counsels were brought in from Britain on a continuing basis, and as a matter of course the former masters under colonial rule continued to advise their emancipated wards.[44]

It is obvious that foreign advisers will continue to play prominent roles in the more complex, more sophisticated sectors. Highly sensitive financial decisions, technical judgments in intricate, involved, international negotiations, complicated bargaining with tough foreign firms, potentially fatal decisions in the law-and-order and external and internal security spheres require outstanding expertise, and foreigners continue to be indispensable. To be sure, African leaders are developing the means to contain and control foreigners intent on taking advantage of their opportunities. Still, the more sensitive tasks connected with the care, feeding, and protection of the goose that lays the golden eggs cannot be entrusted to incompetents, novices, or partisan camp followers.

Discussion of the key role of foreign advisers to governments in developing countries is not complete without consideration of ambassadors and high commissioners from the former colonial or other patron powers. Before Castro, the United States ambassador to Cuba was said to be the second most powerful person after Batista. This special position was reflective, of course, of the overall dominance if not control by United States interests in all vital sectors of that small island off the coast of the North American colossus; it may be said that it was reflective of the quasi-colonial status of Cuba. That relationship had, and in many instances still has, its parallels on the continent of Africa. The ambassadors of France in her former colonies, the United States ambassadors to Liberia and possibly to the Congo (Kinshasa) once Belgian influence was reduced, and the British high commissioners to Britain's former colonies and protectorates constituted, of course, vital links in the patron-client relationship that characterized the first independence decade or decades.

For different reasons in some respects, for similar reasons in others, the ambassadors of the Soviet Union and Communist China also played key roles in the policymaking of Ghana under Nkrumah, in the Republic of Guinea for a time, in Tanzania, and on Zanzibar. When Ghana and Guinea

joined, at least nominally, in a union, their respective ambassadors to the
union partner were given cabinet status. Actually, this experiment failed.
But though not formally given cabinet status, the British high commissioner
to Kenya for at least a decade after independence certainly "represented"
a larger share of the country's wealth — the European settler stakes —
than did any other single individual elected, appointed, or just tolerated.[45]
Under the disposition prevailing in most of French Africa, the internal
elite status of the French ambassadors could scarcely be disputed.

The Traditional and Landed Elites

Elites drawing on tribal-traditional ways alone or principally are steadily
being pushed to the periphery toward oblivion. Stripped long ago of the
substance of sovereignty, they are now being deprived of the remaining
vestiges. Either through legislation or through direct administrative action,
their remaining privileges are being undercut and reduced; the pitiful
resources left to their disposal after the voracious appetite of colonial rule
had been satisfied are being absorbed by the secular government or by
private interests. Today, their competitiveness depends mainly on their
ability to coalesce with secular elites to ingratiate themselves, to effectively
serve secular rulers.[46]

Only in a few remaining pockets do traditional rulers and their associates exercise anything remotely resembling sovereign powers; northern
Nigeria and Senegal are the outstanding examples. We recall that the economic basis for traditional rule in both areas is peanut (groundnut) production, and Donal O'Brien shows in his excellent study of the Mourides
of Senegal, that the marabouts achieved their position of eminence largely
by default.

> This pre-eminence results partly from the fact that European-run plan-
> tations, of the kind which developed in the Ivory Coast, were never a
> success in Senegal. An experimental venture was launched by a French
> company in 1921, attempting the mechanized cultivation of groundnuts
> with a European staff and an African work-force, but the price for ground-
> nuts was found to be inadequate to support European salaries, and the
> experiment was abandoned in 1925. Thereafter the administration left the
> cultivation of groundnuts to African producers, and of these the most
> important were the *marabouts*. When the Senegalese Government in 1966
> established a list of "large-scale producers," on the basis of annual ground-
> nut tonnage, twenty-seven of twenty-nine were *marabouts*, and twenty of
> these twenty-seven were Mourides *shyyukh*.[47]

The emirs of northern Nigeria basically derive their pre-eminence from
the same source. Had not British interests preferred not to assume direct
control over peanut production, the much discussed indirect rule would
have been an empty gesture. Eventually, proceeding from that point of departure, the northern rulers were able to convert their economic opportun-

ity into modern coinage. New privileges were carved out, and secular power positions were developed, including a share of the control over the entire federal system of Nigeria.

What of the landed traditional aristocracy? As we have shown, for the majority of the people of Africa land and subsistence control go together, and he who controls the land controls those who depend on it. The ability to banish a person from the source of his and his family's subsistence or the ability to deny access to land — powers used throughout Africa before the advent of Western concepts of legality and still used today — must be perceived as power of life and death in the estimation of the hapless peasant. Russian, southern European, and Latin-American history shows conclusively that even outright reforms or changes in status of servitude and in patterns of landownership and land use do not immediately or necessarily alter the power structure; landed elites somehow manage to hang on to their privileged positions, sometimes for a century or more. Africa offers no exception. Again, Donal O'Brien makes this perfectly clear. Though his illustration is drawn from Senegal, the point has general validity wherever traditional or religious elites have secured effective control over land:

> The power of the *marabouts* as *lamans* has ... now at least nominally been abolished by national legislation. The Law on the National Domain of 1964 ... suppresses all rights of eminent domain, and gives each peasant the right to the land on which he now works, without obligation to any superior. The state becomes the national proprietor. This law was explicitly designed to end exploitation of peasants by *lamans* and others, the place of the *laman* being assumed by an elective Rural Council. ... These councils were not yet (1967) established anywhere in the Mourides zone, however, and the law had yet to have its real effect. Even when the councils are elected, they are likely to be controlled by the same *marabouts* who previously exercised the function of *laman*.[48]

It is interesting that Soviet theory regards the landed aristocracy in Africa as the most powerful deterrent to socialist development. Professor Potekhin, citing northern Nigeria, Cameroon, Ethiopia, and Buganda as the only instances where a class of "landlords [is] exploiting a dependent peasantry," argues that it is only in those areas that "non-capitalist development" is encountering significant opposition. In his view, elsewhere on the continent the absence of social classes based on means of control as potent as land makes it possible for socialism to be adapted directly from peasant society.[49]

To a considerable extent, the potential of the landed elite is circumscribed by alternatives to service on land they control — alternatives that exist within range of mobility of the subsistence agriculturalists. Given the slow rate of development of industries based on agriculture — the slow rate at which capital finds its way into the interior — existing social control patterns based on land are not likely to change in the near future.[50]

VI

Pressure and Interest Groups

The essence of political democracy is that the politicians are subordinate
to the public, in whom are vested the fundamental rights of free
criticism, opposition, and dismissal. A political system in which the
public surrenders these rights to a political party must have the same
evil results as an economic system in which the market is subordinated
to a guild of business men.

ARTHUR W. LEWIS
POLITICS IN WEST AFRICA

"The People" and Groups Generally

Prime Roots of Pressure

In developed systems the role, function, and social position of groups competing for power or to secure a share of the wealth or both are likely to follow certain established patterns. Their conduct is governed by generally accepted rules; even their aims and objectives are formulated by reference to standards developed and accepted over long periods of time. Accordingly, public officials rely on codified concepts, firm expectations, and the corresponding predictable outcomes in their dealings with pressure and interest groups or with leaders and spokesmen of such groups. To these known patterns must be added the personal variable, the social prejudice, and the idiosyncratic tendency that motivate the decision maker to tip the scale for or against given groups. Given the rather close relationship that pressure and interest group leaders and spokesmen seek to establish with the top echelons in order to maximize their opportunities, the ability to identify with the leader's or the high office holder's idiosyncratic inclinations or his socioeconomic self-interest, may well prove to be the decisive difference between pressure group failure or success.

In the relatively unsettled, open-ended, experimental social settings of the developing world, relationships are much less formal. Far greater weight may have to be attached to a highly individualized perception among decision- and policy-makers of what a given group represents, what it seeks, what type of threat it poses. Unknown is the level of effectiveness or potential among such groups. In the underdeveloped setting, the capability of groups to compete for shares of the wealth drops off sharply as one moves down the social hierarchy.

Developed or developing, no system features groups clearly and precisely separate and distinct from others pursuing similar or related goals. In fact, there may well be overlaps between groups pursuing detrimentally opposite goals. Since groups and goals overlap, individuals move back and forth across associational boundaries; the same individuals pursue diverse interests in different groupings. Even contradictory goals may be pursued by the same individual in the same organization or group. Therefore, in the open-ended experimental setting of the typical African economy it would be most inappropriate, if all groups were to be thought of as firmly embedded in permanent molds.

On balance, everything points to an elitist interpretation of pressure and interest group behavior in Africa. Even in the developed systems where the rank and file possesses the means to check on the leaders' conduct, those leaders, unerringly locating the ladder to power and influence, all too soon become separated from their original base. The high incidence of illiteracy and the absence of an effective and independent press more quickly and more strikingly widen the gap between leader and follower.[1] The argument that the masses possess the ability to engender influence on public policy by their own, more or less spontaneous means can safely be discounted. Because the boundaries are fluid, the goals confused and confusing, opportunities for rulers to resort to deception, misinformation, obfuscation, and suppression if necessary are more than adequate to neutralize that potential should it materialize.

Why then do we concern ourselves with pressure and interest groups? Because even in an inchoate state they are important instruments of rule, and as such they do play an important part in the entire power and influence game generally termed *politics*. The way they play their part, or parts, is different from the way it is depicted in the standard treatment. The lines of command and communication, the goals and aspiration of leaders and their immediate supporters are different from those usually reported or described, but they are an important ingredient of the dynamics of politics. To an extent they are the key to an understanding of the dynamics of distribution of wealth, hence the distribution of power and influence.

The People

Ever since the first ruler discovered the value of identification with "the people," whatever his frame of mind or ideological orientation, the rhetoric of rule has included the ritual bow to the sovereign will of the people. Actually, the will and social power of the people is easily limited and controlled; the demands of the masses are easily channeled and manipulated.[2] Masses have thrown off the restraints only where the control apparatus was already critically weakened by other forces and factors or where it had already disintegrated.

While Western theorists and propagandists of Western democratic ideas pay lip service to the sovereign mass, socialist, Communist, and other social revolutionary writers seem inclined to view the masses as quite capable of staging effective assaults on established rule, always, of course, under appropriate leadership.[3] Attempts to organize mass action are legion, but so are unsuccessful uprisings.

On the continent of Africa no combination of segments of the masses can expect to overcome even a modest show of force by the established rulers. Where masses appear to have been successful — say, in a demonstration or riot — the probability is that someone organized the action, directed it, and exploited it. It has not been difficult for those in control of the law-and-order apparatus to seek out and neutralize, if not disarm or destroy, agents of unrest and revolt, as a rule.

Soviet Russian, Communist Chinese, and black anti-imperialist, anti-neocolonialist writers leave advanced futile prescriptions based on the potential of the masses to support revolutionary acts. To an extent such prescriptions may be the product of a false analogy that equates the African peasantry and urban workers with the substantially different Russian or Chinese peasantry.

Whether of Western or Eastern origin, some of that populist rhetoric has been acquired by contemporary African political thinkers. Understandably, the ritual of rule in Africa requires the same bows to the "will of the people" that have resounded through the market places and public forums of the older countries. Whether a given policy advances the people's rights and interests or hinders them, whether it inaugurates some form of democracy or closes the door to free expression, it will be couched in terms that suggest popular approval.

Fictitious or not, the people's will is nebulous enough to allow its conversion into support of almost anything ruling groups may want to do. If public policy decisions originate with the people in more than a geographic sense, close inspection of each particular instance will reveal that it actually stems from only a minute percentage. Most likely it originates with a special interest group situated high within the social structure. Africa's peoples cannot be regarded as more than a backdrop for special pressure and interest plays or as a general ritualistic reference point for public oratory.

Analysis of mass potential should recognize that communications between the masses, however defined, and the decision- and policymakers — the legitimized and self-styled representatives of the people — are quite open-ended: there is no limit to articulation, and any interpretation of what is being said is as valid as any other. In these circumstances meaningful communication of practical consequence to the exercise of power and influence can be conducted only with reference to very specific demands clearly understood by all directly concerned, with a minimum of static and distorting interference. Great public policy issues are susceptible to so many interpretations that any solution of a question, no matter how irrelevant or unrelated to articulated public or mass demands or vaguely perceived or registered expectations, can be so construed as to appear to be a direct and true response to popular pressure.

Granted that one can conceptualize such expansive popular interest blocs as consumer interest or farmer interest. Public opinion polls and surveys conducted in a few areas tend to lend credence to the concepts. Purchasing power, however, is actually limited to a small segment of the total population.[4] More broadly, educational and employment demands and demands for certain critical amenities such as water and light medical care may be regarded as mass pressure sources. But none of these can readily be converted into sources of power and influence remotely similar to those at the disposal of the elite or the organized pressure and interest groups.

From time to time a relatively free election is conducted and numerous members of parliament, incumbents, are defeated. Many are tempted to attribute the defeats to popular or mass pressure, a kind of uprising at the polls; events in Kenya and Tanganyika (not Zanzibar) were interpreted that way. Was it *wananchi* (people) power that defeated a number of sitting deputies of Kenya's ruling political party in 1969? One glance at the list of fallen reveals that none had occupied a position of substantial power. In Tanganyika a victim of oppositional efforts was quickly returned to his place at the top.[5] The African adaptation of the British practice of permitting candidates to run where they please, or better, where the truly influential allow them to run, is a convenient means of preservation of privilege and established power. In Africa this device is backed up by manipulation of the election results themselves by such means as ballot stuffing and other outright violations of the written election code.[6]

Can Africa's masses be organized and trained to defend social revolutionary achievements? As we have said, it is doubtful whether the people ever really approve measures taken in their behalf except in a collective sense. Beyond that Karl Deutsch, actually discussing another question, seems to imply that mass organization in Africa may indeed hasten state disintegration where a "rapid increase in social mobilization and political assimilation [is] faster than the process of civic assimilation to the common political culture of the community . . ."[7] In different terms, even the seemingly most mass-directed African ruler, the Nkrumah or the Sekou Touré or the Nyerere, will think more than twice before he unleashes the forces vaguely hinted at in Deutsch's formulation.

Groups

There is, of course, no difficulty in positing the existence of groups in general, and there are no barriers to prevent verbal formulations and ascription of group characteristics and group goals to any segment of any population anywhere. A serious problem arises only when the power potential of a group is to be identified with some precision. Here an enormous gap separates theory and practice. In theory the possibilities are boundless, and nothing, unfortunately, prevents us from attempting to project onto the African scene our beliefs and suppositions, drawn usually from our Western experience. For example: "A rise in the level of overall power in the society is frequently viewed by crucial sectors of an emerging nation as much more vital than any question of the distribution of power."[8] "Crucial sectors" of a nation are, of course, incapable of viewing anything at all, and the thesis that any sector however defined will prefer a rise in "the level of overall power" to an increase in group or sector power stands contradicted by accumulated evidence.[9]

Application to Africa of concepts like consensus is hazardous in the extreme. Everywhere consensus functions as an intellectual and often a propaganda screen, covering up fundamental disagreements among contending factions or subgroups. Unless approached with a high degree of precision, the term *consensus* leads to confusion of the presumed positions shared by a fictitious public with the rather specific goals and objectives of highly motivated and specifically directed groups that cluster around essentially transitory issues. One consensus, in other words, blends into another, possibly a contradictory one, while the analyst is busy formulating his generalization on the first. Much of the discussion of consensus in Africa actually deals with trivia. Issues that matter in the power and influence context rarely if ever reach a point of agreement among contenders that would warrant use of the term consensus. (If absence of active opposition is taken for consensus, then there was consensus on captivity and torture among concentration camp inmates under Nazi rule.)

Pressures analytically assessable are exerted on behalf or in pursuit of specific interests. Interests too vaguely perceived have no analytic value; they may not even have theoretical value. Specific interests relate to the goals and expectations of individuals in a certain order of priority, again adjusted to individual needs. To be sure, this approach may be a form of reductionism, but reduction to a point is needed if we are to contact reality as it pertains to the less developed world. Physical security for self and family can be presumed to be near or at the top of the individual's sense of priorities. Where physical security is not at stake, economic security, even survival, may rank highest. It is possible that there may never be enough of such security as far as the individual is concerned. Of course, I am not suggesting that these considerations are the sole motivational factors explaining human behavior. What I do suggest instead is that they are high enough on the scale of values to warrant elevation to a core issue in power and influence analysis.

Whatever individual and thus group expectations and interests may be, numerous forces operate to constrain, delimit, divert, frustrate, and nullify some or all.

The Government of this country [Zambia] is ultimately concerned with the welfare of everyone of its citizens, whether he be miner, fisherman, railwayman, civil servant or in any other calling. It matters little whether he lives on the line of rail or in the remotest corner of the country. Just as the common man is the strength and hope of this nation, so it is the duty of Government to foster and protect his interest.[10]

These sentiments are understandable but substantially misleading; none of the governments here analyzed, or any government for that matter, can actually embark on implementation of that declaration. This particular statement was issued in response to certain recommendations made by a commission of inquiry on wages and working conditions in Zambia; but the constraints on the policymakers are enormous, and the interests of economically vital segments of the population, such as miners and railway workers, will have to be evaluated ahead of the interests of economically marginal groups. The arithmetic of economic poverty or, as in Zambia, imbalance compels attention and sets guidelines for priority treatment of the interest group in direct conflict with public rhetoric.

There will always be a disparity between what government leaders want as public officials and what they can hope to accomplish in that capacity. However, government leaders also act as individuals. Under the restraints that economic exigencies impose on them, individual survival interests may assume greater importance to them than to cabinet officers in more highly endowed economies. The combination of scarcity and individual interest on the decision- and policy-maker's part sets the stage for fulfillment of higher pressure and interest group ends.

The outcome of the struggle for recognition is normally determined by the way the merits of given demands are perceived at the top. Those whose services the ruling group deems essential for its own survival, individually and collectively, are most likely moved to the top of the pecking order. Highest priority is accorded those whose expertise is deemed essential — for example, higher civil servants, leaders of the military, and the police.[11] The claims of these groups, in turn, are affected by the general situation that confronts the country: the level of earnings and allocation of resources generally among other groups (workers, the lower salaried, and farmers) is governed somewhat by the perception of how wide a gap between high and low income is compatible with the ruling group's survival and security interests. Ideological considerations, even recommendations of commissions of inquiry created to adjust wages, prices, working conditions, and other aspects of the economy subject to pressure and interest group demands, are ranked as deemed appropriate at the top.[12]

In Africa conditions are more favorable for the few in possession of requisite skills and information than they are in, let us say, the United States. Wealth, though important, can be matched by knowledge and skills far more here than in the advanced societies. Pressure in support of interest group demands does not originate in a vacuum and is not based exclusively on good intentions. It does not unerringly locate the points in state and society where it is likely to bring results. Characteristically in developing countries information required for effective pressure group action is difficult to come by. As we have suggested, there is a real world to which pressure must be applied, there are real points of decision- and policymaking to which pressure groups must direct attention. In the real world, more likely than not pressure points are located in the spheres of illegitimacy and extralegality. Probably bribery and corrupt practices, informal friendships, or favoritism are required methods. Strict libel laws that require reliable proof in support of allegations prevent the press, where it is so inclined, from publishing guidelines on the subject for the benefit of the general public. The public interest, in other words, must be content with the bare bones of economic and fiscal information. Meanwhile, the few who are privy to state secrets, with access to the skills of lawyers whose concept of public ethics may be heavily colored by the requirements of their profession, enjoy the fruits of what amount to privileged positions.

In African pressure and interest group or power and influence arithmetic, mathematical equations that social scientists use to evaluate relative potential of interest do not apply. The element of Africanization creates a situation in which Africans with virtually no financial support can insinuate themselves into positions of influence, while foreigners or members of non-African minority groups, such as Kenya Asians, may find their considerable potential actually severely restricted. Yet it is doubtful whether in the crunch, when hard and fast policies are set and decisions are to be made, the foreigner who represents great wealth or wealth-producing potential does not command sufficient weight to overcome the impediments of his nominally foreign status, assuming, of course, a rational economic setting.

In the absence of effective legal or conventional restraints, government normally can overcome private pressure in Africa. The economic punch at the disposal of government in Africa exceeds by far that at the disposal of governmental agencies or individuals who hold office in the advanced countries. The conflict of interest element alone is an index of the disparity. Virtual absence of precedence and the ambiguity of whatever precedence there may be, renders it practically impossible to determine, let alone enforce, conflict of interest rules in Africa. We shall return to that below. The combination of a friendly government official and a clever individual with a few pounds or francs at his disposal, or sometimes with none, is a very strong combination indeed and may secure rewards for a given interest, individual or group. The relative inefficiency of government agencies established to process even only the most pressing demands, further affects the situation. This inefficiency is compounded by lack of information, or an information overload at the center, and the time lag resulting from inefficiency.

By the time a given demand has been formulated, pressure processes devised, and pressure points identified, the economic situation, always being precarious, may already have changed to the point where the demand is irrelevant, impractical, and unfulfillable. Price fluctuations may completely destroy the bases for interest group demands within a short period of time because of the sensitivity of an economy that relies on only one or two commodities and because of the immediacy of such fluctuations for secondary industries — the multiplier effect that after a drop in world price transmits the shock waves throughout the economy at a rate several times that of the drop itself. In other words, in the less developed areas pressure and interest group plays are highly personalized and ephemeral; much huffing and puffing may be followed by no response whatever. Attribution of ideological goals to social and economic pressure more likely than not may be a matter of gazing up the wrong tree.

If any sense of realism is to be maintained, pressure and interest group goals must be related, not to avowed ideological prescriptions or published articulations, but to the practicality of the demands measured against the reality of scarce resources, inexperience, inefficiency, the corroding effects of bribery, and corruption — all of which as we have seen, consume major shares of public funds. Opportunities for redress of grievances exist in Africa, but the probability of given grievances being brought to bear at the right pressure point at the right time are extremely low for those interests not deemed critical to the survival of the ruling group, as perceived by the key decision- and policymakers. Perception in this case is not revealed in public addresses, writings, or even interviews with visiting social scientists.

Entrepreneurs, Producers, and Middlemen

Neocolonialists

In *The Great Powers and Africa,* Waldemar Nielsen asserts, quite prematurely: "By the end of 1968, all of Britain's former African territories had been decolonized except one, Rhodesia . . ."[1] If decolonization is to mean anything at all it must extend to the basic socioeconomic features of colonialism, and we know that independence does not necessarily alter these features. Some progress, of course, has been made; some fetters have been thrown off, and others have been loosened somewhat. In any event, decolonization, like Rome, is not achieved in one day, one year, or one decade. Because the basic relationships between the former colonial centers and the newly independent states have not changed drastically, in certain critical areas the same or very similar pressure and interest processes with few exceptions are at work after as before independence.

Independence does open the door to interests other than those from the former colonial control power. Moreover, economic systems have changed in scope and direction, many assuming multi- or international characteristics. Now more than ever before pressure and interest groups of foreign identity might represent multinational combinations; many operate across international boundaries. Increasingly they operate behind indigenous facades, often through local representatives, under various legal disguises. In economically weak states such groups carry more weight than the economically marginal local groups, while in the more stable states they are on a par with indigenous groups that enjoy the support of local authorities. On balance, as long as capital and especially foreign exchange are of the essence, foreign owners and managers of the comparatively larger, more concentrated, more venturesome, and more efficiently organized foreign capital resources will be accorded special advantages over opposing indigenous interest groups.

Talcott Parsons offers a useful analytic aid in the assessment of the comparative role of foreign interest in the new states. Testing money for its symbolic value, he suggests that acceptance of the symbol may well be as consequential for social behavior as is acceptance of the substance. In his view, if the symbolic value of money is to play its proper role "specific definition and institutional acceptance" are required in four basic respects: category of *value,* category of interest, definition of the situation, and a normative framework of rules. If institutionalization of the symbol-reality relationship has not progressed enough to have generated substantial consensus in society, certain high risks are incurred. Loss of confidence in the value is one; economic collapse is a possible consequence. If we accept that money — that is, wealth available for power and influence purposes — are critical in a system, what will be the social consequences where those in positions of power lack faith in the local money values. If the currency of power and influence in Africa consists largely of foreign exchange, foreign bank accounts, and foreign economic opportunities, a far greater accent on foreign economic processes and sources of wealth would be indicated than is suggested in the nation-building rhetoric of independence. Loyalty tends to follow monetary value as long as that value remains as expected.

There is substantial evidence that among those who occupy positions of power few have much faith in their own national currency, which enormously enhances the potential of foreign pressure and interest groups. Foreign corporate interests, banks, trading houses remain positioned at the control points of the power and influence flow. Of course, they already started with an advantage, since the colonial system had been geared to accommodate their interests above all others. As in all social conflict situations, the exact disposition of foreign influence potential is subject to a certain amount of bargaining. It is important to note, however, that this bargaining takes place across national boundaries, across the boundaries of economic systems. Bargaining is not necessarily terminated or even impeded with a new decree purporting to limit the operations of foreign corporations or personnel on African soil, for decrees have a way of being ignored or circumvented. In other words, decrees that attempt to redistribute or transfer wealth or economic opportunities are meaningless unless they reflect reality.

The potential of foreign pressure groups varies with the economy and the degree of dependence on foreign capital, foreign know-how, and so on. It is greatest in those sectors of the economy that depend on foreign support for development or even sustenance. That the large expatriate trading interests shaped the economies of Africa is generally accepted. Not accepted are the enduring consequences of this historic fact. The deep involvement of these interests in local retail trading, the direction of trade, the credit and banking system, and the transport system enables them rather consistently to resist and even counter nationalist pressures.

The effective relative position of a given foreign pressure or interest group probably corresponds closely to the ratio of export-import trade to overall Gross Domestic Product of the host country. To the degree that foreign groups dominate export and import, that sector must be moved up on the hierarchy of power, above ideology, propaganda, nationalist rhetoric, or party political programs. With it to the top go the associated interests, such as mining and plantation. Following these are the secondary or subsidiary economic sectors, based mainly on the primary sources of production of wealth.

The importance of export-import associated foreign interest groups deserves to be underlined. Kuznets notes that the economic structure of small nations is typically less diversified than that of larger units. This narrowness may be true also of such large but as-yet economically unbalanced national units as Nigeria and the Sudan, which suggests certain important internal consequences for the interest and pressure confrontations in these states. More groups must compete within narrower as well as fewer economic areas or sectors, and "Foreign trade is of greater weight in the economic activity of small nations than in that of larger units," or ". . . the smaller the country, the larger the ratio of exports and imports to total output."[2]

The existence of multinational corporations, of internationally interlocked directorates that span the continent and extend around the globe, raises questions about the typical analytical model that ranks national rhetoric and political party propaganda first and places such ephemera as party programs at the center of what is called the polity. Whether or not the international boards of directors actively engage in conspiracies, as some ardent anti-colonialists would insist, the existence of combinations of interests cannot, of course, be denied. Expressed in terms of economic substance, these combinations generate a potential of impressive proportions, not beyond fairly accurate assessment if one considers aggregate capital or ability to achieve monopoly control in a basically dependent economy. The ability to freely dispose of internationally acceptable currencies in the monetary as well as in the social, power political sense may alone warrant lifting these interests far above local political parties that as parties are known to have encountered difficulties in securing minimal operational funds.

The international dimensions of the system were most clearly recognized by Ambassador Darlington, who represented the United States in Gabon and who correctly perceived a system in which French business interests, French administrators and technicians, and French policymakers in Paris combined to compete successfully against the more conventional Gabonese interests. His summary statement is a classic commentary on the situation.

> The French Government and French business work together in a compact system. The fuel that makes it run is French Government aid which year in and year out pays the salaries and other expenses of a host of French-men-administrators, financial experts, agricultural advisors, engineers, doctors, teachers, judges, to name only a few. It also finances all manner of capital projects and economic and engineering studies and buys equipment from bulldozers to hypodermic needles. French aid is not only large but admir-ably carried out. The many projects that I observed seemed well selected and effectively and tastefully executed.[3]

This appraisal suggests that in French-speaking Africa *la présence fran-caise* should be interpreted to mean total penetration of all aspects of public life that matter in the pressure and interest group context. Since decision- and policymakers must continuously relate to these parameters, it is only with difficulty that one can understand how analysis of what is termed politics in such states as Senegal or the Ivory Coast can rely mainly on noneconomic, nonfinancial matters. Clearly the emphasis should be shifted if our understanding of reality is to be advanced.

In most countries foreign pressure and interest groups at one level are represented locally in chambers of commerce.[4] In competition with so-called political groupings, chambers of commerce dispose of hard power and influence currency. It is possible to talk broadly of party political slogans, ideological propositions, historical platitudes, and generalizations. But the language of trade and finance is comparatively exact. An individual Senegalese can bank on a given rhetorical promise and retreat from it with the greatest of ease, unless he has annoyed the power holders beyond reprieve, but banking on a commercial venture with hard cash permits retreat only at a price.[5]

Complexities of finance and commerce, the marginal level of operation of indigenous entrepreneurs, and of the local government for that matter, adds to the potential of organizations that virtually function as power and influence exchanges for the controllers of capital and skills, know-how, and foreign connections. Few arguments are as eloquent as those that suggest that the well of public finance may run dry in certain conditions. In French-speaking Africa the local, French-dominated Chamber of Com-merce is positioned better than any other body, public or private, because, among other reasons, they are situated at the end of the hot line from Paris.[6]

In Senegal "the groundnut industry constitutes a coordinate oligopoly acting in the same way as a monopoly, when taken as a whole.[7] Groundnut processing, the largest industry in Senegal, is the domain of three big producers and a few smaller ones; all belong to the *syndicat des huiliers,* an association that coordinates the policies of its members. Because of the high concentration of economic activity in one sector around one commodity, and because French interests are controlling, in Senegal and the Ivory Coast the potential of combinations of government boards, private associations, chambers of commerce, and informal meetings of big business and government representatives exceed by far the potential of local parliaments, if not cabinets, legislatures, and administration put together.

In the Ivory Coast, coffee, cocoa, and cotton are the mainstays of the economy. French private interests dominate in all three, sharing decision-making prerogatives with government agencies but having the last word most likely because these products are linked to world market prices, and French interests are strategically placed astride the international lines of communication and control.[8] Since manufacturing and processing still are mainly in foreign hands, the options open to national governments that seek to encourage small indigenous producers are severely circumscribed. To remain competitive, groundnut shelling, cotton ginning, and coffee and cocoa cleaning require considerable capital and skill. Only the large foreign houses possess the requisite capital, equipment, and trade outlets; negotiations between government and small indigenous producers therefore would be unrealistic if conducted without knowledge and approval of the foreign interests.

Of considerable consequence are the personal preferences of local rulers, the products primarily of their educational and socioeconomic backgrounds. Put differently, foreign interest groups enjoy special advantage if their demands can ride to the top on reference power — French in this case.

Beyond personal inclinations is the iron law of economic survival. Since the legal-constitutional, administrative, and economic infrastructural components of the state apparatus having been arranged under colonial rule, decidedly to facilitate continued French domination, to attempt to prematurely cut the umbilical cord would require economically suicidal tendencies on the part of the local rulers.

As time goes on and radical changes are rarely introduced, dependence on foreign interest mounts. The International Bank's assessment of the situation in the Ivory Coast is typical: "Manufacturing is one of the fastest growing sectors of the Ivory Coast economy, surpassed only by transport and forestry." "Manufacturing is almost entirely in the hands of French companies, mostly subsidiaries of large French enterprises."[9] If one considers that about 80 percent of total manufacturing output is produced within a circle of 50 miles around Abidjan, the potential of the foreign pressure and interest bloc in one country becomes even more apparent.

For reasons outlined, foreign pressure and interest groups in English-speaking Africa play a lesser role in the new state systems. How much less is, of course, difficult to determine, but the aggregate potential of French interests is nowhere matched by British interest groups and combinations. In part this imbalance flows logically from the different style of rule and administration, itself a reflection of British preoccupation with more lucrative opportunities elsewhere in the world. Only in Kenya and, of course, in European-dominated South Africa, largely because of the high concentration of British settlers, did Britain invest more substantially, mainly in industry.[10] As a result, employers', trade, and company associations and the chamber of commerce in Nairobi and the towns in the agriculturally important highlands constitute a pressure and interest factor of significant proportions.[11] As long as the government of Kenya wants to remain competitive vis-a-vis Europe and South Africa in high-quality agricultural production, European interest groups in the agricultural and related processing sectors can count on sympathetic hearing for their demands in policymaking circles. This favored position is reinforced by the typically weak position of African business and industry; the growing manufacturing industry of Kenya will continue to lean on British and, secondarily, other Western capitals for some time to come.[12] Britain's entry into the European Common Market will somewhat broaden the range of options.

In summary, European pressure and interest groups, as distinct from European participants in rule at the decision- and policymaking levels, warrant placement very high on the pressure and interest totem pole at both the international and the national levels. Their strength derives in the first instance from their intimate connection with the financial wellsprings in London, New York, Paris, Brussels, Rome, or Frankfurt and their high standing in the estimation of foreign bankers and other sources of credit. Not the least important weapon in their arsenal is the ability to draw on the home government and private sources at home for bestowal of substance largesse honors, or opportunities for enrichment in favor of cooperating Africans.

To demonstrate the pervasively international dimensions of pressure and interest plays in the African states, we have treated foreign interests as essentially homogeneous. We have spoken of French or British interests. We generalized about Belgian, Portuguese, or even South African interest groups or demands. None of these groups or blocs of groups, of course, constitutes a solid phalanx in all respects on every issue. In crisis conditions, French interests in Algeria consolidated. At the time of maximum peril to life and property, approximately between 1960 and 1964, Belgian interests firmed up considerably, and intragroup differences receded temporarily. Generally, European interests tend to coincide under the impact of Africanization drives, but even under extreme stress conditions certain fundamental differences remain. Governmental bodies in the metropolitan centers differ with their own nationals employed in overseas headquarters.

Beyond that international or high-level multinational financial interests — major investment and banking houses, for example — take a stance different from that of those whose operations are confined to the European metropole or to the overseas territory exclusively. Similarly, trading interests differ from manufacturing, banking from entrepreneurial, large trader from small or intermediate trader, and so on.

Under the rubric "French interest" one must include excolonials who have blended completely into the local scene, have lost all substantive ties to the mother country, and would be at a total loss should they be compelled to return home. Kenya, Zambia, and, of course, Rhodesia and Southern Africa generally contain similar elements to a greater or lesser degree. These people have become committed to the interests of the local elite. It is they who are pressing for open-door policies throughout Africa. In Senegal, the Ivory Coast, Gabon, the Malagasy Republic, they are pressing for an increase of aid from the United States and other outside donors, primarily in the expectation that such aid would lead to a diversification of interests, increased competition, and a lessening of direct control over the economies by the metropolitan centers. Principally, foreign interest groups diverge over profit perspectives. At the time of the Congo upheaval, mainly between 1960 and 1962, Belgian interests divided over the issues of the financial economic feasibility of Katanga's independence. Those who stood to profit by continued mining in Katanga, and in Katanga only, were inclined to cast off into the wilderness the relatively unprofitable remainder of the huge colony and with it get rid of the enormous external and internal debt burden. Belgian interests at home and abroad that did not directly benefit from mining in Katanga but stood to lose if economic collapse became the fate of the remainder of the territory took a different approach. The battle was joined in Belgium, in the parliament in Brussels, between the political parties, and in the cabinet.[13] Kenya's progress to independence is marked by similar splits within the British interest group camp, with corresponding battles in the House of Commons in London and in the British cabinet. Britain's political parties also mirrored the struggles.[14] Evidence is mounting that Portuguese settlers differ with financial, trading and manufacturing interests based in Portugal.[15]

Other Strangers

Hidden beneath noble, positive-sounding shibboleths such as national independence, freedom or self-determination of people, or racial sovereignty are eternal and universal quests for scapegoats, self-advancement, domination, and exploitation. Nationalist pressure to secure for Africans all or most economic opportunities is not difficult to understand given the injustice of colonial rule, but it, too, has its shabby side. Justified or not, pressure directed against foreign or alien competition, like pressure against indigenous minorities, all too often is a form of officially sanctioned larceny; it is always injustice.[16]

Drowned out by protestations of economic national self-defense or national fulfillment, racial equality, or even social justice are the cries of the cheated and misled victims of colonial shortsightedness if not duplicity, Africa's expendables in the imperialist drive for economic dominance. Brought to the continent, invited, recruited, or tolerated under colonial auspices to build the railroads, help operate the mines, generally provide semiskilled but cheap labor, then again tolerated and even encouraged as petty or retail traders and utilized as artisans and clerks to support the European superstructure, these unfortunates, most of whom come from Asia and Europe, find themselves suddenly reduced to candidacy for expropriation, deportation, and expulsion.

They have been led into a gigantic trap. Their socioeconomic raison d'être began to evaporate with the termination of direct colonial government. Originally of some importance to the extractive, exporting economies, later of some value as clerks, traders, and artisans in the European urbanized enclaves in Senegal, Ivory Coast, Kenya, and Zambia, the economic policy shifts that accompanied independence suddenly laid bare the social anomaly of their existence. Unlike the larger European traders, planters, and businessmen, they could not retreat to prepared defenses. Instead, their vulnerability increased from month to month. To the unsophisticated, retail trade or petty artisan skills appear to be within the immediate range of African capability. If it should turn out that this is a miscalculation, the risks are estimated to be relatively low. Accordingly, politicians in search of popularity are all too prone to advocate drastic measures against these unfortunates.

Opportunities for group pressure to stem this trend, possibly to reverse it, arise only in a few cases. If international trade wars should get out of control, as has been predicted, African economies will be hit hardest; then even the more nationalistic or race sovereignty-oriented African policy planners will be compelled to reexamine the utility of the commercially and financially astute foreigners in their midst.[17] But then it may be too late.

During the colonial era, a division of benefits evolved whereby Europeans secured for themselves the lion's share of the wealth, leaving a lesser share of income to the more numerous Asians, with a small segment of Lebanese and Syrians sandwiched in between. Europeans dominated the more highly capitalized industries, the larger trading houses, banking, mining, railroading, and shipping, while Asians and Levantines had virtually to themselves the retail trade, interior road transport, and other secondary or tertiary opportunities. Europeans and Asians operated in tandem, though they were not rewarded equally on a per capita basis. Independence broke up this combination, and Europe virtually abandoned their Asian partners.

Whereas highly placed Europeans managed to extract satisfactory settlements, Asians went empty-handed because they lacked the leverage that the respective European home governments provided for the protection of British settlers' and businessmen's interests in Kenya and Zambia, or those of French entrepreneurs, colons, or even petty traders or artisans who wanted to return to the metropole. Asians and *petits blancs* from Europe did not begin to approximate the "golden handshake" — the very handsome settlement negotiated for the benefit of British higher civil servants as a price for independence.[18] Unlike their former European partners, Asians were compelled to negotiate from weakness, considering themselves fortunate if they could depart with a fraction of their inventory or investment.

A major drawback in the Asian position and a major detriment to their ability to exert pressure on African decision- and policymakers relates to what might be termed the international linkage multiplier. In Kenya, for example, although Asian capital invested in enterprises incorporated locally exceed in the aggregate that of Europeans, the European in the Kenya economy, in external as well as internal respects, stands to benefit from the overall dominance of British capital based in the United Kingdom and deployable under favorable conditions in support of Kenyan objectives.

The multiplier reinforcing the European position must be several times that of the Asian community which can count on neither the Indian nor the Pakistani, nor any other major source of investment capital in the world. Thus, one may be misled by a straightforward assessment of influence potential of diverse pressure and interest groups, or group survival potential, based on monetary units alone — that is, without careful consideration of the differential multiplier.[19] Clearly, £100,000 at the disposal of a British trader with access to British banks and investment circles is worth more to the African policymaker than the same amount at the disposal of an Asian retail trader.

To an extent Asians have invited their current tribulations. Clanishness accentuates their outward ethnic distinctiveness and sets them up as easy targets for misdirected public wrath. Asians excluded Africans from their own inner councils. They also have excluded their African hosts from apprenticeship in trades and skills under their control. In these respects the Asians behaved no differently from the petty Europeans, especially the French or the white settlers in former East Africa and in present-day Southern Rhodesia, South Africa, and the Portuguese possessions. The French overseas have been notorious in banding together in defense of their positions, jealously guarding trade secrets, and exercising inordinate deliberation before admitting Africans to positions that could enable them to advance from potential to actual and active competition.

Asians who hold positions that require secondary education or less are likely to be swept away by the mounting tide of African school-leavers. The intensity of the threat is illustrated in Table 15-1.

TABLE 15-1. *Citizenship Status of Pupils Enrolled in Secondary Schools in Kenya (1966)*

Form	Total	Africans	% total	Non-African* Non-citizens
1	24,108	20,515	87	3,593
2	18,503	14,975	83	3,528
3	11,210	7,902	72	3,308
4	7,068	4,263	60	2,805
5	1,356	807	60	549
6	948	537	57	411

*Non-citizens includes other than Asians.
SOURCE: Kenya Ministry of Education, 12 *Triennial Survey,* 1964-66 and 1966, 79, table 12.

The relatively low percentage of Africans in the higher forms indicates that Asians in otherwise vulnerable positions, and barring mass expulsion, may have a period of grace. The potential of similarly situated groups elsewhere on the continent probably can be calculated by reference to the same index.[20]

Much has been made of the matter of the citizenship option offered to the Asians by the government of Kenya in 1962. From available data in 1968 it would appear that among the employees in commerce, transport, communications, manufacturing, and repairs, about a third of the Asians were citizens, but in the services group — that is, all the professions — which accounts for nearly 40 percent of all the Asians and Europeans, very few from either community were citizens. Data on earnings and opportunities to accumulate capital may explain the problem. Of those earning enough to save, fewer opted for Kenya citizenship than was true of those in the less fortunate categories. Clearly the citizens were more likely to attempt to form pressure and interest groups than were the noncitizens. However, in that they could count on stronger ties to the outside world and their higher economic status the noncitizens were not helpless. Also governing their attitude in this respect was the fact that professional skills are marketable elsewhere — in Britain, for example, or in India — whereas commmercial inventory and trading skills are not, related as they are to the special East African conditions. Also relevant were caste considerations, which relate, in turn, to ability to assimilate.

In short, a decision on Kenya citizenship depended on an Asian's calculation of his chances to establish himself and his family elsewhere at a position comparatively better than the one he would be occupying in Kenya, precariously, and at the mercy of a black majority. Younger Asians with high skills had a better chance to start out fresh than did older ones; yet older people had accumulated more capital, had stronger ties within the Asian community, and possibly were less vulnerable to African pressure, at least for a while.

In Kenya in 1968 the sum total of jobs that could conceivably become available to Africans with the removal of Asians amounted to about 6 percent of the reported total employment; in other words, at stake were the jobs of about 36.6 thousand Asians. Of these, 28.4 percent were in commerce and included jobs held by several members of the same Asian families. In the special case of Kenya, abrupt transfer of many of these positions from Asians to Africans was an invitation to disaster.

Asian electricians, carpenters, plumbers, and skilled craftsmen generally were vital to the crucial tourist industry, including transport and communication. (Absence of technical support forces may be the prime cause of failure to get tourist industries under way in West Africa.) In any case, this transfer involved about 10 percent of all employed Asians in Kenya. Assumed that several thousand positions could be closed down on the debatable grounds that since they primarily serviced European luxury interests they were of low public value, it is doubtful whether more than 5,000 jobs actually could be transferred to Africans from that source. Even then it is equally doubtful whether a substantial number of these would hold their positions for a reasonable period of time.

What is true of craftsmen is perhaps even more true of managerial positions. The 6.6 thousand directorial and managerial positions reported for Kenya in 1965 could be regarded as open to Africanization only if the Kenya authorities were prepared to substantially lower their expectations of industrial and manufacturing output as well as their standards for the public service sector. Philosophically, the costs of determined prosecution of the Africanization program may be well worth the gains in popular satisfaction. But if that satisfaction is short-lived while revenue and general levels of economic activity slump sharply, the costs may turn out to be prohibitive.[21] Most likely, expulsion of a substantial segment of the Asian population from East and Southern Africa would yield only temporary relief from African mass pressure, from the scourges of unemployment and poverty, while sharply increasing the economic burden through imbalance and instability.

Technically, all foreign groups operate, of course, within the legal limits of the new states. The majority of foreigners in the new states are subject to national jurisdictions, judicial systems, local laws, immigration regulations, and so on. Yet, reminiscent of experiences of Armenians, Greeks, Cypriots, and Jews at different times elsewhere in the world, some foreigners manage to carve out jurisdictions of their own, operating economically and for all practical purposes legally in a no-man's-land. From that favored position some manage to exercise pressure on relatively weak and impressionable governments. Among the more fascinating and successful operators in that twilight zone are the Lebanese and Syrians, a few Cypriots, the Levantines generally in West Africa, and the Ismaelis of East Africa.[22] Though not equaling their more successful kinsmen, considered above, even the rank and file in these groups appear able to generate considerable leverage by virtue of international ties. They are not powerful. Their influence, as a rule, does not enable them to affect major public policy decisions and they actually may not even be interested in many of them. But they seem able to impact local policies and decisions sufficiently to protect their group interests, at least for a decade or two.

Their principal resource is trading skill supplemented by an unusual talent for engaging in complicated financial juggling and manipulation, not necessarily beyond the bounds of legality. Their effectiveness is further augmented by strong kinship ties with other Levantines in similarly strategic positions elsewhere on the continent, in Europe, and in the Middle East. In a way they operate a kind of transnational underground railroad for financial and commercial purposes. This underground and the strong position of Lebanon as a potential haven for illicit funds in search of safe depositories commends the channel to the growing number of corrupt politicians, civil servants, and other operators throughout Africa.

The network yields numerous advantages, giving the group the edge over many of their more powerful competitors and providing entrees to high government circles in need of their services. Syrians and Lebanese have been instrumental in laundering illicit funds obtained by corrupt politicians through complex transfers of ownership. Through their compatriots elsewhere they acquire superior intelligence about affairs in other African states. By the same token, they seem to be well placed to act as agents of dissemination for African regimes. As foreigners they are less clanish than East Africa's Asians; they are prepared to reside in African quarters, learn to use local vernacular, and generally mingle more freely with black Africans — all of which may explain why this group has managed to function quite effectively within a potentially if not actually hostile environment.

Like the East and South African Asians, the Levantines are much better attuned to indigenous consumer tastes than are the West Europeans. They are more inclined to assume the risks inherent in extending credits to penurious African customers, they work longer hours than do competitors from other groups, and they are willing to accept the privations of living in isolated communities in the interior. They are reputed to be highly skilled in customary local styles of negotiation, including, allegedly, the African variants of collusion, bribery, and induced corruption.[23]

In a relatively small country like Ghana, large Lebanese and Syrian firms with an annual turnover of at least £200,000 can be expected to buy a great deal of influence, if influence is for sale. Even if the Ghanaian

Lebanese community totals only 1,600, its per capita effectiveness in the circumstances warrants a rather high rating, always assumed, of course, that the group is able to withstand the perennial and now ever-mounting pressures in the wake of the drive to Africanize business opportunities.

"Compradors?"

If the amount of pressure a group can bring to bear on public officials is a product of its value or utility to these officials, the indigenous African businessman cannot expect much in the way of concessions. To be sure, the trend, particularly in nonsocialist countries, seems to favor increased allocation of resources to indigenous enterprise. Governments in Nigeria, Senegal, Ivory Coast, Kenya, and several of the North African states have launched varieties of programs to assist fledgling native entrepreneurs in getting a head start. Still, the rise of the African entrepreneur is likely to be agonizingly, irritatingly slow. The aggregate share of the national wealth at the disposal of internal pressure groups is likely to remain organizationally fragmented, scattered in direction and purpose, and generally ineffectual. They will remain tied to the apronstrings either of dominant foreign capital or of the state. In either case they will not be able to gather for their cause the social force that propelled their counterparts in earlier European systems to hold their rulers for ransom.

Actually, the odds against the African entrepreneur's developing the economic punch necessary to alter public policy in his favor are lengthening as the euphoria of independence gives way to workaday reality. Whether he consciously seeks to imitate the European businessman or whether his behavior is the unavoidable consequence of private enterprise, the African businessman, manufacturer, or investor, outwardly at least, will continue to resemble his counterpart in the Western world. It may be more than resemblance; it may be a form of commitment. Suspicion along these lines motivated Nkrumah to call him *comprador,* agent of foreign domination and exploitation.[24] Misplaced though this epithet may be, it is possible that the plant of African private enterprise cannot thrive in any setting other than an essentially open, decentralized — Western — economic one. Possibly the pressure and influence language these interests can employ falls on deaf ears if the economy is centrally directed or controlled. If they are to survive, it may be mandatory that government be more than sympathetic to their demands; it must be committed.

African entrepreneurs, businessmen, small industrialists, investors, traders, and middlemen bear the scars of colonial neglect. As we have seen, colonial rule was rigged in favor of foreign enterprise. If any economic opportunities remained for Africans, it was for one of two reasons: either the Europeans did not care to enter the particular sector, most likely because it was not profitable, or Europeans simply were not available in sufficient numbers to launch a project and see it through the difficult initial phases. Predictably, the desire to cast off restraints imposed by foreigners, to improve their competitive position on their own home grounds aligned many African businessmen and would-be entrepreneurs with the national independence movement.

After independence, and notwithstanding the appearance of black faces in government offices, the economic bases of most of the new states remained in European hands. Indigenous entrepreneurs, many of whom fought hard to survive the discriminatory practices of the colonial era, now found themselves still compelled to do the bidding of foreign owners or managers of capital. Predictably, this was and remained a source of deep dissatisfaction. The experience colored their attitude toward government and gave their particular kind of pressure and influence behavior its distinct quality. Even though they remained true to their preindependence association with the African nationalist movement, they began to oppose it now that it was nominally in control of, hence responsible for, economic policy.

Their opposition to their own governments was not difficult to understand. Not only did their own leaders — they mistakenly regarded them as such — fail to produce the largesse popularly associated with independence, not only did they seem to welch on the promise of transfer of economic power into African hands, but all too soon they also allowed a rapidly expanding public sector to strangle the embryonic private sector. Weak to begin with, African private enterprise could not hope to maintain its precarious hold on its rather minute share of the national wealth, let alone carve out new opportunities and improve its overall position, if checked and opposed by the overwhelming resources at the disposal of the directors of the public sector. The bases for effective influence plays were steadily shrinking.

In French-speaking Africa and in such areas as the Congo (Kinshasa), Kenya, and Zambia, not to speak of Southern Rhodesia and South Africa, the position of indigenous entrepreneurs was further impeded by the presence of European settlers — colons in French areas, *petits blancs* (the poorer layer of the European class) in North and West Africa, East Africa the barriers against indigenous enterprise were rendered even more impenetrable by the interposition of the thick layer of Asians and Levantines.[25] At one level of competition African entrepreneurs encountered the overpowering presence of giant foreign-owned banking and trading monopolies in addition to the economic forces mobilized by the state. At another level, they were and for some time to come will remain hopelessly outdistanced by the lesser foreigners discussed above.[26]

We are familiar with the roots of their dilemma. Lack of education or relevant training clearly is a prime cause of African business failure.[27] Too many indigenous entrepreneurs lack even the most elementary perceptive talent to allow even instinct to guide them through the thickets of public and private law, accounting, and export and import. The basic rules of business management often are not understood, as the Dotsons have shown in their analysis of Zambia, Rhodesia, and Malawi. The intricacies of the money economy are beyond the ken of many.[28]

Africans attempting to enter the business world are chronically short of capital, an inevitable and persistent consequence of a poor start. To be sure, the rapidly expanding economies — albeit expanding only within relatively narrow geographic areas and in an unhealthy, lopsided fashion — generated lucrative opportunities only for those alert enough to take advantage. On occasion, nothing but quick wit was pyramided into small fortunes. However, unless taken into partnership with more experienced, more adequately financed foreigners few of the get-rich-quick types survive. In any case, most of the more lucrative opportunities are snapped up by nimble foreigners before the African is aware of their existence.

In the eyes of the new leadership in government offices, one particular tendency characteristic of African entrepreneurs detracts from their potential as significant partners in the development of the economy. They seem to be disinclined to enter areas that development planners consider vital. Unwilling to take risks, unprepared to postpone gains, they shy away from pursuits that might accrue to the benefit of the local economy in the short run but do not yield substantial profits for years. Manufacturing attracts few African owners of capital. Instead, they direct their energies toward high-yield opportunities such as real estate and apartment house and office building construction and rental — all areas of marginal value to national economic growth.

The portrait drawn by Samir Amin of the *"commercant senegalaise"* (Senegalese trader-businessmen) more or less fits African entrepreneurs everywhere. "Accustomed to see among themselves great success followed by resounding bankruptcy, obliged to convert all of their financial resources and to reduce their cash holdings to a minimum, the Senegalese trader-businessmen are pushed toward adventurism, toward the search for the miraculous business coup." Small wonder if Amin also found that nearly all Senegalese enterprises have their own government for their principal client, or, more precisely, their business partner is their own state treasury.[29]

The specter of sudden bankruptcy keeps the African businessman very close to his government; if at all feasible, he seeks a permanent protective relationship with the state. Insecurity motivates him to press beyond mere reduction or curb of foreign competition. He envisions permanently reserved domains within which he need not ever fear the wily Lebanese or, as in Senegal, the astute *maures,* or the versatile small French trader, or the thrifty, far-ranging Nigerian, or the diligent Togolese, or, in East Africa, the accomplished Asian or Arab.[30] After all is said and done, the expulsion of hapless Nigerians from Ghana, the elimination of the Lebanese and

Syrians, and the denial of certain spheres of activity to Asians, or their expulsion, are likely to be pyrrhic victories for indigenous entrepreneurs. Their reservoir of power is running dry, and they may be unable to exploit the opportunities created on their demand.

Amin notes that the African experience differs from that in the Middle East, in Asia, and in Latin America, where the large land-owning class together with the trading class created by differently motivated or differently behaving capital gave birth to a substantial indigenous capitalist class.

> The absence of these particular structural prerequisites in black Africa constitutes, in our opinion, the historical obstacle to the birth and development of national capitalism. Under the conditions, peculiar to black Africa, the germ of a type of feudal structure, or pseudofeudal structure, where it is found, has produced another form of development: not toward the formation of *"la grande propriété foncière capitaliste"* but rather toward *"formes d'organisations socio-politiques* sui generis," of the type of religious brotherhoods, like those of the Mourides.[31]

This statement is confirmed outside Senegal. What appeared to be organizational efforts among the Ibo and the Yoruba in Nigeria had actually distinct economic undertones. So have organizational and associational efforts among the Ga, Fante, and Ewe in Ghana and Togo, among the Baulé in the Ivory Coast, among the Luo in Kenya.[32] Invariably, if ethnic rationales could not be worked to advantage, indigenous capitalists fell back on the next available support, the state.

In some respects the interests of African businessmen and of public policymakers converge. Treasury officials are keenly interested in conserving always critical foreign exchange reserves. High tariff barriers and the resultant reduction of imports, a pressure goal of local entrepreneurs — except, of course, importers — brings the two sides together.[33] They will part company, however, if the local producer fails to make progress toward replacing the foreign suppliers. All too often he does fail. Moreover, while struggling to achieve the mutually desired goal local business and manufacturing demands ever greater subsidies. Invariably the performance of the small businessman is disappointing to government officials anxious to make progress toward development goals that exceed by far the capabilities of African private enterprise. Assurance from indigenous entrepreneurs that eventually they will be able to repay the government for substantial long-term subsidies, costly protective legislation, equally costly tax relief, and so on remain unconvincing.

With some notable exceptions African business sinks to the level of mendicant in its native environment. Plagued by inexperience, capital shortage, and mounting losses, pressed by consumers to produce goods formerly imported and to do so at lower prices, the African businessman shifts to proposition government on other than business or financial grounds. Under one disguise or another he relies on personal favoritism, ethnic

affinity or kinship, or spurious joint enterprise with a public official —
all of which opens wide the doors to fraud, which in turn renders the private entrepreneur vulnerable to blackmail.

Amin points out that African businessmen's demands for tax relief are
not justified in any case. They already enjoy a low tax load, and accounting
procedures being what they are it is easy to escape taxation altogether.[34]
Again, fraud tends to follow such conditions as night follows day. Inquiries
made after relatively corrupt regimes were overthrown in Nigeria, Ghana,
and Sierra Leone provide eloquent proof that indigenous business enters
into illicit if not illegal relations with office holders as a matter of course.

In Nigeria, for instance, when it was discovered that a native firm of
contractors had garnered lucrative deals though not qualified to perform
the work called for, a spokesman for the firm confessed: "The Corporation as well as the consultants, knew from the start that as an African firm,
we had not accumulated surplus capital and the flexibility of operation as
would be expected from the older and more experienced firms.[35] This partnership in crime, or at best in misconduct, creates a special relationship
between the source of pressure and the target. Whatever the precise position, in the pressure and interest group context African business may well
be committed to sail in the wake of the biggest ship, be it foreign or domestic. By all available indexes, the frail crafts of African private enterprise will be swamped by the tidal wave of economic distress pouring over
the continent.

For completeness sake, mention should be made of African migrant
workers and traders, who account for up to 10 percent of the total wage-
earning force in some West African economies. Although they disposed of
some influence at the time of independence, mass expulsions, rise of xenophobia, and persecutions mainly in the Ivory Coast, Ghana, Nigeria, and
Zaire have dramatically underscored the progressive deterioration of the
power position of that group.[36]

16

Bureaucrats and Guards

Bureaucrats

We have seen how the top echelons in the civil service, the principal sec-
retaries, and more generally the superscale salaried personnel manage to
convert inside knowledge, superior skill, and career head start into formidable command positions in state and society. What of the rapidly growing
army of lesser bureaucrats who staff administrative positions below, from
the national level on down to the village? Indications are that they had
entertained high hopes that independence would yield rich personal rewards; now they are among the most frustrated, the most disillusioned.

Educated, comparatively well trained, situated at or near centers of decision making and astride official channels of communication, the typical
bureaucrat is likely to have a far greater awareness of the enormous shortcomings of the African successor governments than has any other partici-
pant. Often he alone has been part of government before independence, and
he alone therefore is in a position to compare performance before and
after. Trained to operate a relatively sophisticated, advanced administrative
machinery in the tradition taught him by his European predecessors, he
senses deterioration and decay ahead of anyone else. At the same time
he is dismayed to discover that his own economic status and well-being,
instead of beginning to approach those enjoyed by his European model,
actually deteriorate also in relation to conditions characteristic of groups
he regards as comparative — politicians, professionals in the private sector, businessmen. The social security associated with public service by
European standards he now learns is not within the means of the system
he is now asked to serve.

The African civil service, one must remember, was created specifically
to serve colonial ends. It was brought into being to administer economic

exploitation and its local ramifications; it was expected to serve primarily European, not African, interests. The implications of this and the other above-mentioned experiences are clear. Rooted in an essentially alien tradition, the African lower level bureaucrat now must conclude that independence may indeed have left him holding the bag. He is, in the circumstances, disinclined to generate much enthusiasm for the new regime. He is bound to strive to prevent or even sabotage measures that tend to further aggravate his social, economic, and professional tribulations. He is likely to resist measures that in his view tend to contribute further to the destruction of the world he has come to know.

For a while the new rulers were able to exploit the conditioned reflex of the well-trained former colonial public servant. Throughout the continent African civil servants struggled loyally to cope with the mounting burdens placed on their shoulders by increasingly corrupt, all too often incompetent and wasteful leaders. They served willingly without insisting that they be accorded at once the social security and other perquisites that the rulers of Russia, Germany, Japan, and China had found necessary to bestow on their civil servants during the difficult period of economic scarcity and growth.[1] But loyalty exacted on those grounds is of dubious quality. Only a small setback is required to turn it into hostility; only a very thin line separates willingness to serve one set of rulers from the desire to secure a more accommodating alternative. Beneath the docility, abstinence, and self-denial that literature seems to suggest typifies the African bureaucrat, and notwithstanding the wide gap separating civil service compensation from that of the African farmer or worker, the African middle and lower level beauraucrat may well be one of the prime sources of social revolutionary unrest on the continent.[2]

The new leaders are sensitive to the threat from that direction. Efforts are under way to pacify the administrative soldiers, to exhort them to further sacrifice in the interest of national development goals by reference to future rewards.[3] But neither the standard appeals to patriotism nor elaborate constitutional or statutory measures will distract the hard-pressed African bureaucrat from pursuing his personally vital interests. To attempt to legislate him out of the sphere of public controversy, as was done in Ghana in 1971, simply is futile.[4] For many reasons the bureaucratic genie, once released, will not agree to return to the bottle.

First, the nominal transfer of authority to African leaders so improved the relative position of African higher civil servants as to render them virtually invulnerable to pressure as a group. Their advantage will accrue somewhat to the benefit of the bureaucracy as a whole. Second, expansion of governmental activity after independence has sufficiently enlarged the public service to rank it quantitatively as one of the strongest pressure groups.[5]

Third, the experience of the first decade after independence has demonstrated conclusively that loyalty, obedience, and devotion to the common good under prevailing conditions do not pay dividends. Wage and salary review commissions, special inquiries, and arbitration commissions meet, find conditions unsatisfactory if not critical, but regularly fail to produce needed improvements. If some adjustments are made they are usually minimal, and in any event inflation quickly nullifies most or all of the gain.[6] Fourth, as government and administration become more complex, as the realities of economic life impress themselves ever more urgently on the rulers, the value of bureaucratic experience rises sharply and so does the pressure potential of the group as a whole. Fifth, the rapidly spreading cancer of corruption, uncheckable and uncontrollable nearly everywhere, so it seems, eventually wears down even the morally and ethically most dedicated holdout. The record since independence demonstrates that no regime has been able to stem that tide. Those in possession of inside information on what transpires behind the scenes find it increasingly more trying to resist the temptation to convert knowledge into personal gain.

Deteriorating social and economic conditions, combined with the absence of strong moral and ethical leadership and restraints, place enrichment through corrupt practices in a different light. It quickly becomes the thing to do. Increasingly those in position to avail themselves of the opportunity will seek to obtain a modicum of social security by augmenting their income through illicit channels. Obviously, since at least two parties are required to consummate bribery, involvement of the African civil service corrodes the only effective safeguard against total immersion in corruption on a societywide basis. Rapidly being replicated on the African continent is the invidious United States type of alliance between public servants, mainly at the state level, and criminal elements, syndicates, hoodlums, and other sharp operators.

Still, the service as a whole continues to press for a larger share of government support, notwithstanding that in most countries the overall share going to the administrative sector has long ago exceeded economically permissible limits.[7]

Dumont succinctly expresses the problem: "The principal 'industry' of these countries at the moment is administration. It is not productive and simply adds to general costs. Such costs should be reduced but in fact are swollen to the point where personal expenses alone absorb 60 percent of the internal income of Dahomey."[8] Another illustration of this form of fiscal elephantiasis is Senegal. In 1963, 48 percent of current expenditure in Senegal went to administrative personnel alone (including local municipal employees).[9] In this as in similar cases, the public service, in particular the middle and upper level officials, are turned into a privileged social class that soon develops a vested interest in construction of strong defenses against rival claimants from less favored segments of the population.

Deteriorating economic conditions and increased unemployment exacerbate the intensity with which less favored groups will contend against the privileged bureaucracy. One of the periodical salary review commissions in Kenya recognized the implications of this situation for social peace and stability when they noted that the necessity of accommodating ever larger numbers of secondary school-leavers would inexorably compel government to depress salaries or else invite bankruptcy.[10] The repercussions of such a policy should be clear. The higher civil service will throw the lower paid groups to the pursuing wolves rather than court reduction of their own share of diminishing resources. Inevitably the higher civil service will become detached, eventually alienated from the rank and file.

If firm lines are not drawn, the ensuing cycle of salary and wage increases, mainly for the public service, is, of course, an invitation to economic disaster. Each year Senegal consumes most of its revenue on administration at the expense of funds for investment and development. Indications are that this depletion is replicated throughout the continent, with exceedingly few exceptions. Portions of government expenditure earmarked for constructive and productive purposes will decrease, while demands for ever more generous support from the relatively unproductive public sector will grow in intensity. Ironically, as the public salary and wage component expands it becomes ever more critical for the survival of governments because of its sheer numbers coupled with its proximity to the top, while at the same time it will become ever less relevant to the socioeconomic needs of the country as a whole.[11]

To expect vigorous countermeasures from the higher policymaking senior servants would be unreasonable. Whatever must be done to bring distribution of income and privilege back into some kind of socially acceptable equilibrium would require a sense of self-sacrifice that no group in power will engender voluntarily. Cuts of official salaries, imposed in some countries from time to time on highest officials, must be seen to be believed.

Ghana attempted to cut the knot, though it is difficult to assess with what degree of devotion. Going beyond the normal, routine transfer of hapless low-level clerks, plans were prepared to regularly dispatch to the inhospitable bush some of the senior civil servants. The thought was that this action would tend to counteract the unfavorable impact of sharp income differentials between the higher bureaucracy and the masses, partly by bringing central government services closer to the theretofore neglected regions, partly by acquainting higher decision and policymakers with their human responsibilities. The plan ran into a stone wall of resistance. The aversion to a move into the interior — a personal catastrophe for personnel accustomed to the relative comforts of urban living — turned out to be virtually incurable.

Again, calculating the likely effect of substantial salary and wage increases in the public sector on consumer price indexes generally, the same government in 1971 decreed a reduction in government subsidy of the highest paid senior servants. In the main this decree meant termination of subsidized housing or a rent increase.[12] For the lower paid the plan was to reduce the cost of housing, food, and transportation and improve working conditions, a most difficult task in prevailing conditions.

In all probability the disease will overcome the antidote everywhere. Middle class housing will remain unobtainable for the majority of those who might afford it; cost of transportation will rise; and food prices will either increase as food becomes more scarce, or staples will be as scarce as luxury imports. Cuts in ministers' salaries or removal of subsidized housing will not actually lighten the burden on the treasury; whatever savings may be effected will be more than balanced by the losses to corruption.

The Guards: Interests and Traditions

In addition to power, social demands grow out of the barrel of a gun. Since the beginning of time armed guardians of the realm, whatever its nature or size, have been tempted to use their weapons to advance their own individual or group demands. From palace revolts to broad-based social revolutions, armies, regiments, or companies have converted or attempted to convert physical power into material gain or some kind of social security for themselves, individually or collectively. Armed action has been undertaken to effect social change, follow whims, or steal. In contemporary Africa, ordinary lieutenants or even sergeants have come to regard their weapons, a handful of tanks, an artillery piece or two, together with a company of soldiers, a sufficient coin to gain access to the center of government, overturn regimes, even change entire social systems.

Elsewhere we considered the elite echelon of the military as rulers. Here our prime concern is with the military as a broader pressure and interest force competing primarily for benefits intrinsic to their professional mission and their socioeconomic status. For several reasons only tentative conclusions can be offered on this subject at this point in time.

With only one or two exceptions, and leaving aside the European security forces in the southern region of the continent, Africa's armed forces have not yet completed the transition from colonial auxiliary to principal instrument of power and control. Officers corps are still in process of formation; officers are still subject to sudden, on occasion substantial and dramatic, promotional changes (situations that also apply to the rank and file). Military traditions as they bear on modern military service are typically foreign, principally of European origin. Also foreign are the values and perspectives and consequently the interests of the armed forces as a whole and the ways in which those interests are formulated and advanced.[13]

European examples inspired organizations of African veterans of World War II; Ghana's and Nigeria's contributions to the Burma campaigns and

French Africa's contribution to the North African campaigns organized to secure for themselves what Great Britain and France were prepared to offer their own.[14] In addition to bonuses, pensions, and the like, the ranks, officer candidates, and officers expected generous and prompt promotions into positions to be vacated by Europeans.

It was taken for granted that salary increases would be fully commensurate with the new ranks — that is to say that Africans expected to receive the same pay as did their predecessors. As J. M. Lee reports: "[N]owhere is the retention of 'Senior Service' expatriate salaries more obvious than in the security forces themselves. Particularly among the officer cadre there has been a deliberate policy of comparability with metropolitan armies."[15] Expectations along these lines appear to have been responsible for the collapse of the *Force Publique* in the former Belgian Congo in 1960, and they brought on the rapid loss of discipline and military efficiency in all of the armed forces in former colonies.[16]

In pursuit of these goals few of the armed forces could fall back on the time-honored, convenient rationale of national defense. Only the Egyptian military, following successive defeats by the Israelis, could convincingly invoke it. The Kenyan and Ethiopian forces, the Sudanese, and the Congolese (Kinshasa) came closest to warlike action. In none of these cases could demands for a greater share of resources, including increased logistic, infrastructure support, extract much of any consequence from the African regime itself. Only substantial foreign aid, mainly from the United States, Great Britain, France, or the Soviet Union, and to a lesser extent from other European countries, could begin to meet the expectations of the increasingly restive African armies. Even then the nemesis of African economies, foreign exchange shortage, coupled with the equally urgent requirements of the productive sectors helped to dissuade spokesmen of the armed forces from pressing their demands too firmly while the country was under civilian rule. In this respect, higher officers emulated the example set by their European mentors, who had managed somehow to convey to their African counterparts the same sense of restraint that traditionally guided the armed forces in Europe to keep direct pressure on civilian authority to a minimum. Until successful coups spawned different perspectives, postindependence African officers toed that line.

The Imperial Forces of Ethiopia may not fit the general mold for several reasons. Ethiopia has enjoyed a form of independence longer than any other African state. Even the colonial relationship to Italy before World War II differed in critical respects from that experienced by all of the other European possessions on the continent. The Ethiopian military actually had been engaged in combat in defense of a sovereign, independent country against an invader and later on actively participated in the liberation of their occupied homeland. During the intervening period units of the disbanded Imperial forces fought the occupying power as guerillas.

This record has enabled the Ethiopian military alone to speak of an unbroken military tradition. It also explains why in the Abyssinian culture political authority below the imperial throne itself and military power have long been synonymous.[17]

Stature and prestige have made it possible for the armed forces to expand steadily. Even if the emergency over Eritrean insurrection or secession never had arisen, expansion could have been justified on other grounds. High social status has made it possible for the force to enter spheres normally reserved to civilians — for example, literacy campaigns, road building, and community development.[18]

COUPS AND MILITARY INTEREST

Takeover by the military, the successful coup, terminates the colonial tradition of subservience, alters the perspectives of the military regarding state and society, and in all probability radically transforms the soldier, officer and ranks, into substantially different socioeconomic units. Purely professional concerns now become contaminated and blend into ordinary human urges. Dividing lines between duty and right become blurred. Colonial legality is finally cast aside and with it, regardless of rhetoric to the contrary, goes civilian legality as a rule; and when legality goes, the concept of authority also is subjected to revision.

In the context of our examination of pressure and interest groups, what major, overriding interests or motivations are at the root of military coups? What *are* the real aspirations of coup leaders? Leaving aside the problematic and analytically quite elusive psychological explanations — lust for power and so on — we do have an abundance of imaginative, persuasive explanations from scholars, equally well-informed journalists, and military writers.

Western accounts of coups are prone to accept on face value plausible but transparent postevent attempts at rationalization by coup leaders themselves. Little if any mention is made of the fact that coups of necessity require that officers violate their code of honor and are palpably guilty of acts of treason or sedition. Analyses by socialist or Communist writers and accounts from the pens of the displaced civilian rulers themselves (e.g., Nkrumah), are slanted differently. In their view only right-wing officers are scoundrels. Officers who espouse leftist policies are, of course, defenders of the legitimate aspirations of the oppressed people and can therefore do no wrong.

Postcoup explanations from the perpetrators insist that the military are crusaders against corruption, bribery, debauchery — in fact, against virtually all social evils and shortcomings.[19] But this would be a prime example of the *post hoc, ergo propter hoc* fallacy. Even explanations that attribute coups to a desire to improve conditions of the armed forces themselves must be suspect. Certainly, the immense poverty of Africa places special burdens on the paymasters and quartermasters of the armed forces, but the needs of the armies simply have not been that pressing during the decade of independence preceding the rash of coups.

A major problem with most nonparticipant explanations of coups in Africa is that they assume a degree of consensus among coup leaders before the revolt, which to the informed observer must appear highly unreal. Circumstances in which coups must be planned in order to be successful tend to discourage neat, plausible consensus formation. Coup planning is a stealthy, secretive, increasingly hazardous business (note the executions in Ethiopia 1960, Ghana 1967, Sudan 1971, Morocco 1972). More often than not, discussions must be conducted with persons whom chance has brought together. Procedures must of necessity concentrate on the rawest, technically most critical tactical requirements. In all probability individual and group survival interests shared by diverse and at times actually otherwise incompatible factions are the major spur for military intervention and takeover. The proof of this incompatibility is offered sometimes within weeks, sometimes within months.

If one were to test the Ghanaian, Nigerian, Congolese (Kinshasa), Sudanese, Ugandan, and Moroccan coups or coup attempts for that ingredient — personal survival interest — some persuasive evidence would be available. In Ghana in 1966 the leading officers reacted to the threat emanating from the special Soviet and East German trained and equipped Presidential (Body) Guard Regiment.[20] They also reacted to the rumored plan to consign the regular armed forces to certain disaster in what obviously would have been a futile attempt to liberate southern Africa from staging areas in Zambia. Nigerian conspirators in the first of the 1966 series seem to have acted to forestall what they perceived as imminent threats to their careers, mainly from northern Nigerian military and civilian leaders.[21] The northern inspired countercoup later in 1966 appears to have been similarly motivated; northern officers as well as politicians feared for their futures in an Ibo-led, centrally controlled Nigerian state.[23] Revolts in the Congo (Kinshasa) prevented the removal from command positions of a small group of officers. The first of several coups in the Sudan in 1971 clearly sought to forestall elimination of all Communist and Communist-leaning officers; the second of that series took place to prevent a massacre of anti-Communist officers. The 1971 Uganda coup, and at least one of the Sierra Leone series, served to prevent the arrest and removal of several officers under suspicion, rightly or wrongly, of having enriched themselves through corrupt practices.[23]

In short, physical security and career interests of key conspirators surely precede lofty, even idealistic collective group goals. To overlook this very human explanation is to risk substantial distortion of the origins and direction of the events themselves. There are, of course, broader interests, the most pressing of which probably are exploited by the principal conspirators to forge effective alliances. But even alliance formation relates most likely to the strategic and tactical requirements of the moment. Attention focuses first on other commanders to round out the military effectiveness of the coup group; the need for tanks, artillery, fast armored vehicles to transport troops, key communication personnel, and access to secret files determines the final composition of many such alliances.[24]

Closely related to individual survival fears are considerations of group (tribal) survival. This thesis, too, is grossly overworked. All too often tribal interests enter massively only after the event; appeal to ethnic group solidarity then operates more as an insurance against a countercoup. In any case, the ethnic background explanation of African coups must be evaluated with much reserve.[25] It deserves to be considered, though, provided the cause of a coup is not mistaken for the effect.

The Nigerian situation with its Ibo-Yoruba-Hausa-Fulani-Tiv-Efik juxtapositions seems to be the classic case. Developments following the 1966 Ghanaian coup, including the unsuccessful "minicoup" of 1967, clearly reflect frictions along what for want of a more appropriate term can be called tribal lines. The Ga-Adangbe, Fante, and Ewe tensions and conflicts there have parallels in Senegal, Kenya — Luo versus Kikuyu versus Kamba — Zambia, Uganda, and Congo (Kinshasa). Largely as a result of deliberate design by the Belgians, the Congo problem produced a military establishment ridden with tribal dissention and murderous jealousies.[26] The Sudan, torn by Arab-Black strife and civil war, obviously is subjected to stresses based on race. Again, identification of that source as a prime factor in military intervention is another application of the *post hoc, ergo propter hoc* fallacy. The successful coup brings to the surface internecine strife along tribal lines within the armed forces, but racial or ethnic tensions do not necessarily cause or trigger coups.[27] Tribal friction is endemic, and there must then logically be interminable shifts of power and series of coups for decades on end.

Frequently cited as causes for military action against civilian regimes are fissures along professional lines — officers against noncommissioned officers — and interservice rivalries. None is plausible, because the conditions that such explanations refer to lack the sense of urgency one would think is required to motivate men to risk their lives. They are plausible explanations only in the abstract, after the event.

What of explanations along ideological lines? Indications are that leaders of the initial 1966 coup in Nigeria, the coups in Libya, Somalia, and Sudan, and the unsuccessful attempt in Morocco in 1971 shared social revolutionary or at least reformist concerns. But here again, the postcoup, or postattempt, explications are accepted too readily.

Africa's armed forces do not as yet contain enough officers sufficiently strong intellectually and sufficiently trained to stage a coup primarily or even principally on ideological grounds. Conspiracies along these lines must surely fail, for at best only a minute group of officers could be contacted and brought to participate actively without causing alarm, without drawing attention to the conspiracy. Such an enterprise could succeed only if by chance a group of ideologically united officers were to be so distributed within the services as to bring together unobtrusively, plausibly whatever strategic and tactical support is required.

Chances that this sort of hookup can be accomplished anywhere on the continent are virtually nil. The Major Nzeogwus are ephemera. The young Ibo officer whose assault on the northern Nigerian leadership triggered the 1966 events in Nigeria was *sui generis*. Apparently a romantic of sorts, zealous in his opposition to corruption and other notorious shortcomings of civilian rule, he found himself quickly and completely isolated shortly after the coup.[28] This cutoff should have surprised no one familiar with the socialization processes of the Nigerian military.

By Major-General A. K. Ocran's own published account, the group of officers responsible for Nkrumah's overthrow in 1966, mainly then Major Afrifa, Colonel Kotoka, and Ocran, actually gave no thought in an organized, systematic fashion to ideological matters. Nor was there the remotest ideological tie to link the principals in the conspiracy nor these to other general officers or the police command who eventually were drawn in. All of the principal military conspirators were men of integrity (disregarding for the moment the awkward point about a soldier's oath), but ideologically motivated they were not.[29] It is quite apparent, from all available evidence, including Ruth First's excellent summary, that many of the social and philosophic concerns alleged to have been at the root of the Ghanaian action were formulated or discovered *after* the event.[30]

Indications are that Colonel Nasser also was far less ideology inclined than subsequent accounts would want us to believe. In that connection, events in Morocco, the Sudan, Libya, and Egypt suggest extreme caution where Islamic traditions are strong. These especially tend to blur ordinary ideological considerations.

Whatever the background, motivations, or precoup objectives, once in possession of the keys to the treasury, the leadership of the armed forces is compelled to increase military appropriations. Justified or not, rank-and-file demands or expectations for salary increases and other prerequisites can be ignored only at risk of further mutiny or rebellion. It matters little to the soldiers whether the years of neglect applied only to the forces or whether, as has generally been true through Africa, salary and wage freezes rather equally disadvantaged all public services. Officers who participate in the government are expected to secure a larger share of benefits for their men.[31] Salary increases and promotions go hand in hand. While civilians, among whom cabinet ministers were most visible, managed to acquire enormous wealth in many instances, and all too frequently by illicit means, the bulk of the armed forces were compelled to accept a life of self-denial, comparatively speaking. Takeover by the military becomes a signal for a reversal of that state of affairs. In addition, dissatisfaction with living accommodations and with the quality and quantity of arms and equipment serve as powerful spurs to further pressure.

Postcoup budgets predictably reflect the new sense of national priorities. Unleashed to seize the controls, the guard must now be pacified and promptly so. The first post-Nkrumah budget for 1966-67 provided substantial increases for the armed forces, mainly at the expense of the vast army of civilian and paramilitary support troops mobilized by the former president to secure his regime. The shift was significant; allocations were transferred from one set of clientele to another, from one type of support troop to another.[32] That precedent was followed by the coup leader who overthrew the second civilian regime in 1971.

When in 1971 Federal Commissioner of Finance for Nigeria Chief Awolowo resigned, he listed in his final report rising defense expenditures as one of the "critical problems" for his ministry. At about the same time, the army chief of staff on a shopping tour for modern arms in Europe announced: "We are reorganizing our army and must buy the best arms for the defense of Nigeria."[33] These two events and the chief of staff's comments are indicative of the horns of a dilemma that prods most of Africa's military leaders in similar positions of power and control. The core of the problem was articulated appropriately also at that time by the permanent secretary in the Ministry of Economics Development, who warned that defense expenditures, although necessary, had to be kept within reasonable bounds "if the nation's ability to deliver the goods in other important spheres is not to be impaired."[34] The choice of words was apt. It is indeed a question of delivery of "goods" being dispensed to diverse client groups.[35]

Five years after the 1966 coup, allocations for the Ghanaian armed forces totaled N$\cancel{C}$40.4 million as compared to N$\cancel{C}$1.8 million for the Ministry of Labour and Cooperatives.[36] This in spite of the pressing need for solution of the unemployment problem, critical shortages in other vital sectors, and the continuing drainage of foreign exchange as a result of staggering indebtedness to foreign creditors.

The position of Nigeria's armed forces relative to other groups competing for resources was enhanced enormously by the exigencies of the civil war. Enlarged from about 8,000 in 1967 to more than 200,000 by 1971, its maintenance cost consumed between one-fifth and one-fourth of the total budget, ranging up to one-third at one point.[37] On conclusion of the civil war, and notwithstanding other obvious needs in state and society, defense and security were classed "as of the first order of priority."[38] It was the translation of this order of priority that rang alarm bells in the more responsible financial and economic development planning circles. Given the staggering backlog of needs inherited from colonial rule and from the decade of civilian misrule after independence — needs exacerbated by the civil war — reduction rather than increase of military expenditures should have been the first order of the day. But reduction could have been accomplished only with demobilization down to the pre-civil-war level or at least not far above it.

Ironically, the same economic constraints that militated against increased allocations of resources to the armed forces also militated against absorption of 100,000 or more demobilized troops into the economy. In absolutely no way could employment opportunities be found for more than a minute percentage of that group. Figures on enrollment in secondary schools, optimum available employment opportunities, and assumed maximum growth of the economy indicated an excess of job seekers over opportunities in the neighborhood of 100,000 in the early 1970s.[39] Demobilized soldiers, barely literate, most likely illiterate, without steady employment are tempted to resort to the one skill they have acquired: they use their weapons either to revolt or to rob.

Injecting former soldiers into the civilian economy poses vexing problems. In Nigeria a raw recruit receiving the lowest army pay earned £N 17 5s per month, which in 1972 was approximately 8 times the per capita income of the average Nigerian. Pay for soldiers with some experience exceeded the pay for skilled employees in industry and commerce. In Uganda a private earned £285 per year, and in Ghana £300 in 1968.[40]

To the Nigerian military regime, by 1972 still in a state of shock over the bloodlettings, coups, and countercoups between 1966 and the end of the civil war, it clearly seemed the lesser of several evils if the armed forces were fully retained for a while. It seemed politic to devise new, even ingenious rationales to justify maintenance of the status quo rather than risk aggravating further the already weak economic condition of the country. Premature demobilization appeared to be an invitation to a social upheaval of the first magnitude.

Of course, such policies bear an exceedingly high price tag. Unfortunately, the price is rising steadily because armed forces victorious in actual combat expect more than maintenance of the status quo ante. They expect more comfortable barracks, more elaborate training facilities, and higher salaries all around. Firm commitments in these respects, including social security arrangements for armed forces personnel and their families, are taken for granted. The inevitable losses and leakages are compounded by insufficient experience in the administration of the swollen force and by the consequences of the impact of the military psychology on fiscal and economic matters. Somehow additional sources of finance must be located.

In Nigeria revenue from mineral oil production, though increasing sharply after the civil war, was expected to remain behind overall requirements to sustain the recovery effort, yet make up for losses incurred during the internal upheaval, and ensure a minimum economic development program to secure future progress. Consequently, the military leadership had to turn itself into a pressure group for increased production in all established sectors. They also were compelled to seek increased foreign aid wherever available. Whatever their ideological inclinations or idiosyncratic preferences, the spokesmen of this particular pressure group in Nigeria as elsewhere tended to opt for policies favoring relations primarily with the more affluent West.

Meanwhile, expenditures by the defense establishment skyrocket. In Nigeria between April 1970 and January 1971 it totaled £N 102 million; the initial vote of appropriation for the entire fiscal year was a mere £N 38.8 million. At the same time, a commission appointed to review wages and salaries was expressly enjoined from examining the military and the police.[41] A new battle was joined, in Nigeria perhaps more than elsewhere, but the effects of the new disposition make themselves felt wherever officers have acquired the means to force open the treasury over the objection of more rational civilian counsel.

J. M. Lee has calculated that "any government wishing to maintain a single battalion of infantry might be required to pay up to £400,000 a year in salaries alone." He adds: "To put such a battalion in the field, with appropriate stores, travelling arrangements and training facilities, might cost at least another £200,000.[42] (Here is one reason African regimes are disinclined to go to war.) Small wonder if the armed forces share of state revenue is rising sharply everywhere. Lee reports that the Congo (Kinshasa) army received "one-sixth of the state revenue in the first fifty-six months" following seizure of power — 25 billion out of 150 billion Congolese francs. The same source estimates that in 1967-68 in French-speaking Africa, 8 out of 15 states had provided the army with between 15 and 25 percent of their resources. "Mali, Guinea, Chad, and Cameroon were prepared to spend up to a quarter of their budgets for military purposes."[43] The full significance of these percentages becomes apparent if they are read against the background of ever rising costs in other, economically critical sectors, and if they are considered in light of steadily deteriorating world trade conditions and generally rising budget deficits.

Following a coup or the victorious outcome of a civil war, the armed forces' insistence on high priority consideration of their grievances becomes ever more strident; higher civil servants still intent on balancing budgets and making social ends meet financial resources find that the new class of politicians in uniform is considerably less flexible in its demands and in bargaining posture than the previous civilian leadership. Generals and colonels, it turns out, are less inclined to brook resistance than are civilian cabinet ministers. Beyond that, the transformation of the military from service status to that of master of the house begets new group interests and new demands. Inexorably, power also corrupts the military.

Of the major sources of corruption, two may be singled out as most pervasive. The first is universal and simply relates to the human impulse to maximize social security and well-being while the opportunity lasts. Having already broken the law of the land by the act of insurrection, the officer in position to implement his wish can easily improve his personal fortunes by bending lesser legal barriers. Evidence is mounting that general officers and colonels in Africa are following closely in the footsteps of their analogues in Latin America. Unfortunately, dependence of each succeeding regime on the armed forces tends to discourage the few post-military governments Africa will see from probing into the financial acitvities of military commanders. The world is not likely to witness the kind of investigation that military regimes in Ghana, Sierra Leone, Uganda, and Nigeria conducted to discredit their civilian predecessors. (The post-coup Nigerian inquiries tactfully refrained from examining questionable operations of civilians allied with the new military rulers.)

Because none of the economies aside from Egypt and the Union of South Africa produce more than incidental material support for their armed forces, the lion's share of budgetary allocations earmarked for the forces eventually ends up in the hands of foreign suppliers. In the United States the military consumption potential coupled with the economy's capacity to meet that need has enabled the armed forces command to become brokers for industry and commerce and increasingly actually representatives of private interests. But the African military commands usually have very few plums to bestow, a situation that reduces their capability to participate in internal pressure plays. They have few favors to trade for benefits, votes, and general support for their purposes unless they manage by fraudulent means to divert funds allocated to the services.

In Nigeria, for instance, officers were reported to have accepted inferior equipment from foreign suppliers at grossly inflated prices, and the difference was split among the partners.[44] Forces in the Congo (Kinshasa), Morocco, Egypt, Sierra Leone, and Nigeria at one time or another and in diverse ways appear to have contrived to increase their share of the wealth by illicit or illegal means with some increment of their pressure and influence capabilities vis-a-vis other contenders for power. Still the net gain to the forces as a whole from that direction is negligible.

Increasingly, a greater proportion of the African military appears to discard scruples and join the parade of claimants for public funds for purposes wholly extraneous to their mission. Interestingly, once they are in control of information media, many of the uniformed, self-appointed precoup scourges of bribery and corruption turn out to be quite remorseless in their endeavors to suppress evidence of armed forces misconduct. Predictably, if censorship is imposed by the military, it is represented as defense of law and order, always in the public interest. In light of the trend it is prudent to heavily discount as indexes of armed forces pressure potential even dramatically high financial allocations to the military. Funds diverted from their authorized purposes tend to be lost to the group as a whole and serve mainly, if not exclusively, the interests of individuals.

It is important in this context to focus on one additional line of argument advanced by analysis of the military in Africa. They state that somehow at one point in time the military as a group entered into politics whereas prior to that entry it was outside politics.[45] As noted elsewhere, this argument is possible only if one takes a rather vague and exceedingly narrow view of *politics*. Considering the nexus between economic resources and maintenance of a military establishment as integrally related to politics, and considering also the possibility that politics without economics is a form of social entertainment, the entry of the military into politics is a nonevent. If they required pay, promotions and expansion, equipment facilities, housing, and so on, they along with all other demand and interest groups were in the political arena from the moment of their inception as a group or an organization. The fact of their deep involvement simply was concealed from view by a screen made of a convenient social fiction — namely, noninvolvement of the military in politics. By the same token, if the military never really was outside politics as here conceptualized, it never really can depart from it. In my view it never really does depart.

Lineup of military interest groups throughout the continent as they relate to the competition for limited resources will find in most favored positions those who have directed access to the principal decision and policymakers and who dispose of the most potent means of generating pressure. In that hierarchy, those who are in control of the military communications network (the intelligence gathering function), have the edge, assuming always they are efficient enough to take advantage of their opportunities.

Agricultural Producers

Even in a comparatively stable and settled society, distinctions between diverse layers of agricultural producers become blurred as one group invariably blends into another. In Africa, still very far removed from any kind of stability, identification of clear definitional boundaries separating peasants from farmers may be intellectually satisfying but is wholly impractical for the development planner. Yet references to an African peasantry abound in political literature, suggesting a conviction abroad that the African peasant represents a solid social force, ready to engage or be engaged collectively in some kind of social action.

The International Economic Association at its 1961 meeting in Addis Ababa offered four classificatory groupings for agriculture based on stages of development: (1) purely subsistence activities; (2) mainly subsistence but with some sales for cash; (3) largely or mainly commercial agriculture; and (4) entirely commercial. The report of the association sees "a great majority" in stage (2) where the value of their subsistence production exceeds that of their sales, and finds that the main process now going on is between stage (2) and stage (3). It notes that probably in the Ivory Coast, Ghana, and Nigeria a good many African producers have moved into stage (3).[1]

At a different level, Nkrumah in attempting to identify operationally meaningful class distinctions refers to peasants as "those who cultivate negligible areas of land, and are often forced to sell their labour power to become seasonal workers."[2] To him the agricultural social structure consists of the following major and sub-groups.[3]

> The exploiting classes:
> (1) plantation owners
> (2) "absentee" landowners
> (3) farmers (comparatively large property owners)
> (4) petty farmers

The exploited classes:
  (1) peasants
  (2) rural proletariat

Nkrumah's classifications do not quite correspond to those employed by more orthodox Marxists. Soviet academician Potekhin, for example, differentiates between "planters and rich peasants managing their farms on a capitalist basis" as against peasants who follow either collective-traditional or socialist modes of production.[4] Western writers seem to be less concerned with such distinctions and use both terms interchangeably.

For our purposes, peasants are wholly or mainly occupied in subsistence agriculture and do not own all or most of the land they till and derive their livelihoods from. They do not differ materially from the lowest in Nkrumah's "exploiter" class, the petty farmers.

If aggregate wealth and numbers alone were the keys to success in the struggle for power, the African peasantry and the farmers should be the dominant force on the continent today. Together they produce by far the largest share of the continent's wealth, account for some two-thirds or more of the population, and in 1964 were reported to account for 39.4 percent of total GDP of the continent (at factor cost), excluding South Africa.[5] Typically they generated nearly all of the foreign exchange needed to keep state and society together. The majority of the peasantry, however, are out of touch with the modern cash economy.[6]

Peasants

In spite of its manifest weakness, the peasantry has been projected into the struggle for power in Africa as something akin to the Great Silent Majority discovered by political party strategists in the 1970 federal election in the United States. Of course, neither in the United States nor in Africa does citation of the great silent majority signify intent to involve it actually and directly in decision making. The intent usually is solely to persuade whoever needs to be persuaded that the mythical majority is behind the self-proclaimed spokesman. So it is with the African peasant.

Kwame Nkrumah was such a spokesman, self-appointed, perhaps, but increasingly popular. Reassessing the prospect for social revolutionary change on the continent after his fall, he visualized the situation as follows. "In Africa, the peasantry is by far the largest contingent of the working class, and potentially the main force for socialist revolution. But it is dispersed, unorganized, and for the most part unrevolutionary. It must be awakened and it must be led by its natural class allies — the proletariat and the revolutionary intelligentsia."[7] This rather broad perspective is generally shared by Soviet and Communist Chinese theoreticians but stands in marked contrast to Nkrumah's performance when as ruler of Ghana he had the opportunity to translate theory into practice. After his fall, *the African Communist* speculated that one of Nkrumah's major tactical errors may have been his failure to apply the formula recommended by Frantz Fanon; he should indeed have organized the peasants in defense of his regime.

By all indications anyone banking on the African peasantry to support revolutionary action is likely to be disappointed. In the real world the African peasant has little chance of taking on his antagonists, be they Nkrumah's bourgeoisie, Fanon's feudal leaders, or just plain capitalist imperialist exploiters. This for a number of reasons, several of which Nkrumah recognized: illiteracy, lack of access to capable leadership and to organizational technology, and as a group extreme susceptibility to fragmentation usually along ethnic lines, causing them to be easily set one against another by extraneous interests. To the modern economic planner, socialist or capitalist, the African peasant serves two prime functions. To the extent he is engaged in production of an export crop he contributes to the foreign exchange fund. Beyond that he is a source of low-wage labor, which as the need arises can be returned to its home base without cost to government in terms of unemployment compensation, welfare payments, and the like. The wage labor function characterizes the greater part of the peasantry as here defined.

It is possible that Nkrumah's "peasants," if ever they can be detached from the farmers, especially the wealthier ones, will provide the ideal setting for the social revolution he envisaged. "The countryside is the bastion of the revolution," he wrote somewhat hopefully. "[It] is the revolutionary battle field in which the peasantry together with their natural class allies — the proletariat and the revolutionary intelligentsia — are the driving force for socialist construction and transformation."[9] The vision is reminiscent of the Russian revolution, but hardly relevant. Can the African peasantry really be separated from the dominant large landowners, planters, or farmers? Can it really be separately organized and separately led? Available evidence points overwhelmingly to the defeat of any such design in this day and age, on the African continent.

The talakawa of Northern Nigeria, the wananchi of Kenya, probably all peasants and smaller farmers, are and for a long time to come will remain in the firm grip of the traditional overlords and their successors.

Oginga Odinga, unofficial spokesman of East Africa's rural masses, entitles one chapter in *Not Yet Uhuru* "Peasants in Revolt."[10] It is significant that this very chapter illustrates not the revolutionary potential but the impotence of the African peasantry. What Odinga actually shows is that peasant dissatisfaction with colonial land and agricultural policies at best provided the real revolutionary elements — principally African trade union leaders, ex-servicemen, and a few wealthy African businessmen plus a handful of local Indian militants — with a base for their assault on colonial rule. Odinga shows that in Kenya the peasantry, including the

Mau Mau movement, far from being an instrument of revolution, served as a mere tool of urban and urban-led militants, most of whom were quite unrelated to and disinterested in rural affairs.

All too often revolutions are attempted or staged on the peasants' back. This was the case in the great revolutions in Russia and China and is the case in Africa now. Illustrations abound, cases in point are Mulele's short-lived revolt in Congo (Kinshasa), the Hutu uprising in Rwanda, Oginga Odinga's attempts in Kenya, the more modest efforts of the Northern Elements Progressive Union in Northern Nigeria (in the fifties and sixties), the ill-fated attempts by the Sudanese Communists in the seventies. The very thought of social revolution seems to repel the African peasant as it does the African farmer. Like all masses, peasants can be moved to violence, but that is not saying that they can be relied on to sustain actual revolutionary action. In these circumstances, weak as it is the African peasantry can be discounted as an effective pressure group. At best it serves as a foil for others.

Farmers

Unlike the American farmer, the African farmer has not been able to institutionalize his potential. There has not been an opportunity, for example, to develop the legal-constitutional web of federalism favoring rural power that characterized American politics for more than a century. The African farmer was just coming into his own during and following World War II, mainly in West Africa and somewhat in East Africa, when his efforts to capture the strategic control points from the departing colonial administration were frustrated by a colonial counterstrategy that allowed urban-dominated forces to secure all command positions. It appears to have been established policy under colonial rule to interdict if possible the formation of truly independent and effective pressure groups in the agricultural sector primarily to ensure favorable bargaining conditions for white settlers, especially in the labor market.[11] (Herein lies one of the most important but generally obscured differences between the American (1776) and African "revolutions.")

In any case, the legal-constitutional channels through which rural forces of European origin seized and maintained power in the United States never materialized for the black African farmers. They did materialize, of course, for the European farmer in Rhodesia, Portuguese Angola and Mozambique, and South Africa. Consequently, African farmer interests had to contend with their antagonists — mainly commercial, bureaucratic, industrial, and in some places ideological — on a straight power basis.

Unprotected by well-entrenched institutional safeguards, African farmer interests, like that of peasants, is quickly dispersed, divided, and cut down to segments where it can be contained with relative ease. Only where the need for foreign exchange is truly desperate and where farm groups are highly concentrated can substantial pressure plays be mounted.

Anyone who wants to divide the farmers in order to dominate and control them can count on assistance from the ubiquitous middlemen and other parasitic interests who attach themselves in large numbers to the farmer and his product and who interpose themselves between the farmer and his principal customer, the government. The African farmer is compelled to deal with government, for alone he is unable to reach his markets, which pending development of the economy at home continue to be located primarily overseas. Without government assistance he cannot begin to cope with the staggering technical problems of marketing, export, or transport; mastery of the complexities of international commerce and finance is totally beyond his capabilities.

Undoubtedly, capitalist economic policies cultivate and exacerbate the class divisions within the farmer group that sap its collective potential. It turns out to be quite easy for government to skim off, under one pretext or another, substantial portions of farm income, especially income earned by large-scale farmers.

An inventory of farmer interests must include, of course, maximization of net income — that is, income after taxes, after the middleman's take, and after administrative overhead. Steadily deteriorating world market conditions make this maximization a matter of desperate urgency to ever growing numbers. The farmer must simultaneously decrease the cost of his own basic food and supplies, both of which are caught up in the inflationary spiral at home and abroad. He must reduce the cost of loans needed to tie him over the lean period between harvests. But wherever he turns he encounters the intermediaries, the layers above him, who seem to thrive on his weaknesses, foremost his economic dependence, his lack of education, and, it must be added, his gullibility and imprudence when in possession of large sums of cash. All of this drives the African farmer further into the arms of government, as does his desire to enjoy undivided possession of productive land, a desire fanned in part by the exigencies of modern cash economy and in part by other modernizing influences that promote individuality over the collectivism characteristic of traditional life.

The best known case of landhunger turned into an explosive social demand arose in Kenya. There the drive for land quickly became fused with other issues, acquiring revolutionary momentum in the process. The Kenya story has been well covered in the so-called *Dow Report,* in Odinga's and Jomo Kenyatta's books, and in several government papers published after independence.[12] One glance at the maps accompanying the *Dow Report* graphically illustrates the sources of deep emotional commitment to land: in this case as in so many others large tracts of the most fertile land had been alienated from the traditional users. In the circumstances "[L]and

and all it had come to stand for, remained an emotional force capable of creating a degree of unity among the otherwise divided Kikuyu."[13]

Because land alienation had, in effect, drawn a black-white dividing line across the Kenyan landscape, race inevitably became a focal point for contention. Racial sensitivities were not far removed from emotions fed by deep-rooted tribal and traditional attachment to land as a prime source of prestige and as a tangible insurance against the uncertainties of life. Race remains a major source of tension as long as Europeans are permitted to remain ensconced in prominent positions in the economy generally and in agriculture in particular.

In Zambia, Kenya, and the Ivory Coast, for example, government revenue continues to depend to a critical extent on the comparatively high productivity of the European element in the economy. Because European run or owned farms and plantations are more efficient, hence more of an asset to an ailing economy, governments continue to display favoritism toward Europeans, inevitably stoking resentment along racial lines in the process. African farmers will not forget the indignities that Europeans inflicted on them under colonial rule. It is difficult for them to shed the past when the competitive advantage Europeans enjoy after independence resembles so closely their monopoly position of colonial days.

The drive for land continues even after the race issue should have become defused by large-scale emigration of Europeans. After several thousand of the white farmers had departed from the Kenya highlands, which Kikuyus and others had coveted so ardently, the animals roaming the surrounding game reserves became the target, along with the preserves as well as the tourist industry based on both.

The massive Kenya Land Settlement Scheme, though remarkable in many respects, actually fell far short of popular expectations.[14] The scheme, a product of the Mau Mau rebellion and its aftermath, yields impressive statistics, which unless interpreted and heavily discounted could all too easily invite overly optimistic assessment of farmer interest group potential. By 1965 Africans owned and operated 750 large-scale farms, which covered some 600,000 acres. However, it seems that actually, quite like other creations of the postindependence era, the farms turned out to be more of a liability than an asset to African interests.

The financial requirements accompanying transfer of the farms from European hands exhausted the meager resources of Africans, leaving them with very little working capital to cope with the initial demands posed by the wholly unfamiliar operation. Loan repayments quickly proved to be beyond the exhausted resources. Lack of skills to run large and complex farms added to their woes; although semispecialized skills had been acquired by many of the Africans, the broad-gauge, overall command of large-scale farming had yet to be developed. In its 1966 review of the then-incipient program the Kenya government noted a sharp drop in production, to about 20 percent of pretransfer levels. Not included in this accounting were the deterioration of the means of production, the land itself, the equipment, the cattle, and the houses taken over from Europeans.[15]

The focal point in any political-economic analysis of the farmer's pressure potential at the national level remains his contribution to foreign exchange earnings, modified by the degree to which alternate sources of revenue are being developed. Since the trend indicates continued dependence on agriculture, primarily because of the high cost of and generally poor prospects for industrialization, the pressure environment is likely to remain substantially unchanged for decades to come.

Like the colonial administration before, African rulers must regard as a policy aim of the highest priority the containment of farm pressure for an increased share of the wealth. A successful or even partially successful farm revolt in all probability would spell economic disaster. This possibility determines the outer parameters of farm pressure potential. Government must seek to maximize agricultural production while holding to a minimum farm income; where the line cannot be held, government must recapture some of the increment granted through increased taxation. Widespread inability to exact revenue by these means compels adoption of a rather firm if not rigid stance vis-à-vis farmer demands.

All too often the reality of the situation is obscured by fantasies about capital being generated in the farm sector through increased income accompanied by forced saving; the stratagem is expected to result in sharply increased productivity but fails consistently. Plans along these lines must remain on the drafting board for want of appropriate infrastructure, underdevelopment of the requisite fiscal apparatus, and absence of a social and economic climate that could generate sufficient confidence to encourage saving and induce investment.

The inevitable contradictions are increasingly reflected in the public rhetoric of policymakers. As wild promises and pledges give way to sober assessments of a rapidly deteriorating situation, farm resentment builds up, creating a climate of suspicion and hostility that invites repressive measures in turn. For some time to come, development strategy is constrained to motivate the farmer to increase production without granting him anywhere near the reward he expects or has been led to expect. At the same time, revenue extracted from the farmer will, to his further dismay, continue to be applied to the solution of pressing social and economic problems in the more troublesome urban concentrations. Unfortunately efforts to apply surplus from agriculture to achieve a modicum of economic diversification also accrue, by their very nature, mainly to interests in or near cities.

In these circumstances only a few special groupings of African farmers actually have prospered. (Measured by colonial standards, nearly all of Africa's farmers have experienced some improvement in their per capita income, but in terms of rising costs and increasing taxation few even approach the plateau of economic satisfaction.) Compared with farmers in developed countries, the African farmer is steadily losing ground.[16]

Frequently mentioned examples of success are the West African cocoa farmer and the East African coffee planter. Concerning the cocoa farmer, the widely cited phenomenon of the amazingly successful small farmer tenaciously clinging to his allegedly age-old position in Ghana, or Nigeria is a myth. To be sure, small farmers are everywhere. They are, however, extremely weak, increasingly at the mercy of predators in government and commerce, and generally fighting a losing battle. The large-scale farmer dominates. In Nigeria, for example, inequality in land distribution resulted eventually in 9 percent of all farmers holding more than one-third of cultivated land in the 1950s.[17]

Superficially viewed, the position of the large-scale African farmer in West Africa would seem secure because he remains indirectly the prime source of badly needed foreign exchange. Judging by official statements at budget time, everything seems to revolve around him: he must be supported; his enterprise must be rewarded; government through research and experimentation must help him solve production problems, improve his land and his crop, improve transportation facilities to expedite marketing and export, and so on. In reality, the wealthier the farmer, the more securely he will be tied up in the web of government; as an interest group even this category discovers that most bargaining chips are on the side of government and administration.

The large-scale cocoa farmer typically employs wage labor drawn mainly from neighboring countries. This importation brings in its wake problems of immigration, residence and work permits, and international financial transactions — workers' remittance of earnings across national boundaries. As Polly Hill has pointed out, even the small-scale cocoa farmer (in Ghana) can be classified as businessman.[18] This designation is even more appropriate to the large-scale farmer who operates with borrowed capital, engages in complicated banking maneuvers, issues leases, even establishes branches. The ramifications of this type of operation bring him into direct contact with government and administration to an extent that it becomes difficult at times to determine where the private sphere ends and the public one begins.

The position of the East African coffee grower, another example of relative prosperity and success, is somewhat different, but the social end effect of his operation is the same: he, too, is unable to escape the impositions of nonfarming interests. His product accounts for about 30 percent of total export earnings in Kenya (1970), for 18.2 percent in Tanzania (1966), for 58-60 percent (1970) in Uganda. Severely restrictive policies enforced under colonial rule limited the area an African coffee farmer was permitted to cultivate; even the number of trees he could grow was limited by statute. Compelled to keep his operations at a low level, the East African coffee farmer, if he hoped to remain economically alive, was forced to become more efficient.[19]

Still the coffee farmer remained comparatively weak, especially where European planters remained the favorites of government.[20] Beyond that the rough winds of international trade, world price fluctuations, and changing consumer tastes in the developed countries set in motion additional forces that were totally beyond his control or ken. Today, like the West African cocoa farmer, he, too, is firmly hemmed in by government, administration, commerce, and finance. If he is to successfully prosecute his interests he will have to penetrate the thick intervening layers of local government officials and functionaries, middlemen, purchasing agents, traders, and bankers.

Cooperatives seem to be the answer to the farmer's prayers, but like all other forms of organization in developing areas they seem to be endowed in literature with more interest and pressure potential than they actually deserve. The fault lies mainly in overreliance on legislative instruments that give them their start, in misinterpretation of the intent behind the laws, in overconfidence in the ability of administrators to implement whatever the intent really is.

To be sure, agricultural cooperatives serve many useful purposes. It has been pointed out, for instance, that the cooperative is "socially and politically desirable because it encourages producers, for example, to be self-reliant, thrifty, and ready to submerge individual interests for the greater good of a community of producers." The same source also finds that "participation in co-operation is economically desirable because it acquaints producers with the problems of markets and of business organization, and so enables them to see their problems as producers more intelligently in the larger setting of economic life; it also may widen the range of alternatives open to them."[21] The actual record of performance of cooperatives in Africa has actually been quite disappointing. No one, of course, expected them to secure at once a greater share of the wealth for their membership, but they have not done well as interest group outlets either.

Agricultural cooperatives came into existence under colonial rule mainly to combine the meager capital resources and limited skills of indigenous farmers struggling to free themselves from the traders, middlemen, distributors, and processors whose interests were directly contrary to theirs but whose resources were far superior. For obvious reasons they had virtually no chance to unfold their potential until after independence.[22] But weaknesses inherent in nearly all organizations started by former subject peoples to improve their lot against overwhelming economic odds locally and internationally stunted their growth and development even when they enjoyed at least nominal support and encouragement from African governments.

In Tanzania, for example, it appears to have been official government policy to accord local cooperatives "monopoly rights over collection and distribution of certain commodities."[23] Yet in practice cooperatives there were mere service adjuncts for government. The seeming paradox is illustrated in the following comment by one observer: "Co-operatives are themselves major economic groups in most districts, but they have not functioned as organized interest groups for cash-crop farmers."[24] The reason is that throughout Africa farm cooperatives, like most other organizations that exist along the periphery of power, are unable to defy the prevailing law of political-economic gravity; if they promise even the slightest economic benefit, like a successful small businessman in the United States they are penetrated at once by the revenue-hungry larger patronage system.

In fairness to government and administration, it must be remembered that at this stage in their development the typical African cooperative constitutes an extremely poor investment risk. It may indeed be a liability to government if left uncontrolled and unsupervised.[25]

Whatever the background or explanation, the African farmer organized in cooperatives or operating individually finds himself in the position of the hare racing the tortoise. He is firmly sandbagged by officialdom, by political parasites and leeches clustering around all sources of patronage; he is hamstrung by regulations more exploitative than regulatory. As a result his energies and those of his true representatives are sapped. Far too many fronts must be attended to, too many palms greased, too many predators fended off.

Lacking access to physical force, farmers must generate economic force. There really is no alternative. Yet experience shows that government quickly counters any attempt to create an independent pressure campaign chest. Specifically, the ruling circles recognize the threat were their golden goose to achieve a substantial measure of economic independence. When the cocoa farmers in several regions of Ghana attempted to create an independent war chest in order to strengthen the producers against the Nkrumah regime at the national center, the regime countered first by neutralizing then by subverting and eventually by capturing potential donors, foremost key traditional rulers and their financial supporters.

The African farmer generally is not the world's most efficient producer. Increasingly he must turn to government for assistance. Staggering losses threaten when disease strikes the cocoa tree, and only massive countermeasures by government-sponsored agencies can stem the tide. Only government intervention can control the cost of labor. Like the Senegalese peanut farmer, the cocoa producer is perennially squeezed by seasonal cyclical movements of money and commodity and always in need of financial support — loans to tide him over lean periods and to enable him to buy equipment and, when necessary, plant or replant. In practice, this need can be met only out of government resources, which tends to reduce the overall potential of farm groups. Independent credit and thrift societies have been proposed to widen the margin of independence, but the chronic absence of fundamental incentives to postpone gratification, to save, and to invest has frustrated efforts along these lines.[26]

It would be a mistake if one were to regard the pressure play between government and officialdom on the one hand and the farmer on the other as strictly a bilateral two-party proposition. Beneath the cover of government office or, perhaps better, behind the government facade operate myriads of private and semiprivate, legal as well as illegal interests, all seeking to extract from the agricultural milk-cow something for themselves.[27] It is not even advisable to accept that groups officially labeled as farm connected, such as farmers' unions, are in fact representing farmers' interests. In order to obtain whatever is required, the African farmer frequently finds that he is dealing with officialdom in a private capacity. To put it differently, money flowing into agriculture tends to stick to more fingers than does money flowing into commerce or industry. The farmer's relative lack of experience and technical developments, as well as his educational deficiencies, prevent him from detecting deceit, misrepresentation, and fraud, thereby opening up vast opportunities for the sharp operator who approaches him in the guise of a representative of distant, impersonal authority.

A commission of inquiry looking into disturbances in Western Nigeria in 1968 found that many of the witnesses who offered testimony on behalf of the farmers were, in fact, not farmers at all. It turned out that nonfarm interests had discovered the pressure potential emanating from the much-abused farm community, had maneuvered themselves into positions of power within farmers' organizations, and had indeed encouraged riots and acts of violence against persons and property but principally to further causes unrelated to basic farm interests.[28] What were the recommendations for elimination of this condition? The commission urged that effective organization of farm interests would require "educated leadership." This would, of course, be no improvement at all.

Instead of being exploited by outsiders wholly disinterested in his welfare, the farmer would by this formula simply be handed over to bureaucrats or technical advisers or a combination thereof. Unfortunately, bureaucrats are not incorruptible. Moreover, their perspectives on economic affairs in general and of agricultural matters in particular are characteristically at odds with those held by the producers themselves. Chances are that for the farmer the "educated" spokesman is no spokesman at all.

Additional traps are set for the African farmer. Poorly or not at all represented, he may find himself deeply engaged in battles of dubious value to himself personally or to his group. This situation is not new. Rural masses, peasants and farmers, perhaps because they usually are not too sophisticated, have been exploited by sharp operators since the beginning of recorded history. It seems that in 1966 the farmers of Northern Nigeria allowed themselves to be persuaded that elimination of Ibos would immediately improve their lot, a mistaken belief that appears to have triggered a very bloody massacre at that time. It is most doubtful that th massacre bettered the peanut planter's fortunes by one shilling. One must hope that such history will not repeat itself in East Africa, but the portents of race war fanned by demagogues among the rural masses are visible. The targets are the Asian merchants. One observer's comment on the topic is instructive not only on African-Asian race relations but also in regard to the interest group prospects of the East African farmer generally.

> Those who took the initiative in challenging the Asian merchants were not the ordinary peasants, but the African "entrepreneurs" in the countryside, who found the Asians standing in their way. These entrepreneurs, by appealing to the peasants and telling them that they were "their men," as opposed to the Asians, who were "outsiders," managed to use the co-operative to strengthen not only their own economic position but also their political control over the countryside.[29]

Soon thereafter the cooperatives were converted into alternate instruments of exploitation of the agricultural producers. (Incidentally, the author seems to have reference to farmers rather than to peasants.)

Assumed that farmers somewhere on the continent manage to organize themselves independently, can they hope to eventually generate sufficient pressure potential to compel acceptance of their demands? The farm vote obviously has lost its value in all but a few countries, since elections have gone out of fashion nearly everywhere on the continent. While elections were still in vogue, mainly, of course, before independence, the farm vote of necessity blended into the traditional vote. Alliances between farmer and tribal-traditional interests were a prominent feature of electoral campaigns in Ghana between 1951 and the early 1960s. In Uganda until the one-party system was proclaimed there, the Kabaka Yekka represented the interests of the traditional Baganda elite as well as the interests of wealthy Baganda farmers.[30] Similar constellations such as the Action Group and the Northern Peoples' Congress emerged in Nigeria; indeed, traditional rule-farmer alliances characterized rural politics in virtually all countries where multiparty elections were still conducted.

Nkrumah insists that alliances between traditional rulers and large-scale farmers are one of the mainstays of imperialist rule on the continent.[31] His thesis tends to be supported by scholarly evidence, which suggests that the famed British system of indirect rule relied strongly on just such a combination in Uganda as it did in Northern Nigeria, and French rule appears to have benefited greatly where combinations along these lines could be engineered.[32]

Except for the minute group of countries where governments still are being elected honestly and fairly, the sole remaining element of farm leverage is denial of farm product to government and consumer generally —

that is, influence through deprivation. As in all other pressure plays, considerable skill, organizing ability, and, of course, effective leadership are required. Exceedingly few farm organizations or movements appear to have been able to put together the required combination, although motivations to resort to this form of pressure certainly have been high and are increasing.

Aside from the famous cocoa holdout in the then Gold Coast in 1937-38, perhaps the outstanding example of this tactic was the peanut farmer strike in Senegal in 1965. But once again we have reason to believe that the prime force making this particular strike possible is to be found in the traditional-religious sphere. In all probability the marabouts and their organizing ability constituted the critical element here.[33] Be that as it may, farm prices and related conditions were the issue. Since independence cocoa farmers in league with interested traditional rulers appear to have engaged in some kind of concerted action from time to time, but this point cannot be established with certainty. It is possible that food shortages, held to have contributed to Nkrumah's downfall, according to some observers, also may have been artificially induced as a form of farmer protest.

Different socioeconomic conditions in French-influenced areas have differently affected the pressure environment for farmers. In the Ivory Coast, for instance, indigenous farmers must cope with the presence of French competitors who, unlike British settlers in Kenya, remained even after independence under the direct protective umbrella of the French control element in the new African regime. Until recently (about 1964) this protection was balanced by advantages that flowed from the protective status agricultural products from French or former French territories enjoyed.[34]

On balance, however, indications are that the African farmer in the Ivory Coast, where he has attained the highest level of prosperity, may not encounter much support or sympathy in the future if the drive to industrialize the country and diversify the economy through industrialization is allowed to proceed unchecked. It is significant that no alarm seems to be reflected in official references to the flight from land, in favor of the cities, which in the absence of substantial technological improvement hemorrhages agriculture. Portents of things to come are conveyed in the comment, probably from a French technical adviser to the Ivorienne government, that urbanization is not a serious problem in part because such developed countries as the United States and the Soviet Union also experienced it. (!)[35]

Given the deteriorating conditions that affect the African farmer deprived of the protective shield of a guaranteed French, and beyond that European, market, and given the African farmer's proven though temporary inability to compete successfully at home or abroad unless protected and subsidized, it is quite possible that development planners in the Ivory Coast, in Senegal, and certainly in the less productive areas of the former French empire are prepared to let African agriculture find its natural level as soon as revenue-producing alternatives have been secured. In those conditions the farmer's plaints are likely to receive sympathy only as they signal imminent shortfalls in revenue or serious food shortages.

Criticism to the effect that governments are not doing enough to shore up African farming misses the central problem. Again, Kenya's spokesman for the opposition, Oginga Odinga, indicts his country's government for failure to support the farm cooperatives, for permitting Europeans to purchase lands after independence, and for granting to foreigners incentives they were unwilling to grant Africans.[36] Similar criticisms are made continuously throughout the continent for entirely understandable reasons: governments really have little choice, given prevailing social philosophies and socioeconomic development targets. This would include, in all probability, a government led by Odinga as it included the government led by Nkrumah.

In the final analysis the conditions likely to govern Africa's position in the world, especially regarding export of agricultural commodities to the more highly developed countries, is such that no African regime can allow agricultural interest groups to negotiate directly with customer nations and international combinations. Unlike the European farmer who has somewhat dominated negotiations surrounding Britain's entry into the Common Market, the African farmer, as noted, has no real leverage left. Affecting the outcome of negotiations between producer and consumer countries, such as the on-going discussions with the British Commonwealth, the European Common Market, and the United States, will be government decisions that reflect not so much the farmer's interests as those of treasuries or ministries of finance. The prime objective of African diplomatic negotiations must after all be preservation of the foreign exchange balance or what there is left of that. The colonial heritage has firmly tethered African agricultural production to the industrial nations. The resultant client status spells economic thralldom for the African farmer for a long time to come, notwithstanding official pats on the farmer's back.

18

Labor

Historic Roots

Except for certain sets of circumstances and only in exceedingly few national systems, African labor relates to its antagonists and bargaining partners or opponents as butter does to the knife. It does not have much to show for several decades of organized effort to improve its position. Although wages have increased slightly, cost of living has risen more sharply. Wages are well above whatever income the African peasant can secure, but they are dismal if compared to compensation paid to labor's principal competitors for a share of the economic pie. Government and business, the bureaucracy and public enterprises, and even foreign enterprises seem to do far better by any measure than does labor.

Independence, of course, by itself brought labor no real gains whatsoever. To the contrary, soon after the new flag had been raised, organized as well as unorganized workers were promptly harnessed to the national chariot and were exhorted relentlessly to strive for goals essentially unrelated to traditional trade union interests. Substantial relief is nowhere in sight, whether the system be capitalist or socialist. The feeble economies simply cannot bear the added strain of wage increases or substantial improvements in working conditions, at least not as currently constituted.

Only after a certain plateau of economic productivity is reached can African labor expect material gains, and then only if radical social changes have first altered the overall socioeconomic control structure. Since indications are that the distance separating the worker from what he may regard as his just reward is still lengthening, it would seem that a chapter on pressure and interest fortunes of African labor should perhaps not be carried further. But the story is worth telling if for no reason other than it illustrates once again the considerable difference between shadow and substance as African social organizations are concerned.

Observable reality has not prevented a certain euphoria to permeate literature on the subject. This attitude can be traced to liberal observers' practice of a form of ideological wishful thought or self-deception and to an inclination of number-oriented students of social organization to be overly impressed by large concentrations of people. We have reason to believe that many if not most of the ideological garments worn by African workers' organizations were furnished by sympathetic emissaries dispatched by British Labour, the French political Left, socialist as well as Communist-led Western trade unions, and equally well-meaning partisans and agents of the socialist countries of the world.[1]

Whatever the source of inspiration or guidance, it was widely assumed that African labor would take on the emissary's ideological coloration, but it has done so only in exceptional circumstances and then only in a most superficial manner. As a rule, labor and labor organizations remained what they had been from the beginning, ideologically aimless and colorless, still captive social organisms, and extremely vulnerable, therefore, to exploitation and abuse.

Labor's historical role in the reduction of foreign control also has been exaggerated. To be sure, workers, and in some cases trade unions and certainly individual trade union trained leaders played a part in the march to independence. But it was only an auxiliary and short-lived performance. At best African labor can be credited with providing the spark that kindled the flame of independence in isolated cases — for example, in the 1947 railway strike in French West Africa.[2] Most important, unlike workers in the industrial countries the African worker did not have to sacrifice part of his wages for scores of decades to facilitate capital formation, which, in turn, eventually furnishes a solid basis for real independence. In time he may be called on to do just that, but with the exception of a few special industrial contingents he has not yet been in that position.[3]

As the past performance of African labor has been misconstrued, so has its future. One example of a form of analytical quantum jump, based perhaps on misreading of the Russian Revolution, may suffice to illustrate the point.

> In spite of the small percentage engaged in wage-labour, the workers hold a strategic place in the economies of the new nations. Because they are concentrated in precisely those industries and services on which economic development depends, they have the potential directly to influence and even control the political machine.[4]

The accuracy of this prognostication is doubtful. Indeed, it is most doubtful whether political machines are that committed to economic development, and if they are whether they are susceptible to influence and control by labor. The opposite seems to be true.

Whether class distinctions can be drawn in Africa today also is very debatable, in particular whether African labor possesses class consciousness to a degree sufficient to motivate and then sustain it in a drive for power. As we shall show, it is not even certain that labor can launch, let alone sustain, a concerted action in pursuit of limited labor-related objectives in most of Africa. Actually, it should be most difficult for the realist to detect even the barest outlines of class among Africa's workers unless, of course, he takes a very broad view of the term. Rather than class consciousness, we may be witnessing simply ordinary human reaction to insecurity or economic deprivation, reflections of an ordinary desire to keep body and soul together. Even where the language of class warfare is heard one should keep in mind that the cock's crowing does not by itself bring the morning.

A former member of the British Communist Party seems to go beyond this pessimism, if pessimism it is, when he asserts quite firmly that

> there is not now and never has been any such thing, politically or economically, as a working class. There are workers, wage-earners, by the million, but neither in theory nor in practice do they have any class identity of the kind that Marx describes. They have a life-style, they have powerful clan-like local and craft allegiances, but a sense of class-in-action they do not have.[5]

He was speaking of labor in one of the world's most highly industrialized nations, Great Britain, though the words were intended to apply far more widely.

In Africa the myth of the working class is kept alive by empathic Soviet and other social philosophers highly motivated to give the worker his due and committed, quite rigidly as a rule, to a specific point of view. The myth also is sustained by African social thinkers not yet intellectually free to formulate their own positions. Dr. Nkrumah appears to fall into that category.

Partisans and prophets of social revolution, always impressed by numbers, bank heavily on the workers. Superficially they seem to have a point. As Ioan Davies notes, they are numerically strong enough to be credited, at least in theory, with some pressure capability, and they are strategically placed so as to be able to do some damage in sectors critical to economic development. However, quantification often distorts reality. Although engaged most intensively in relatively few but critical sectors, the heaviest concentrations of workers in nearly all countries occur in state-owned or state-controlled enterprises. This places the theoretical revolutionary spearheads securely under the direct supervision and control of government. As for the remainder of the work force, they are typically far too scattered in medium-sized to petty enterprises to score much of an impression.[6]

The true dimensions of labor's potential as a contender for a share of the wealth are sketched in a United Nations Study of West Africa. It is noted there that in the 1960s out of a population of about 93 million the "work force" was between 45 and 50 million. Of that total, "the bulk . . . is engaged in unpaid agricultural employment while the proportion of salaried and wage employment to total economically active population ranges from about 10 percent in the French-speaking countries to over 20 percent in Ghana." The study found that wage employment was highly concentrated in urban areas "where the population is growing at nearly three times the rate of over-all population growth." Other points were that "only a very small proportion of the available labor force [was] skilled manpower, while the dominant, low and unpaid categories of the working force are virtually illiterate."[7]

Specifically, the percentage of high- and middle-level workers and salaried employees in West Africa ranged near 20 percent of the work force total. In Ghana in 1960 this number amounted to somewhere between 30,000 and 40,000. In Zambia between 1965 and 1970 the comparable figure was in the vicinity of 50,000, with over 96 percent employed in the mining industry.[8] In Nigeria total wage-paid employment in 1962 was about 930,000; of these about 300,000, or in the early sixties, 2 percent, of the economically active population belonged to trade unions. By 1964 the total had risen to 367,000, but so had the number of unions; moreover, many of these unions were not, in fact, trade unions at all.[9]

In prevailing conditions it would be a colossal misreading of the situation if these minute percentages were to be perceived as tips of icebergs. In many cases the exceedingly small and fragmented groups of wage earners have no fundamental support to fall back on — none whatever. Even published figures on trade union membership must be treated with considerable scepticism. For a variety of reasons discussed in this study — among them low funding and low skill orientation — trade union statistics deserve to be ranked well below the mean government statistical performance level.[10]

Whatever one's estimate of the overall numerical strength of labor, or whatever the pattern of strategic location or concentration, conditions of economic scarcity dictate to the new governments extreme caution in entertaining any substantive requests from labor. Simply beyond reach in most countries are wage increases, improved working conditions as they call for substantial expenditures, and such luxuries as social welfare, social security and retirement provisions, workman's compensation, unemployment compensation, and the like. Only token allocations are possible unless other, more urgent considerations enter into the picture. Foremost among these considerations in favorable circumstances can be the imminent loss to government of substantial revenue or investment.

Relative Bargaining Position

Neither peasants nor workers are able to bargain effectively without organization; that is why trade unions came into existence. The vast majority of Africa's trade unions, however, are ephemera, controlled usually by combinations of corrupt officials or by employers or their agents. Memberships range from a hundred to a few thousand, and even these numbers may be scattered in dozens of enterprises and in many localities.[11] Unions have numerous other basic weaknesses and deficiencies, some of which we shall return to, but they also have certain opportunities and assets that to-gether — in favorable conditions, one must always add — may spell suc-cess, however limited and temporary that might be.

Among the strategically best situated unions are those of the railway workers. (Railways were among the earliest technological, quasi-industrial contributions of colonial rule to Africa, which endows railway workers with a kind of historical seniority.) By the nature of their work they are in regular contact with outsiders and are, of course, highly mobile. Most likely their frequent exposure to crews loading and unloading at port railway terminals has infused many of them with social revolutionary thought. We referred earlier to the probability that railway workers in French West Africa may have sparked the independence movement there. Similarly, events in the Sudan in 1971 revealed the growing strength of the Sudanese Communist Party, which is based largely on the local railway workers' union.[12] Yet the odds are against successful prosecution of strictly economic demands even in this seemingly favored group.

The 1961 railway and port strike in Ghana, based mainly on Secondi-Takoradi, graphically illustrates the importance of transport workers as compared to other segments of the labor force, and the limits of that im-portance if countered by the weight of the state. It demonstrates that even in conditions singularly auspicious for a successful rising the collective strength of rail and port workers is not sufficient to overcome the phalanx aligned against it. In this strike, led by their respective unions and supported by interested groups from outside the labor camp, the workers at first seemed to score some successes. But their success was deceptive. They had only succeeded in frightening a caretaker group of ministers left in charge of the government while President Nkrumah was out of the country. They had scored momentarily only because at that point their collective hands were at the throat of an already ailing economy.

Like most of the less developed countries, Ghana depended heavily on bulk exports such as minerals, timber, and diverse agricultural commodi-ties, mainly cocoa.[13] Until local capacity to process these commodities de-velops sufficiently to obviate bulk export at or near current volume, the transport sector obviously can claim high priority treatment up to a point. That point was reached very quickly in this instance. It will invariably be reached very swiftly in others whenever labor demands threaten to adversely affect an economy's international competitive position or to upset the in-ternal disposition of power by setting dangerous precedents that others in-tent on challenging the ruling group might follow. For some time to come governments will display extreme sensitivity toward such challenges of its authority. As is well known, almost instinctively now, in ruling circles all over Africa, labor's shored-up demand for an increased share of the wealth may not be contained forever. Any substantive economic concession can cause the ultimate break in the dikes.[14]

Mine workers enjoy similar comparative advantages, again only in favorable conditions. The Zambian mine workers, for example, have been able to improve their per capita income and to a modest degree their working conditions generally, mainly because they too have their hands at the throat of the golden goose. Incidentally, in Zambia mine workers compel special attention for yet another reason: government there appears to have been persuaded that their comparatively high income tends to boost the economy, in particular secondary industry, through their rising propensity to consume.[15]

Of the two major categories of wage earners, the public and the private, the public one clearly has the edge. The reasons for this edge are quickly summarized. Indigenous employers are few and far between. Foreign employers outside the mining industry require a relatively small labor force, because government policies favor capital-intensive enterprises for investment purposes. In the circumstance, the public sector increasingly represents the major source of employment for African workers. It is the crucible that merges the interests of organized labor and the public service against the producers, the rural majority. This alignment is borne out by the total budget allocation to wages and salaries in certain countries, mainly in French-influenced Africa.[16]

In Nigeria about 1965 government and public corporations employed over half of all wage earners. The situation was similar elsewhere on the continent. Needless to say, this situation gave the national decision-making echelon, mainly in the economic and financial spheres, a controlling edge in determination of labor policy and industrial relations.[17] Characteristically, public sector perception of industrial relations, wage policies, and working conditions inevitably take on a public or national interest coloring, however and by whomever such interests are determined. More likely than not, noneconomic considerations will vie with economic ones, and in the absence of cost accounting and similar checks the noneconomic are likely to crowd out the economic.[18]

The presence of the large public sector labor force posed a problem for Professor Potekhin, for he recognized at once that labor employed by a social revolutionary regime, such as Nkrumah's in Ghana before 1966, could not well be treated as a working class locked in a struggle for its rights against capitalist exploiters. The problem for the Soviet Africanists arose over the contradiction posed by the obvious dependence of so many of Africa's economies on Western capital. Ghanaian workers in privately owned but nominally publicly supervised and controlled gold mines, or in construction engaged in furthering Western-Ghanaian joint enterprises, could not in the circumstances very well be regarded as suitable targets for social revolutionary appeals to the working class.[19]

Strategically the advantage of the government-controlled working force lies in its heavy concentration in relatively narrow sectors such as mining, quarrying, construction, and transportation. As long as African economies depend on outside support, mainly from Western sources, the large segment of the labor force within government's direct control is not likely to be unleashed to generate pressure on foreign-owned or operated enterprises over wages or working conditions.[20]

Tribalism and Race Relations

Ties between trade unionism and traditional and tribal organization often are extremely close. With few exceptions African trade unions remain integrally linked to traditional patterns of loyalty, reflecting in their internal structure many of the clan and caste divisions and conflicts characteristic of traditional African life.[21] This link produces, in turn, a curious ambiguity, even a dilemma, for progressive, modernizing trade union leadership. In order to prepare for all-out battle against its detractors, socioeconomic antagonists, and the array of forces at the disposal of government in particular, unions must regroup, reorganize, reform. The patterns started under colonial rule must be radically altered. But as soon as reforms are under way — if they are permitted at all — the individual worker's overwhelming need for personal guidance and support in a rapidly changing environment drives him back into the arms of traditional rule. Where return is no longer possible because traditional rule also is disintegrating, he falls back on tribal ties, the last remaining link to group identity and succor.

If trade unions follow him they become deeply compromised if not bogged down in conflicts and contention basically counterproductive to their avowed raison d'être. Concern with tribal allegiances and practices is incompatible with the requirements of collective bargaining, for it invariably leads to fragmentation and dissension. Yet the attraction to the more familiar, more personal tribal life remains, actually increasing with the individual's mounting fear that he might be cast adrift in an alien, hostile world. Rather than betting his slender resources, pennies actually, on the demonstrably doubtful ability of union leaders to obtain for him higher wages or improved working conditions, the basically insecure worker seems to prefer to commit whatever surplus he can garner to support funds administered for his ultimate benefit by his tribal association. There is evidence that he will opt that way even though his contributions under tribal schemes may be higher than union dues. The explanation goes beyond mere insecurity or lack of confidence to the knowledge that social security, including provision for birth, sickness, death, and retirement, are manifestly beyond realization, no matter how strong a trade union may be.

Thus the trade unions are denied the funds needed to improve their bargaining positions and are deprived of opportunities for demonstration through aggregation of workers' savings in order to provide direct value to the individual. Trade unionism is swept up in a vicious circle: "[it] is deprived of funds because the services which it ought to render are provided by non-industrial organizations supported by the workers, and it cannot provide rival services because it has no funds."[22]

Incidentally, availability of the tribal alternative is frequently exploited by lesser trade union functionaries who are fearful that consolidation and amalgamation of splintered and fragmented unions will eliminate their offices. They hang on to their perquisites by pointing a finger at the top leadership, accusing it of trying to submerge ethnically distinct membership in larger them = dominated amalgams. Unfortunately for trade unionism, fragmentation is precisely what divide-and-rule and patronage oriented interests may have in mind.[23]

Where race relations still are a major problem, trade unionism both thrives on and suffers from its consequences. Because white foreigners are slow to leave in Zambia, Kenya, Senegal, and the Ivory Coast, trade union leadership, wrapping itself in the mantle of Africanization, has been able to attract support on the grounds that reduction of foreign presence means advancement of indigenous interests. Like all the other strategies, this one, too, falls short of success. First, fear of being abandoned to a traditionally hostile tribe often exceeds xenophobia directed at Europeans; in other words, in the eyes of a black miner the white miner who enjoys certain privileges may pose a lesser threat than does a fellow worker from another tribe. Second, if as in Zambia and Senegal trade union leadership is on the verge of converting anti-European feelings into political leverage at the national level, the regime invariably counters with mobilization of the relatively disadvantaged and jealous rural masses to whom the wages of urban-public and mine workers are veritable fortunes.

Environmental Impediments

We have already commented on the usual ineffectiveness of the strike. Strike performance to date warrants the generalization that a chance of success in the use of this weapon exists only if it can be related to broader social issues. In a few specific instances strike organizers were able to persuade workers that their individual and group misfortunes were traceable directly to official and private corruption, theft, and general mismanagement of the economy by those in command positions. In other words, labor was able to identify with broader social protest. This identification appears to have been the reason that massed labor action in close cooperation with other disadvantaged and aroused groups scored some successes in Upper Volta in 1966, in Nigeria in 1963-64, and in Senegal in 1969. It is noteworthy that the protracted but comparatively successful 1963-64 general strike in Nigeria gained momentum not over a wage issue but over the broader issue of relative social deprivation. This point emerges clearly from a statement by the chairman of the Joint Action Committee, which had been formed in an attempt to weld together feuding factions in the labor movement. "We don't attempt to justify the unions' position in economic terms or to say just where the Government is going to find the money. That is their job. All we can see is that they are spending plenty on themselves. It's time we got our fair share."[24]

Similar considerations sparked the Ghana strike in 1961. Yet after the dust had settled, the net result in terms of real economic gains, a matter of prime interest to workers, invariably was a disappointment. The Ghana workers had succeeded in persuading the government there to withdraw a 5 percent levy on their income, but within months of the strike settlement prices skyrocketed; the cost of living increase ranged above 30 percent in a single year. In these conditions dues payments to unions assumed murderous proportions if measured against the average worker's household reserves. Such is the fate of labor throughout the continent. A strike may even succeed in sweeping a regime out of office — always assumed that powerful allies can be found — but the worker's pay is eroded nevertheless and increasingly at a sharply accelerating rate.[25]

Strikes are difficult to sustain on the continent for yet other reasons — reasons reminiscent of organized labor's early history in the developed countries. Neither union reserves nor the workers' economic staying power begins to match that of their adversaries. A strike very soon runs out of energy when weekly wages are the sole means of keeping body and soul together. The lack of staying power expressed in low monetary reserves and low food stocks for strikers and their families, combined with employer and government penetration of the labor ranks and lack of physical striking power (arms), prevents the more highly concentrated South African blacks from taking advantage of their relatively advantageous position as the mainstay of South African industry.

The strike potential is further undermined by what might be termed the fickleness or unreliability of nonlabor allies and the general disinterest or even apathy of the masses. After all, it's within only a quite limited arena that labor's contributions are critical enough to generate a degree of leverage in ruling circles. Even a general strike leaves the vast majority of the population quite unaffected. As long as government can manage to compensate for shortfalls in critical skills and services, not much is left for labor to mobilize in its support.

The high percentage of industrialization combined with the overwhelming dominance of mining in the Zambian economy might suggest different interest pressure and achievement prospects for labor. Certainly, Zambia's economic profile — an economy 95 percent of which is devoted to mining extraction and processing of copper — would suggest a relatively high sensitivity to labor pressure, hence a high strike potential, in both public and private sectors. This does not seem to be the case, however. Even in such a favorable setting labor's potential is continuously drained, and its social thrusts are diverted from natural goals and objectives. Like their brothers everywhere, labor leaders as well as rank and file seem to be incapable of escaping the swamps of tribalism. The more than 73 tribes, depending on one's definitions, are not susceptible to consolidation. Tribal and linguistic differences have splintered the labor movement enough to dilute its potency below the point of effectiveness as a major pressure force.[26] Not even the presumable common concern over favored treatment of white miners and railway technicians has served to overcome internecine strife.

In 1969 all strikes and stoppages were banned by law, and severe penalties were provided to punish violations. At the same time wages and prices were frozen, as much as possible, pending promulgation of a new, avowedly more equitable formula on prices and incomes. But unrest cannot be stayed by such devices. Disparities in salaries of white European and those of indigenous workers remained glaring, while the rate of Zambianization, in the mines and along the line of rail remained provocatively slow.

Continued pressure to alleviate these conditions ran into steadfast government opposition. It remained government policy to regard acceleration of the Zambianization process as permissible only in the lower ranks — mainly unskilled — where, of course, few Europeans had ever worked. Acceleration in high-skilled positions was deemed incompatible with overriding economic requirements and expectations. Moreover, retention of a certain percentage of European miners and railway engineers was regarded as mandatory for safety. It was more than a coincidence that at a time when pressure for Zambianization reached one of its periodic boiling points Zambia's productivity was set back for a year or more by the mining disaster in the Mufulira mine.[27] This alone let a great deal of air out of labor's balloon.

Substantial unemployment can always be expected to adversely affect labor's potential while enhancing the bargaining opportunities for business and industry and for government. Private sectors do not yet represent a major source of employment, even if, as in Kenya in 1970, the government may insist on a 10 percent across-the-board increase in employment. This increase did not materially improve the situation in Kenya; the overall wage bill remained static, and pressure for more jobs continued unabated.[28] The true prospects of African labor for decades to come were forecast in the *Kenya Development Plan 1970-74.* "Minimum wages are necessary to avoid exploitation of labour. On the other hand, if minimum wages are raised too rapidly, the effect must be to exclude growing numbers of people from employment."[29]

It has long been established that organized labor cannot hope to counter this government and employer gambit unless it can enlarge its aggregate share of total wealth to sustain strike action. Even then, the pie to be fought over is not large enough in the typical African case. The as-yet fragile economy might well be smothered by overemployment.

It might seem at first glance that the growing tendency on the part of African regimes to assume at least partial control of foreign-owned enterprises, including mines, would improve African labor's bargaining prospects. Actually, black labor seems to lose when properties are taken over by the state, in whatever form. While dealing with relatively cautious, if not timid, foreign employers, and assuming that government either refrains from intervening directly or exercises extreme restraint, black unions do have a slight edge. However, as soon as Black African owners or managers appear at the negotiating or bargaining table, if they appear, the situation changes dramatically.

Even if nationalization does not take place, African labor is losing ground relative to the limited progress made before and shortly after independence. The trend in favor of military cum civil service government and increased state control short of direct takeover is apparent and is not likely to be reversed barring radical reversal of investment and aid policies by the rich countries.[30]

Organizational-Structure Impediment

The marginal existence of African trade unions — they are close to the center, of course, in the realm of propaganda — has prevented the emergence of an effective corps of union leaders. Actually, beneath the veneer of organizational solidarity trade unions in Africa are cans of worms.

The generals of labor, paying lip service to the workers' interests, are engaged instead in pursuit of personal, or at any rate, nonlabor goals. As for the rest — the middle-level leadership, the captains and lieutenants, so to speak — the chronically depleted coffers compel those who can to follow their leader's example and also extract some personal gain. Lesser union leaders seek to secure their union base by exploitation of ethnic or even racial tension and by what is known in United States union circles as "drinking fountain radicalism." In the process much energy is wasted, petty squabbles are blown up to major proportions, and, as noted above, the fracturing process that promotes ever smaller and therefore ever weaker unions is accelerated.[31]

Berg has offered the most incisive view of the inevitable consequences of this type of leadership. Energy and scarce resources are consumed in futile combat against internal rivals. Duplicity and conflict of interest necessitate transfer of the inevitable machinations and maneuvers from the shop floor, where these struggles "might at least have the effect of raising trade union consciousness," to "the backroom and political corridors at home

and abroad, at the palace level so to speak." The main effect on the rank
and file, Berg concludes, "is confusion." He continues: "The instruments
of battle, moreover, are hardly such as to elevate the moral tone of the
trade union community. Little black bags are much in presence and there
is buying and selling on a wholesale basis."[32]

What are being bought and sold are, of course, jobs, promotions, and
petty offices in the union. Beyond that, money paid to union officials can
and does purchase the amount of labor peace that is possible in the circumstances. Major cornucopias for African unions since colonial days have
been the treasuries of Western trade unions, principally those in Great
Britain, France, and the United States. Recently, Soviet money appears
to have found its way into the same channels.[33] Substantial evidence points
to the United States Central Intelligence Agency as a source of considerable
funding for pro-Western trade unions.[34]

There is a certain irony if this dependence of African workers and their
unions on outside, mainly capitalist donors has survived into the postindependence period. The new leaders' refusal to financially back up their
unions compelled most of the leaders to accept outside funds when offered. The consequences were predictable; Africa's labor movement was
compromised.

Unfortunately, the structural-functional shortcomings of African trade
unionism cannot be eliminated or corrected with money. The constantly
rising curve of technological innovation, combined with the effects of trade
wars among the great and middle powers, along with yet additional factors
that debilitate most social organisms on the continent augurs ill for the
labor movement in this part of the world. Eventually, independent union
financing may well become a permanent casualty and with that, the movement itself.[35]

To contemplate dues shop or checkoff systems in prevailing conditions
would be compounding labor's travails. Such systems would accomplish
only a further increase of individual take by upper and lower officials. Even
where dues shop systems are adopted, as in Zambia, ethnic factionalism,
corruption, the confused and confusing ideological dilettantism of leading
officials, and in Zambia the nationalization programs initiated in 1969-70
tend to defeat any determined effort to provide adequate financing for the
unions from inception.

The list of internal organizational and structural defects and impediments
can be extended ad infinitum. Union discipline poses a special problem. No
matter what the terms of an agreement with management might be, leaders
cannot count on being able to deliver on their pledges. It is extremely difficult for them, to insist, say, on minimum levels of performance, rate of production, punctuality, or regularity.[36]

As one moves down the ladder of power and influence, in particular as
one descends to the level of mass or masslike organization in the African

environment, leaders or agents either representing or purporting to represent a given following most likely will become inexorably detached and will pursue their own goals and interests. As these goals and interests relate to the group interests the leaders are supposed to represent, a certain metamorphosis can be expected to occur. Group goals in the labor movement, for example, may be converted to such agent goals as maintenance of office and access to additional income. In blunt language, the corruptibility of the agents of pressure and interest is likely to increase in direct proportion to the size of group membership as modified by the level of education prevalent in that group. Failure to calculate this factor into the overall assessment of African trade unionism is one of the major shortcomings in the literature on that subject.

The end effect of all this must be that the trade unions will remain consigned to the nether regions in the power and influence structure. Instead of developing and acting out a meaningful role as labor's interest representatives, union leadership in order to survive will have to allow itself to be prostituted. At best they can hope to play the role of faithful, loyal support elements whose prime function will be to promote and implement official policy. When labor refuses to play that role it may not even count on partial recognition and acceptance of even moderate demands. It is clear from the foregoing, as it has been clear all along, that African labor cannot hope to exact specific and significant gains unless it can locate and cultivate truly powerful allies.

19

Tribes, Regions, and Towns

Tribes

In Chapter 11 we reviewed some of the analytical and some of the practical operational problems that arise from the use and abuse of the term *tribe*. We showed that like race, caste, or ethnicity, tribe is in dire need of reinterpretation, and that in its traditional form, it is an extremely undependable analytical tool. One reason is that as a concept the word has been immersed for so long in popular lore and social mythology similar to race, cast, or ethnic minority. To accept lore or mythology as hard evidence is, of course, always poor research strategy.

Scholarly or not, tribe is in any case a form of culture bias, for in its current use in the Africa context the term is rooted quite evidently in Western social consciousness. In its literary existence it is a reflection mainly of Western European demographic mapping endeavors. Earlier we cited the possibility that as an abstraction the concept may mislead the observer to mistake yet another shadow for substance on the African landscape.[1] In other words, one must doubt whether the concept can be operationalized beyond pure social theory and outside the realm of propaganda or, with Lasswell, outside the realm of symbol manipulation.

It is most doubtful whether any African grouping that draws on ethnic, racial, caste, or color characteristics alone can actually generate sufficient pressure on decision- and policymaking circles to exact significant concessions. When demands of that nature seem to have been prosecuted successfully, it is advisable to look beyond the obvious or apparent explanation, usually alleged tribal or ethnic political strength, and to test for something more substantial and more enduring. The truth of the matter usually is not far away. In Africa, as in the United States or India or anywhere else, one need not scratch the tribe or racial group or caste too deeply to

262

uncover more substantial interests or concerns — subsistence interests or physical security interests, for example. If not economic, the compulsions that underlie what is perceived or described as tribal behavior may be detected more readily with the tools of psychology than with those of psephology. Whatever one's methods, clearly in this matter the risks are always great that the bottle's contents are obscured by labels.

Accept for a moment that tribal considerations govern to a significant extent the behavior of African pressure and interest groups, so that one might be justified in using tribal designations to distinguish one type from another (tribal from religious, or tribal from social caste, or tribal from color based). Then another caveat must be kept in mind: in no known case does pressure along such lines emanate uniformly from all sections or from all social strata of such groups. Rarely do benefits obtained accrue to more than a minute percentage near the top of the group hierarchy.

Most likely, what appear to be manifestations of tribalism may be nothing but eternal quests of the oppressed, the exploited, and the disadvantaged for a place in the sun. The desire to promote associates or kinsmen to positions of influence has been a characteristic of all social groups since the beginning of time. All groups everywhere seek improved living standards, which includes more ample supplies of amenities, such as drinking water, schools, medical assistance and facilities, electricity, transportation, and, most important, employment or other economic opportunities. Even the least modernized sector in the remotest corner of the continent is today at least dimly aware of the value of education. Tribes that insist, through their spokesmen, on control of land they believe is theirs, are simply following in the footsteps of generations of peasants around the world.

As a concept if not a slogan, tribe has been an instrument of colonial rule if not colonial deception for a century or more. The social consequences are still with us. Today as before, invocation of tribal rights or interests, for whatever purpose, may be no more than a subterfuge or a tranquilizer. In South Africa, for example, the entire system of internal colonialism, in addition to apartheid, rests on mummification of so-called tribal traditions. If ever there was any substance to tribe, it has been subverted by decades of debilitating, degrading colonial experience. Traditional ways have been perverted until they ceased to reflect genuine human concerns; pristine interests in the environment and in the appropriate human response, essential ingredients of tribal organization, have been warped, distorted and bent to serve wholly extraneous designs on the economic product or the labor of the common African.

Ever since colonial administrations, foremost the Belgian and the French, established classifications of peaceful and rebellious tribes, recognizing the peaceful and crushing, at times brutally, the rebellious, tribe has been reduced to an instrument of administrative convenience. Rebellious tribes were, of course, always those who persisted in occupying valuable lands or potential mining regions coveted by foreign interests, or those who stubbornly insisted on remaining astride convenient access routes to sources of wealth. Peaceful tribes were those whose leaders were prepared to accommodate foreign exploitative designs on local sources of wealth.[2]

If not an instrument of administrative convenience, tribe has served as a rallying point in electoral campaigns. This device, in turn, persuaded some observers to conclude, going by the rule "where there is smoke there must be fire," that there must be some substance. To be sure, electoral appeals, especially at the grass roots level, often were emphatically directed at ethnic concerns.[3] It is significant, however, that no reliable evidence has been produced to show that electoral outcomes were indeed influenced in a causal way by considerations properly identifiable as tribal in the strict sense of that term. More likely, if elections were conducted honestly the votes were cast not along tribal lines at all but along socioeconomic interest lines; the privileged sought to protect their advantages, while the underprivileged sought to improve their positions. That certain blocs of votes had in common certain characteristics was not a reflection necessarily of tribal identity and solidarity but purely coincidental, a remnant of the past rather than an index of the present. One need only examine any one of these alleged blocs for differentiation along lines of internal social stratification. Interests of tribal leaders and the elite element in general may not at all be those of the inarticulate masses below.

In any event, before one attributes any voting behavior characteristics to election outcomes it is worth recalling that as a rule elections on the continent have been conducted fraudulently, and electoral successes were scored by securing the cooperation of key leaders at the local levels — chiefs usually, or other well-placed local functionaries. The key to success in these cases was not so much persuasion of electors, or voters, but efficient organization of the fraud — ballot stuffing, malicious and illegal invalidation of opposition votes, falsification of results at all levels, elimination or incapacitation of opposition election officials, or outright intimidation of voters.[4]

Tribe-associated interests seem to break along a poor-rich dividing line. In Kenya, for example, the Rift Valley and Nyanza region lead all others in production potential as the Kalenjin and Luhja clusters possess more effective resources than competing groups in the poorer north and along the coastal strip.[5] Similar juxtapositions can be identified in the Ivory Coast.[6]

In Kenya, the Kalenjin group is Nilotic and sandwiched between contending groups in the Rift Valley. In their search for ways to construct alliances in order to resist competition or domination by other groups, Kalenjin leaders seek to align with kindred clusters such as the Kipsigis and the Luo in the Nyanza region. Always the ultimate aim seems to be more to secure positions for leaders at the top than to economically better the masses.[7] What emerges here is a pattern of economic interest contention among leaders who for their own purposes prefer to camouflage their activity with tribal language and symbolisms.[8]

The rich-poor juxtaposition most likely carries over into other spheres. Unemployed members of one group may be persuaded to identify for pressure purposes with wealthier members of the same group — the solidarity appeal — but they can be expected to go along only up to a point. Luo farmers will follow Luo intellectuals, but not everywhere and not at all times. Social class stratification must come to Africa eventually, and what may now be a form of wishful thinking on the part of deposed leaders or revolutionary aspirants to power may soon become the prevailing pattern. The tribe will be the first casualty.

Language or fears and apprehensions centering on language have long been major rallying points for what appeared to be tribal pressure groups. Language has been prominently featured where it is believed or assumed to be the key to economic gain — for example, in public administration, the civil service, in skilled trades, and in labor unions. But even here other factors such as education and religion usually are involved.[9]

At first glance associations of miners in Zambia, Northern Nigeria, and Ghana may appear to be tribal, and pressures emanating from these groups may appear to be tribe-oriented. On closer examination different conclusions seem indicated. For example, a study of Zambian towns shows that tribe, like neighborhood and Christian fellowship, does play only a subordinate role, principally at the level of personal friendship and marriage. It fades into the background or is submerged altogether in hard bargaining for economic advantage.[10]

In the Zambian mines — as in the South African mines, incidentally — tribal elders (functionaries) occupy privileged positions that they are loath to surrender. The coalition politics in which they engage to protect their positions appear to be tribal but actually follow factional lines based on considerations apparent to the student of group dynamics but possibly not to the student of tribal ritual.[11] Yet a rather curious and circuitous route leads us back always to tribe as the alleged source of conflict.

The accident of the Zambian Bemba tribal cluster's being located along the economically strategic copperbelt has advanced the myth of tribal pressure there. Tribalism was seen as the source of demands from that group for improved wage levels in the mines, because it emanated primarily, if not exclusively, from one single identifiable group. More likely, agitation among the Bemba is economic in the first instance and relates not to tribal but to the racial, black-white juxtaposition characteristic of southern Africa generally. It seems that in the mines more than anywhere else black workers are offended by white conduct if not by white presence.[12]

Tribalism has become almost synonymous with Nigeria. To an extent this identification is traceable to the colonial strategy of divide and rule. Indeed, the Nigerian case may be the classic illustration of misapplication of the term. Unfortunately, the consequences of British manipulation of the three major groupings under the banner of tribal division prevented realization that behind terms like Hausa, Ibo, and Yoruba were innumerable subidentities pursuing a wide variety of diverse and divergent interests. Long after it had become apparent that the major divisions reflected only administrative constructs, the old adage retained currency: *omnia Nigeria in tres parte divida est.* But Nigeria, like most other African states, is far more complex than that. Most important, the complexities relate to tribe only incidentally, if they relate to tribe at all.

While the postindependence constitutional arrangement was under discussion, both the colonial and the indigenous Nigerian leadership had been bombarded with petitions, expressions of deep concern on the part of diverse minorities throughout the country that their interests might be compromised permanently in the proposed federal design. Though couched understandably in tribal terms — petitioners assumed that this was the accepted formula — the fears expressed actually were minority fears pure and simple. As such they did not differ from fears expressed by religious, cultural, ideological, economic, and other interest groups anywhere. They addressed themselves to discrimination in employment and fears of administrative oppression, cultural deprivation, and religious intolerance — Muslims fearing domination by Christians or vice versa or pagans fearing both.[13]

Many of these fears were justified. Ibos were a distinct minority in Northern Nigeria, as were Yorubas; Ibibio and Tiv, Kanuri, and dozens of others found themselves for one reason or another surrounded by presumed or perceived hostile majorities. But if any solidity accrued to these groups as a result, it was only in passive response, and that does not translate into substantive tribal pressure potential.

Even the catastrophic Nigerian civil war was not the tribal confrontation that partisan propagandists and uncritical outsiders wanted the world to believe. To be sure, atrocities had been committed, but it would be difficult to attribute them to tribal factors. In its fundamental causes the civil war resulted from a showdown among detribalized elite elements who were ready to assume a nationalist posture founded on a desire to rule a modern state as they saw fit. Had Biafra emerged fully as a state, no one would have been able to recognize in the control structure the tribal origins of the dominant group, the Ibos.

The aftermath of the civil war, as well as numerous incidents reported while it was in progress, should have established beyond doubt that modernization had long ago destroyed the vestiges of tribalism among the elite responsible for the outbreak of that conflict. Only the shell had survived to serve as a springboard to national independence and power for a wholly alienated group of corrupt politicians, some temporarily uprooted military officers, and a sprinkling of professionals and intellectuals. Beneath the thin veneer of macroethnic superficiality several branches of the once cohesive Ibo complex had long split off, pursuing different goals along different paths. The occasional riot with tribal overtones was but one of many symptoms of social problems that increasingly shake all of Africa to its foundation.[14]

At least one observer seems to believe that instead of lessening tribal and traditional ethnic tensions, modernization for a time at least tends to exacerbate them, reviving the tribe as a basic social organism in the process. This notion, too, is the result of exaggerated perception of nonevents. The contention is that increased expectations and, as these fail to be satisfied, increased frustrations seek relief in ethnic protest. What is actually happening is something quite different. Lack of social mobility has riveted the vast majority of Africans to traditional areas, concentrating them around their customary sources of existence. Even concentrations of migrants in urban areas are likely to have a common ethnic background. All that is incidental, however. What is at stake in the protests is physical survival, a share of the wealth. It is what protesting masses have in common throughout the world.[15]

Ethnic group social protest for several reasons is likely to be more articulate and more specific at local levels. In less developed or underendowed areas people feel deprivations more acutely at the local level; that is, they may not be aware at all that the national economy is near bankruptcy or that foreign exchange reserves are running low, but they will approach rebellion when there are no schools at all. Actual or presumed consequences of ethnic bias are more visible locally, which is one reason local politics so often take on an intensely personal character. It is only at the local level that the individual can bring into focus the identity of a decision- or policy-maker, hence his ethnic origins and specific official acts attributable to him. It is only at the local level that the individual citizen who considers himself ethnically aggrieved can relate specific acts to particular officials whose ethnic identity is, of course, well known.[16]

Social protest along ethnic lines, aside from specific demands for placement in certain key positions in the public sector, usually is quite inchoate. It is virtually impossible for strictly tribal demands cast in specific terms to advance far beyond the village, at best beyond the district level. Demands classifiable as tribal are parochial by definition. They have little if any bearing on the major public policies of concern to officials at intermediate and higher national levels of government. Preservation of customary legal jurisdiction over certain social offenses and questions of land tenure, marriage, divorce, and inheritance increasingly become entangled with broader questions of civil and criminal law, civil rights, modernization of agriculture, and so on. Even demands for equity in employment in both the public and the private sectors break on the resistance of those already established and fearful of having their precarious gains nullified by majority reaction to further demands from minorities.

One may be justified in suspecting that invocation of the tribal issue is the modern African equivalent of the exploitation of religion in connection with the quarrels between the Stuarts and the Tudors in England. When in Zambia in 1971 what were referred to as "Bemba politicians," alleged that the ruling group around President Kaunda practiced discrimination against their tribe, they could not have been serious; the Bemba do not constitute an entity solid enough to be discriminated against. What was really at issue was the right of oppositional elements to consolidate themselves in the guise of a popular movement versus the right of the regime to prevent the attempt. To a lesser degree the complaint, couched in tribal terminology, reflected the impatience of the younger elements with the older independence generation who seemed to be disinclined to surrender their power.[17] As religion before, tribalism now is invoked to help mobilize support for purely factional assaults on the power structure.

Regions and Towns

The belief that in the context of social conflict political forces can meaningfully be distinguished from nonpolitical ones has prevented us from noticing the emergence of new contenders for a share of the wealth and eventually of power. In the United States, for instance, attention has been riveted for so long on political parties and elections that the emergence of far more potent and more efficient instrumentalities of public and private competition for socioeconomic advantage went virtually unnoticed for decades. It has been only very recently that the role of the giant corporation has been adequately recognized in public affairs. Along with the large corporate bodies in the private sector, the cities and the states have become progressively more active in the competition for public and private funds. Still, much of this maneuvering remains obscured from public view by traditional rhetoric about the so-called political arena.

The situation in Africa is quite similar, except that the myth of the potent political party as an instrument of government has been laid to rest nearly everywhere. Into the vacuum, along with the governmental apparatus, the public corporations, and the larger private enterprises, indigenous and foreign, step the regions and the larger cities.

In a federal system, such as the one that governed Nigeria for a while, entrenched constitutional clauses may guarantee to administrative subdivisions (regions in Nigeria) certain perquisites of power. Armed with those advantages, these subdivisions can compete for resources more effectively than can groups not so endowed — tribes, religious organizations, or political parties, for example, or the cities and towns. But as Nigeria has demonstrated, constitutional guaranties are no defense if the superior force at the disposal of the central, national regime is deployed against constitutionally autonomous units in earnest; both the Western Region and Eastern Region regimes eventually collapsed when seriously challenged. Things are different if instead of controlling power the aim of regional, city, or town leadership is merely to press for a proportionate share of available resources and for improvement of the economic base in general. As can be expected, here also a certain pecking order governs prospects of success.

Not far below the outer shell of the vaunted tribe are the principal urban concentrations historically associated with large ethnic complexes (e.g., Ibadan, the capital of Yorubaland in Nigeria; Kumasi, the capital of Ashantiland in Ghana). These centers must compete with the national capitals (Lagos and Accra, respectively), for scarce resources. Gradually an entirely new and different pattern emerges in which groups and entities traditionally not regarded as capable of participation in politics or in pressure and interest group contests make their appearance.

Here again vast inequities have developed, making it advisable to examine the political landscape of each and every state for true, as distinct from apparent, centers of gravity. Here, too, the rich are likely to become richer while the poor are dropping further behind. The distorted computer image of the moon is applicable here also.[18] It would dramatically underscore the growing cleavages that separate towns in economically favored sections from those in the disadvantaged economic hinterland. In Ghana the Kumasi-Accra-Secondi-Takoradi triangle would be most prominent. In Nigeria it would be the Lagos-Ibadan-Benin triangle, or the oil, cocoa, and palm product region; in Senegal the peanut belt, in the Ivory Coast Abidjan and the hinterland of cocoa production, in Zambia the copperbelt and the line of rail, and in Kenya, of course, the Highlands. An image of the Congo (Zaire) along these lines at least for the first decade of independent development, would show an enormous mass centered on Katanga and supported by a dwarfed body, the rest of the Republic. Such a presentation could be based on per capita income, tax contribution, real estate value, and bank deposits.

Tested for actual as against proposed or projected distribution of resources, the new, post-civil-war Nigerian federal setup quickly reveals the handicaps under which the several states enter the race for scarce resources. It becomes apparent at once that at the top of the pecking order will be the area along the Lagos-Ibadan axis in the west, the midwest, and Kano State in the north, with the remainder scaled down and ending with the state that has the poorest chances of survival and hence constitutes the poorest risk for investment, development, and allocation of resources.[19] This pattern is replicated in every single country throughout the continent, the grim heritage of lopsided, inequitable if not mindless distribution of effort and resources under colonial rule. The grimmest survival of that approach is the expanding urban blight.

Census data for the late fifties and early sixties indicate that towns and cities of 20,000 or more inhabitants accounted for only 1-4 percent of the total population of Burundi, Ethiopia, Uganda, and Tanzania, 6-8 percent of the total of Kenya, Madagascar, and Somalia, and 14 percent of the total in Zambia.[20] Indications are that urban areas in Africa will grow sharply with commensurate increase in pressure potential.[21]

As everywhere else in the world, the major urban centers on the African continent reflect historic trade, migration, and security patterns, with one significant difference. In Africa with few exceptions the patterns did not reflect indigenous requirements. Urban concentrations grew mainly around foreign points of debarcation and foreign administrative and commercial headquarters, located nearest the most convenient port or rail facility.

Since export-import trade still is the principal if not sole cash-producing activity in the former colonies, and because money supply tends to be greatest at points of entry into an economy, major African cities loom far larger. The economic volatility of the major African cities, hence their

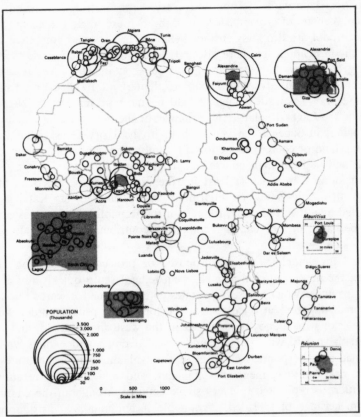

FIGURE 19.1   *Major Contemporary Urban Centers*

SOURCE: Paden and Soja, *The African Experience*, Vol. 1. Northwestern University Press, 1970. After Map 10 in *The Geography of Modern Africa* by William A. Hance. Copyright ©1964 Columbia University Press.

appetite for services, investment, and administrative care, is far greater in proportion to the hinterlands than is true elsewhere. This disparity finds dramatic expression in demands for housing, medical and educational services, and facilities in per capita terms.

The dynamics of African development, however, are such that demands from that direction quickly outrun available resources. The magnetism of urban riches, as the squalid living conditions in Africa's cities are perceived in the rural areas, is rapidly producing conditions approaching chaos in the leading capitals.[22] Unlike the similarly hard-pressed larger cities in the developed countries, African metropolitan centers do not yet possess the economic underpinning needed to take up the slack and provide temporary relief for, say, the unemployed. At the same time, the presence of disproportionate numbers of educated persons in the private and public sectors, principally in administrative capacities, increases the demand for costly public services, amenities, and construction.[23]

Indications are that African cities will have to join cities in the developed countries in pressing for funds for relief of the masses descending rapidly into more abject poverty than was their lot at their points of origin in the rural areas. But the required funds will not be forthcoming for decades, because other priorities consume the attention of fiscal authorities. The likely result will be coalitions between upper strata urban and financial interests operating behind a facade of token concern for the plight of the cities.[24]

The only ray of hope comes from the self-interest of urban authorities intent on creating a more favorable environment for revenue-producing industrial and commercial operations. Possibly the higher administrative, government, and private sector executives will develop a commitment to improve their immediate working environment, but that is doubtful aside from the single road leading from the airport, a better bridge or two, and one central avenue. As sources of pressure the major cities, and in some cases regions, will become progressively more insistent on receiving a fair share. Allocations will have to increase if only to avert serious unrest and costly disruptions in the vicinity of key governmental offices, sensitive if not nervous industrial and commercial headquarters, and economically vital centers of manufacturing and processing. Also of critical importance in this respect, of course, is the strategic location of Africa's major cities, most of which control access and egress to and from the country.

The critical question remaining is how increased allocations will be oriented. Will they at least partially provide for the substantial urban and suburban growth anticipated, or will they be stopgap measures always too little and too late? Apparently the answer to that question lies in the ability of city leadership, public and private, to free itself from national, central government administrative bondage and from the patronage bondage as well in order to be better able to devote its energies to tasks more reflective of its communal responsibilities.

20

The Educated, Organized Religion, and Political Parties

The Educated

Africa's educated are in a precarious position. Behind them a tidal wave of illiteracy gathers, expanding inexorably, threatening to obliterate eventually the modest achievements of Africa's renaissance.[1] Ahead of them, and probably appreciated by them more keenly than by the rest, yawns the ever-widening gap that separates most of Africa from the developed world. In such conditions ability to perceive the future can be disconcerting. It certainly generates frustration, and frustration characterizes particularly the vanguard of the educated, the African intellectuals. On the whole they are probably among the world's least stable, hence least assessable and predictable, aggregation of human beings.

Aside from the few at the top, who have found a degree of security for their lifetimes, the majority of the highly educated, the brighter and more gifted among the graduates of secondary schools, the university graduates, and probably also the unsuccessful university students, are becoming increasingly aware that they may indeed be heading for an abyss. What is by no means clear is the direction the inevitable reaction will take, although one can be sure that intellectuals far more than ordinary humans will not respond to cataclysmic events or probabilities in predictable fashion. Least likely to act predictably is the African intellectual who, unlike his counterpart in the developed world, is reaching the threshold of revolutionary change at a point when the world around him shows signs of wanting to fall apart.

At least so it must appear to the young graduate preparing to begin a career. The alien institutions inherited from colonial days crumbled in most cases within a decade or less, creating a sense of indirection and insecurity if not a vacuum. If legislative, judicial, and administrative reference points

272

vanish altogether or undergo complete metamorphosis, whatever remained for phychologically satisfying individual orientation was all too often a mere shell. The intellectual still imbued with a desire to see order and stability emerge, moral and ethical standards further developed and preserved, and traditional values retained or adopted cautiously to serve modernity discovers that he is fighting a losing battle; he is increasingly alone. The African novel and the African poem, in that they seek to deal with the workaday world, speak eloquently on that subject. So does nonfiction, with some notable exceptions.

Edward Shils and his disciples created the artificial African intellectual, the student who is firm in his convictions, intent on following a narrow and straight path to success, usually leadership in one setting or another.[2] He fully understands his purpose and function in society; he knows what he is about. Nothing could be further from the truth.

In the face of overwhelming odds, and unless he is one of the few who can financially afford the luxury of clinging to principles and ideals, the African intellectual devises highly individualistic means of survival; in effect, he emulates the chameleon as he adapts to his environment. The gift of articulation enables him to persuade himself and others that whatever his response to reality may be, it is wholly rational and entirely consistent with his status and social obligations. It is the articulated rather than the real intellectual, student, or generally educated person who is the object of most if not all opinion and attitude survey. In other words, what is often analyzed and discussed is only the long shadow of an emphatically transitory social entity.[3]

Raymond Aron, speaking of French student radicals in the Paris riots of May 1969, commented wryly that once the excitement of the riot had died down, the radical student leaders "who represented nothing returned to nothing."[4] This comment might apply also to African student leaders and activists, with very few exceptions, after each and every one of the riots or disturbances that have rocked the once-staid African campuses with *increasing frequency*. This assessment, of course, is not shared by the activists themselves. Like the American students who persuaded themselves that they had been instrumental in forcing the retirement of one United States president, the African student also engages in heroic fantasies, mistaking his marginal role for that of a catalyst for leadership. The self-deception is reflected rather uncritically in some survey research findings on student behavior and motivation.[5]

In real life exceedingly few African university students qua students ever attained command positions in movements of any consequence; few ever penetrated to the inner perimeters of political parties, including opposition parties. Fewer ever reached the true pinnacle of power. The few exceptions succeeded not because of their student status but in spite of it. The Nkrumahs, Azikiwes, or Kenyattas were lifted into power definitely not on the shoulders of university students; actually, they had long shed their student roles when they made their decisive moves.

Literary treatment of so-called student power is often mystifying. Students are boldly credited with having wrought changes "in the authority structures in Africa" or with importing ideologies to the continent. No persuasive proof has been presented. Most likely, it is the old fallacy at work again. Students press demands, a riot ensues, followed by a change of or within government. Overlooked because it probably was not a research focus is the infinite array of genuinely causal factors.[6]

It is always possible, of course, that a nervous and insecure regime can be stampeded by a public opinion mouse. The mere threat of a student disturbance at the only or principal institution of higher learning in the country has prompted governments as strong as Nkrumah's in 1963 to put troops on alert. Regimes in the Congo, Senegal, the Ivory Coast, Ghana, Nigeria, and Kenya, to mention but a few, took drastic steps to quell student unrest or put down threats of insurrection. Most significant, however, is that no substantive concessions are ever made, and none are made on a permanent basis if demands go beyond purely academic concern. Even then concessions are not made generously.[7] After a few collisions the effective power structure closes in on the feeble student movement, laying bare the true measure of student power. If after a show of strength, however insubstantial, students appear to be coopted into the ruling circle, careful scrutiny of the event will reveal that what have been coopted are not students at all but the socioeconomic moths and butterflies that inevitably emerge from student cocoons. What the survey researcher often examines is nothing but an abandoned cocoon.

Masked by on- or off-campus rhetoric are the usual down-to-earth economic interests. Regardless of the radical revolutionary posture students are wont to assume while not burdened with responsibility and while acting out the expected role of social activist, they eventually discover that career prospects for revolutionaries are exceedignly poor. Thus for the overwhelming majority no real alternative exists. The product of the university must reorient himself, and promptly so, if he wants to climb up the ladder the established order has prepared for him.[8]

If students want to influence public policy, again as students and not as stalking horses for nonacademic, noneducational causes, they must find allies. Alone their chances of being heard where it counts are extremely poor. Unfortunately for them, what on purely ideological grounds may appear to be their natural allies — the opposition-oriented leadership element in the worker and peasant movements and organizations — in the real world turn out to be their natural antagonists, antiintellectual to the core. There may be some justification in this attitude.

It has been said that higher education in Africa results in *zweckentfremdung,* alienation from an initial purpose.[9] For a variety of reasons, higher education in Africa does tend to remove the end product from his natural environment. This is true more in French than in British-influenced areas, but the tendency is apparent everywhere. Perhaps the trend is a reflection of the development syndrome that sees modernity lending a hand only to the educated, lifting only him into the present, leaving the rest decades if not centuries behind and in poverty and ignorance to boot.[10]

Professional associations and informal groupings of doctors, lawyers, and teachers are also under a cloud for approximately the same reasons that apply to the educated generally. Their position is aptly summarized in the following vignette of Kenya's Bar.

> It developed as part of the elite colonial society, its leaders were the leaders of the Asian and European communities in political and public affairs, and the bulk of the work was for these communities. [The Bar] had been deliberately excluded from professional contact with the African part of society in 1930, and inevitably thereafter, its interests in that part of society and its problems waned. . . . Increasingly, it saw itself as an integral part of the elite, and, as such, entitled to share its privileges, particularly that of self-government based on the English pattern.[11]

Granted, the situation in Kenya is unique, or fairly so: a long tradition of racial dualism before independence, to be followed by an African-Asian-European attempt at mutual accommodation. Still, the Kenyan model is fairly typical; social and economic dualism continues even in uniracial Africa, with a black or indigenous elite rising only gradually to become part of the foreign or foreign-dominated reference and peer group. After all, it has been only since the late fifties and early sixties that lawyers, doctors, and university professors have been trained on the continent in appreciable numbers.

Still, as economic interest groups Africa's professionals need not fear much. Their prime interest will be satisfied as long as demands for their particular skill remain high. A rate of remuneration not too far below the salaries and fees their European counterparts overseas obtain (above in some instances) seems assured, barring severe national economic setbacks, of course.

SCHOOL-LEAVERS

Virtually leaderless, relatively inarticulate, but potentially far more explosive than university students are the graduates of secondary schools, the most potent element in the general category of school-leavers. They are the product of a drive initiated shortly before independence and accelerated by the African successor regimes. Growing at an alarming rate, sufficiently educated to be conscious of a life better than the one that had been their station — and remains that of their fathers — unwilling, therefore, to return to the rural areas, and almost totally averse to manual labor, they constitute the ideal material for the demagogue.[12]

The sheer momentum of the education explosion, fueled constantly by the conviction among Africa's new leaders that education equals development, hence brings closer the solution of their most urgent problems, predictably generates even greater demands from below for expansion of educational opportunities. As a result, the process of disgorging from more and more schools ever larger numbers of graduates into stagnant, at best sluggish economies continues without letup. More specifically, each year employment must be found for ever increasing numbers in a nonexpanding, comparatively narrow wage-earning sector. One estimate is that the number of young people entering the labor market is at least twice that of workers withdrawing. It is predicted that the ratio will increase to about three to one by 1980.[13]

Wisely or not, the surplus migrates to the cities, and to the larger ones at that, with all attending consequences and side effects. But it is by no means clear what form the expected protest will take. The temptation is great to regard these candidates for discontent and disillusionment as the core of social revolutionary action in Marxist terms, the vanguard of the proletarian revolt.[14] More likely, by all appearances the leadership element for this segment will be drawn from the more highly trained and educated who went beyond secondary schools. Yet the record shows that even they cannot retain mass following.

A special source of frustration for school-leavers is that their education and training lacks relevance to social, economic, and technical reality. Lack of funds, of staff, and of adequate motivation, combined with the tenacity of the European rear guard, have permitted maintenance of the colonial pattern that pretended to prepare Africa's youth for tomorrow by passing on to them relics of Europe's past. By such means hundreds of thousands of expectant youngsters have been and in many cases still are being prepared for positions that either have not yet materialized on the African scene in sufficient quantity to meet demand or may never be part of modern Africa. This irrelevance is true across the board, including, incredible though this might seem, vocational training in agriculture.[15]

To call these unfortunates "surplus intellectuals" (as has been done) may be inappropriate. More accurately they are, in the main, semieducated and semitrained, and as such are candidates for recruitment into the broader army of disaffected, disillusioned opponents of whoever is in power.[16] A surplus of the semitrained, mostly university level, can convert into a classic revolutionary spearhead (as noted earlier, for a brief period only) unless absorbed, continuously and commensurate with the expected steady increase, into relatively unproductive, supernumerary positions that the state creates for that purpose.

Quantitatively, this segment of the work force is quite small, probably not ranging above 3 percent of the total work force in any given country and below in most. But the position of a highly trained person in a preponderantly unskilled environment looms as a glittering prize to the hundreds of thousands below who are unqualified but quite pretentious. The situation approaches the revolutionary threshold where prospects for relief of mass unemployment among potential wage and salary earners drop below a certain level.[17]

In many instances the erroneous impression has been formed among job seekers that Asians or other foreigners, including Africans from other states, constitute the sole obstacle to fulfillment of their immediate demands. Once the more volatile and articulate among the employables or the unemployed are persuaded that adequate opportunities can be provided through mass expulsion of foreigners at the middle-level manpower range, the revolutionary situation reaches a critical stage.

Obviously, for some time to come development aspirations will not be matched by available means. In the circumstances an overly precipitous promotion of the semiskilled into more highly paid positions — an appealing formula in the eyes of hard-pressed office holders — seems inadvisable. To ensure even a moderate rate of progress toward development goals, it is mandatory that certain minimum standards of performance be maintained in the more critical sectors. Certainly, allowing performance standards for high-level manpower positions to deteriorate further forecloses all opportunities for increased production of wealth, an absolute necessity for relief of the burgeoning demand for employment.[18]

Organized Religion

It should surprise no one if organized, Western-spawned and supported religion encounters difficulties in independent Africa and is, in fact, under increasing pressure to abandon the more visible pressure and influence vantage points acquired originally with the active support of colonial government. Eventually it may have to retreat from all direct participation in public affairs, for from the more critical perspective of rejuvenated Africa the conduct of the Western churches and missions in the past has been strange indeed. It is still difficult to reconcile such conduct with avowed Christian objectives in many parts today.

The shabby treatment that foreign religious enterprise accorded the indigenous rituals and the traditional-religious and religious functionaries is difficult to forget. Nor is it possible to conceal the churches' and missions' intimate identification and affiliation with colonial rule at the source in Europe and in the annexed territories. Nor will it be possible to hide the high incidence of hypocrisy that manifested itself in church and mission failure to practice what they preached. With notable and on occasion heroic exceptions, the record of Christian churches and missions on the continent in such matters of social justice as race relations and economic exploitation is a stain only time can remove.

Perhaps the most fundamental error committed by the Western bearers of the universal message of divine love lies in what can only be termed racist assumptions about divinity. In an overwhelmingly black or certainly non-white environment, they quite seriously advanced the proposition that the Son of God, hence by implication God himself, the Virgin Mary, and all of the angels always were and still are white; as they were portrayed graphically they most likely showed Anglo-Saxon or Germanic characteristics. It is doubtful whether Africanization of the clergy, of the mission staffs, and of the heavenly hosts will suffice to bridge the relevance gap created over centuries of cultural and psychological tactlessness and insensitivity.

This alienation and continued affiliation with churches overseas, a financial necessity for all churches except those in European-ruled southern Africa, pushes organized religion toward the end of the pressure and interest group queue nearly everywhere. Perhaps the belated shift to a more universal concept of religious responsibility on a racially neutral basis will help to buy time. It is possible that sceptical African observers will be impressed by growing church opposition to apartheid, to continued control of Southwest Africa by the Republic of South Africa, to Rhodesian intransigence on matters of black self-government, and to continued Portuguese domination and control of Mozambique, Angola, and Guinea-Bissau. One may ask why foreign affiliated banks and trading houses, having compiled a similar record, do not suffer the same fate. The answer is simple. Organized religion is expendable; or so it seems in all respects but one — education.

Significantly, the value represented by organized, Western-affiliated religion in this respect has very little to do with its avowed spiritual mission. Summarily put, in a setting too poor to even begin to satisfy popular demand for schools and teachers, church and mission schools and modest to adequate funding with their ready-made staff still remain the only worldly answer to the prayers of African parents too poor to send their offspring to private institutions.[18]

In light of this value, and until sufficient locally supported and operated alternatives materialize, Western-financed organized religion may entertain some hope that its needs, at least with respect to education, may encounter sympathetic consideration at the top. Where education is less highly prized, or where performance of church-supported schools is strikingly inadequate, pressure potential will, of course, drop off correspondingly. The position will become untenable as the financial shortfalls experienced by the mother churches at home begin to affect their direct and indirect operations abroad. Actually, the repercussions of financial stringencies have already reached the continent, and several denominations have been compelled to raise needed funds locally; for obvious reasons this task cannot be very productive.[19] Things will become progressively more difficult as the African cultural and psychological awakening spreads, posing radically new and different demands for the clergy and the missionaries, white or black.

As the financial and technical value of Western churches and missions depreciates, Africa's secular leaders will be inclined to examine more closely than ever the sociopolitical propensities of organized religion in general. In particular they will begin to assess more realistically what many of them regard as subversion, at best opposition potential. A decade ago, Nkrumah placed the churches under a magnifying glass and actually imposed numerous restrictions on church officials. Eventually his ideological associate, Sékou Touré of Guinea, followed his lead, as did Mobutu in Zaire.[20]

Events in the Congo region and in Zambia tend to substantiate fears among the new leaders — many of whom, incidentally, obtained all or part of their education in Western-supported schools or missions — that unless organized religion is placed under tight restrictions it might get out of control for reasons not necessarily related to foreign influence. The 1964 holy war of the Lumpa Church in Zambia and its bloody aftermath revealed what aggregate religious pressure can do once the basic content — the clergy, the liturgy, and the ritual — is Africanized and the entire structure is detached from its Western moorings.

The Lumpa revolt and similar uprisings elsewhere demonstrate that the African offshoot could easily convert or be converted by interested parties into a social protest movement. Such a movement would be far broader, far more popular, and more dangerous to stability and security than any action of the original churches since the religious wars and interventions toward the end of the last century.[21] Similar considerations, incidentally, have led leaders in Muslim areas to restrict the activities of Western missions from the point of initial contact to this day.

The position of organized manifestations of Islam on the continent has been quite different. Missionary activities and proselytizing, though intense and widespread, do not appear to have enjoyed the same measure of financial support from their parent churches — Middle Eastern in this case — as did Roman Catholic operations from theirs. When large sums began to flow from North Africa to the south, the underlying motivation was less spiritual than political conspiratorial. When aid was offered to factions in Chad and the Sudan — from oil-rich and ideologically aggressive Libya, for instance — the intent appears to have been to render support to insurrection rather than to strengthen the religious presence of Islam. It is likely that the century-old memories of Arab slave raiding in black Africa and the accompanying atrocities and indignities render the links between the sources of Islam and its African variants extremely brittle and tenuous.

Moreover, Islam is more than a mere religious expression; it is a way of life. As such, it blends into the African traditional structure and life, where religious and secular concerns flow together to constitute one indivisible whole. In the less developed and less modernized regions immediately south of the Sahara, from Senegal to Chad, the African branches of Islam are, in fact, *the* traditional structure. As such, their pressure and interest group propensities are virtually indistinguishable from the conservatism of traditional demands everywhere. Their relative importance vis-a-vis other groups contending for scarce resources is coterminous with traditional interest group activity in general. (We considered the unusual case of the Senegalese muridiya earlier.)[22]

A Note on Political Parties

We trust that we have dealt persuasively with the myth of the potent political party in Part I. As a means of interest aggregation the African party is no more effective than it is as an instrument of power. The reasons are roughly identical: those already in supreme command fear rivalry. To protect themselves and their positions they tend to interdict formation of any kind of grouping that can conceivably spawn opposition. Where conditions are not yet ripe to prohibit political parties, one may take it for granted that all potential rivals are hamstrung in all essential respects. Taken together with the environmental and technical difficulties that affect all organization building in developing areas, all political parties, including the so-called ruling ones, are thereby kept chronically short of operating funds, talent, and all other prerequisites of effective party activity in the traditional sense. It is obvious that these shortages render most unlikely the parties' interest aggregation and articulation propensities except in one important respect: the self-interest of the party bureaucracy, the functionaries, and, of course, the top leadership will still be served.

Thus, as a means of bringing interests and demands to the decision-making and policy-planning surface, the typical political party on the continent with exceedingly few exceptions possesses all of the efficiency of a fishing net badly tattered and frayed and as open beneath as at the top. Per chance something might cling to the solid rim, but such a chance is unlikely. Financial anemia, managerial inefficiency that increases with distance from the capital, and lack of leadership talent combined with the other characteristics of developing societies make it virtually impossible for the leadership to remain in meaningful contact and communication with the so-called grass roots. In fact, grass roots would be an inappropriate term in the absence of any proof that there is any substantive connection or link between the bottom and the top, leaving aside rhetoric and political theory, of course.[23]

It is most unlikely that any organization so afflicted will be able to attract and maintain a body of supporters constant enough to warrant description as membership. As for votes cast in elections — a commonly used basis for assessment of party strength — there is no evidence either to suggest involvement of anything more than a most transitory, casual relationship with specific party organizations or candidates.

As for the tight inner circle of middle-level functionaries who make use of the party, including the so-called mass party, for their own ends, it is extremely likely that it will always be captive, wholly or substantially dependent on whoever controls patronage. Even if development proceeds and a degree of prosperity is attained, as in the Ivory Coast, the gravitational pull from the center will become stronger rather than weaker as central governments throughout the continent tend to accumulate means of control at a rate far greater than the rest of their respective countries combined. Consequently, the stamp of central authority and interest will be implanted ever more firmly on whatever partylike formations may take shape, under whatever name they may be brought into existence, for whatever purpose.[24]

What of the personalized political machine as an instrument of interest aggregation and pressure? The cases open to close analysis — Nkrumah's machine, for instance — show quite conclusively that they feed exclusively on patronage dispensed from above with all that this entails.[25] As its name implies, the machine serves its creator or manipulator. Only to the extent that the supreme dispenser of patronage allows freedom of action can the lesser leaders and functionaries pursue their own interests, always looking over their shoulders, of course. Leaving aside wholly personal demands and idiosyncracies, it is obvious that high on the list of demands are retention of privileges and perquisites, income, legitimate and other, and beyond that preservation of the system that brought them their good fortune. Like the party but more so, the machine must strive to eliminate rival organizations. Understandably, for general comfort and convenience of those in control, arrangements are sought to secure access to sources of wealth on a permanent basis.

Such access is assured by the nature of things. As we have shown, the machine is oiled by funds extracted openly on a regular and continuing basis from the public treasury, from captive or dependent private sources, and by stealth, through bribery and corruption. These sources hardly are conducive to interest group behavior along ordinary lines. An organism kept alive by such means will be oriented primarily if not exclusively to serve the individual or group whose hands are at the controls. It has been said that in "Liberia the True Whig Party is very much alive and, unless it is realized that it is from the Party and not even from a personality as great as President Tubman, that authority springs, Liberia cannot be understood."[26] It was not at all difficult, of course, to understand Liberia while President Tubman was alive and in control, provided one did not allow *the appearance* of the True Whig Party to deceive one into mistaking the shadow for the substance.

VII

Public Decision
and Policymaking

Even freedom, that most precious gift of all sometimes means little
more than the power to decide how you would cut your cake
if you had one.

KIMBLE, cited in Anton Rupert
PROGRESS THROUGH PARTNERSHIP

21

Decision and Policymakers

Problems of Definition and Identification

A group of scholars who gathered at a professional meeting toward the end of the decade that had seen a veritable explosion of conceptual and methodological innovation in the social sciences asked themselves whether political science had not perhaps created a monster that was now about to swallow its children. It would not be historic to discover that a multitude of scholars had become so fascinated with an idea, a concept, or a major thesis that all alternate ways of viewing reality had been blotted out. It is conceivable that this blindness has occurred with regard to government, its corollary, authority, and the operational manifestations of decision and policymaking. It should not be ruled out that a commitment to formality and rigidity, to artificial typology and purely theoretical classification may indeed have created an intellectual vortex that swallows up all or most contrary propositions or, at best, forces them into firmly set patterns of thought.

Thus, the word *government* conjures up visions of individuals and groups located in clearly identifiable offices, formulating and executing policies in a set manner, transmitting messages through clearly delineated channels in the form of directives, under a great variety of names, in a distinct fashion to specific targets. To the reader even vaguely familiar with living government and authority today this is not a convincing portrayal; in much of professional literature the decision- and policymaking landscape is etched far too precisely — so precisely, in fact, that it may have no practical bearing on reality. In the context of the less developed world, attempts to draw sharp distinctions between governmental and nongovernmental spheres, between legal-authoritative and effective-authoritative, between public and private, or even national and international may be doubly hazardous.

It is not our purpose here to attempt to resolve all definitional ambigui-

285

ties arising from the study of decision and policymaking. The number of possible, even plausible conceptual and methodological approaches and combinations one could employ is limitless. The subject area becomes manageable, and perhaps also intelligible, only if confined to a specific sector, but even then the field still is wide open, since it is by no means settled what portion of the totality of social activity is included and what is excluded under the heading of decision and policymaking. A common error in decision-making analysis, for example, credits individual decision makers with abilities no human possesses, including dictators in totalitarian systems. Further, a frequently overlooked point is that decisions not made or made but not as intended may play as important a role in the entire process as do decisions made and deliberately so.

Whatever one's point of departure or focus, it can be safely accepted that someone somewhere within the maze of command headquarters formulates and promulgates policies on matters of broad public concern; someone somewhere makes decisions that eventually will impact on state and society. The making of public policy and of relevant decisions is a fact, and an important one at that. While it may be difficult to resolve the picture in every detail, several major features and characteristics can be discerned. We may not be able to generalize on the precise identity of the personnel, may not be able to designate with precision the exact locus from which given policies and decisions emanate, may be unable ever to detect with certainty all relevant influences or inputs, and yet learn something about the process by asking, not who, but why and to what end.

Public decision and policymaking are the penultimate steps in what power politics is all about. Contending forces seek to secure specific objectives. Eventually the successful ones obtain satisfaction. They receive their share, which in this particular context is the ultimate step. Patterns of reward and punishment and of resource allocation, patterns in which benefits are bestowed or denied are discernible and reveal the concrete outcome of politics; as Lasswell has formulated it, decision and policymaking determine who gets what, when, and how. While the inner workings of the political process often may remain concealed from our view, except in relatively trivial and inconsequential small group situations, the broad outlines of the product of that process are accessible and reveal the direction in which a given regime or system is traveling. For that purpose analysis of decisions actually made should prove far more rewarding than rhetoric about what seems desirable.

The quest for identification of the actual locus of decision and policymaking, or of the actual person or office, often proves futile because of the difficulty inherent in drawing distinctions between public and private interest or even between public and private sector. The distinctions are quite blurred at the individual level of, say, cabinet officer, a high-ranking civil servant, a dictator, or an industrial tycoon. Public and private interests become quite intertwined at that level, neat legalistic distinctions under such headings as "conflict of interest" to the contrary notwithstanding.

In 1969 a Nigerian economist complained that "resources" were being transferred to government at the expense of the private sector.[1] At work here is the fallacy of mistaking legal-constitutional divisions for real ones. Evidence is quite persuasive that in the Nigeria he referred to, and in less developed areas generally, resources ostensibly being transferred — allocated away from the private sector — eventually end up in private hands once again. Even where it is not a direct case of misappropriation of funds or of stealing or of some other more discreet variant of theft, funds alleged to be transferred in the public interest simply are not at the disposal of the public, not even at the disposal of the public's representatives, whoever they may be.

What is actually transpiring is a replication of the classic conjurer's trick. The public official or decision maker is seen stepping into a box labeled *public sector,* only to emerge, to the spectator's amazement, from a second box, *private sector.* (The discovery is made usually only by chance and is called, quite inappropriately, a conflict of interest scandal.) How is the feat accomplished? With mirrors, of course. The change is accomplished in the dark, all movement concealed from the spectator's view, and while the observer confidently assumes that the official is still concealed in the *public sector* box.

We noted earlier that in discussing various approaches to identification of the ultimate controlling power elite Dahl inquired whether such endeavors do not perhaps produce a regressive theory that leads us inevitably into the trap of always suspecting more power leaders, or rulers, behind those already identified. This suspicion could apply also to studies of decision making. Actually, Dahl surrenders too quickly.

Social science seems to be at bay with respect to power, rule, and decision analysis, partly because it is not prepared to penetrate the defenses established by those it seeks to identify. For instance, it seems to stop short of examining the social purposes and functions of libel laws, laws to protect the privacy of public officials, national security laws, and legislation or measures alleged to maintain law and order. To cite but one illustration, the facade created to conceal massive confusion of private and public interest in the late Tubman regime in Liberia was not seriously examined in social science coverage for decades. The long-standing refusal of most United States senators to agree to full disclosure of private financial ramifications of their public role is another case in point. That such information can be effectively concealed from the public in spite of an independent and extremely efficient and vigilant press speaks volumes.

Following the tracks of money, however, leads us to additional complications. As we have shown, lines of power and influence, and consequently of decision and policymaking, crisscross national boundaries almost at will.

Few policies of major public consequence are devised that apply exclusively
to the national domain, and few decisions at that level are made purely
within the national context. The entire subject matter, therefore, must be
regarded as extremely fluid and certainly multidimensional.

Fundamental Economic Determinants

A fundamental determinant of public policy and attendant decisions is, of
course, the dominant mode of production. Noting the comparatively wider
distribution of income in peasant economies, Helleiner concludes that decision making in these settings must also be widely dispersed.[2] An opposite
conclusion could be equally plausible. Because income is widely dispersed,
the power and influence component of income is more highly diluted.
Hence, relatively modest but highly concentrated accumulations of wealth
can assert themselves more effectively than is possible where large and disparate concentrations of income and wealth offer competition, opposition,
and too many diversionary opportunities for predatory officials and leaders
to contend with.

It is too early to draw firm conclusions, but the steep increase in production of mineral oil in Nigeria not only could revolutionize the power structure there but also could drastically alter the decision- and policymaking
environment in the process. Export trade, which dominated the society
and the state for decades, may give way to export per se, through wholly
different channels, by radically different procedures and different means.
Not too many countries, however, can expect significant alterations in the
mode by which their primary source of income is produced.

The Personal Dimension

More pervasive as an environmental input is the personal dimension of the
African decision and policymaker. Although we do not reliably know who
he may be in all cases, we do know in what climate of opinion, information,
and knowledge he must operate.

In considering the time-space relevance of the United States President's
annual state of the union message to the Congress Aurelio Peccei argues
that our (Western) time horizons may be too short for our purposes. He
attributes this state to "our elective political institutions and their reliance
on popular consensus within the sphere of the nation-state, and also the
mercantile and hedonistic leanings of our Western society."[3] Of course,
Peccei had in mind systems that dispose of far greater numbers of mature
and well-trained occupants of high-level positions and enjoy far stronger
social underpinnings for policies and decisions than is characteristic of less
developed areas. The situation is analogous to a space probe that misses its
objective because its programmer failed to take into account that the target

is in motion while the probe is under way. The degree of accuracy in aiming developmentally at distant targets should be far higher in industrially advanced systems.

The average decision maker aims for objectives within his more immediate, personalized range of vision. He is likely to accord highest priority to projects that in his judgment offer the greatest promise within his active lifetime. Decisions of minimum personal consequence to the decision maker and his immediate support system are likely to be postponed or shelved altogether. Such ambivalence was characteristic of Kwame Nkrumah. Freed from the burdens of producing immediate results, with a target date in mind well beyond the career lifetime of the decision or policymaker, economic calculations and prognoses can be quite generous, even extravagant, and wholly impractical.

One source of the problem is the ability of the African decision and policymaker to create the universe within which he functions very much to his own liking. Corrective factors are few and, unfortunately, can be silenced all too easily. In certain respects the African decision and policymaker can create his own environment, tailored, of course, to accommodate his own preferences and predelictions. It is entirely possible that major policies and related decisions pertain to wholly personalized instead of objectively determined universes.

For that reason, some scholars invite false leads by insistence that leadership analysis be closely correlated with broader social and natural environmental factors and forces.[4] For example, linkages to kinship and other groups need not materially bear on the behavior of decision makers, partly because these environmental factors still are not sufficiently assertive and homogeneous to coalesce in time to affect policy and decision, and because chances are that the individual in question may be quite oblivious of what concerns the scholar. The argument that because ruler or official X operates in country or society Y he must behave in Z fashion cannot be more than pure conjecture at this point. It may always remain conjecture.

The analytical hazards of rash theorizing on the person-environment nexus are illustrated in an International Bank for Reconstruction and Development (IBRD) report on the decision-making system under Nkrumah.

> Although the [Nkrumah] government's stated organizational principles were specialization of function and clarity of responsibility, the actual practice was to increase centralization of decision-making at the top, with division and isolation of operating agencies at the bottom.[5]

It has been argued that in the underendowed environment, decentralized, autonomous decision making may be the better of several choices partly because of the high costs of centralization. The Ghanaian experience tends to contradict this argument. As it developed, the system worked to separate and divide the local subsystems, allowing the central leader to play one against the other.

In actual practice, decentralization means proliferation of relatively impotent, fragmented, probably atrophying decision units. Few if any of the local or subunits possess information adequate for reasonably realistic determination of the reality around them. Decisions are made without regard to adjacent sectors, without reference to past experiences, which are not accumulated or evaluated, and without regard to probable future developments. In the aggregate, decisions so made will certainly have an eventual impact on society but will scarcely have a decisive influence on contemporary events. In the present context most crucial, the hiatus between lower and upper echelons leaves the upper one very much suspended in air and, as we have said, all too frequently following their own noses.

Isolation from reality in principal decision- and policymaking groups can assume astounding dimensions, as was demonstrated during the last years of the Nkrumah regime. One of the most critical environmental inputs in Ghanaian policy formulation and its ramifications was the matter of balance of payments. There is evidence that this problem was not fully perceived until 1965, because no single agency had a complete inventory of the rapidly growing external debt obligation. Such perceptual aberrations, of course, are not unknown in the more advanced countries, but in the African economic setting the consequence can be catastrophic.

Decisions and policies, however false and inappropriate, once made and cast into legal form assume a rationality all their own. Subsequent actions are compulsively related to them; the error becomes an ironclad fact, an input, sets standards for years, and sows the seeds for subsidiary decisions likely to issue forth for decades.

Where they are intent on obtaining facts, decision makers in Africa simply find it most difficult to break through the barriers of incompetence. Of numerous illustrations one can cite, the following may be regarded as typical and reliable, partly because the intent was not to discredit a regime but rather to render a major economic sector — namely, the critical railway system of Nigeria — more economical and efficient. The Commission of Inquiry into the Affairs of the Nigerian Railway Corporation found that the chief accountant of the corporation, surely a most important person in Nigeria's export-import system — did not understand elementary concepts of accounting and revenue control and did not comprehend "what was meant by physical control of revenue receipts, and even after he had the point explained to him, he maintained that it eluded him."[6] A French banker offered this comment on the same theme. "The countries [in French-speaking Africa] ask us to give aid, to invest. My board asks me about a certain country in Africa. I must report that there are no accounts, or, if there are, they may be plus or minus one million dollars."[7]

It is at this point that the full weight of decision making at the international level, as distinct from the national and local levels, can be appreciated. In international finance, international trade, banking, investment, and mining, transporting, marketing, and processing of basic raw materials, in the movement of primary products on which most if not all economies depend, decision makers in Paris, New York, Washington, London, or Zurich, are likely to be far better equipped than are their African counterparts in Dakar, Abidjan, Accra, Lagos, Lusaka, or Nairobi.

Even in relatively favorable conditions African decision makers still are far removed from reliable data. In Nigeria for instance, the large increase of revenue from crude oil has necessitated allocation of substantial resources to creation of a more competent Nigerian corps of revenue and production analysts; Zambia encounters the same problem in assessing the facts pertaining to the copper industry there. Ghana is said to have lost millions because of poor intelligence on its own cocoa crop.[8]

The role of expert advisers in this regard cannot be underestimated. Although he addressed himself to affairs in the United States, Karl Kaysen offers what seem to be the most pertinent remarks on the subject. In discussing the "commitment" of certain presidential economic advisers to certain models and theories (e.g., the theory of the competitive market), he writes:

> The role of the economist in policy formation in these areas is almost diametrically opposite to that envisaged in the formal theory of policy-making. ... He functions primarily as a propagandist of values not as a technician supplying data for the pre-existing preferences of the policy-makers. Some of his propaganda is directed at those participants in political decision-making to whom the advisers are directly responsive, aimed at shaping their values in the direction of the adviser's own. Much of it is directed through his political superiors to other participants in the political process — including the general public — and the adviser becomes, in fact, a supplier of arguments and briefs which seek to gain wider support for economists' political values.[9]

When the advisers are tied in with the enormously more competent, because better equipped, foreign enterprises that provide the major share of a government's revenue or are indirectly responsible for a major share, the impact of that input can be assessed as equal or superior to that of all indigenous sources of advice combined.

Sir Arthur Lewis has pointed out that there is absolutely no reason to regard the African leader as any more noble — or any more honest, for that matter — than his analogue in the developed world, and he, we know, well deserves closest supervision and control.[10] Moreover, the African engaged in decision and policymaking usually lacks experience. Therefore, it may be more productive to distinguish sets of decision makers not as Western or non-Western, a conceptual dichotomy that has long dominated social analysis, but on grounds of accumulated experience in positions held, training, and related qualities. In the real world an experienced person in a key position, willing to surround himself with competent advisers, and, equally important, endowed with a personality and mind that permit him to accept advice may be far less prone to embark on irrational adventures than one who is embedded on paper in a solid complex of institutional checks and balances yet is totally inexperienced, entirely at sea intellectually, and temperamentally averse to accepting advice from anyone.

There is room for doubt, of course, about what is and what is not rational. It is possible for a decision to be declared irrational by one set of standards yet be eminently rational by another. Harsanyi reminds us that it is possible for a very rational person to make wholly irrational decisions, and, in turn, what at first glance may appear to be irrational may actually work quite logically toward a long-range goal hidden from the observer's view.[11]

It is possible also that the only meaningful measure of a decision's rationality may be that related to objective economic considerations: Is the decision in line with the resources required for its implementation? If not, have provisions been made to secure the requisite resources? In that framework what has been termed "disjointed incrementalism in policymaking — a term quite prominent in literature on African rule — will not be of much consequence. Behind the facade of illogical and seemingly irrational rhetoric, and even reported decision making, there could be entirely rational progress toward well-defined objectives, discounting the zigs and zags of economic planning and development. The bread-and-butter decisions, on resource allocation, import-export, mining, taxes, royalties, are less disjointed than meets the eye.

Yet if one accepts that data are unreliable, when they exist at all, even what Oscar Lange terms "methodological rationality" may be little more than a form of shadowboxing. We may recall a reference made earlier. "Someone bases his plan of travel on the official time-table but fails to reach his destination, because contrary to the information given, the train does not stop there." This statement, we noted, illustrates methodological but not factual rationality.[12] Can one apply the distinction to developing countries? Can one distinguish between methodological and factual rationality when the facts are too unreliable to attach any substantive significance to methodological rationality? For instance, is there much point to such distinctions when the methodologically correct and rational development plan simply fails to reflect to any appreciable extent, especially in critical respects, vital economic facts?

Too much can be made of methodological rationality, too little of evidence of irrational methodological or factual decision making. Decisions made under the Nkrumah regime, irrational in both respects by Soviet as well as American expert judgment, had enormous, long-range repercussions

— for example, steeply rising cost of servicing ill-advised loans, skyrocketing costs of equipment needed to operate uneconomic enterprises, increased cost of capital, or the cost of unplanned urbanization where such urbanization did not necessarily increase productivity. The cost of methodologically as well as factually faulty decision making, in other words, may be far higher in the more vulnerable economies of the developing world, and a closer look at the sources of personal decision making may be warranted.[13]

It is clear from the writings of many a biased and personally involved observer that their assessments of the decision makers in Africa, or in all underendowed societies, are based not on considerations of rationality at all but on wishful thinking. Social scientists in particular have their sources of inspiration in wishful thought when they substitute abstractions of their own invention for the matrix of events from which decisions arise. Erratic decision making in such a setting can then be considered quite rational, as is demonstrated so charmingly in Alice in Wonderland.[14]

Obsession with abstractions has led to exaggeration of the role and importance of ideology and social philosophy in public policy formation in Africa. The abstraction was allowed to determine behavior since it was given that if a leader said he was a socialist it followed inexorably that he had to behave as a socialist would. This is putting the cart before the horse. The record of decisions made is uncovered quite easily, and there is no need, therefore, to speculate on the nature of the pattern of decisions or on the social philosophy of the decision makers in question in terms of the decisions made as distinct from decisions attributed to them by some social scientists intent mainly on providing support for abstract theoretical assumptions.

Obvious from the record is the decision maker's preoccupation with considerations of personal security, physical and economic. It would be exceedingly shortsighted not to consider this an environment where the alternatives to officeholding often are either exile or retirement to ignominious existence in the shadows. Not to calculate the effects of bribery and corruption on decision making would be folly. The task of identifying motivation is further complicated by the deficiencies of all officeholders who are moved into positions of power and influence by considerations often quite unrelated to the office they are to hold or the qualifications associated with it. The gap between an African officeholder's perception of the tasks associated with his office or of the policies he is to apply or follow or implement is no less yawning than that characterizing many an officeholder in the United States or Great Britain.[15]

It is most difficult, if not beyond available analytical tools in most instances, to determine how much a given policy decision is steeped in philosophy and how much it reflects the policymaker's commitment to certain forms of creation of personal wealth. As one United States senator has put it, it was not "conflict of interest" that prompted him to support causes dear to the oil and gas lobbies but "identity of interests" (Senator Long, Louisiana). Assumed for argument's sake that Kwame Nkrumah's interests in the development of the Ghanaian economy were identical with his personal interests, it still strains credibility too much to accept that the confluence of interests was pure coincidence. The answer to the puzzle is provided, of course, by analysis of the policy alternatives if viewed in light of the personal-public interest identity hypothesis. For instance, if considerations of a personal nature had not been involved in awards of the more substantial contracts, would feasibility studies of projects have been omitted nevertheless, would the need for secrecy, for concealment of projects from the critical eyes of experts, have been mandatory? The same hypothesis applies to the controversial public policy decisions of the principals in the first Nigerian Federal Republic as it does to personally rewarding decisions made by leaders everywhere.

Out of this mix comes the reality of decision making in underendowed areas. Lack of experience, pressures of the type discussed, the force of persuasion applied by hucksters (economic propagandists) constantly invite flight from reality in public oratory, rhetoric, and official formulation, and in the material used in many a Ph.D. thesis and many a theoretical treatise. Andrewski's comments are worth quoting in that connection.

> As on so many other points, there seems to be a vicious circle here, because the tendency to fall into word magic when talking about economic problems may well be due to the hopelessness of the situation. The phenomenon of flight from reality into some kind of make-believe can often be observed in communities facing insurmountable difficulties; and it seems to square well with Malinowski's theory of magic; the main point of which is that even people living on the most rudimentary level of culture think rationally about processes which they can control, but fall into an autistic mode of thinking when dealing with completely unmanageable and unpredictable phenomena. Given their means, the Tobrianders (as described by Malinowski) are very logical about how to build a canoe, but adopt irrational attitudes towards the weather or disease.[16]

Thus one need not endorse the extreme of rationality or irrationality or the extreme of philosophic underpinning or none. It is quite possible, in fact persuasive in the circumstances, that a mix exists, that decision making more often than not relates to that mix, or to several mixes, of diverse compositions. African leaders do not differ from their less experienced counterparts elsewhere; they are relatively rational on matters within their ken but take flights from reality on subjects beyond their experience, expertise, or knowledge. As we suggested earlier, this dichotomy applies equally to African intellectuals and nonintellectuals; it does so alone on the strength of the record compiled by intellectuals in the more highly developed societies. Increased reliance on quantified data, on rather unperceptive, unimaginative empirical investigation has obscured the central importance of the personality in decision making.[17]

At independence, social structure as it bore on public policy was in a primordial state; a universe was yet to be created. The analogy of the physical universe may be appropriate. As a universe cools, vapor turns into substance. The atoms, still moving about excitedly, gradually settle down to assume their new shapes. Only after this state occurs do theories about atomic behavior derived from settled conditions become relevant. Much social science theory derived from conditions in the developed world was applied prematurely to Africa, often with ludicrous results. Both developed and less developed systems are wracked by turbulence caused by excited social and human atoms but to different degrees, and the mix of vapor and cooled-off substance exists in different proportion.

In tropical Africa the vaporous often prevails, because the settled or traditional element progressively loses importance while alternate elements are still in process of formation. The foreign or expatriate element, though an active force, still is alien to the body politic of the developing system.

Traditional institutions lose importance first because of the nation-based institutional change — never a revolutionary change, as is often asserted. Next, the modernizing influences disorganize and disestablish traditional institutions and ways. Then the nation-state turns out to be inadequate as a means, or framework, for the solution of pressing problems. In their hearts decision makers become aware of the fundamental irrelevance of the nation-state to the solution of their basic economic problems, but for a variety of reasons their public postures cannot yet reveal that insight. Nevertheless, the basic irrelevance or insufficiency of the national framework affects their willingness to allow social conditions to control their options and behavior at the policymaking levels. In Africa we may be in a middle period where international forces are beginning to affect national ones, and where decision makers are gradually becoming cognizant of their ambiguous position between two conflicting worlds. The orderly world of traditional social science theory simply is not the world in which they must make their decisions.

Astonishingly, although evidence of the primacy of economics in determination of decision makers' behavior abounds, social science continues to produce works that pretend that other forces have been sufficiently identified to warrant generalizations.[18] In any case, the decision makers are feeling their way, are still highly impressionable, are shopping around, and the result is ad hoc impromptu policy formulation modified only by exigencies of budgets, debt service obligations, and the like.

While there are, of course, vague perceptions of the adverse impact of foreign influence and control on the freedom of decision in the new states, there is as yet no clear understanding of how that influence or that control could or should be restricted or eliminated. One should certainly not mistake the occasional article, speech, or interview for a consensus of decision makers. The economic systems are still too undefined, to cite one source of dispute and uncertainty, to permit formation of hard and fast decisions on the precise point where foreign influence can be dispensed with; in fact, in certain conditions its continued toleration might incur unacceptable psychological sacrifices.

Perceptions of propriety in modes of acquisition of wealth vary more widely among African decision makers than among their counterparts in the developed countries. Curiously, in these respects the Africans are credited with perceptions more firmly rooted than those of their models, for reasons that remain shrouded in mystery. The truth lies somewhere between Andreski and Apter or Riggs; probably closer to Andreski. Hoselitz cites wealth, education, and political power as conferring the highest social status in all except the most primitive societies.[19] Aside from the wide range of possibilities that list includes, and also leaving aside the vexing problem of definition of what constitutes *political* power, the list probably is as useful as any other; it may come closest to the core of what really motivates African decision makers.

One of the prime tests of certain ideological positions is the economic payoff from specific policy decisions. To distribute income or to raise revenue is a matter dealt with quite simply in a policy speech. At the level of budgetary decision making it turns into quite another matter. Before these two major options materialize, a number of hard decisions must be made that are likely to stand in direct contrast to the ideological desire to equalize wealth, for instance. First, productivity of the economy must be increased. In other words, before wealth can be distributed, wealth must be provided and secured. Before that can be done, foreign control must be reduced. This, again, requires policy decisions substantially unrelated to those designed to meet ideological objectives.

There is absolutely no reason to believe that African decision makers are better informed than their counterparts elsewhere. The effects of cost of living increases on social stability or the consequences of tax increase or reduction on production are mysteries not always understood by experts. The relationship between price increases and wage and salary freezes usually is perceived dimly but not understood in all important respects.

Examination of major policy addresses by principal African policymakers reveals a paucity of references to such elementary facets of international economics as the reality of the financial situation in which a given country may find itself. These leaders' speeches often suggest that sheer determination on the part of government and people is adequate to surmount all obstacles in the path of rapid development. To say that these are speeches meant only to reassure or exhort the uninformed public is to suggest that among themselves the same individuals discuss economic affairs more rationally and intelligently. No evidence of that exists, with a few notable exceptions. Significantly, the best informed and ablest individuals do not necessarily find favor as advisers to those who hold supreme power.[20]

The exigencies of the struggle to survive seem to prevent economically more astute leaders from emulating Nkrumah's example of inconsistency. He was quite capable of saying and writing that the United States AID program and the International Bank were tools of the CIA and imperialism, while at the same time he requested major loans from the United States and the Bank. Similarly, President Kaunda and President Nyerere moved to nationalize foreign enterprise as they invited foreign investors to bring their capital to their respective countries.[21]

One final comment on this subject. The notion that African, or black, brown, or white people apply different thought processes derived from the color of their skin, is most difficult to support. Do African leaders — decision and policymakers — actually, and as a matter of fact and not as a matter of conjecture or speculation, see the world differently; or are their views and perspectives simply those of the long-oppressed, humiliated, and exploited, and as such not materially different from views expressed by similarly positioned people elsewhere in the world? Professor Potekhin, the late eminent Soviet academician and specialist on African affairs, offered some cogent remarks on that subject. He pointed out that according to the concept of *negritude* white and black people have a different way of thinking: "the European's way of thinking is analytical and logical while the Negro African is intuitive. This, implies," Potekhin countered, "two methods of cognition, and cognition by means of comparison and intuition is Negro-African cognition. These anti-scientific ideas lead to absurd political conclusions."[22]

22

Major Policy Options and
Alternatives

Policy Determinants

Undoubtedly, most if not all of Africa's leaders are highly motivated to move their people as rapidly as possible into the 20th century. This for a variety of reasons. There is a conviction that the development gap disadvantages Africa's masses and that it must be bridged if the economic, social, technical, and cultural voids left by colonial rule are to be filled. Foreign control and influence must be reduced and foreigners replaced as rapidly as is practical; corollaries are diversification of the economies, expansion of economic and diplomatic bargaining potential, strengthening of internal defenses, and development of the African personality or whatever other regional or local ethnic variant can be identified. Perhaps nation-building is a major source of policy, but that is quite doubtful. Nationalism is a concept too nebulous to lend itself to specific policy formulation but seems to play a role as a distant divinity. The Nkrumahs may be the last of a generation of leaders intent on achieving continental unity in their lifetime, though goals of regional unity or cooperation still inspire occasional policy decisions.

It is possible to speculate whether race and ethnicity actually are prime factors in policy formation, though they do generate much rhetoric and propaganda. That racial sensitivities are widespread there can be no doubt, especially along the divide that separates European-dominated from black Africa. In that zone especially, reduction of European domination certainly, its complete elimination possibly, must be a wellspring of many a policy attempt. More than an attempt has not yet been risked. In this respect as in most others the overriding necessity of continuing reliance if not dependence on outside assistance has had a softening effect on otherwise hard attitudes. Indeed, dependence becomes itself a major source for policy formation.

It is difficult to determine with precision how conscious of these sources Africa's leaders are. More important, it is impossible to determine how well prepared they are to devote time and energy to understanding them better, or even adequately. Nkrumah and Touré clearly extended themselves in this respect, but they seem to be the exception among those who held or still hold actual power.

Public relations requirements direct governments to couch whatever they intend to do in language likely to appeal to the greatest number. Since the supply of words is virtually inexhaustible for all practical purposes, the sky can be the limit. Verbally, mountains can be moved, water made to spring forth from rocks, and leaders can walk on the waters. In the realm of propaganda, means need not be reconciled with ends.

In the real world, however, options are not unlimited. They are especially restricted on the continent of Africa. However appealing or grandiose an idea might be, if it is to be of any practical value it must touch ground somewhere, sometime. Contact with reality alters many intentions. At the policymaking level such contact causes reordering of priorities, narrows the range of choices, and brings closer to the policymaker the consequences of his acts. Human nature being what it is, we can confidently assume that as with any other policymakers, self-interest rises on the scale of values as risks become more real and more imminent.

The high incidence of personal rule on the continent suggests that considerations of personal safety are at or close to the top of the priority list, followed by the interests and demands of the principal support troops. Somewhere in the background, vaguely perceived most of the time but keenly noted on occasion, are considerations of general interest. Even these in all probability translate into security considerations in the minds of the command element; the masses must not be neglected to the point where an explosion becomes a possibility. That realization of possible mass dissatisfaction is a source of policy is clear; what is not at all clear is whether the threat is taken seriously enough to consume much policymaking time.

Aside from official pronouncements, memoirs, and autobiographies that contain extremely vague references to the public interest, satisfaction of consumer interest, and public welfare generally, very little evidence is available to suggest in-depth concern with fundamental social questions. Threats of uprisings seem to be attended to on an ad hoc basis. Rulers are secure in their knowledge that mass control and, if need be, suppression of revolts are purely military and police matters. In this respect Africa's leaders are, of course, no different from the typical heads of state or heads of governments in the developed world.

A common error in policy analysis of African regimes is to take foreign policy declarations too seriously. As in the realm of internal propaganda, foreign policy postures can be assumed at very little or no cost. The poorest country can advocate redistribution of the world's wealth; a regime that lacks military force to secure its own position internally can generously formulate military defense or attack plans for the entire continent. Thus the strong positions that certain of the more militant states assume on the South African and Rhodesian as well as the Portuguese colonial questions are in most cases actually extremely cheap. No significant costs are incurred, no substantive resources need be committed or shifted. The exception is Zambia, where special conditions that arose from the act of separation of the territory from Southern Rhodesia from the economic network created under the former Federation of Rhodesia and Nyasaland (Rhodesia, Zambia, and Malawi now) make extremely costly defense measures economically plausible. The foreign policy stances taken by Nkrumah, by the Algerian regime, by the Egyptians, and by other militant regimes far removed from the battleline should not be mistaken for actual policy decisions; they are dreams, propaganda ploys, at best suggestions and recommendations for the future.

Next to preservation of the self and of the immediate support group, the overriding, compelling objective, the policy problem that demands attention at the risk of disaster is posed by the constant presence of the financial wolf at the door. In technical terms, highest priority attaches to policy options that relate to the immediate task of meeting current obligations.

Before long-range plans can be seriously considered, before unproductive pet projects can be financed, policies must be devised to reduce the crushing debt incurred by all of the former colonies and in many cases increased as a result of imprudent spending practices adopted immediately after independence. Beyond the public debt — that is, beyond the obligations incurred or accepted by governments toward foreign and domestic creditors, mainly foreign — there are the private debts. Investors, originally invited to satisfy the capital hunger of finance-starved colonies, insist on regular and punctual servicing of their investments, including loans and other credit arrangements. In the absence of a strong private sector, and in any case compelled by the chronic shortage of foreign exchange, governments must also assume responsibility for this servicing.

Indeed, foreign exchange is the fulcrum of policy formulation. The foreign exchange fund at a given regime's disposal for free policy formulation — that is, excluding foreign exchange already committed — is the ball and chain on the policy feet of African policymakers. (A different analogy might compare this particular impediment to the narrow hem of the traditional Japanese kimono; the effect on the individual's freedom of movement is figuratively identical.)

"If," it has been said, "the Trojan Horse had foaled, horses today would not need hay." Much of the literature on policy planning and formulation as related to African governments is that iffy, as are most prognostications from the governments themselves. Schumpeter considered that gap between what is and what ought to be when he wrote: "The spirit of a people, its cultural level, its social structure, the deeds its policy may prepare — all this and more is written in its fiscal history, stripped of all its phrases. He who knows how to listen to its message, here discerns the thunder of world history more clearly than anywhere else."[1] Indeed, the fiscal history of a regime or of a country follows a logic quite distinct from the public face or posture a government may assume. In that respect there is no room for assumptions about wooden horses foaling.

The iron laws of fiscal restraint operate ruthlessly, though their force is not always immediately apparent. As a rule regimes intent on profligate spending can manage to do so only for a while and never without cost to high-priority projects and to the detriment of tasks that should have been attended to but were not because the necessary funds had been diverted. The day of reckoning cannot be avoided indefinitely.

Some wholly impractical policy proposals seem to make sense to some observers, perhaps because they are disinclined to engage in cost accounting or are simply not concerned with the economic dimensions and costs of great social myths. One such myth is that of modernization. World Bank experts, sensitive to the hazards inherent in applied mythology, have warned against "modernization for the sake of modernization."[2] Yet, the concept seems to have overpowering attractions for certain leaders, as it apparently has for a large number of development specialists. Regardless of costs, some countries expend enormous efforts to replace entirely serviceable machinery merely to modernize. Construction of skyscrapers is authorized where real estate values do not call for that type of land use and where the expense, therefore, may actually widen the gap between means and ends. After all, the investment is not returnable, as far as the public wealth is concerned, perhaps for decades; perhaps it will never pay. In many parts of the continent modernization of government machinery, social processes, and institutions and procedures amounts to little more than a very expensive but wholly superficial facelifting.

Most likely, modernization carried out without regard to costs produces hordes of white elephants: hotels without tourists and, incidentally, without maintenance and adequate supply; schools without adequately trained teachers or without teachers worth the name; hospitals without modern equipment, inappropriate for the tropics, and unsuitable for available technical skills. Equipment introduced for the sake of modernization frequently falls into disuse, and doctors and nurses may not be found in sufficient numbers to staff the hospital.

Uneconomic modernization clashes with the imperative of economic restraint dictated by available resources. Economically sound but unexciting projects are likely to be delayed in favor of projects that bear the superficial mark of modernization and pseudoprogress. It is scarcely a secret that in practice modernization all too frequently means preference for the immediate, dazzling, prestigious expenditure at the expense of a potentially

more valuable but delayed-benefit project that will not accrue to the benefit of the officeholder or at best only to his memory. (It is an intriguing
question how many African leaders devote much time and effort to devise
policies whose realization will be delayed beyond their time, and do so in
the expectation of credit in the annals of history.) Unemployment, the most
cultural reform, which is tedious, long range, and unexciting. Instead, following the mindless modernization theory, glittering pseudoreform projects
are launched that consume scarce resources, leave agriculture essentially
as is, and make no appreciable dent in unemployment. A form of surro-
gate modernization: it looks like it, consumes resources like it, yet produces no significant change for the better.

Like pseudomodernization, pseudodecolonization has its hypnotic attraction for the leader in search of spectacular success. To demonstrate to
himself and his people that he has thrown off the shackles of imperialism,
anticolonialism and anti-imperialism can turn into a consuming passion regardless of economic costs. Often the issues are joined over the question,
actually an imperative, of agricultural reform. In light of colonial practice,
to promote agricultural growth instead of industrial growth bears the hall-
mark of surrender if not sell-out of the fruits of independence. Sir Arthur
Lewis has calculated the dimensions of the dilemma for one country alone.
To initiate meaningful agricultural reform, not mindless modernization,
farmers would have to be offered incentives of the magnitude of the Nigerian oil bonanza; hundreds of millions of dollars would have to be found
for that purpose alone.[3] Yet the expenditure of such sums would bear the
imprint of preindependence colonial policy, which banked almost exclusively
on agriculture, and on one crop at that.

Acceptance of the status quo is an exceedingly bitter pill to swallow.
Few governments seem prepared to assume the risk; the government of
Kenya is one.[4] Yet in 1963 the same government through its propaganda
outlet, the dominant party, also promised flatly that "[the party] intends
that every child in Kenya shall have a minimum of seven years "free education." A group of independent analysts estimated that the cost of such an
ambitious program would be well over triple the figure set by the government, which raises questions about the proposed posture on agriculture
as well.[5]

Perhaps the most pervasive influence on policy, leaving aside the aforementioned human frailties and other consequences of social pathology, is
the increase of hard-headed, independent-thinking pragmatists at the policy
planning level. The awareness is spreading that a contradiction of enormous
proportions exists; if any substantive headway is to be made with the mandatory assault on poverty, the contradiction must be faced and not explained away.

Simply stated, the contradiction arises from a growing desire, born of impatience, to attack poverty through restructuring of the basic production

relationship on which state and society are founded. Such restructuring cannot be accomplished without a capital formation program of truly gargantuan proportions. Realists know that this end cannot be attained without assistance on a major scale, mainly from sources inclined to be antagonistic to the concept of fundamental social change.

To accommodate both diverging prongs of the policy fork, both sides must make a number of conceptual, philosophic, and ideological concessions, even if the foreign side happens to be socialist, as the Soviet Union has discovered in numerous instances. The African side must be prepared to postpone indefinitely the notion that sovereign independence must be rigidly interpreted. It must also devise ways and means of overcoming lack of confidence among potential donors of needed capital. The foreign side, in turn, must be prepared to accept what by all appearances, though not necessarily in substance, seems to be an anticapitalist stance. Put differently, foreign observers will have to ask more frequently "what do they do" instead of "what do they say."

Professor Lange provides a socialist formula for the accommodation by dividing economic policymaking into two principal parts. One part addresses itself to socioeconomic structure, including the basic question of production relationship; the other is restricted to current economic policy questions, development of existing production processes, and secondary adjustments and changes in the distribution of income and the like.[6]

The result of such accommodation may be a policy condominium. Because neither side is able to override the other and still make progress toward its objectives, a compromise must be effected. To be sure, nationalist rhetoric will continue to enunciate goals and intentions that to the realist must seem wholly inappropriate if not outright irrational. Leaders will continue to proclaim their intent to bury capitalism while requesting more investment, or they will insist that the mutually exclusive goals of national independence and Pan-African unity be pursued simultaneously. The thrust of the times will see, in slightly altered form, a repetition of a phrase used by a newspaper commentator who was examining the curious policy postures adopted by Sudanese leaders in 1971. "Without actually renouncing any of its socialist aims, the revolutionary Government of Maj. Gen. Gafaar al-Nimeiry is quietly trying to restore confidence in the private economic sector and persuade it that it has a place in the Sudan."[7]

Holt and Turner advance as one of their major hypotheses that development policies require that governments make a determined, explicit effort to adapt the social system to its material environment — "the adaptive functional requisite."[8] In the world of African finance and economics generally, the most relevant material environment for the first few decades, possibly the first half-century, is international in scope and involves foreign forces far more than domestic ones. (Since this is a source of embarrassment for African regimes, policies adapted on that premise must of necessity be camouflaged. Incidentally, the center of the adaptive function is the national capital with all that such a place entails.)[9]

In the final analysis, the principal wellsprings of policy are to be sought in the sphere of resource allocation, but identification of resources must precede allocation. Policy priorities are determined by the nature of the source or sources. Resources are not allocated indiscriminately for any purpose that comes to mind. Instead, a major share of available resources are already spoken for. The free fund is extremely limited and must be regarded as a reserve for the committed fund in the very likely event that the committed fund proves insufficient. Such shortages can result from any one of the numerous contingencies that characterize the policy climate in Africa today, including erosion or shrinkage due to world market price fluctuations in the principal export commodity, mismanagement, and inflation.

Fiscal Policy

Whatever ideological disguise power and politics may assume, and whatever all too rigid academic treatment may do to them, the unvarnished truth will emerge under the acid test of fiscal policymaking. At that point nebulous rhetoric and wishful aspirations must give way to hard decisions. If they do not, disaster usually is imminent.

Of the various misconceptions that surround fiscal policy in Africa, the first to be corrected relates to the artificial distinction most analysts draw between public and private financial management. Theoretically, fiscal policy is management of public funds derived from revenue and expended by or through public bodies. As we have shown, the reality is different. Everywhere on the continent fiscal policy must of necessity become deeply involved in private economic affairs at home and abroad, primarily because private capital and enterprise still remain the principal sources of economic dynamism and vitality, ranking far above the comparatively sluggish, inexperienced, and disoriented public competitor. Moreover, the private sector has the advantage of direct access to the principal centers of commerce, industry, and finance throughout the world.

Kindleberger has pointed out that one reason the reality of African fiscal management is so readily obscured is the analysts' excessive preoccupation with the technical side of fiscal policy at the expense of the real side.[10] Robson and Lury, for example, in their otherwise significant survey, *The Economies of Africa,* tend to completely overlook that in most if not all countries, a prime function of public fiscal policy is to further the interests of foreign private capital.[11] Further, they inadvertently convey a false impression with the deceptively persuasive comment that "[F]iscal policy has generally been the main instrument through which governments in Africa have operated hitherto."[12] This formulation conceals, though certainly not intentionally, that in Africa *government* must be interpreted broadly to include not only the public but also the private sectors, both foreign and domestic. In other words, fiscal policy also serves the invisible government — the trading and financial interests, for example. Indeed, fiscal policy may itself be regarded as a negotiable instrument subject to hard bargaining like any other commodity.

Once it is recognized that monetary power cannot be separated from fiscal management in the special conditions found in Africa, it becomes clear in what direction fiscal management must proceed. Private power is securely ensconced at the roots of the money tree from which governments hope eventually to harvest fruits. Without control over the root system, fiscal policymaking is bound to be ineffectual socially as well as economically. The reality of this situation is expressed charmingly in the Kenya Development Plan for 1970-74, in which the assumption that seemingly underlies the entire plan is that private capital will be available. However, it is eventually admitted that if "any of these general assumptions should fail to materialize, this would affect the whole economy . . ."[13] It most certainly would.

It is extremely important to remain aware that it is foreign more than indigenous capital that is involved. Under the laissez-faire doctrine, developed countries restrained public fiscal authority from entering the private sector.[14] That was on the assumption that the private sector performed as expected. When it failed, as in provision of steady employment, government assumed a share of the responsibility, largely through fiscal measures. African private enterprise being what it is, the major share of the responsibility for enlargement of employment opportunities everywhere falls on the shoulders of foreign capital, making it the partner of government with concomitant effects on fiscal policy and planning.

Then there is the other major bane of government and administration that we have encountered throughout our examination of public power: the regrettable fact that government often is totally blind. Efficient management of finances and money is difficult enough when reliable and adequate data are available. When none are available, or when the reliability is too precarious to place much trust in data, or when data are few and far between, policymaking is reduced to a form of guesswork, albeit sophisticated guesswork at times. As Stolper has put it, it may be a matter of "planning without facts."[15]

In such conditions overreliance on centralized fiscal policy management could be disastrous. Centrally originated errors, compounded most likely by macrothought propensities characteristic of all government, are likely to be far greater and more far-reaching in their consequences than are those committed by private enterprise whose built-in correctives probably function rather automatically. Holt and Turner draw our attention to the experience elsewhere in the developing world where fiscal decision makers, like policymakers, are severely handicapped by limited perception of the reality they are expected to cope with.[16] Knowing little if anything about such variables as velocity of money circulation, the early British, French, Chinese, or Japanese policymaker was unable to assess the immense funds tied up in the subsistence sector or in the narrow but economically and fiscally important zone between that and the small-scale exchange economy. Then as now in Africa, accounting procedures were hopelessly inadequate, frequently downright misleading.[17]

The full measure of the weakness that afflicts fiscal policy and planning is revealed in the following complaint.

> Unless the importance of the accounting function is recognized and given the highest priority in the allocation of human and financial resources and there are provided adequate accounting teams, who will ensure value for the money, *the remainder of the public service* is automatically rendered impotent.[18]

This statement is underscored by the findings of a UN agency. "The growth of the public sector in African countries has not, however been accompanied by adequate development of fiscal and financial statistics."[19]

In such conditions not only are fiscal and monetary policymaking propensities of government bodies severely circumscribed, but forecasting or projections of social and economic development and change also may well turn out to be fallacious. Major wellsprings of concern are the cyclical movements of prices, of monetary circulation — a reflection of the growth and harvesting cycles of the commonly dominant agricultural sources of income — and they dictate high-priority and timely compensatory measures. Yet successful implementation of countercyclical fiscal policy also calls for a number of technical measures that are difficult to get underway in the underdeveloped countries at the present stage. One such measure is the development and perfection of the technique of economic forecasting. Tripathy notes that in addition to weather, the terms of trade, which may fluctuate wildly, and the absence of an adequate national accounting system, which could be used as a basis for national budgeting and economic forecasting, are major drawbacks in any effort to provide against cyclical fluctuations of the economy through fiscal and monetary adjustments.[20]

In the circumstances, caution is indicated in all assessments of public policy designs, for unless based on real figures involving real monetary resources fiscal policy is a meaningless exercise; it is but a form of public entertainment. To stave off disaster, appropriate fiscal policies must be supplemented or accompanied by substantial control of resources owned and operated by the better equipped private, most likely foreign element.

As things are, fiscal and monetary policy is a far less potent instrument of governmental power than is commonly assumed. Fiscal policy performance still is far from the goal envisaged by the more sanguine, more enthusiastic social engineers now entering the ranks of government. It is far from being an accurate and dependable tool. More likely than not fiscal management takes the form of a haphazard skimming off the top whatever revenue cream is conveniently assessible; all too frequently it represents a form of financial strip-mining. It cannot be regarded as a direct line to the controlling nerve centers of any society, unless one views the motley and minute group of beneficiaries of direct monetary handouts and other economic favors as the essence of state and society. In the fiscal management of social conditions it is possible that the unreliability of data and the lack of adequate information on activities elsewhere in the economy, in areas far removed from policymaking centers yet of critical importance to policy, may place some regimes in the precarious position of a person throwing a boomerang in the dark to bring down an unseen target.

Walter Heller's comments on goals he ascribes to fiscal policymakers in data-saturated United States may provide us with a glimpse of likely effects of uninformed policy planning in African conditions. Speaking of the United States, he posits as firm goals and commitments to guide policy planners such elusive and difficult targets as "social justice," "political stability," "best possible utilization of human resources," or "equal distribution of income."[21] These goals may have some substance in the United States. There is much room for courageous talk on such subjects where as a rule no one expects immediate delivery on promises, where, in other words, no immediate payoff is expected, where rhetoric is king. But as has been demonstrated so vividly in Latin America, those who control not word manufacture but effective power seem prepared to act and act violently as soon as rhetoric threatens to be translated into actual policy. Quite regularly, as soon as the line that separates rhetoric from practice is crossed, these interests call in the military to set things right.

A government intent on providing a modicum of social stability through fiscal measures designed to effectively redistribute income may in the end achieve the opposite. This kind of approach tends to be counterproductive, mainly because in order to be effective in the typical African setting the goals Heller outlined — a form of economic blood-letting — must first be approved by the victims. They dispose of sufficient means to stay the surgeon's knife; so if they are not consulted, capital flees at once or in any case ceases to be available locally. If they are consulted, they have the means of offering determined opposition, including uprisings and overthrow of the regime.[22]

Inevitably, the nexus between fiscal policy and development is broken when policymakers and supporting civil servants, hard pressed for funds, fall back on less costly segmental approaches, always at the expense of long-range aggregative goals. Unfortunately, by the time such patchwork policies begin to pay off, if they pay off, debt services, inflation, and other ravages have taken their toll. However, broad-gauge, aggregative measures, such as injections of purchasing power through massive, wide-ranging infusion of funds or massive shifts of funds from one sector to another, in prevailing conditions serve merely to enrich one sector while driving up prices and imports to the dismay of the remainder.

In the typical African setting, money supply is relatively inelastic in the short run, partly because production is afflicted by institutional rigidities that impede the free flow of human and material resources from one sector of the economy to another. Therefore, artificial injection of purchasing power into receptive sectors simply pushes up prices of relatively inelastic domestic supplies, while buoying imports supported by consumers of high priced imports. Thus much of the multiplier effect relied on by fiscal policy planners who want to crank up the economy is actually not allowed to become operative or is exported abroad; that is, its benefits, if any, accrue to non-African economies. Realization of this problem encourages preference for segmental over more comprehensive approaches.[23]

Careful assessment of the diverse options open to policy planners counsels caution before one accepts either a wholly aggregative or a wholly segmental approach. At any rate, whichever approach is selected given the paucity of data and the tenuous status of the essential cause-and-effect nexus in the developing systems, policy designed to affect distribution of power more likely than not will be segmental and will be confined to relatively small portions of the power and influence spectrum. Inevitably, ambitious broad frontal assaults on social injustice, inequity, and so on, will likely peter out at a very early stage.

The foregoing caveats apply perhaps even more to revenue derived from mineral oil, as in Nigeria, than to revenue derived from the more common sources of financial supply. It is never just a matter of applying oil riches to social reform, as Libya perhaps illustrates best. More likely than not, fiscal policies designed to alter the social structure through massive ingestion of oil revenue toward, say, redistribution of wealth may result only in a severe case of national financial indigestion. One remedy, which Sir Arthur Lewis prescribed, recommends that revenue in excess of immediate, basic, and current requirements be paid into a separate development fund where it will be used without economically unhealthy, possibly hemorrhaging effects on purchasing power and thereby on the price structure or the balance of payments.[24]

Diversion of excess revenue from current consumption should also remove it from the grasp of shortsighted manipulators of power and influence, although, as we have shown, such exploitation is difficult to avoid in Africa. If revenues set aside for development become mere revolving funds for private use, the objective Lewis envisaged will not, of course, be achieved. In any case, the flow of large amounts of cash into an economy not basically prepared for the infusion will most likely release throughout state and society shock waves that themselves will affect the distribution of power. For these reasons, students of oil-rich countries are well advised to delay in forming generalizations until the body economic in question demonstrates a capacity for proper and peaceful digestion.

Indeed, caution may be in order regarding all generalization on fiscal policies anywhere on the continent except in South Africa. For instance, in Zambia in the 1960s and early 1970s the governing factor in fiscal policy probably was that mining companies paid the largest proportion of taxes. This imbalance coupled with the perennial problem of fluctuations in the price of copper, which in turn drastically affects the companies' incomes, sets certain limits for fiscal policymakers. In such conditions planners who want to commit too large a portion of revenue obtained during fat years may find severe and critical shortages in lean years.[25]

The margin for maneuver is exceedingly slim in most of the countries under consideration, and in the realm of fiscal policy there is indeed many a slip betwixt the cup and the lip. It is a very long way from brave policy pronouncements to concrete results. Ideological propositions, after all, are concerned with power and influence, primarily in social and economic respects. All schemes arising from broad ideological prescriptions must eventually be paid for if they are to acquire any substantive meaning. It would be well, therefore, if one viewed with considerable scepticism the widely espoused notion that fiscal policy may be a convenient means to secure reordering of social relationships if not actually to alter drastically the prevailing power structure.

Classical theory of fiscal policy held that neutral fiscal policy and a balanced budget were essential for economic growth. Reaction to this classical theory among writers on economic theory and relevant fiscal policies for underdeveloped countries held that free play of market forces and a balanced budget were counterproductive in developing societies. Instead, fiscal policy was to be used to bring about a balanced society or a balanced economy, and interference with the market forces was essential as a means for survival of poorer countries. Free play of market forces, it was argued, would inevitably exacerbate the differences between developed and underdeveloped countries, Hence, it was held, government intervention was required. This theory was based on the assumption that there was a governmental structure and a mechanism to achieve the desired goals.

The reality of politics and economics in tropical Africa, however, indicates that the governmental mechanism required either does not exist or, where it may exist, consists of external forces as much or more than internal forces — in *Afrique Francophone,* for example — and of economic forces more than what we traditionally regard as political forces. Also, the limits of power in tropical Africa are such that governments, given all the skills and good intentions ascribed to them by theoreticians, cannot hope to exercise the kind of discretion needed to achieve the desired goals.

Classical fiscal policies were influenced by a simple set of reasons, and these were the reasons of capitalist development — in short, maximization

of profit opportunities. Such a simple set could be translated rather easily
into fiscal policies. Countervailing social forces (the workers, etc.) did not
yet dispose of the political weight required to effectively oppose these
policies. Fiscal policies in underdeveloped countries, however, are tenuous,
delicate in their origins, and uncertain in their social as well as economic
background and reasoning. Assumptions about social ends, rights and
privileges, domain of government (the public versus the private sector),
and so on, have not yet been thought out.

Since there are no clear concepts of where one is coming from and where
one is going, remedies usually cannot be devised. Where they are devised,
usually by outsiders who base their prescriptions on conditions quite different, even alien, they cannot be implemented for lack of skill or because
of the confusion surrounding social ends and purposes. Consequently, to
leave decisions on public policy to government as traditionally defined is
to consign the future of millions to organisms poorly or not at all equipped
to handle the task.

What conclusions can one draw from this? The real, true partners in the
power hierarchy as well as the issues over which fundamental struggles
are waged must be identified, and ways and means must be found to bring
these forces into a working relationship uncluttered by traditional concepts of government and politics.

The Budget

"The Government," writes Stolper, "has an immense influence on the *allocation of resources* directly and indirectly; and ... almost everything the
Government does has a direct or indirect reflection in the budget. *The
budget is the central document for economic policy;* and it is the major
policy instrument."[26] One basic question we have posed is whether "government" is a subject or an object. We have suggested that it is more an object,
an instrument perhaps, a tool. Government is used; it does not exist separate from nongovernment; it is inextricably intertwined with all other
agents and agencies engaged in the struggle for power and influence. Only
in the less perceptive writings of political scientists and, of course, in
establishment propaganda does government acquire a distinction all of its
own: the Leviathan, the colossus, a monster or a giant, lording it over
private pigmies.

As we have demonstrated, government is less sovereign, less national,
less public, and less separate and distinct in reality than its literary image
suggests. It is extremely open, hence vulnerable to foreign influences if not
control. One should never succumb to the process of reification to the extent
of failing to recall the human content of government, the concrete substance behind the abstract shadow. None of the human actors or players
associated with government can be viewed as entirely, or even substantially

separate and distinct from the mainstream of society. Nor in thinking about government, should one leave out of account that in all probability a highly educated high-ranking government official will be oriented far more toward a social class that spans the public and private sectors than toward one based exclusively on the public sector. In fact, this attitude is more likely in the embryonic, experimental, and extremely fluid African setting than in tradition- and custom-encrusted developed systems.

Therefore, in effect, when key personnel in government and administration are engaged in budgetary decisions they cannot and probably will not cast aside personal or class interests and commitments and prejudices regarding such fundamental questions as distribution of wealth, production of wealth, and modes of production. Perhaps most important because it occupies so central and seminal a position, foreign exchange will remain the cement that binds public policymakers to private interests, for without the active cooperation and good will of private entrepreneurs and investors most foreign exchange reserves will dry up rather quickly.

Always to be kept in mind is the regrettable fact that public funds do not complain when diverted illegally or improperly to private advantage or for other unauthorized purposes. Someone of authority must blow the whistle. Unfortunately, for battle purposes, Africa has too few individuals sufficiently well situated to be able to detect abuse and sufficiently adept at avoiding the usual deterrents to criticism of the powerful and influential.

Thus, accepting Stolper's point but interpreting *government* more broadly than he does, one can take the position that, unlike the rather nebulous fiscal policy, budgets are far more than mere instruments of government policy. Appropriately designed and meticulously and realistically executed, they could in otherwise favorable circumstances serve as effective instruments of social policy. At the same time they will always remain susceptible to influences and pressures from outside government. Indeed, it would be a serious analytical and conceptual error if even in connection with the comparatively rigorous budget procedure the open-endedness of government were to be ignored or even just slighted.[27]

Budget policy, therefore, should be regarded as very much a part of the struggle between and among pressure and interest groups. In fact, it should be recognized instead as the fulcrum of that struggle. The facade of propriety, the mythical conflict of interest barrier, the equally hoary myth of public fiscal neutrality must not be allowed to stand in the way of persistent and diligent inquiry into budgetary affairs. In other words, our attention must not be diverted from determining the precise identity of the hands in the public till. Of those there are far more than superficial analysis of budgetmaking brings to light — especially in Africa.

Rimmer recognizes this problem:

There are, then, powerful forces at work which tend toward the increase of government expenditure, and whose connections with the enlargement of the productiveness of the economy are tenuous if they exist at all. In any country, it can seldom be true that the Budget represents a concerted social purpose; it is much more likely to be a forum for interest conflicts in the society — between the old generation and the young, the urban population and the rural population, the wage-earners and the farmers, civil servants and private persons, the rich and the poor. Out of these conflicts and their budgetary repercussions economic development may conceivably occur, but it occurs as a by-product of the political processes rather than as their designed results; and macro-economic design which abstracts from the real political forces underlying budgetary changes, substituting unobjectionable but inoperative political aims of its own, inevitably appears in retrospect to have been naive. The designers did not know the reality they were trying to shape; they did not know the score.[28]

It is time, then, to recognize the budget as a playground for what is colloquially called wheeling and dealing, something the rigorous social scientist of yesterday could not even think about let alone utter in public.

One source of misperception of the role and function of the budget in Africa is the mistake of accepting budget figures on their face value. Budget speeches everywhere are notoriously inaccurate, euphoristic, and utopian, and, most important, they conceal far more than they reveal.[29] Budget figures must be augmented by data on other public revenue and expenditure activity. Accounting deficiencies and methodological weaknesses in identifying and consolidating all relevant fiscal activities, among others, render budgets even less reliable than is commonly accepted even among experts. Most important, these same shortcomings sufficiently muddy the waters for very substantial amounts of public money to be whisked into private coffers without the public's becoming aware of it. J. M. Lee refers to the experience in French-influenced areas.

> In francophone states, there have been such important budgetary difficulties that it has become almost a necessary condition for economic health and for continued French support, that the budgets should be managed under a system devised by French business consultants, Société Internationale d'Études de Recherches et d'Organization (SINORG).[30]

The extent to which the publicly visible profile of a budget can be subverted to purposes other than those revealed in the budget speeches of ministers of finance is noted in a comment from a distinguished Nigerian authority on the subject, Chief Dina. Addressing himself to the relationship between the current and the more long-range capital budget in Nigeria, he draws special attention to the loopholes through which up to 30 or 40 percent of a total capital budget can be bootlegged into the operational budget. This diversion is accomplished by means of the supplementary estimates "through which a number of capital projects which have either been rejected at the budgetary exercise level or have never been considered at all at this stage are surreptitiously admitted on to the capital budget programme."[31] Aside from raising havoc with the development plans, the practice enables the elite to slip additional funds into the more accessible current budget where they can be directed more expeditiously to secure the power and influence ends in the game that real-life budget-makers are obliged to play.

Taxation

Traditionally in Africa, in addition to serving as a means of financing government operations, including future development, taxation is viewed as a means of reducing unstabilizing spending propensities at the consumer level, of equalizing or adjusting income, and of encouraging certain desired economic activities and practices over others. But taxation also functions as an instrument of punishment and reward — intimidation by threat of additional tax levy or reward by tax reduction or nonimplementation of existing rules and regulations.[32]

No discussion of tax policy and tax administration in Africa is meaningful unless one takes into account the operational deficiencies and short-comings characteristic of all policy implementation on the continent. They are likely to affect tax collection more than other, more manageable, government operations — more than collection of duties at points of entry, for example. In the area of taxation there is a very wide difference indeed between plan and execution.

At the lower, mass level, many factors contribute to the problems with taxation, as both a fiscal revenue-producing and a social regulatory or policing instrument. Some are endemic; others are traceable to inexperience and confusion at the top. It may well be that taxation in Africa is a classic demonstration of the hazards inherent in employing too many cooks. The list of experts who had a hand in the design of tax policies on the continent from colonial times through a transition period to the present ranges very far and very wide. It starts with the quietly efficient civil servants in London, Paris, or Brussels, who devised schemes to safeguard colonial rule and protect metropolitan interests, and it extends to the parade of hired experts and technicians from capitalist, socialist, and in-between systems, who eventually were joined by African authorities.

Most fundamental by all indications is the combination of widespread illiteracy, the comparative novelty of cash taxation, and poor communications, further compounded, of course, by the effects of experimentation at the top and, of course, the ubiquitous incidence of corruption and bribery. It should hardly be surprising in the circumstances if among the masses taxation is perceived as a wholly unwarranted intervention in their private and collective affairs and probably as a direct threat to their existence.[33]

Obviously, in a setting where annual per capita income ranges between $100 and $200, and considering the opinion climate, tapping low-income brackets will be both impolitic and unrewarding. Given the likely reception of a new levy, what may appear to be a paltry increase in taxation can in the circumstances easily trigger, and indeed has triggered, many a riot.

Thus the search for revenue and for social policing effectiveness will concentrate at the higher income levels where power, influence, revenue sources, and reward opportunities for high officials and politicians converge. Action there seems mandatory in response to the ever widening gap between rural and urban areas, between the more highly developed and favored and the comparatively backward and neglected sections, as well as to the universal differential that separates the poor from the rich.[34]

But taxpayers of substantial means still are few and far between everywhere north of the black-white divide. The best prospects in black Africa are where relatively wealthy European settlers or other high income earning foreign personnel still are available, as in Kenya. There some fat still remains to be trimmed from that source through individual and corporate tax.[35] In Tanzania, though, not much is to be gained; only 0.2 percent of all taxpayers paid income tax there in 1965.[36] In such settings, other means obviously must be found if the power and influence pyramid is to be reshaped.

Countering social equalization objectives are considerations of capital growth. At a time when sources of capital are drying up all over the world, income tax levied at the higher brackets is increasingly viewed as a deterrent to new investment. In Senegal, for example, well after independence less than 5 percent of all fiscal revenue was derived from income taxes.[37]

During the colonial era and the period immediately following, an illusion of income regulation by taxation was maintained through what appeared to be heavy taxation on incomes but was, in reality, mere subterfuge. In 1966 Zambia derived nearly 60 percent of gross taxation from income taxes.[38] Yet the substantial incomes of mining corporations were left virtually untouched by local levies. Only after royalties on mineral production and other revenue sources were tapped a few years later could one seriously speak of taxation as a social policy instrument.[39]

Kamarck draws attention to the most probable consequence of overall inefficiency in tax imposition and collection: all too often the wealthy slip through the numerous loopholes, and the system ends up subsidizing them at the expense of the smaller, poorer fish who cannot manage to squeeze through the net. Moreover, Kamarck notes that the bulk of government revenue most often comes from indirect taxation of one kind or another, and that hits the poor in particular.[40] Table 22-1 illustrates a portion of the problem.

TABLE 22-1.   *Tax Paid by Income Groups in Western Nigeria*
(1965-66)

(1) *Income* *Group (£N)*	*(2)* *No. of* *Taxpayers*	*(3)* *Percent of (2)* *Paying Tax*	*Percent of* *Tax Being Paid*
1-50	624,443	75	40
51-99	194,246	24	19
101-199	46,725	0.5	10
200-299	18,409	0.2	6.2
300-499	9,157	—	4.5
	Percent of tax paid decreases as income goes up, rising again slightly at the £N1,000 level.		
1000-1499	1,788	—	3.0
1500-3999	2,096	—	11
4000 and over	80	0.3	2.5

SOURCE: Aluko in Nigeria, Western State, 1969, 176; table 5, exhibit "J."

In the case illustrated above, a regressive tax rate seemed the only way out because it was possible to rely only on the poorer taxpayers to meet their obligations. Given the relative helplessness of the African farmer or peasant, all too often a fact known to the world only in isolated instances, brutality becomes a standard administrative method.[41] The social consequences are predictable; eventually some blood will flow.

It has been argued that a clash is inevitable when tax policy and tax collection are in conflict, when, for example, ideological aspirations to achieve income equalization clash with the productivity imperative.[42] Nkrumah came up against this conflict partly because of the technical difficulties in modifying well-established methods of tax collection and partly because he and his supporters were unable to resist the temptation to use the tax device to punish or restrain potential opposition elements.[43] Thus one of his programs to effect the export-import balance through taxation simultaneously called for increase of the purchase tax, reduction of imports, and lowering of the level of spending on luxury goods. The intent was not only to encourage a shift in consumption habits but also to cut down the potential of the core of political opposition, the middle and upper class bourgeoisie.[44]

At a different level, taxation is used to equalize income distribution in a broader regional and administrative context. Tax policy played a critical role in the evolution of the Nigerian Federation, for instance.[45] Incidentally, nearly everywhere the salaried groups provided the most convenient and accessible target for income tax collection when funds run low. In Senegal and Dahomey, for instance, this source was used time and again to help make up budget deficits.[46]

Clearly, as a social planning device taxation remains a two-edged sword, especially where its application is more or less unpredictable or beyond central control. "Where the margin between subsistence and market economies is very slight," writes Due, "imposition of taxes may simply encourage people to retreat to the subsistence sector." Preventive prescription poses several dilemmas, as Due points out.

... the framing of the tax structure must give particular attention to the minimization of adverse incentives effects and maximization of incentive reactions which further the attainment of the goal.

Unfortunately, two major dilemmas are encountered: In the first . . . the type of tax that most successfully recovers for the government a portion of the gains of the rising national income is the type that is most likely to interfere with incentives. Second, the general tax environment of an under-developed economy is unsuited to a high degree of perfection of the tax structure. Various significant features of such an economy include low levels of literacy and record keeping, inadequate numbers of trained tax administrators, unsatisfactory land title situations, limited use of bank accounts, and the importance of the subsistence segment of the economy, the output of which is difficult to ascertain and value.[47]

Development Planning

In light of our discussion it would seem that long-range planning in Africa at this point in time is an exercise in futility. The mortality rate of first-generation national development plans is phenomenally high; prospects of survival for the second generation are extremely poor. Consistently, events overtake plans, many times well before the plan has gotten under way. Yet to ignore development planning would be a serious error.

It seems obvious that some kind of planned development is unavoidable if Africa is to cope with the debilitating consequences of colonial rule and its aftermath. Only effective planning and plan implementation will serve to minimize the tendency of entrenched power and interest groups to ma-nipulate everything within their reach to their own advantage. Put different-ly, something of considerable value would be learned if analysis of develop-ment planning were to indicate that regardless of philosophic, ideological, or socioeconomic content of plans, conditions in Africa for the next decade or so are such as to frustrate each and every attempt to organize an effective attack on the most pressing and urgent problems in a rational manner.

Development planning might be examined for two aspects: the degree of realism reflected in planning, and the power and influence consequences of plan implementation. Reality testing will tell us something about the probabilities of plan success, while power and influence analysis will lay bare the principal reasons entrenched interests seek to block implementation. Since constitutions cannot be expected to become operative if the prevailing distribution of effective power fails to correspond with the assumptions made in the legal document, development plans must remain unfulfilled if they fail to take adequately and directly into account the distribution of the very instrumentalities plan designers assume to be available to overcome expected resistance and facilitate plan implementation.

Still, "the best laid plans of mice and men . . ." could be the epitaph for most if not all of Africa's development plans, yesterday, today, and tomorrow. The difficulty starts with the absence of adequate and, perhaps most important, appropriate development theory. Most published theories are pure armchair strategies with very little bearing on the conditions that actually prevail at the level of implementation. Perhaps it is true, as the Nigerian economist Aboyade (1969) believes, that really no theory appropriate for national plans exists, only theories appropriate for plan segments, and he doubts even that.[48]

Not much of a theory can really be expected, considering the mix of minds usually engaged in theory making. Social scientists and economists mostly but not exclusively ever since political scientists have concerned themselves with development all too often seem to have lacked opportunity to familiarize themselves with the practical conditions they generalize about. At the other end of the spectrum are bureaucrats, in the United Nations, in African regional organizations, and in several national ministries or planning commissions, who appear to be professionally committed to camouflaging reality.

Curiously, or significantly, economists and development bureaucrats when cornered seek to explain their departure from reality by the disarming excuse that the economic design could have been implemented had it not been for the politicians. The shoe is on the other foot. Plans fail because political reality, as we understand it here, has not been taken into account.[49]

Actually, it is not difficult to appreciate what might well be the root problem in development theory. As a rule plan conception and plan design take place in a kind of no-man's-land between financial, industrial, and commercial reality on the one hand and academic theory or in some cases social doctrine on the other. What Andrew Schonfield suggests for the developed countries might also be in order for Africa: first, the true partners in the enterprise planned for must be identified; second, the true relationship must be fudged; that is, it must be integrated and any basically antagonistic relationships varnished over. In the developed countries the true partnership combines state and private enterprise.[50] In Africa it comprises, first and foremost, government, domestic private enterprise, and foreign capital and enterprise, including banking, world financial centers, markets, and processors. Once these partners have been identified, the problem is, of course, by no means solved. To coordinate so diverse and divergent a grouping of interests is tantamount to driving a cart drawn by oxen, donkeys, and wild horses. Schonfield recognizes this difficulty and recommends, quite realistically, a wheeling and dealing approach so that the more pressing development problems can be solved. Obviously this requires a reigning in of the wild horses of the revolutionary apocalypse along with the plodding draft animals of academic rigor.

If wheeling and dealing is the method, it is clear that not all ingredients in the development brew can be regarded as fully equal in value and importance. No plan can begin to approach fulfillment if it does not reflect the all-pervasive unequal distribution of means of production and means of control of wealth, the schism that separates rich from poor and foreign capitalists from their weaker African counterparts. Nor can one ignore the urban industrial and rural agricultural gap nor the separation in space as well as in time of the administrative and political control center from the hinterland.

All official protestations to the contrary will not help. For instance, a declaration contained in the 1970-74 Kenya Development Plan asserts that revenue redistribution is from the "nation toward the rural areas" and "rural development [is] the underlying strategy of the whole Plan." Such strategy would be an invitation to national bankruptcy if actually undertaken.[51] The Zambian Plan for 1966-70, the Senegalese Plan for 1969-73, and the Nigerian Plan for 1970-74 follow that pattern of euphoristic and overconfident articulation of improbable goals.[52] At the same time there is no shortage of candid assessment, often from the pens of the principal authors of the deceptive plans. Dr. Aboyade, a leading Nigerian economist and foremost among development plan architects, has written abundantly on the subject and can serve as crown witness to prove the point that the extreme elasticity of plan language as well as the sweeping assumptions and patently false premises that afflict many a plan should not be taken too seriously.

In one of his many critical examinations of development plan premises, Aboyade draws a bead on one of the more pervasive sources of confusion, the so-called modernized-subsistence sector dichotomy. His argument is that if planning is to be productive, attention must be shifted to the more salient dualism comprised of a capital and profit economy on the one hand and a capitalless operation typical of the subsistence sector on the other. This dualism implies that development is not so much a matter of technically improving — superficially modernizing — a backward and technologically inefficient agriculture as it is a matter of either capitalizing agriculture — so that the no-wage, no-profit sector is altered to conform to the wage-profit pattern in the so-called modern sector or, the reverse, adjusting the wage-profit sector to the capitalless sector.

In hard political-economic language, if development planning is to attack the source of the predicament a rather massive redistribution of wealth is unavoidable, with concomitant reduction of foreign dominance, which, as we shown, thrives on maldistribution or one-sided distribution of scarce resources. But there is a gigantic fly in that ointment: Is restructuring of the economy on the prescribed scale compatible with the iron laws of capital flow and investment? Will outside capital docilely follow the route determined planners indicate?[53]

Another authority on planning sees the problem quite differently. To him, the ideal plan calls for a combination of the following ingredients.

(i) To make available for economic development the maximum flow of human and material resources consistent with minimum current consumption requirements;

(ii) To maintain reasonable economic stability in the face of long-run inflationary pressure and short-run international price movements;

(iii) To reduce, where they exist, the extreme inequalities in wealth, income and consumption standards which undermine productive efficiency, offend justice and endanger political stability.[54]

The fallacies inherent in that program are apparent. Whose consumption requirements set the standards? What is "minimum level of consumption?" How much inflationary pressure is acceptable and why? When are inequalities of wealth and income unacceptable? What justice is offended and at what point does "offense" commence? The answers to these and similar questions indicate why development plans go awry.

An outstanding Nigerian, Ayida, considers the urgent question of regional inequity or maldistribution of resources and developmental capabilities within a national framework as a major planning impediment. "The most difficult objective to reconcile with rapid growth is the need for 'balanced development,' or the gradual reduction of the disparity between economic regions in the country. The reduction cannot be accomplished by planning for stagnation in the relatively more developed parts."[55] In other words, the dilemma that faces the development planners in this particular respect is that one cannot have one's cake and eat it too.[56]

If development planning should not be regarded solely as a means of promoting balance and equity, one should also note that economists, sociologists, and political scientists differ widely on what is and what is not desirable in social engineering. The Parsonian view, for instance, holds that coherence of society is a prime function of the common processes of socialization. To Mancur Olson, "[t]hey contend that it is mainly the similarities of values, norms, collective attitudes, and role expectations that holds a society together. If people are brought up to want the same things they need not fight each other."[57] Olson counters that the most stable and most coherent society encourages significant differences in tastes and desires, especially with regard to private goods. This, he suggests, drives one to the conclusion that it might, in fact, be the proper task of government — and of development planning by implication — to develop these differences, and where they are indigenous to develop tribal differences so that they may become functionally valuable in the modern context. Modernization then does not mean creating a consensus, socialization of wants, formation of common values, and reconciliation of conflicts, but deliberate, planned, purposeful cultivation of differences, within certain bounds, of course.

On a different plane development planning suffers from critically defective international vision. Planners can ignore the tridimensional distribution of power among international, national, and local centers only at the risk of total planning irrelevance. Somehow the connections between economic planning and world market conditions, between capital requirements and the supply situation, and similarly vital aspects must be taken into account and incorporated in the plan.

On a regional basis thoughts of coordinating diverse and divergent national economies or segments of national economies will remain unproductive unless adjusted to reflect the complexities and contradictions arising from the sharp cleavages between diverse and divergent European-instituted systems on the continent. For instance, no talk of plan synchronization is possible if French development clocks continue to run backward, as seen from the regional integrationist perspective. A justified question is why one should assume that African socioeconomic interest groups together with their domineering foreign partners should differ from their feuding, for centuries warring, and still highly competitive European counterparts at home.[58]

In a way plan implementation is like attempting to submerge an inflated air mattress in water; as one part is pressed down, several other sections pop up and out. There is much simplistic theorizing on how to submerge the entire mattress, but the feat cannot be performed unless many hands act in concert and simultaneously to the same purpose. The analogy with planning is complete if at the same time the waters turn turbulent, a storm is brewing, and the required hands will not coordinate. One such combination of recalcitrant forces and adverse circumstances surrounds the very popular so-called attack on poverty.

Any planned assault on this disease is frustrated by what has been termed "the vicious spiral of poverty." The spiral starts with persistently low labor productivity, which depresses per capita real income, which in turn stunts the developmentally essential capacity of the economy to generate savings. The problem is further compounded by an extremely marginal propensity to consume (a very slight decrease in income may terminate consumption of anything but the most essential commodities or services). The result is a critically low increase, if any, in capital formation and in the other production factors in relation to size and rate of growth of the working population. Inescapably, labor productivity and per capita income will be depressed further.[59]

Realistically, energetic and effective development planning is a luxury few of the countries of Africa can afford in ordinary conditions. At best it is an economically marginal exercise; only a relatively minor setback need occur, a modest drop in the world price of the prime commodity, and the storm signals are hoisted. While at one point sweeping social or economic reform plans may seem feasible, a relatively minor downturn in the terms of trade (the ratio between export earnings and import costs) will abruptly change the planning climate, causing postponement of reforms and a return to the established, tried, and proven procedures and ways of doing things. Usually this regression means a return to traditional sources of revenue, imperialist or not.[60]

Low purchasing power alone poses an insuperable obstacle to development planning. For ideological, prestige, and economic reasons, industrialization continues to be a major feature in most national development plans. Yet it is technically not feasible to introduce into poverty-stricken areas the kind of industry Africa can afford and needs. One reason is that markets will be too costly to reach.[61]

Thus plans designed to effect significant shifts from agriculture to industry are defeated from the outset. Conversely, plans to develop land and modernize agriculture may siphon off capital needed for infrastructure and for industry, which is needed to secure a greater degree of independence. A decision not to interfere with population growth leads to sharply spiraling expenditures for social services, which will again divert funds from economic development, while neglect of nonagricultural activities "will maintain and increase the pressure on land."[62] No matter how carefully a plan seeks to compensate for each area of neglect, the results will materialize only during the plan period when they will incisively alter the plan environment, leaving clusters of problems unattended and encouraging resistance to further planning.

The bureaucracy will feel disadvantaged by a policy of land development; they suspect, and rightly so, that this policy will eventually require their transfer from the comforts of city life. A hands-off policy on population growth, however, will tend to enhance the growth of the bureaucracy, making the power structure even more top-heavy, while neglect of nonagricultural activities will simply abandon to their fate the growing landless proletariat and the unemployed. Plans to diversify agriculture run into difficulties when no farmers can be found to experiment with the alternate crop, when no local organization can be created and made operational to promote and sustain alternate production, and when production discipline, required to sustain new modes of production in an experimental environment, is absent.[63]

A rather basic point is that no plan can be implemented within even an approximate range of its targets without the skills, the institutions, and the operational infrastructure indicated in the plan itself. Realistically seen, few if any of the continental systems possess adequate capabilities in these respects. As a World Bank assessment puts it: "regardless of the pace of training and administrative reorganization, the time lags involved in building institutional capacities are such that this will remain a relatively scarce resource, and any future commitment of public sector effort should be carefully assessed against competing claims and the overall institutional capacity of Government."[64]

Rampaging inflation affects planning in numerous ways. For instance, the relatively inefficient African farmer may find it more difficult than expected to develop land allocated to him if inflation drives up the cost of farming.[65]

What impact has Africanization on a given plan? That replacement of expatriates with Africans temporarily reduces efficiency and output there can be no doubt. Since plan fulfillment even to a reasonable degree requires high performance in critical sectors of administration, business, and industry, Africanization for some time to come is very likely to slow things down if it does not cause actual disarray.[66]

If implemented, all plans can be expected to affect the existing power structure *but not necessarily as envisaged by the planners.* Neither Soviet planners working in the USSR in the twenties and thirties nor Ghana planners in the fifties and sixties created the social system they envisaged. In the Soviet Union many eventually were devoured by the monsters their diligence produced as a side effect.

Measures to artificially alter the critical components of the power structure in predetermined form inevitably turn out to assure plan failure. Few if any planners even estimated the social cost of plan fulfillment; in all probability they were unaware of such cost. Increasingly, planners in developed countries calculate these costs into their estimates.[67] In underdeveloped countries the most critical cost factor is investment loss or reduction of capital inflow. This factor, in turn, increases the probability of social unrest and revolution, adding to the social cost once again.

Aside from the reservations dealt with earlier, modernization remains a pandora's box on other counts. Beneath or behind the facade of modernization rhetoric lies the reality of the seven-eighths of the cost-price iceberg. Very brave words have been spoken on the subject, but modernization cannot be planned meaningfully on an overall national, economic systemwide basis. Very few sectors of state and society can stand the infusion of large doses of modernization without severe repercussions. In all likelihood modernization of a given sector or sliver of a sector merely means papering over the existing patterns, shifting the modus operandi of the powerful and influential into new positions, endowing them with new titles, but not altering the substantive bases at all or barely so. In other words, reform can be devastatingly expensive.[68]

Quite possibly Holt and Turner are correct in arguing that "the technology most appropriate for the developing societies is not yet available — has indeed not even been invented."[69] Applied to the modernization tasks, this argument may imply that the exercise is indeed futile, for if modernization means anything it means accelerating what would develop normally at a slower pace. Such acceleration, for reasons spelled out earlier, requires a very high level of skill and a very well developed technology. Not even considered is the resistance to be expected from traditional forces whose potential is minimal in positive respects but who can raise havoc by passive resistance.

Along with constitutions, party programs and platforms, and government manuals and handbooks, plans have contributed to a false image of the decision- and policymaking environment. Imperceptibly, analysts have slipped from consideration of initial development efforts to evaluation of actual performance while actually dealing with dreams and intentions. In the process they have endowed government with far greater potency, even reality, than may be warranted by the performance record. Consequently, if plans are actually translated into action, government, said to be the driving if not controlling force behind the plan, looms large in the decision and policy-making framework.

The ultimate reality of planning in the African context is shaped by considerations of wealth and income, of capital formation and investment. "A Plan without a large budget surplus will get nowhere; whereas a large budget surplus can work wonders even without a Plan."[70] To obtain the requisite surplus, capital must be found. No matter hat the ideology or form of government or the plan or its design, capital cannot be squeezed readily from the already overtaxed resources. Usually only two major reservoirs can be tapped: unpromising domestic income and wealth or foreign capital.

Investment Policies

In state after state attempts to increase capital by investment in public enterprises has failed to yield the expected results. Often it has ended in failure. In advanced economies capital formation is easier because the basic, prerequisite seed capital is already there; it has been accumulated after decades, even centuries, of saving through sacrifices on current consumption or by other means. With surplus capital, public enterprises can be seen through the initial stages of unprofitability. In underdeveloped economies consumers are already so near the minimum level of subsistence, are so poor, that postponement of consumption simply will not yield enough to warrant the dissatisfaction it inevitably generates. Current incomes are not large enough to justify the administrative expense of instituting widespread saving. "Merely to provide for rapidly growing population, acquisition of the primitive tools and simple housing now enjoyed can use up most of the savings."[71]

Thus if a meaningful investment program is to get under way, the requisite capital will have to be imported. If it is to yield anything of value in terms of the current and, because of the population increase, mounting need, it must be channeled into truly productive, capital-yielding enterprises. African governments simply have neither the skills nor the capital to obviate the foreign investor, let alone surmount the formidable obstacles in the way of domestic capital formation where, as in Ethiopia, Senegal, and parts of

Nigeria, traditional forces constitute an effective veto bloc.[72] For obvious reasons traditional owners of investment capital seem to be disinclined to apply their wealth to social change in their own sphere of influence. They prefer to invest elsewhere, either in urban commerce and industry or abroad. In the less developed areas indigenous capitalists generally seem to prefer to "pile up their savings abroad, legally or illegally."[73]

Few investment policy planners actually can persuade themselves that the capital that might conceivably be recaptured by Draconian measures of foreign investment and saving controls can actually be applied to domestic capital formation within a reasonable period of time. What Samuelson calls the "qualitative distortion of investment," is a chronic problem in Africa. Capital is squandered on unproductive schemes (apartment houses and office buildings) that yield high incomes to a few. This income is not applied, in turn, to domestic capital formation but is invested again in the very narrow range of schemes attractive to the few.[74]

The admonition, advanced by the government of Nigeria on promulgation of a decree on investment policy and related matters, that investors should come to regard Nigeria as "an important economic proposition" and not as a mere adjunct "to vast international operations" is no substitute for creation of important economic propositions. This is not saying that countries such as Nigeria lack profitable opportunities for foreign and domestic investors. It is merely noting the need to solve the "chicken or the egg" dilemma in investment policy: substantive investment will follow, not precede, profitable opportunities. Since raw material extraction has been curbed and controlled in places taken over by the state or whoever acts for the state, this particular area may now be closing as a channel for foreign investment. Alternatives of equal attractiveness to free foreign capital are few and far between. Only the future will tell whether centrally controlled capital from the socialist countries can become a viable substitute.[75]

23

The Name of the Game:
Access to Wealth

Beyond specifics is the general; beyond particular steps taken by governments lies social policy or philosophy. More concretely in the context of this book, beyond technical measures and adjustments, usually undertaken on an ad hoc or piecemeal basis, lie the ultimate rewards sought by individuals and groups competing for supremacy in the power and influence game. In this chapter we examine the fabric of policies and approaches that relate to the ultimate payoff for the efforts analyzed and described in the earlier parts. Consistent with our sense of realism, we disregard the overt message conveyed by the pattern, the mythology and rhetoric of alleged reward and punishment. Instead, we concentrate on the fabric itself, the strands from which it is woven, and the purposes it is to serve.

Man's ability to deceive himself and his fellow man about his intentions seems limitless. One may doubt, for instance, whether as a general rule there is much more to the pursuit of power than the quest for material advantage, conceding always, of course, the exceptions that prove the rule. But this point need not be argued here. Suffice it to say that overwhelming evidence indicates that the keenest and most widely held of all interests, the quest most generally, universally, and diligently, even ruthlessly pursued, relates to physical survival in its simplest form and to acquisition of wealth at its most sophisticated. In between lie concern over maintenance of minimum levels of subsistence, social security, economic betterment, and the like. Certainly if the Russian and Chinese social revolutions have established anything conclusive, they have provided proof of man's irresistible urge to secure for himself and his kin, and beyond that for his social group, a larger share of the wealth than his government (his fellow men acting in some capacity through some channel) is prepared to concede to him.[1] The most visible, the most concrete manifestation of that overriding interest is

found in and around the contest for that portion of the wealth that is
realistically available for distribution as individual or corporate income.

In scarcity-ridden Africa, realistic availability is indeed the watchword.
On paper all the liquid economic assets of a state could be distributed on
a per capita basis to every man, woman, and child. In reality only a very
small portion can be disposed of in that manner; the bulk of the liquid
wealth must be applied or reinvested to meet the social goals set by the col-
lectivity or its institutional expression — the government or, more realistically, the ruling group. This means capital development and formation, debt
service, research and analysis, defense, public services, and other similarly
pressing social uses.

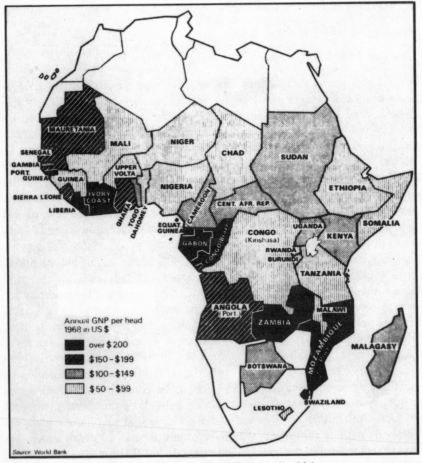

FIGURE 23.1   *Degrees of Poverty in Africa*

SOURCE: "Africa: Minerals or Oil—or Aid," *The Economist,* January 30, 1971,
20.

In analyzing what, in effect, is a public response to private demands, we are not concerned with the power politically meaningless statistical concept of per capita income computed on a national basis, for it conceals those critical symptoms that must be understood if incomes and wealth distribution policies are to make sense. It conceals, for instance, the stark disequilibrium of income that all of Africa inherited from colonial rule. Instead of inquiring into per capita income, we ask: Whose capita gets the income and why? Furthermore, we are not interested in income so small that it cannot buy appreciable amounts of influence or power in strategic places. We are concerned mainly with actual or potential concentrations, or blocs, of income or wealth or of means of acquisition of wealth large enough to tip the scales of decision and policymaking at national and international levels.

An exhaustive treatment of this particular subject is not possible within the limits of this study. We can only explore the linkages among incomes policy, power, and politics by reference to a few representative illustrations from a select group of countries. In each case different facets of the general problem complex will be highlighted to provide a reasonably well-rounded picture.

Incomes and Wealth Distribution Policies

When it comes to public discussion of the facts of life pertaining to the who gets what, from whom, when, and how, we are as reticent as the Victorians were on the subject of sex. Our store of euphemisms to conceal from public view otherwise obvious transgressions seems inexhaustible. The record shows that Africa's leaders have been well taught in that respect, or they are learning very fast. While the general public is deceived in regard to particulars by tireless invocation of such taboos as conflict of interest, those in position to get away with it are almost at will tapping the public treasury and other restricted portions of the wealth of the nation.

A hue and cry surrounds public executions of petty criminals, and small-time profiteers and embezzlers are pilloried through sensationally embellished pseudorevelations and published exposes. But the legal-constitutional provisions devised by the departing colonial regimes partly to protect the public fund are either circumvented or violated outright behind a virtually impenetrable screen. Behind that screen an entirely new class has arisen in Africa, not unlike those that arose, protected by identical verbal camouflage, in the developed societies at a comparable point in time. That new class now must be reckoned with.

Incomes and wealth distribution and allocation policy has two distinct facets, one covert, the other overt. Neither should be confused with pseudo-policies, which should be consigned solely to the realm of social myth.

We dealt somewhat with an aspect of the covert face earlier in discussing corruption,[2] but there is much more.

Covert policy in this regard involves closing one eye, or looking the other way. It is characterized by acts of omission as much as commission; it is a practice of benign permissiveness toward favorites of the governing group. It is a form of legitimization of misconduct by the select few accompanied by stern reaction to similar or identical behavior on the part of the not so fortunate or those out of favor. Except these unfortunates, the guiding rule in this game is to live and let live.

Prior to independence and after a brief flurry of last-ditch defense of their rapidly crumbling positions the colonial regimes moved to accept the rule and willingly extended the benefits that flowed from it to their African successors. In a way, the ensuing pattern may be described as a partnership in systematic diversion of Africa's wealth. A prominent feature of that arrangement is discretion. Grand larceny, wholesale embezzlement, and large-scale diversion or conversion of wealth to private purpose went unexposed, with the exception of misconduct by such rogue elephants as Nkrumah and Touré, or habitual spoilers or nonplayers or otherwise accommodating players such as Bokassa (Central African Republic), and, of course, excepting avowed opposition leaders with a genuine social revolutionary bent.[3] As revealed in Ghana and Nigeria, the partnership extended even to the setting up of false fronts to permit joint illegal transactions.

From a very broad historical perspective, and in fairness to the more public-minded African and foreign architects of this facet of incomes and wealth policies, something can be said in its defense. First, retaliation probably would have followed any challenge of the expressed desire on the part of many of the new rulers to secure a substantial degree of control over independent funds at the earliest possible opportunity. It was all too clear that colonial rule had been a thinly disguised form of largescale theft. Second, many European administrators and some businessmen sympathized with the African position that only a massive transfer of funds directly into Africa hands could counter the effects of continuing dominance of foreign elements in their midst. It seemed plausible that if anything of the kind were to be done it would have to be on a scale commensurate with the task ahead. To stave off economic retaliation, especially abroad, a kind of strike fund seemed a reasonable measure of self-defense. In that sense establishment of false fronts to facilitate transfer of substantial funds seemed quite legitimate, even though it was of questionable legality or outright illegal. Alas, the funds so diverted were rarely applied to the avowed ends.

Within limits set by considerations of self-preservation, the live-and-let-live rule also governed relations among the African elite, including opposition elements provided they, too, were prepared to play by the rules.

TABLE 23.1   Africa: Population (Mid-1969), GNP Per Capita (1969) and Average Annual Growth Rates (1960-69)

Country	Population (1,000)	GNP Per Capita (US $)	Growth Rates Population (%)	Growth Rates GNP Per Capita (%)	Country	Population (1,000)	GNP Per Capita (US $)	Growth Rates Population (%)	Growth Rates GNP Per Capita (%)
Nigeria	64,560	—	2.6	-0.3	Senegal	3,790	200	2.2	-0.1
Egypt, Arab Rep. of	32,501	160	2.5	1.2	Rwanda	3,650	—	3.1	-0.8
Ethiopia	24,769	—	2.0	2.3	Chad	3,510	—	1.5	-1.3
South Africa¹	20,218	710	2.3	3.8	Burundi*	3,475	—	2.0	0.0
Congo, Dem. Rep. of	17,900	—	2.1	0.2	Somalia*	2,730	—	2.5	1.5
Sudan	15,188	110	2.9	0.6	Dahomey	2,640	—	2.9	0.9
Morocco	15,050	190	2.9	3.4	Sierra Leone	2,510	170	2.0	1.2
Algeria	13,349	260	2.4		Togo	1,896	100	2.6	0.0
Tanzania²	12,557	—	2.6	1.6	Libya, Arab Rep. of	1,869	1,510	3.7	21.7
Kenya	10,890	130	3.1	1.5	Central African Rep.	1,518	130	2.4	0.0
Uganda	9,500	110	3.0	1.7	Liberia	1,480	200	2.8	1.3
Ghana	8,341	190	2.5	0.0	Mauritania*	1,136	140	2.2	4.6
Mozambique	7,539	210	1.8	3.3	Lesotho*	930	—	2.9	0.0
Malagasy Republic	6,656	110	2.4	0.0	Congo, People's Rep. of	880	220	1.5	2.3
Cameroon	5,736	150	2.1	2.0	Mauritius*	799	230	2.4	-0.4
Angola	5,430	210	1.3	1.4	Botswana*	629	—	3.0	1.0
Upper Volta	5,278	—	2.2	0.1	Portuguese Guinea	530	260	0.2	4.3
Rhodesia	5,090	240	3.2	0.4	Gabon	485	320	0.9	0.6
Ivory Coast	4,942	240	2.8	4.7	Reunion	436	660	2.9	4.5
Tunisia	4,919	230	3.0	2.1	Swaziland*	410	180	2.9	3.2
Mali	4,881	—	2.1	1.2	Gambia*	360	110	1.9	0.7
Malawi	4,398	—	2.6	1.0	Equatorial Guinea	286	290	1.8	4.7
Zambia	4,020	290	2.6	5.4	Comoro Islands	270	130	3.7	4.2
Niger	3,909	—	3.0	-0.9	Cape Verde Is.	250	120	2.5	-1.6
Guinea	3,890	—	2.7	2.6	Ceuta and Melilla*	165	320	0.9	3.5
					French Territory of Afars & Issas	93	600	1.5	6.1
					Sao Tome and Principe	66	310	0.3	0.2
					Seychelles Is.*	51	—	2.2	-0.5
					Spanish Sahara*	48	270	1.8	4.4

¹Including Namibia.
²Mainland Tanzania.
—Estimated at less than 100 dollars.
*Estimates of GNP per capita and its growth rate are tentative.

Note: 1966 GDP per capita figures for Nigeria were US $83 and for Tanzania US $72. (Survey of Economic Conditions in Africa, 1968, New York, 1972, 5, table 1.)
SOURCE: World Bank Atlas: Population, per capita product and growth rates. Published by the International Bank for Reconstruction and Development 1971.

Overt incomes and wealth distribution policy is considerably less dramatic. Its impact on the power and influence structure is more difficult to fathom. Because its data base is far broader, more substantial sums and more people are involved, and a greater variety of transactions must be traced, it turns out to be a far less dependable foundation for social analysis. Yet it has its fascination. Within certain limits such policy reveals the general outline of a new power and influence dispensation, or at least it augurs certain realignments, telling us something about the scope and nature of the economic rewards certain groups can expect in ideal conditions.

Inclusion of both covert and overt policy in our analysis implies that the scope of the inquiry must of necessity be rather extensive. Indeed, so conceived, incomes and wealth distribution policy cuts across the entire spectrum of public policymaking, engaging all major and numerous smaller organs of government and administration, both formal and informal, official and unofficial. Like fiscal policy, it also cuts across the dividing line between the public and the private sectors. Recognition of the side-by-side existence of two types of such policies should prevent one from mistaking overt protestations for actual commitments, thus attributing to individual regimes more governance, more purposefulness, and more design and clear intent than they themselves might want to claim. However, a fair number of policymakers in positions of some consequence are quite aware of the implications that flow from the inevitable inconsistencies and contradictions. They are genuinely concerned and highly sensitive to the imperative of reform in the manifestly injustice-ridden and highly explosive sphere involving the distribution of wealth, of means of production of wealth, and of income.

Significantly, the most eloquent and most sure-footed formulations of the broad, basic social problem associated with economic inequities are advanced from the United Nations perspective — a position not burdened by fiscal responsibility outside the limits of its own organization.

> Extreme inequalities in the distribution of income and wealth are detrimental to economic development insofar as they reduce the nutritional, health, and living standards of the people, create an excessive demand for imported luxury consumption goods, further an excessive transfer of funds abroad and prevent the growth of internal markets. Where such conditions exist, fiscal methods are appropriate to bring about more equitable distribution of incomes and channel additional resources into economic development.[4]

On a similarly unrealistic plane but from within a government directly concerned comes another appraisal of what must be done. One observer reported that the government of Senegal for some time has taken the position that wages must be frozen until farm income can be brought to the level of the workers and the civil servants. The official position is that "wages can be raised only in proportion to those of the underprivileged farmer." Put differently, as the government saw it, if the economy was to be successfully converted from a France-oriented supplier economy to one that serves Senegal directly and as a whole, the minimum to be achieved with respect to income distribution was establishment of a "fixed relationship between the standards of living of our 'quasi-classes.'" This rhetoric was balanced by the expressed realization that wage increases most likely would adversely affect the competitiveness of Senegal's fledgling industry, maintain or even increase unemployment, drive up the general level of prices, and worsen the terms of trade.[5]

Shortly after independence the government of Kenya pledged itself to correct "past imbalances without endangering citizenship guaranties and rapid development." But they recognized that in "correcting these imbalances, measures must [also] be taken to avoid the emergence of antagonistic classes among the Africans themselves as development proceeds."[6] Four years and the length of one plan later the same government noted that "[t]here are at present inequalities of income between a small number of highly remunerated individuals on the one hand — large farmers, people in business, politics, the civil service and certain professions — and the great mass of the people on the other."

To cope with the problem, the Kenyatta government did not call for a Maoist cultural revolution. Instead it offered, in measured terms, that it would "continue to be the policy of the government to insure that the higher income groups in the population contribute increasingly, by way of taxation, towards the objective of reducing the income gap between rich and poor *to a socially acceptable level within a reasonable period of time.*" Meanwhile, the government through its rural development measures would "ensure that the standard of living of those with low incomes grows at a faster rate than the average."[7] "Thus," the statement concluded, "the Government will follow the policy of simultaneous levelling downwards and levelling upwards."

Additional targets for intervention were the widening gap between income levels in the towns and in the rural areas, especially the gap between urban and rural workers. This problem was to be tackled at several fronts: urban wages were to be controlled within certain limits; living in the rural areas was to be rendered more attractive to encourage development of income-producing enterprise; prices were to be kept reasonably constant; and taxation was to be brought into play as a last-resort leveler.[8]

Typically, the reasons such ambitious programs could not be effectuated in the foreseeable future were contained in the previous development plan, published four years earlier, where it was noted that the "rate at which arable land can grow through irrigation and other land reclamation schemes is limited and indeed requires capital to accomplish." The productivity of land, in other words, tended to force development in an undesirable direction with predictable consequences for income and wealth distribution between the urban and rural sectors.[9]

The full dimensions of the task ahead emerge even more clearly in view of a 1966 prediction that by the year 2000 "Kenya would have little more than 1.3 acres per person of potentially productive land."[10] Inevitably, this land shortage would increase the pressure to expand the wageearning sector, with predictable consequences for the existing disequilibrium. At about the same time, yet another perspective suggested that "the desire to enlarge the share of the wealth of the unskilled vis-a-vis the skilled conflicts with other national priorities as well as with the strong bargaining position enjoyed by the skilled who do have employment alternatives hence greater market value," a fact of African life we encountered earlier.

In the 1970-74 plan, determined government intervention to direct and reinforce incomes equalization measures is recognized as unavoidable. In that framework incomes policy was to address itself simultaneously to business profits, prices, and productivity, consumer price structure, and wages.[12]

Viewed differently, conflict situations are arising from income inequalities between "skilled persons and capitalists" and "unskilled workers and peasants."[13] The discrepancy most frequently discussed is that between Europeans and Asians and between Asians and Africans.[14] A glance at the income tax item in the annual estimates for 1968-69 suggests that in Kenya some rather large incomes were earned. Out of a total government revenue estimate of K£65,018,400, K£21,000,000 derived from income tax.[15] Various compilations show a sharp preponderance of non-African over African incomes, ranging from a ratio of about 30 to 1 (including Asians and Europeans) in 1957 to 100 to 23 to 1 in 1965 (Europeans-Asians-Africans).[16] In 1965-66, only 5,689 taxpayers paying graduated income tax in county council areas earned over K£600 per annum![17]

Incomes discrepancies in areas where sharp racial clashes have occurred, as during the so-called Mau Mau period, generate more pressure than might be present where similar or even greater gaps have developed but racial conflicts have been held to a minimum, as throughout French-speaking Africa.

Zambia faces some similar but many different problems. The urban worker's income was eight times that of the subsistence farmer, creating a gap far wider than that separating the urban Zambian from the comparatively well-off European. The income differential between the Zambian mine worker and the average farmer was staggering: by 1970, while the miner could earn up to $1,000 per year on the average the farmer saw about $5 cash per year, not counting the value of the crop and the amount he and his family consumed.[18]

Lack of alternate productivity to compensate for the heavy concentration on mining created a consumer goods shortage that continuously buoyed price levels. The resultant inflationary pressures further stimulated demands from the mine and urban workers and the clerical and junior executive personnel as well, leading the Zambian president to predict a period of violent confrontation between the disadvantaged rural masses and the remainder.[19] However, it was the high income position of the 50,000 mine workers, in addition to the 70,000 whites and their purchasing power, that helped to prime Zambia's still feeble secondary industrialization effort. African mine workers, railway workers, and farmers continue to press for a greater share of the country's copper-produced wealth, while policy planners move to expand government control over the economy to ensure more rapid development of copper and other industries, more rapid Zambianization, and more effective prosecution of the high-priority disengagement from Rhodesia.[20]

If improvement of the Zambian share or shares of the national wealth means anything, it means wage increases and increased farm income. Realistically, Zambianization of the economy does not mean capitalization of a Zambian middle class for a long time to come. Since the Zambian post-independence regime, like so many other African regimes, is historically rooted in trade union agitation, it was initially committed to act on the wage front. Yet in view of the low productivity of all industry outside the mining industry, substantial wage increases in secondary industries over the already high existing levels were uneconomical. Zambia's leaders could do little more than follow the example of their colleagues elsewhere and confine their activity in the spheres of incomes equalization and redistribution of the wealth mainly to rhetoric and to only minor adjustments or paper reforms. To the extent that monetary advances were within the capability of the economy or, more precisely, could be afforded by the particular industry, the general fund out of which they were to be paid was, of course, quickly depleted by a sharp increase in the labor force — labor attracted by the larger incomes fund, by inflation, and by higher cost of living.[21]

The exceedingly perceptive Nigerian Development Plan for 1970-74 did not ignore the causes assumed to have led to the collapse of the first federation and the ensuing bloody civil war. It listed as two important objectives "the active promotion of a great and dynamic economy on the one hand and the establishment of a just and more egalitarian society on the other," but it warned that "[s]imultaneous pursuit of economic growth and distributive equity cannot be successful without a carefully formulated incomes policy."[22] Because of the immense difficulties in allowing state, society, and the economy in particular to resolve through natural processes the anomalies in incomes and wealth distribution, government intervention was frankly postulated as a fundamental prerequisite. Again, the realism in this particular plan breaks through in the passage immediately following. "Unfortunately in the Nigerian context, Government has not been able to play this vital role in a systematic manner; nor has the focus of intervention always been guided by the requirements of economic development and social change." The author of that passage must indeed have had his tongue in his cheek.[23]

Paradoxically, or perhaps quite plausibly, the typical approach to income regulation and equalization is to devise nets that inevitably prove insufficient to catch all but the smallest fish. In other words, measures to secure a modicum of social justice, usually tend to hit the already disadvantaged. The larger fish, as every school child knows, are most difficult to catch. In the social realm there is reason to believe that all too frequently they are not meant to be caught. The escape route most commonly used by that species is known as tax evasion.

For more than a decade Nigeria, one of the more adequately documented examples, has struggled with this debilitating African disease. Elaborate measures to equalize or adjust grossly unfair and inequitable income distribution through taxation consistently fell short of expected goals, largely because of the ease with which they could be circumvented. Predictably, it is the already well-situated rich who are able to contrive evasion while the lower level poor pay the tax.[24] In Western Nigeria about 1966, between 85 and 90 percent of all taxes — property, income and head tax — were paid by persons who earned less than $300 per annum.[25]

At a different level the largest single item in Nigeria's federal, regional, and local government expenditures in 1965 was "Personal Emoluments."[26] This item is characteristic of Africa. It is of some power political consequence where "emoluments" favor the police or the military, as they do increasingly in coup-afflicted countries. In the 1970-71 Federal Estimates for the Federal Republic of Nigeria, the overall share of "emoluments" in the total budget fell from around 33 to 13 percent. However, the shares going to police and "defense" remained high at 58 and 30 percent of their respective budgets, rising probably at a much faster rate than military regimes are prepared to admit.[27]

The relative power position of an expanding military and police officers corps together with their augmented and still rising share of total national income does signify accretion of the aggregate potential at the disposal of the two branches but does not necessarily signify an actual net increase of monetary power and influence purchasing potential. In Nigeria augmented compensation did provide individual soldiers with enough funds to improve the propensity to consume, but neither enlisted ranks nor officers could accumulate enough to be of any consequence power politically unless they, too, resorted to illicit means. There is some evidence that a class of nouveau riche in uniform is in process of formation. By the laws of socioeconomic kinship an improved, financially invigorated group base means reinforced vested interest and generation of a pressure momentum that tends to drive the group leadership to seek and secure further advantages.

For obvious reasons official rhetoric in Senegal attempts to fudge the provocative differential that separates industrial workers and commercial employees on one side from the administrative staff on the other, and also misstates the facts pertaining to the unhealthy relationship between rural and urban workers. Given the limitations under which Senegalese regimes must operate in their campaign to equalize incomes or narrow gaps, such a strategy of obscurantism might be prudent at this point in time.[28] In the opinion of one observer, differences in salaries between industrial and commercial workers and office workers alone raise profound "human, moral, psychological, and technological" questions that are most difficult to resolve, because the means required for this particular conflict resolution have not yet materialized.[29]

The same source, incidentally, provides evidence that Parkinson's Law also operates in Africa. The creeping proliferation of government offices has buoyed the demand for typists, which, in turn, has driven up typist remuneration. The result is that typists earn as much as their European predecessors whom they replace, and they rank above African traders and skilled mechanics who work in far less pleasant conditions.[30]

High living standards along the coast have produced a psychological attachment to European standards to the detriment of any significant policy shift in favor of the rural sector. The disparity is illustrated by the fact that while 52.2 percent of the income in Senegal is earned in and around Dakar and 1.8 percent in the distant southeast region, retail prices based on 100 units for Dakar reach 110 in the interior.[31] If the several tens of thousands of Europeans working mainly in the larger cities are excluded from incomes calculation, the gap between urban and rural Africans alone would be lower, of course. But as noted elsewhere, the African is not inclined to be satisfied with lower standards; he will continue to press for parity with the Europeans.[32]

Reminiscent of Zambia, the disparity between African and European incomes is one of the most sensitive problems. In 1959 in Senegal, 50,000 non-Africans earned 20 percent of total income, while 2,650,000 Africans earned 77.8 percent.[33] Thus, non-Africans accounting for a fifty-fourth of the population dispose of a fifth of total income ("revenu global des menages"). African farmers and fishermen, three-fourths of the population, obtain two-fifths of total income, while salaried personnel, an eighth of the population, earn between a fourth and a third of total income.[34] The African versus non-African or indigenes-foreign juxtaposition assumes different proportions in the Ivory Coast because of the large contingent of migrant farm workers in the cocoa- and coffee-producing regions. Incomes policy there faces a near standoff between the two sectors as concerns their respective shares of total income.[35] Amin shows that between 1950 and 1965, and regardless of legal sovereignty status, the relative shares of foreign and African incomes did not change substantially, though the gap between them was narrowed somewhat.

TABLE 23-1.

	Urban		Rural	
		(In billion francs	CFA)*	
	1950	1965	1950	1965
Foreign Sector	13.1	55.4	1.1	7.2
Large enterprises	3.6	22.5	0.4	5.0
Salaried employees	6.2	15.9		
African Sector	11.3	60.3		
Rural			32.5	70.6

SOURCE: Amin, 1967, 298-99.
*1965 value.

It is clear that incomes policy in the Ivory Coast, when related ostensibly to equalization of the foreign and African sectors, is far from attaining a goal satisfactory to Ivorienne interests until and unless non-Ivorienne foreigners are extrapolated from the aggregate for the African sector. If they are, however, the share remaining to the Ivorienne segment is exceedingly small, as will be the power potential modified only by the degree to which the native policymakers are prepared to favor Ivorienne nationals over foreigners, African or non-African. Incomes policy, however, cannot incisively attack the prominent position of the large French-owned and operated enterprises without also attacking the very foundations of the economy as currently structured.

Do the better-situated Ivorienne families command sufficient incomes to generate significant power political purchasing power? An article written to attract consumer goods distributors to the Ivory Coast, thus probably weighted on the side of optimism, reveals the virtual absence of an influential indigenous middle class.[36] As for the rural-urban incomes juxtaposition, at independence the share of wageearners in the public and private sectors representing less than 10 percent of the total population earned more than the total rural mass representing 80 percent.[37] The situation did not materially improve with independence. To the contrary, current incomes policy, as distinct from rhetoric, reflects a willingness to accept the imbalance as unavoidable.[38]

Some General Implications of Incomes Policy

In view of the dilemma facing policymakers intent on bringing about substantial redistribution of wealth, social analysis has erred greatly by not stressing acts of omission along with acts of commission. For example, failure over a period of time to stem inflationary trends can raise havoc with any attempt to correct imbalances in the distribution of income and wealth. (Quite possibly more than the political revolution that occurred at the end of World War I, postwar inflation in Germany drastically altered the class structure by decimation of the once-powerful middle class).

Inflation always affects income distribution and attacks existing patterns of control of wealth. The lowest income brackets suffer first, especially the unskilled and those with fixed incomes. Skilled workers and technicians, professionals, and businessmen tend to benefit. Simply stated, inflation exacerbates existing inequities.

Inflation is currently being imported into developing countries on a large scale. Foreign suppliers of needed commodities and materials pass on to the consumers — the African economies in this instance — their own increased costs. The African governments are in no position to compensate themselves or their nationals. As a result, the cost of living in the importing country rises, wage demands are pressed, and some increases are conceded, albeit reluctantly. The end result is erosion of whatever gains diverse groups may have secured. Levels of income of the urban masses are especially affected in view of their relative dependence on imported goods.[39]

The other side of that coin is deliberate stimulation of inflationary trends. "Governments are driven to inflation," writes Sir Arthur Lewis, "when they think the political difficulties of raising resources in this way are less than the political difficulties in the way of raising the same sum in taxes."[40] Considerations along these lines, among other concerns, appear to have guided thinking on incomes policy in Ghana during the Nkrumah years. Unfortunately for the regime as well as for the economy in general, the policy went awry.[41]

Whether deliberately or accidentally promoted, from our point of view the most interesting aspect of policy surrounding inflation and income distribution is the element of favoritism. In Ghana civil servants could expect to rise to a modest degree on the inflationary wave via built-in salary increases. The same applies elsewhere; government manages to take care of its own. Left behind, in Africa at least, is the wageearner and, of course, the farmer. The peasant depending on an imported hoe or a bag of fertilizer is simply thrown to the inflationary wolves, though not without some encouraging words from government spokesmen and local officials.

It seems that in the realm of incomes policy especially the road to disaster often is paved with good intentions. By the same token, the graveyard of good intentions may turn out to be a more rewarding area for policy analysis than is the small mound of policies actually implemented.

Long-range approaches to the problem, through taxation, wage policies, land reform, promotion of indigenous middle class or business sectors, and the like, are socially respectable policies. As such they lend themselves to public peroration. They are popular because they promise to benefit the greatest number. However, few if any of these policies have an appreciable concrete impact on the distribution of power and influence in society. Policies designed to cope with immediate economic realities do have such an impact. Invariably such policies are unpopular because they tend to benefit only small, if not minute, and most likely foreign minorities. Public pronouncements on this vital problem complex, therefore, must be analyzed for what they conceal as much as for what they reveal. The number of reserved areas of interests accorded preferred treatment or tacitly exempted from drastic measures — the number and identity of economic and social sacred cows, in other words — must be assessed most carefully.

The scenario for distribution of effective power is substantially different from the one that explains distribution of pseudopower for popular consumption. The pattern favors urban centers over rural areas, the already privileged and strong over the weak, those associated with or involved in major and economically critical production processes over those engaged in marginal work and activities. Foreign capitalists are favored over indigenous ones, except at relatively insignificant middle and low levels.

All of the systems tend to end up favoring the retention, even the further development, of wealth-producing enclaves — islands in the general national economy — based either on mining as in Zambia or on trading and manufacturing as in the more typical system. Enclaves spawn concentrations of powerful agents of capitalism, be they public or private. Social values are formed and shaped in these enclaves, formulated and propagated concepts of justice and equity, of power and influence reflect preferences within the enclave rather than opinions of the country or society at large.

Income distribution thus must be evaluated, as Helleiner suggests, not only in per capita terms but also "in terms of what the differently distributed income buys, what values it strives to achieve, what examples it seeks to emulate." These differences, Helleiner continues, determine influence allocation of resources and determination of priorities or "the demand structure of given blocs of income."[42] Peasant incomes favor demand structures different from those of industrial workers' incomes. In Northern Nigeria or in the interior of Senegal, peasant incomes stimulate demand structures, hence concepts of equity in distribution of wealth and incomes, that differ substantially from those of the more highly industrialized, commercialized, and capitalized southern or coastal regions in the same countries. Of considerable social consequence in this regard is the tendency, which Helleiner notes, for income earned in peasant agriculture to be used up in necessities of life, whereas income earned in the enclaves is more likely to be saved.[43] The implications are clear.

The life-style encouraged by enclave-earned incomes, including luxury goods, modern services, and costly imports, generates a high reward for foreign style of living — that is, high referent propensity, hence commitment to a Western style of life. From that perspective, retention of foreign influences are tantamount to guaranties of continued enjoyment of a favored way of life, which leads to a mutually reinforcing commitment to maintain the status quo ante independence, including a fundamentally inequitable distribution of wealth and of income.

A seemingly harsh but actually eminently realistic appraisal of the situation was offered early in the development decade by Sir Arthur Lewis, when he noted rather candidly that the "lower income groups . . . do not belong to the categories whose promotion is in the interest of growth. In the event income differences and savings activity are considered alone, their income in relation to that of other groups should be reduced not increased."[44]

Politician and planner alike depreciate measures that favor the already privileged and advantaged salaried group situated mainly in the national capitals. Yet modernization favors the skilled; it creates, for example, new administrative positions. Any increase in income at the bottom automatically brings in its wake a further increase in the salaried sector. In 1958 the Senegal regime opted in favor of a 15 percent increase of salaries, while the farmers took an equal reduction. The marabouts helped to keep the lid down. This was the only way, for an equal increase in farm income would inevitably have brought in its wake further allocation of resources to an enlarged corps of administrators needed to cope with the material consequences of the farm bonanza.

Substantial increases in income or substantial changes in the wealth and income distribution patterns, while never adequate to cause significant betterment at the bottom, inevitably will tend to flow to a large measure into corrupt pockets. Regimes are known to have taken shortcuts to siphon off economic gains for the benefit of their own support machinery. In any case, a 10 percent shift from private to state-owned industry, state-owned commercial establishments, or state agricultural enterprise, while not necessarily improving the income position of the masses, will inevitably lead to expansion of government machinery. The salary rolls will devour more financial resources, while productivity will increase only slightly or remain stagnant. If a substantial shift in the distribution of wealth can be effected, it will result only in creation of new bases from which new special interest groups can gain more direct access to the decision- and policymaking machinery. Given prevailing limitations, redistribution of income really means rearrangement of power political support patterns within existing power political parameters. All that happens is that Peter is robbed to pay Paul.

Africanization and Income Distribution

On face value, Africanization should bring about a shift in income and wealth distribution. But replacing non-Africans with Africans in existing jobs does not result in significant changes unless the positions in question are of highest strategic significance and also endow their new occupants with sufficient economic muscle to overcome resistance of entrenched and established foreign interests. This situation is unlikely for some time to come. Positions open to Africanization are not that important strategically.

Certain key positions may not yet find any Africans trained to adequately perform the requisite tasks.

As Africanization proceeds, it will favor the more highly skilled and educated ethnic subgroups within each society. In some cases numerical superiority may be the deciding factor. In Kenya Africanization tends to favor the more numerous and more strongly entrenched Kikuyu; in Zambia, the Bemba; in Nigeria, the western and northern groups; in Ghana, the Fante or the Ewe.

Economic Africanization usually means takeover of foreign owned and operated enterprises, most likely, however, only in the lower ranges. In Ghana in 1968, the Ghanaian Enterprises Decree, typical of similar acts promulgated elsewhere, directed that small businesses under N¢ 500,000 and wholesale under N¢ 1 million were to be transferred into Ghanaian hands within a specified time. This form, more than the more common form of forcing low-level employers to employ Africans in subordinate positions, or even high-level employers to do essentially the same, may eventually result in significant shifts of power and influence if the sector within which the transfers take place remains viable and healthy, and if the new owners and managers generate and sustain a genuine interest in exploiting the newly proffered opportunities.[45]

If it is true that to be power and influence effective Africanization must take place in key economic positions involving more than nominal turnovers of employee or capital resources, it is more than likely that it will favor retention of the status quo ante independence. After all, it will benefit mainly those among the African population who collaborated closely with the former colonial masters. Senegalization, Ivorienization, Ghanaianization, or any other national variant of Africanization in nonrevolutionary conditions will bring to the fore the business elite, the local capitalist, the defender of the status quo. This is not saying that these forces will be uniformly willing instruments of foreign exploitation. To the contrary, they may have a sharper bite than the first-generation leaders who professed social revolutionary objectives but practiced capitalism, usually of the Western variety. Be that as it may, Africanization policy of and by itself cannot be regarded as substantially related to effective shifts in power.

Other Incomes Policy Alternatives

Although basically related to Africanization, the policy objective termed "pyramid dismantling" warrants separate consideration. Zambia's first five-year development plan envisaged the dismantling to be accomplished within the plan period. The aim was substitution of the European with an African apex, combined with progressively accelerating Africanization downward until all control and supervisory positions, especially in mining but also elsewhere, had been transferred into African hands.

The concept of pyramid dismantling, in contrast to ordinary Africanization, suggests systematic change and selective transfer with a view especially to transfer of key control positions in state and society. But structures that could be described as pyramids that one could "dismantle" existed only in European dominated and controlled white settler colonies. There the top of the pyramid was occupied by expatriate businessmen and financiers, senior civil servants, high-ranking expatriate military and police officers, and advisers. It seemed prudent here to avoid precipitate action, which could easily result in serious disruptions of a most sensitively balanced economy. Accordingly, a "proceed with caution" sign was figuratively displayed at all strategic junctions and command posts, including mining and banking headquarters, the vital transportation and energy-producing sectors, and military and police headquarters. Caution was applied wherever expatriates predominated, including high-level government positions in such sensitive ministries as finance and commerce, in the central banks, and in the special and secret services.

Unless reliable Africans take the place of the former occupants of key positions, pyramid dismantling holds certain dangers in addition to disruption and loss of efficiency and productivity. Where Soviet or Chinese influences, direct or indirect, take the place of British, French, or other European influences, the dismantling process can well culminate in the construction of an entirely new pyramid, which could turn out to be a Trojan horse from the point of view of the elite doing the dismantling. To be sure, African policymakers seem confident that they will be able to contain new threats to their independence, but there is room for doubt on that score.

In conclusion, although few African policymakers and leaders are without policy goals and prescriptions, few also have been able to find conditions propitious for untrammeled, unrestricted application or implementation of truly revolutionary designs. Modest shifts in the power and influence structure were achieved by Touré in Guinea, by Nkrumah — though not for long in that case — and by such regimes as Tanzania and on Zanzibar, Somalia, and the Sudan. In general, policy implementation has been more a matter of piecemeal manipulation of whatever happens to be conveniently within reach of the power elite. Showdowns with interests entrenched near or at the top are carefully avoided, and manipulations are confined to the support structure underneath, through relatively small rewards, occasional punishments, concessions, small favors, and the rewards of a middle- and low-level patronage system. Yet the struggle continues; the search for more substantial independence gathers momentum, often under pressure from internal opposition and dissent groups increasingly stimulated from the direction of the Soviet Union and the Chinese People's Republic.

Epilogue

One of the hazards incurred in political-economic analysis is that one becomes associated in the reader's mind with simplistic economic determinism. We hope that we have effectively dispelled any such impression. Nor has it been our intent to suggest that politics in Africa is less complex subject matter than is politics elsewhere. There can be no doubt that a well-rounded view of politics or political behavior requires consideration of insights generated in yet other fields or areas of knowledge such as psychology, sociology, philosophy, or jurisprudence. The essential, indeed the critical point we have sought to develop here is not that the economic dimension is the sole determinant of politics in Africa but that in conditions prevailing on the continent, now and for the foreseeable future, economic forces and factors *tend to predominate* at all levels — local, national, and international. Put differently, in conditions of economic scarcity or poverty, the economic dimension may warrant being ranked higher within the analytical priority structure than may be true in conditions of abundance or affluence. Certainly, analysis so conceived cannot avoid being interdisciplinary.

The point has been made that the legal-constitutional structure under which the former colonies were granted independence was obsolete before the ink dried on the relevant documents. Power politically these documents may have been irrelevant even before. We have attempted to show why political thought on and about Africa went astray.

We also suggest that little may be gained from the study of the more spectacular but developmentally inconsequential factional squabbles, personality conflicts, or other effervescent phenomena of the passing political parade. It is doubtful that much can be gained in the way of gauging the future by theorizing about contemporary regime shifts, the paper-thin ritual of international diplomacy, aimless military coups, or the throes of legal,

343

party political, or administrative systems that are already doomed at birth. Improvisation, series of ad hoc measures, all of an emergency kind and most likely defensive in nature, will be the style of government and politics for some time to come. If that is so, those immediately involved may be better informed and in any case should be allowed to have their way without being subjected to over-the-shoulder gratuitous advice from outside.

If our studies and our concerns are to have any substantive bearing on the outcome of Africa's present travails, our sights must be raised to allow us to come to grips with the analytically more rewarding long-range aspects of development on the continent. To that end realism must replace idealism, or at least idealism, ideology, and euphoristic visions must be heavily discounted and more diligently examined for their economic content. Beyond that, political thought on and about Africa must be cut adrift from its traditional Western moorings. To tether it to the already calcifying tenents of Soviet Russian and Communist Chinese thought or to the mummified remnants of ancient Marxist doctrine would be no improvement at all. It is our hope that this study, limited in scope to enhance its reliability but broad enough to be representative, will serve Africans and Africa's sincere friends abroad in a joint quest for a better understanding of the continent as it really is.

Based on long- rather than short-term phenomena, reflective of historically more consequential events and relationships, the study of politics in all of the less developed countries will be rendered socially more meaningful, diagnostically more rewarding, and intellectually more satisfying to all concerned. Then, and only then, will our deliberations be of interest to Third World leaders and planners, and only then will our studies of Africa, Asia, and Latin America promise to yield anything of lasting value.

Suggested Readings

PART I

The most compact yet diversified discussion on power and related topics is offered in Bell, *Political Power*. Karl Deutsch develops some intriguing themes on problems of perception of society and politics in *Nerves of Government*. On the subject of power and influence, the most thorough analyses may be found in Cartwright's contribution to J. G. March, *Handbook of Organization*, and in Cartwright and Zander, *Group Dynamics*, especially in chapter 32. Also recommended is Gamson, *Power and Discontent*. Lasswell and Kaplan, *Power and Society*, still remains a basic source.

On the interrelationship of politics and economics, Lange, 1963, especially in chapters one and four, updates the classic Marxist position that engenders increasing appeal among African leaders and intellectuals. Heilbroner's *Economic Means and Social Ends* and Myrdal's *The Political Element in the Development of Economic Theory* deal with more current aspects of political economy. Rimmer, 1969, supports the call for a return to political economy by criticizing economists for abstracting their raw material from politics; Mitchell, 1967, strikes a similar note. Brett, 1969 considers the additional variable, rationality.

An additional Marxist source, based on African experience, is Tamas Szentes, *The Political Economy Of Underdevelopment*. Budapest: Akadémiai Kiado, 1971.

PART II

NOTE: In keeping with the purpose of this book, works written by economists are cited here only if they are readily intelligible to the political scientist untrained in economics.

By far the most comprehensive sources on individual countries and territories are the volumes published in the series of *Area Handbooks* prepared by the Foreign Area Studies (FAS) of the American University — in particular those on Senegal, Ghana, Liberia, Zambia, Angola, Mozambique, Kenya, Uganda, and Tanzania. (These and additional volumes in the series are available through the U.S. Superintendent of Documents, U.S. Government Printing Office, Washington, D.C.)

The student of politics and economics will find invaluable the International Monetary Fund's *Surveys of African Economics,* even though they tend to be on the conservative side. Volume 1 deals with the countries in former French Equatorial Africa, Volume 2 with East Africa, Volume 3 with all but one of the countries in former French West Africa, and Volume 4 with Zaire, Zambia, and Malawi.

Reliable, up-to-date information on the economies of countries is conveniently found in Standard Bank, *Annual Economic Reviews.* (The Standard Bank, Ltd., London is an affiliate of Chase-Manhattan of New York.)

The United Nations and affiliated agencies and organizations publish periodic and comprehensive reports and special studies. Foremost are the publications as well as the unpublished records of the Economic Commission for Africa, (ECA).

Of value to the political scientist as well as to the economist are Robson and Lury, *The Economies of Africa,* and the development plans published by individual countries. Though not likely to be implemented as planned, these plans contain most useful data and discussions.

A first-rate companion textbook for the present study would be Kamarck, *The Economics of African Development.*

On the international relations of African states, Nielsen, *The Great Powers and Africa,* and USSR, Academy of Sciences, Institute of Africa, *History of Africa,* provide overviews prepared from two opposing perspectives. Kamarck, *op. cit.,* chap. xi considers the "Diplomacy of Economic Development." Green and Seidman, *Unity or Poverty,* and Wallerstein, *The Politics of Unity,* deal with problems of African economic and political integration and cooperation. So does Virginia Thompson, *West Africa's Council of the Entents,* Cornell, 1972. Guy Hunter, *The New Societies of Tropical Africa,* Oxford, 1962, and P. S. Lloyd, *Africa in Social Change,* Penguin, 1967, offer comprehensive overviews of social, economic, and cultural change.

PART III

Of general relevance is Charles P. Kindleberger, *Power and Money: The Politics of International Economics and the Economics of International Politics,* Basic Books, 1970; and Kindleberger, *Economic Development,* Second Edition, 1965, Part Three, "International Issues." A strong African voice is raised in Nkrumah's writings — in particular, *Neo-Colonialism: The Last Stage of Imperialism* and *Class Struggle in Africa.* Green and Seidman, *Unity or Poverty,* approaches the same subject from a similar position. Franz Fanon, *The Wretched of the Earth,* deals with broader, social revolutionary aspects of Africa's response, as does Nkrumah, *Handbook of Revolutionary Warfare,* London, Panaf Books, 1968.

The relative helplessness of the primary producing countries is brought out in Theodore H. Moran, "New Deal or Raw Deal in Raw Materials," *Foreign Policy,* Number 5, Winter 1971-72, 119-34. Also noteworthy on the subject of neo-colonialism are the contributions by Gavin Williams, Ann Seidman, and Reginald Green in Ch. Allen and R. W. Johnson, *African Perspectives: Papers in the History, Politics, and Economics of Africa,* Cambridge: Cambridge University, 1970, 225-324.

The aforementioned *Area Handbooks,* the IMF *Surveys,* and the economic surveys published from time to time by the UN's Economic Commission for Africa provide the best available overviews of the international position of the African states individually and collectively. Although restricted mainly to West Africa from Senegal to Cameroon, the þiweekly *West Africa* is a must for current information.

PART IV

Kindleberger's *Economic Development* is of importance here also, though he does cover problems of economic development on a universal scale. The noneconomist will be greatly assisted in his understanding of the nature and uses of economic resources especially by chapters 4-7.

On the nature and role of military power, Ruth First, *The Barrel of a Gun,* and Claude E. Welch, Jr., *Soldier and State in Africa,* Northwestern University, 1969, are recommended in addition to other major sources cited in the Notes. Carter, *National Unity and Regionalism,* offers case studies on internal-regional relations. P. C. Lloyd, *Africa in Social Change;* and Alderfer, *Local Government in Developing Countries,* provide background material on the traditional and local levels.

The corrupting influences of money on politics are considered in Wraith and Simpkin, in Scott, 1972, especially chapter 8, dealing with Ghana, and in several essays collected in Heidenheimer's *Political Corruption.* Andreski's *African Dilemma* offers some incisive observations on the subject, as does Dumont in *False Start in Africa,* a significant critique of economic and especially agricultural development in the newly independent states.

PART V

The following are of special value: Lasswell, *Politics: Who Gets What, When and How;* Dahl on power, in Bell and elsewhere; and C. Wright Mills, *The Power Elite.* Sir Arthur Lewis' little volume on *Politics in West Africa,* Dumont, chapter 6, and Andreski deal with the pathology of African leadership, as does Bretton, *The Rise and Fall of Kwame Nkrumah.* Bretton, *Power and Stability in Nigeria,* chapters 4 and 5; LeVine, *Political Leadership in Africa,* Stanford, 1967; and *Dreams and Deeds,* University of Chicago Press; Lloyd, *The New Elites of Africa;* Liebenow, *Evolution of Privilege,* Cornell, 1969, investigate elites in individual countries. W. Howard Wriggins, *The Ruler's Imperative; Strategies for Political Survival in Asia and Africa,* Colorado, 1969, provides valuable insights.

The rise of the African military has generated a growing volume of literature in which that rise is traced, including First, Guttridge, and Lee; assessment of their impact on social change by Welch; and country studies such as Luckham, Miners, and Lefever, and Pinkney.

PART VI

Almond and Coleman, especially Coleman, though somewhat dated, in *Politics of the Developing Areas,* Princeton, 1960, chapter 3, attempt a typology of pressure and interest groups and related problems. Important country studies, containing detailed analysis of such groups, including political parties — all listed in the Bibliography — are Apter (Gold Coast), Austin and Bretton (Ghana), Bretton, Coleman, Crowder, Dudley, Mackintosh, Sklar, and Whitacker (Nigeria), Kilson (Sierra Leone) Young (Congo), Zolberg (Ivory Coast), Apter (Uganda), Bienen (Tanzania). Nkrumah, *Class Struggle in Africa* is representative of the now-classic African socialist view. Kindleberger's discussion in *Economic Development,* chapters 4-7, is especially germane. The *Area Handbooks* serve as convenient reference works on the groups considered in this part and on related aspects, in addition to the works cited in the Notes.

The heavy emphasis on political parties in political analyses during the first independence decade has tended to obscure the often more potent and powerful socioeconomic or bureaucratic interest and pressure groups such as financiers and bankers, business and industry, or the higher civil service. Since all of the above-cited country studies deal with one or another of these groups in varying contexts, the student would be well served in exploring these sources by reference to their indexes as well as the tables of content.

PART VII

Again, Kindleberger, part 25 "Domestic Policy Problems," together with Stolper, 1966, and the policy and development sections in the International Monetary Fund's *Surveys of African Economies,* provide excellent background reading on problems of decision- and policymaking. The several Development Plans cited throughout this study, together with appropriate sections in Robson and Lury, constitute a useful set of case studies. Of considerable value, though of a more general nature, is Bauer and Yamey. Kamarck, chapter 10, also is of special relevance here.

Because the critical mass in public decision- and policymaking, especially in conditions of economic scarcity, is economic wherewithal, and dependent on that financial ways and means, a realistic study of what actually transpires must rely on accounts of what is being done, not what is being recommended or deemed desirable. In that regard, the most useful assessments are again found in the pages of *West Africa,* especially in lead articles and feature stories evaluating development plans, development progress reports, budgets, major policy declarations, and the like.

Notes

CHAPTER 1

1. *New York Times,* July 17, 1969, 38.
2. Pollock, vii; Heidenheimre in Rose and Heidenheimer, 791.
3. Easton, 71.
4. Laing, 39.
5. Heilbronner, 80-93.
6. Helleiner, 1964*b*, 256; and 1964*a* and 1964*c*.
7. E/CN.14/401, 182.
8. An eloquent testimonial to the condition described is contained in the plaint by a chief statistician in the Ministry of Economy Development and Planning in Kenya. In his report on alleged irregularities in maize marketing, he wrote: "If adequate statistics had been available many of the events which gave rise to the appointment of this Commission might never have happened;" and "full and adequate consideration of the maize problem *in Kenya* is impossible because of the lack of statistical data relating to particular aspects." Kenya, 1966*c,* 5-6, italics added.

Soviet Russian Professor Potekhin (18-19) offers some interesting observations on the reliability and accuracy — social accuracy, one might say — of such indexes as *per capita income* calculations:

There is no passing over the fact ... that the way the national income is calculated in the capitalist countries makes for the artificial overestimation of its size and camouflages the explitation inherent in capitalist relations.

The very method of calculating the national income chiefly on the basis of taxation statistics tends to inflate its size, and it includes income from trading operations, services, and other spheres where no material values are actually created. Soviet economists have estimated that the resultant increment is about 25 per cent on the average.

A United States embassy official in Lagos, Nigeria, reported that his office "recently gave up attempting to determine gross national product." He stated that "per capita income" was meaningless. "There is no real way to assess the income of over 70 percent of the population of Nigeria. The best one can say is that the *per capita* income in Nigeria is not as high as that of Ghana." He also commented that census figures produced by the rejected census of 1965 might be reasonably accurate as reflected in the analysis of data on smallpox and other vaccination programs conducted in selected areas. (Noteworthy in this connection is the disagreement among experts called together to assist in the formulation of questions on the 1960 census in Ghana. They were unable to agree on the definition of *tribe.*")

9. Balandier, 47.

10. A study based on Kenya and Tanzania reports that "a negative factor in analyzing power bases of African politicians and their prepolitical occupations is the apparent lack of personal, financial, or political resources of the politicians." Chaput et al, 127. Aside from the misplaced categorization of personal, financial and political, all three, of course, are part of the same thing; the use of power in this illustration is intriguing. The power resources the authors have in mind are identified more fully in the sentence following. "Kenya and Tanzania statistics suggest that only twenty to thirty percent of the politicians had independent power bases in the professions, the trade-unions, private businesses, or church hierarchies." Actually none of the resources cited with respect to most black politicians in the countries in question are significantly independent from the government, a fact of life that brings us closer to the heart of the matter.

11. Dahl, 1957, 201-215.

12. Cartwright, 1965, 3-4.

13. March; Simon, 1957.

14. Cartwright, *loc cit.*

15. Weber, 531.

16. Cartwright, 1965, 5. Dahl, 1957, 203. See also Cartwright, 1965, 11-13.

17. Parsons, *Public Opinion Quarterly*, 1963, 53-54.

18. Cartwright, 1965, 11 and 16.

19. Simon, 1953, 515-16.

20. Frey, 302-5.

21. Bell, 3.

22. Lange, 13.

23. Laing, chap. 5.

24. Lange, 237-40.

25. *Ibid.*, 157-60, especially note 11, 158.

26. Pollock, 323.

27. *Public Opinion Quarterly*, 1963, 54.

CHAPTER 2

1. E/CN.14/370, 19.

2. See Green and Seidman, 93.

3. UN/ECA, *African Economic Indicators*, 1968, 15-16. For further statistical evaluations of Africa's aggregate economic potential, see ST/ECA/109, 47, table 1, in which the projected West African Economic Community is compared with one single European country, Italy.

	West African Economic Community*	Italy
Gross domestic product per capita in US$	107	969
Purchasing power Population density '000 of US$ per square kilometer	1.7	164,510

*Includes 14 countries.

Other relevant data indicate that the combined gross domestic product of 39 African states was the equivalent of less than two-thirds of that of Italy. The purchasing power of the entire East African subregional market is of the same order of magnitude as that of Greece. ST/ECA/109, 1 and 12. The overall African position as compared to that of South Africa in gold holdings in the fourth quarter 1968 was as follows.

Africa)mainly Libya, Morocco, Nigeria) US$	370 million
South Africa	1,243 million
USA	10,892 million

International Monetary Fund, *International Financial Statistics,* April 1969, 13; and ID/CONF. 1/RBP/1.

4. A/6868/Add.1, 5.
5. Nettl, 563-64.
6. E/2158 (Second Committee, 21st session, agenda item 5).
7. Potekhin, 8-9; italics added.
8. Lewis, 1967, 27.
9. Soja, 1.
10. Pye in Pool, 200.
11. Kindleberger, 238-39.
12. E/CN.14/28, 12.
13. E/CN.14/INR/141, 6, especially table 3.
14. *West Africa,* October 11, 1969, 1205.

CHAPTER 3

1. International Monetary Fund (IMF), 1970 (vol. 3), 73.
2. Interview, May 1969.
3. Senegal, 1965, vol. 1, 55.
4. Senegal, 1968, 30; and 1965, vol. 2, map opposite 212.
5.

Distribution of monetary investment by
sector in Senegal, 1959-62 (%)*

	1959	1960	1961	1962
Agriculture	0.6	1.3	2.4	1.8
Energy and minings	38.5	41.4	11.5	6.2
Manufacturing	4.2	6.0	3.1	8.0
Building and construction	2.1	0.8	1.9	2.4
Transport	7.3	7.8	12.5	10.8
Other services	3.6	3.8	3.8	3.8
Trade	7.3	7.5	8.2	6.1
Administration†	36.4	31.4	56.6	60.9

*Excluding nonmonetary investment in the traditional sector.
†Including government-provided education and health services.
E/CN.14/370, table 17, 26.
See also Amin, 1971, 211, table 32; Senegal, 1969, 18-20.

Of the 60.9 percent allocation to administration, the 1968-69 budget projection showed 48.8 percent for salaries of government personnel alone. France, 1969*b* Annexe 40, 292.

6. P. Biarnes, *Le Monde,* January 11, 1969.
7. Nkrumah, 1968, 94.

8. Republic of Ghana, 1967, *Economic Survey,* 112, table vi. Accra: Central Bureau of Statistics, 1968. After the coup, external aid helped to reduce reliance on internal borrowing, but external and internal debts still remained towering obligations. *Standard Bank Review,* September 1971, 15.

9. Hill, 1963; Afana, 54-71.

10. Hance, 113.

11. Bretton, 1962, chap. 2.

12. United Kingdom Colonial Office, 1958, *Commission* [*on*] *Fears of Minorities;* and Nigeria, Northern Region, 1958.

13. Kuznets in Robinson, 14-32.

14. Standard Bank, *Annual Economic Review, Nigeria,* June 1970, 6.

15. Aboyade in Robson and Lury, 134.

16. Kaunda quoted by Jacques Nobecourt, *Le Monde* (weekly), March 17, 1971.

17. UN/ECA/FAO, 8.

18. Berelsford's tribal map lists approximately 100 different groups, including 13 or 14 with a 1962 census population of approximately 50,000 or more. The principal groups at the time were the Tonga (252,938), Bemba (190,623), and Chewa (135-727). Berelsford, 151.

19. Zambia, Finance Division, *Economic Report, 1968,* 33. Lusaka: Government Printer, 1969.

20. Kay, 5; Zambia, 1966*b,* 5, table i.

21. E/CN.14/401, 83.

22. Zambia, Mines Department, *Annual Report, 1965,* 8. Lusaka: Government Printer, 1966.

23. Standard Bank, *Annual Economic Review, Zambia,* August 1970, 9-10.

24. IMF (vol. 2), 166.

25. Soja, 101.

26. The most critical sector — agriculture and livestock (monetary sector) — also had fallen behind plan targets. The trend seemed to be reversed by 1969. Standard Bank, *Annual Economic Review, Kenya,* July 1971, 12.

27. Kenya, 1966*a,* 124; Kenya, 1969, 2-3.

28. Kenya, 1969, 17.

29. IMF, 1969 (vol. 2), 195ff, 208.

30. *Ibid.,* 198, and 200, table 23. By 1970, coffee, tea, and petroleum led the export list. Standard Bank, *Annual Economic Review, Kenya,* July 1971, 2.

31. IMF, 19, (vol. 2), 156ff.

32. *Ibid.,* 174; Standard Bank, *Annual Economic Review, Kenya,* July 1970, 11-12.

33. American University, 1967*b* (Kenya *Handbook*), 74, 80, and 96, tables 1, 5, and 11, respectively; also see Rothchild, 1969; *ibid.,* 1970; and Kenya, 1969, 25.

CHAPTER 4

1. ID/CONF.1/RBP/1, annex 3, map 9.

2. See Foltz, 1965; American University, 1963 (Senegal *Handbook*), 27-30.

3. ID/CONF.1/RBP/1, 120ff: E/CN.4/L/320/Rev. 1, especially 207-8.

4. Oser, 1967, 170-71.

5. *New York Times,* January 10, 1970, 54.

6. ST/ECA/109, 19; and IMF, 1970 (vol. 3), 2, on the crucial role of railway nets in regional cooperation and, eventually, integration.

7. Fitch and Oppenheimer, 126.

8. Zambia, 1966*b,* 8.

9. *West Africa,* April 11, 1970, 399.

10. Bing, 148-52.

11. Berg, 11-12; Dudley in Mackintosh, 402, note 2.

12. UN/ECA/FAO, 27.

13. Kamarck, 86.

14. IMF, *International Financial Statistics,* April 1969, 14-15.

15. E/CN.14/INR/113, 4-5, 8; E/CN.14/401/232, table 9.

16. Kenya, 1965, 7, 28; IMF, 1969 (vol. 2), 176; President Kaunda, *US News and World Report,* December 2, 1968. Zambia, *Public Service Commission, 1968,* sec. 5, Lusaka: Government Printer, 1969; E/CN.14/401, 80-81.

17. Andreski, 72-73.

18. N'Diaye, 63-66, 207-8.

19. Fougeyrollas, 102ff.

20. *Standard Bank Review,* December 1970, 6-8.

21. Lange, 43, note 35.

CHAPTER 5

1. Bryszinski, 204-29; Nielsen, 185, 218-20.

2. Union of Soviet Socialist Republics, 1968. A more detached view is Green and Seidman, 191-99. Nkrumah, 1965, chap. 18.

3. Nkrumah, 1965; Potekhin, 1968.

4. *New York Times,* January 18, 1971, reports that one USAID official who was plagued over a period of years by interminable and protracted debates and wrangles over a relatively trivial matter finally threw away the file, never to hear of the matter again.

5. *West Africa,* March 26, 1966, 341-42; *ibid.,* June 11, 1966, 645-46.

6. *Ibid.;* and Ghana, 1969*b* vol. 1, viii.

7. Kenya, 1966*a,* 41.

8. *West Africa,* December 6, 1969, 1462.

9. UN, *Economic Bulletin for Africa,* vol. 6, July 1966, 17.

10. *Ibid.,* 83.

11. *The Sun* (Baltimore), February 16, 1971.

12. Kenya, 1966*a,* 149-50; Kenya, 1969, 160-65.

13. Kenya, 1966*a,* 42.

14. Stolper, 1966, 282.

15. *Standard Bank Review,* December 1970, 6-8; also IMF, 1968 (vol. 1), 53.

16. Davies, 195; Kilby, 303-4.

17. American University, 1967*b* (Kenya, *Handbook*), 374-77; Potekhin, 43.

18. *Wall Street Journal,* September 7, 1970.

19. Stolper, 1966, 280-81, including note 1.

20. E/CN.14/401, 86.

21. Nigeria, *First Development Plan, Progress Report, 1964,* 20-21. Lagos: Federal Ministry of Development, 1965.

22. *Christian Science Monitor,* June 30, 1969.

23. Diallo, interview, July 1969; also *West Africa,* February 20-26, 1971, 211.

24. Dotson and Dotson, 82; also see E/CN.14/401, 78.

25. Zolberg in Welch, 1970, 10; Lee, 181; United States Department of the Army, *Africa. A Bibliography,* DA,PAM 550-5; *West Africa,* August 31, 1968, 1030; *Africa Confidential,* December 27, 1967. First, 205-21.

26. Andreski, 133.

27. E/CN/14/401, 207, table 2.

28. Huntington, in *Foreign Policy,* Spring 1971, 114ff. Lefever, 205-21; United States, 1971, part 8, 1881-1958.

29. Lefever, *op. cit.;* United States, 1971, part 8, 1907-8 and 2423-24. Bretton in Judd, 452-54; USSR, 32, 422 (and especially all references to Soviet assistance to Algeria, Somalia, Angola, and Mozambique).

30. Lefever, 218.

31. Mabileau et Meyriat, 77.

32. Darlington and Darlington, 138-39.
33. *Ibid.*, and disregarding Egyptian and Libyan assistance.
34. *Chicago Daily News,* November, 1969.
35. U.S. Department of the Army, *op. cit.,* 166, gives comparative data but no effectiveness analysis. On reported Soviet assessment of Somali MIG flying capabilities, United States, 1971, 1948. Additional data on the level of U.S. military assistance to Africa for 1970 are published in *ibid.,* 1953.
36. Nkrumah, 1968, 96.
37. Interview with a non-African technical adviser, May 1969.
38. Nkrumah, 1968, 94ff.

CHAPTER 6

1. E/CN.14/401, 77, table 2.
2. A/6868/Add. 1, 11.
3. Nielsen, 102; also 104, table 8; and Amin, 1971, 308, table 77.
4. Nigeria, Federation, 1970, 135.
5. Standard Bank, *Annual Economic Review,* Zambia, June, 1969, 3.
6. *Standard Bank Review,* December 1970, 18-19.
7. Philip Asiedu, *Washington Post,* December 20, 1970, 8.
8. "Oil, Nigeria's Waiting Game," *West Africa,* February 20-26, 1971, 221.
9. Nigeria, Federation, *Recurrent Estimates Of The Government of The Federal Republic of Nigeria, 1970-71.* Approved, Head 50, 293. Lagos: Federal Ministry of Information, 1970; and *West Africa,* week ending July 23, 1971, 853; also *Wall Street Journal,* November 12, 1970. (The Soviet Union was to loan £225,000 of the total.)
10. *West Africa,* February 20-26, 1971, 221. Schätzl, 57, cautions that effective bargaining can begin only after initial exploration and drilling costs have been covered. Schätzl, 211-12, table B.1 (appendix), illustrates increasing diversification of oil exports, which augments bargaining potential. The advantage of lower shipping cost over Mideast oil is illustrated in *ibid.,* 67, table 20. Kilby, 74, relates several instances of tougher bargaining on Nigeria's part.
11. *New York Times,* November 28, 1970; *Standard Bank Review,* November 1970, 25-26. Standard Bank, *Annual Economic Review, Zambia,* August 1971, 10.
12. *American Metal Market,* November 15, 1967. On the perils of precipitate nationalization, see Moran.
13. *San Diego Union,* July 14, 1968. The comment by a Zambian official was made at a time when white saboteurs from below the border, probably Rhodesia or South Africa, had blown up a strategic bridge on the road to Malawi.
14. *Christian Science Monitor,* October 21, 1970.
15. 1965 (London), 2; italics added.
16. *US News and World Report,* May 13, 1968.

CHAPTER 7

1. France, 1969*b*, annexe 40.
2. For example, Ghana, 1966-67*b*., 27-28, paragraphs 160-65.
3. 1959, 22ff.
4. Helleiner, 1964*a*, 582-610; together with Kamarck, 127-28.
5. Nigeria, Federation, 1967, 290-91. Kenya 1966*c*, 86.
6. Nigeria, Federation, 1967, *loc. cit.*
7. *Ibid.,* 11, 150, p. 259.

8. International Bank for Reconstruction and Development, July 12, 1967, annex 1, 1.

9. Schatz, 1968, 428.

10. Dumont, 82.

11. Kenya, *The Policy on Trade Union Organization in Kenya,* Nairobi: Government Printer, 1965; "Busia and the Unions," *West Africa,* week ending October 1. 1971, 1133. American University, 1968*b* (Tanzania, *Handbook*), 388-94.

12. E/CN.14/401, 186 and 188, table 2.

13. Ghana, 1968*c,* part 3, especially 41*l*46.

14. Finlay et al. in Emmerson, 68.

15. Kilby, 299.

16. Zolberg, 1963, 24.

17. *Jeune Afrique,* June 23-29, as cited in *West Africa,* July 5, 771.

18. *West Africa,* July 19, 1969.

19. UN/ECA/FAO, 1964, 122 and appendix G, 1, and xxvii.

20. E/CN/CAS 5, 16.

21. Zambia, *Report of The Commission of Inquiry into The Affairs of The Lusaka City Council,* Lusaka: Government Printer, 1969; Ghana, 1966-67*b,* 25-26, paragraphs 152-53.

22. Kenya, National Assembly, *Official Report,* May 5, 1965, col. 1841.

23. Kindleberger, 124, italics added.

24. *Ibid.*

25. US House of Representatives, Committee on Banking and Currency, Staff Report for the Subcommittee on Domestic Finance, *Commercial Banks And Their Trust Activities.* 90th Congress, 2nd session, July 8, 1968. Washington, D.C.: Superintendent of Documents, 1968, 22.

26. Suret-Canale, 396ff.

27. France, 1969*a,* 9.

28. Olakanpo; IMF, 1968, 22-23, table 2, lists the total assets of the 14 commercial banks in French Equatorial Africa. Given the combined total GDP for the countries involved, the total of bank assets is impressive. Kenya, 1968, 160-170.

29. Amin, 1969, 172-73, 176-79, and 183; Olakanpo, *op. cit.;* and Kenya, 1968, *loc. cit.;* Nigeria, Federation, 1970, 227-28.

30. Amin, *op. cit.,* 183.

31. Ekukinam, 50ff.

32. Jones-Quartey, 206.

33. Ghana, 1969*a,* January 2, col. 175, Mr. Kwesi Lamptey; *ibid.,* January 30, Dr. Agama.

34. IMF, 1969 (vol. 2), 39ff; Nigeria, Federation, 1970, 19; Kenya, 1969, 558ff.

35. *Marchés Tropicaux,* April 1966, 22ff; IMF, 1969 (vol. 2), 7, 35ff, and 189ff.

36. Ekukinam, 64ff; Central Bank of Nigeria, *Monthly Reports,* give increasing evidence of such support.

37. Zambia, 1966*b,* 14.

CHAPTER 8

1. Suret-Canale, chapter iv.

2. American University, 1967*b* (Kenya, *Handbook*), 638-40; Kenya *Statistical Abstract, 1966,* table, 131, 101-2. Nairobi: Government Printer, 1967. Kenya, *Recurrent Expenditures, 1970.* Nairobi: Government Printer, 1969, Vote: President; also *ibid.,* 1968-69, Nairobi: Government Printer, 1968, and 1967-68. Nairobi: Government Printer, 1967; Kenya, *Economic Survey 1967,* table 8.4, 93. Nairobi: Government Printer, 1966. United States, 1971, 1881-1955.

3. Nigeria, Federation, *Estimates, 1964-65,* head 22, subhead, 35, 37. Lagos: Ministry of Information, 1964.

4. First, 167-68; Miners, 146-47.

5. Nigeria, Federation, *Estimates, 1964-65,* Summary of Recurrent Expenditure Heads, 14. Lagos: Ministry of Information.

6. Ghana, 1966, iv and 1-2; Ocran, 28-39; First, 197-98; Lefever, 55-56.

7. Ocran, 68-84; First, *loc. cit.;* Lefever, 58-60.

8. Ghana, 1964, *Statistical Yearbook,* 106. Accra: Control Bureau of Statistics, 1967.

9. Nigeria, Federation, *Annual Abstract of Statistics, 1965,* 128-29. Lagos: Federal Office of Statistics, 1967.

10. Nigeria, *Development Plan, Progress Report, 1964,* table A.13, heads 636/111; 1955-62 Programme, 636/110.

11. Miners, 130-54; First, 159-69.

12. Zambia, Public Services Commission, *Report For the Year, 1966,* appendix G. Lusaka: Government Printer, 1967.

13. *Christian Science Monitor,* March 25, 1971; *ibid.,* April 1, 1971.

14. Lefever, 55-56; Ghana, 1966, 2.

15. Ghana, 1969*b*, vol. 1, 6-63.

16. Deutsch, 1963, Part 2; Pye, 3-23.

17. Simon, 1953, 509, note 12.

18. Cartwright, 1965, 18-19.

19. Leonard Doob, *Communications in Africa: A Search for Boundaries,* (New Haven, Conn.: Yale University Press, 1961).

20. Fougeyrollas, 45; *Christian Science Monitor,* December 16, 1969.

21. *Mao's China. A Model for Africa,* the title of a pamphlet distributed clandestinely throughout East Africa by an anonymous source; author's collection.

22. Ghana, 1967*a*. This inquiry revealed enormous leakages and slippage in the application of funds intended for communications improvement. Sums allocated in Nigeria to similar purpose prior to the 1966 coup are also known to have been milked by corrupt office holders.

23. Nigeria Mid-Western Group of Provinces, *Report of the Commission Appointed to Enquire into the Owegbe Cult,* 74-77. Benin City; Ministry of Internal Affairs and Information, 1966; Kenya, 1955. Foster and Zolberg, 1971, 19-20; United Kingdom, 1960, 163-170. American University, 1969 (Zambia, *Handbook*), 424. For a different view, see Odinga, 1967, 113-115.

CHAPTER 9

1. Harvey, 238. Native courts had, of course, always been firmly controlled. See Nigeria, Federation, 1953.

2. Recent exceptions, Heidenheimer, Scott.

3. It has been suggested that corruption and bribery are indeed essential to the continuous growth of the economies of less developed countries. Leff, 1964.

4. Sklar in Carter, 1966, 138.

5. Ghana, 1967*d*, *White Paper,* 1; also Ghana, 1967*f*, parts 1 and 2, especially 28-29.

6. Sklar, *op. cit.,* 134.

7. Nigeria, Federation, 1962, vol. 1, 60; Nigeria, 1967. 11/15, 154.

8. Helleiner, 1964*c*, 117, reports a £1 million diversion of public funds through a questionable loan scheme. Equally significant is that the diversion was concealed from published accounts. *Ibid.,* 261, note 26.

9. Scott, 1972.

10. Leff, 8.

11. J. H. Plumb, *Saturday Review of Literature,* February 25, 1967, 41-42.

12. Ghana, 1966-67*b*, 27-28, paragraphs 160-65.

13. Bing, 179.

14. Nigeria, Northern Region, 1953. Bretton, 1962, 169-70; Nigeria, Western Region, 1956, Report of the Commission of Inquiry into the Administration of the Ibadan District Council (*Nicholson Inquiry*). Abingdon, Great Britain: The Abbey Press, 1956, 122 (secs. 389-91). Ghana 1969*b*, vol. 1, v-vi; Behrman, on exchange of gifts, 50-54. Wraith, 11; see also Cartwright, 1965, 16.

15. Mackintosh, 244.

16. *West Africa,* June 8, 1963, 645, on the *Muffett Report* (on Kano).

17. Lewis, 1965, 31ff, especially 33; Wraith, 203.

18. Odinga, 76-94; Jones-Quartey, 23; Sklar, 113.

19. Sklar, 300-301; Ghana, 1966-67*a*, 1966-67*b*; Nigeria, Federation, 1957, and 1962; Sierra Leone, 1968; Nigeria, Western State, 1967.

20. Sklar, 175ff.

21. Commissions of Inquiry, cited in note 19 above.

22. Bing, 177-78: "If there were no Chartered Accountants in England how many public companies would be conducted with absolute honesty? If there were no large class of trained bookkeepers in Britain what British Board of Directors could answer for the integrity of their business?"

23. The story of the Northern Nigerian Bornu extension of the Nigerian Railway illustrates the problem exceedingly well. According to a Tribunal of Inquiry:

1. The original tenders for contracts were made to a firm, NEMCO, in which the chairman of the Nigerian Railways himself had an interest.

2. The railway corporation lost a quarter of a million pounds because the said firm was to be favored.

3. Eventually the Nigerian firm had to be relieved of responsibility for the job, but not before large sums had been collected by it in advance.

4. The advances had been granted on the say-so of the chairman without the usual guaranties that the job would be done.

5. The firm, NEMCO, was said to have its head offices in Enugu. When the chief engineer of the Nigerian Railways sent an assistant there to obtain a certain information, he learned that the assistant had visited the office and "found present there one gentleman who described himself as the accountant. He stated that the Managing Director was in Onitsha, the Business Manager was on leave, the Engineer was in Germany, the Secretary was in Jos and the Chief Clerk was in Port Harcourt having locked the office containing the files and taking the keys with him. The accountant stated he knew nothing about the Bornu Extension or any correspondence relating to it." Nigeria, Federation, 1967, 49.

Comparative cost analysis of similar railway projects			
Project	Estimated Cost in £	Distance in Miles	Cost per Mile in £
1. Bornu Extension	22 million	400	54
2. Kilosa-Mikumi Tanganyika	800.000	46½	17.2
3. Mnyusi-Ruvu Tanganyika	2.2 million	117	18.8
4. Kampala-Kasese Uganda	5.2 million	208	25

Nigeria, Federation, 1960, *Report of Elias Commission,* 42.

24. Dudley in Mackintosh, 398-99.

25. Ghana, 1966-67, 7, paragraph 32.

26. *Commissions of Inquiry,* cited in note 19, above.

27. Nigeria, Federation, 1962, Day 79, 13 and 18.

28. *Ibid.,* 57; Ghana, 1966-67*b*, 13-16.

29. Nigeria, Western Region, Assembly, Official Report, May 29, 1962 (Chief Akerele's remarks).

30. Nigeria, Federation, 1962, Day 79, 20-21.

31. Ghana, 1969*b*, vols. 1-3.

32. Ghana, 1966-67*b*, 69-70, paragraphs 65-92, offers a suggestion about how and when the idea to extract funds from contractors may first have been introduced in Ghana.

33. *Ibid.*, 13-16.

34. Kilby, 78.

36. *Ibid.*, 73ff.

36. Interview with an USAID official, May 1970, who proposed that the U.S. agency restrict its contributions to Nigeria to nothing but development of water resources. This would benefit the country enormously while providing few opportunities for graft. It is possible that aid from the socialist countries offers fewer opportunities for corruption.

37. Darlington, 116-17.

38. *Ibid.*, 153.

39. Odinga, 89.

40. Bretton, 1962, 79, note. Nigeria Federation, 1967, 161.

41. Bretton, 1966, 69.

42. Ghana, 1967*f*, parts 1 and 2, 21-22.

43. *West Africa*, December 5, 1970, 1431.

44. *West Africa*, week ending May 14, 1971, 552; *ibid.*, May 28, 1971, 614.

45. *West Africa*, April 9, 1966, 417; *ibid.*, May 7, 1966, 528.

46. *West Africa*, July 30, 1966, 868.

CHAPTER 10

1. Prest, 143.

2. Bienen, 302, 303, including note 39. Zambia, *Development Plan 1966-70*, 2, outlines shift from line of rail to neglected areas. Nigeria, Federation, 1970, 36; Aboyade, 275-303, (contains useful tabulation of regional inequity factors); E/CN.14/CAP 2/INF 4; Kenya, 1966*a*, 75-76; Kenya, 1969, 166-78.

3. Ghana, 1968*c*, *(Siriboe Commission)*, part 3, 16; Ghana, 1969, February 8.

4. Ivory Coast, 1967*a*, 1-2.

5. *Ibid.*, 24.

6. *West Africa*, November 22, 1969; Nigeria, Midwestern State, *Approved Estimates, 1970-71*. Benin City: Ministry of Home Affairs, 1970, 15.

7. *West Africa*, November 8, 1969, 1327; *Christian Science Monitor*, October 20, 1971; Dina.

8. Lewis, 1967, 9-10.

9. Nigeria, Kwara State, *Recurrent Estimates 1968-69*, Kaduna: Government Printer, 1968, 3.

10. *West Africa*, November 8, 1969, 1327; Schätzl, 175-78.

11. At independence the Kenya *Fiscal Commission* envisaged a "substantial transfer of services" from the central government to the then new regional authorities. Predictably, these authorities quickly became defunct, Kenya. *Report of The Fiscal Commission*, 6. Nairobi: Government Printer, 1963.

12. From a confidential report prepared by a private, non-Nigerian group.

13. Nigeria, *Annual Abstract of Statistics 1965 op. cit.*, 162, table 14.4; 164, table 14.4; 165, table 14.5; 178, table 15.1; Kenya, 1966, vol. 3, 46-47, table 7.3. Ivory Coast, 1967*b*, 91, carte 11. Nigeria, *Annual Abstract of Statistics, 1965, loc. cit.*, 67, table 7.1 shows that by per capita rate of post offices the north is decidedly disadvantaged in the crucial communications sphere.

14. Gould, 1970.

15. Bienen, 302-3, note 39.

16. Kenya, 1966*a*, 75-76.

17. IBRD, 1962, 20.

CHAPTER 11

1. Ghana, 1968*c*, part 3, 3, paragraph 6.
2. Ghana, 1967*c*, appendix 1, 83; also Ghana, 1968*c*, *op. cit.*
3. *Ibid.*, 2, paragraph 23.
4. Bretton, 1966*b*, 211, note 74.
5. Ghana, 1967*c*, 187, paragraph 686.
6. E/CN.14/401, 182.
7. Kenya, Report of the *Fiscal Commission*, 76. Nairobi: Government Printer, 1963. The Nairobi City Council at one time had possessed the power to raise funds directly in the United Kingdom.
8. Balandier, 201-2.
9. *Ibid.*, 202.
10. Berelsford, 141.
11. Trimingham, 188-89; American University, 1963 (Senegal, *Handbook*), 194; Dumont, 135-37; O'Brien, 214-36.
12. Behrman, 31; Amin, 1969, 48; Dumont, 135.
13. Behrman, 67.
14. Kamarck, 33-34.
15. *Ibid.*, citing Hunter 1962, 14.
16. Coleman, 1958, 137.
17. Kenya, 1966*b*, vol. 3, 48, table 3.
18. Bretton, 1966*b*, 32.
19. Zolberg, in Foster and Zolberg, 21.
20. Nigeria, Northern Region, *The Northern House of Assembly* (*Elected Members*) *Electoral Regulations, 1956,* (N.R.L.N. of 1956) Kaduna: Government Printer, 1956, B562 (151-52); Odinga, 113-14. See also United Kingdom, 1960, chap. 6.
21. *Washington Post,* January 11, 1970.
22. Berelsford, 141; Kilson, 256-58.
23. American University, 1967*b*, (Kenya, *Handbook*), 121, italics added.
24. Ghana, 1964, vol. 5, 115.
25. See especially Ghana, 1964, Special Report "E", "Classification of the Population by Tribe," xi-xv, paragraphs 2.1-3.4. The census report notes that in certain conditions classification by language may not be very meaningful.
26. *Ibid.*, xvi, and table 15, 74-79.
27. *Ibid.*, xiii-xv, paragraph 2.3.4. See also Zolberg, *op. cit.*; Wallerstein in H. Eckstein and D. Apter, *Comparative Politics.* New York: Free Press, 1963, 666.
28. Chaput, 24ff.
29. Panter-Brick, 115.
30. Kay as cited in Chaput, 17.
31. Ghana, 1964, Special Report "E", lxxvi, table 4.9.2; Chaput, 15; Foltz in Coleman and Rosberg, 30.
32. Kaunda, quoted by Charles Mohr, *New York Times,* May 26, 1971; Scarrit, 36.
33. Rotberg cited in Chaput, 17.
34. Ghana, 1964, Special Report "E", lxx; lxvi-lxix, table 4.7.4, a-d.
35. "Of the total number of literates among the population, over 66 per cent are literate in one of the three major Akan languages," all three of which are mutually intelligible. *Ibid.*, lxx.
36. See Hans Wolff, "Linguistic Pluralism in Modern Nigeria," *Problems of Integration and Disintegration in Nigeria,* Conference Proceedings, 30-32. Northwestern University, March 31-April 2, 1967.
37. Ghana, *Educational Statistics, 1963-64,* Accra: Ministry of Education, 1965, table 38, and 48-49, tables 22, 23; Ghana, 1964, Special Report "E", 83-85, table 17.
38. *Ibid.*
39. *Ibid.*, appendix C-34, table S 26, and 107-9, table 24.
40. *Ibid.*, xxxv, table 4.1.2.

41. Potekhin is relevant here, although he speaks of society and country rather than tribe.

42. Berelsford, 142.

43. Hailey, Lord, *An African Survey,* Rev. ed. 1956, 685. London: Oxford University Press, 1957. Karl Marx, certainly one of the world's greatest authorities on social power, saw land as "the source of all production and existence." (Lange, 110-111.) See also Kindleberger, 4.

44. Hailey, 685-774.

45. Kenya, "Influence of Land Settlement," 1-2. Unpublished mimeog. paper. Anon.

46. Potekhin, 55.

47. *Ibid.*

48. For a brilliant analysis of the relationship of land tenure to peasant culture, see McAuslan in Widstrand et al, 81-101.

49. Dumont, 125.

50. *Ibid.,* 128; McAuslan in Widstrand, 82-84.

51. Odinga, 13-14.

52. Potekhin, 65.

53. *Ibid.,* 65-66.

54. *Ibid.,* 66; also IBRD, 1962, 66.

55. Hailey, 733-35; Behrman, 48-49, 136-44; O'Brien, 189-213; see also René Lemarchand, "Political Clientelism and Ethnicity in Tropical Africa," *Am. Pol. Sci. Review,* 56 (1), 1972, 68-90. Amin, 1969, 48ff. On planned land reform in Ethiopia, *Washington Post,* September 2, 1971.

56. Behrman, 144; Nigeria, Federation, 1970, 110.

57. Potekhin, 65.

58. Nigeria, Western Region, 1962, 2-3; American University, 1963 (Senegal, *Handbook,* 343; Kenya, 1966a, 129ff.

59. Widstrand, *op. cit.,* 82-101.

60. Dumont, 128, note 1.

61. Ghana, 1969a, April 29-30, col 1532.

62. Nigeria, Western Region, *Report Of The Commission Of Inquiry Into The Sapele Urban District Trust,* Ibadan: Government Printer, 1963. Nigeria, Western State, 1967; Nigeria, Federation, 1962, especially vol. 1, part 4, chap. 4-5. Nigeria, Eastern Region, 1960, *Perkins Report Of The Inquiry Into The Administration Of The Affairs Of The Enugu Municipal Council.* Enugu: Government Printer, 1960

63. Kamarck, 109-10. Potekhin regards this as the opening wedge driven by capitalism into a basically socialist or quasi-socialist traditional system.

64. Nigeria, Federation, 1970, 110.

65. Kenya, 1969, 24; United Kingdom, 1960, 264.

66. Oser, 172-73.

67. *Ibid.,* 189.

CHAPTER 12

1. *New York Times,* August 12, 1969.

2. Bretton, 1966b, 41-63; Ghana, 1968, *Proposals of the Constitutional Commission,* 100, paragraph 369.

3. UN/ECA/FAO, 7.

4. E/CN.14/370, 71.

5. *West Africa,* June 11, 1971, 651.

6. Ghana, 1968, *Proposals of the Constitution Commission,* 83-84, paragraph 310.

7. Peter Adjetey in Ghana, 1969a, January 21, col. 75.

8. Mr. Bediako, *ibid.,* January 23, col. 126.

9. 1961, 226.

10. Lewis, 1965, 62-90.

CHAPTER 13

1. In Bell, 36-41.
2. *Ibid.*, 38.
3. Elites have been identified by reference to their own claims—e.g., Mercier in L. Van Den Berghe, 163ff. One well-known and frequently cited study actually advanced the thesis that the "most influential segment among the [Nigerian] elite is made up of political figures." Smythe and Smythe, 5. Self-perception by the elite is the basis of Scarrit's work, 31.
4. Fred W. Riggs, cited in Holt and Turner, 305, speaks of "an agglutination of values around the powerholders," which, according to him, "tends to restrict differentiation, particularly among the various elites."
5. N'Diaye demonstrates that awareness as far as the student element in the elite is concerned (1969); but see Scarrit, 43.
6. Zolberg, 1966; Bretton, 1966*b*.
7. Hoselitz, 1960, 37.
8. Nkrumah, 1967, 28-34 and elsewhere throughout the book, provides one of the more intimate glimpses of the self-deception.
9. Bienen, 10-11, note 25.
10. Dahl in Bell, 36-41.
11. Hunter in *Christian Science Monitor,* February 25, 1970.
12. Adedeji, *West Africa,* March 14, 1970, 281; April 4, 1970, 363-65; April 11, 1970, 396-97; April 18, 1970, 433; also Nigeria, Federation, 1970.
13. Miners, 131-58.
14. Price, 1971*a*, 370ff; First, 191-200; Lefever, 55-57.
15. Huntington, S.P., *Political Order in Changing Societies,* 194. New Haven, Conn.: Yale University Press, 1968.
16. *Ibid.*
17. Ghana, 1968*b*, 169 and chap. 21 (The Armed Forces).
18. Bediako, in Ghana, 1969*a*, January 23, col. 129.
19. Ghana, Central Bureau of Statistics, *Economic Survey 1967,* vol. 3, table 5. Accra: State Publishing Corp., 1968; Kenya, *Economic Survey 1967,* table 8.2, 93. Nairobi: Government Printer, 1967.
20. Ghana, 1966, iv; Bretton, 1966*b*, 103.
21. Ocran, 28-39.
22. First, 196.
23. Ghana, *Economic Survey, 1967, op. cit.* 111, table 5.
24. Nigeria, Federation, *Estimates, 1964-65;* First, 161, Miners, 119.
25. Nigeria, Federation, *Estimates of the Government of the Federal Republic of Nigeria, 1964-65,* 14. Lagos: Federal Ministry of Information, 1964; First, 429-30; Lee, 94, table 5(a); 95, table 5(b).
26. Kenya, *Economic Survey, 1967, op. cit.,* 93, table 8.2.
27. First, 78-79.
28. See, for example, American University, 1963 (Senegal, *Handbook*), 451.
29. *West Africa,* December 5, 1970, 1419-21.
30. Price, 1971*b*, 399-430; Miners, 34-43.
31. *Ibid.;* First, 3.
32. First, 78; Young, 182, 282-84, 441-42; African Research & Publications Pamphlet, *Congo. Prelude to Independence,* 67-70. London: Goodwin Press Ltd., n.d. (ca. 1960).
33. Miners, 115-29; First, 162ff.
34. Lee, 173-75, table 9; Young, 443, 182, 282-84, 441-52; Lefever, 86.
35. Nigeria, *Annual Report of the Nigeria Police 1961,* 60, appendix B. Lagos: Federal Ministry of Information, 1962.
36. First 61-76; and Lange, 23ff; Nkrumah, 1968, 30-41; Price, 1971*b*, 399-400.
37. Lange, *loc. cit.,* Nkrumah, 1970, 41-46.

38. Luckham in Panter-Brick, 58-77, is seriously deficient in some respects but offers the best analysis of the regional fit in the Nigerian military. Also Miners, 229.

39. Holt and Turner, 336-41.

40. *Ibid.*

41. Ivory Coast, *Journal Officiel . . . Côte d'Ivoire,* January 29, 1969, 128. See *West Africa,* week ending August 20, 1971, 947, for new forms of "cooperation" between France and Africa.

42. Zambia, *Ministry of Labour, Annual Report of the Department of Labour for the Year 1966,* appendix G. Lusaka: Government Printer, 1967; Kenya 1969, 116-17, tables 4.3 and 4.4.

43. Zambia, *Public Service Commission for the Year Report,* 1967, 3. Lusaka: Government Printer, 1968, italics added.

44. Kenya, 1965, 7-9 and 28.

45. Odinga, 311; Kenya, 1968.

46. Bretton, 1966*a.*

47. O'Brien, 202. *Shyukh,* plural of *Shaikh,* a religious leader who has disciples.

48. *Ibid.,* 201-02. *Laman,* originally a client chief who received title to land from his feudal overlord; later, a titled landholder, enjoying far-reaching powers over the peasantry, wishing to use his property (*ibid.,* 200).

.49. Potekhin, 32: "There are semi-feudal, patriarchal-feudal forms of exploitation, and there are capitalist elements which exploit wage-labour, but there is no class of feudal lords opposed to the peasantry, and there is still no class of bourgeoisie opposed to the working class."

50. The protracted struggle over land reform in Ethiopia is a case in point. See *New York Times,* November 4, 1971.

CHAPTER 14

1. Charles E. Lindbloom, *The Policy-Making Process,* 63-64. Englewood Cliffs, N. J.: Prentice-Hall, Inc., 1968.

2. Lasswell, 31-45.

3. Nkrumah, 1970, 80; Woddis, 125.

4. Zambia, 1966*b,* 21.

5. *Christian Science Monitor,* November 28, 1969; *Washington Post,* December 8, 1969. The cabinet-level defeats represented a change only along the periphery of power; all members of the effective control group around Kenyatta were returned.

6. Strict laws on libel and defamation interdict systematic uncovery and public discussion of electoral irregularities, except for isolated and relatively trivial incidents. See Nigeria and Ghana, *Electoral Regulations, op. cit.;* see note 4, Chapter 21.

7. Karl W. Deutsch, *The Analysis of International Relations,* 195-96. Englewood Cliffs, N. J.: Prentice-Hall, Inc., 1968.

8. Frey, 303, note 5.

9. *Ibid.*

10. Zambia, *Government Paper on the Report of the Commission of Inquiry Into the Mining Industry,* 1. (*Brown Report*). Lusaka: Government Printer, 1966.

11. It has been noted that the reward systems in many of the new states are more discriminating in favor of the top echelon than was true in France shortly before the Revolution, Dumont, 1969, 78-87.

12. Kenya, 1967, 27.

CHAPTER 15

1. Nielsen, 35.

2. Kuznets in Robinson, 18-19.

3. Darlington, 38.

4. *Ibid.*, 115-17.

5. Amin, 1969, 172-79.

6. Interview with UN official, Dakar, May, 1969.

7. Pfefferman, 1968, 38.

8. IBRD, July 12, 1967, annex 1, 1.

9. *Ibid.;* Amin, 1971, 220, table 40; IMF, 1970 (vol. 3), 247 and table 10.

10. Kenya, 1968, 135, table, and elsewhere; Rothchild, 1969, 17-18.

11. Kenya, 1968, 144-52. Of greatest influence probably, is the Federation of Kenya Employees.

12. Unless Kenya chooses to repudiate external debts and expel the economically dominant European element. See IMF, 1970 (vol. 3), 209, table 29.

13. African Research & Publications Pamphlet, 43ff. Legum, 48-49, 52ff, 58-63.

14. Mboya, 129-36; Blundell, chap. 15; Odinga, 176-81.

15. Wheeler in *"Three Revolutions," Africa Report,* vol. 12 (8) 1967, 61-62; American University, 1967a (Angola, *Handbook*), 209-10, 259-60.

16. Rothchild, 1969-70, 10.

17. Malmgren, 115-143.

18. Oser, 195-96; Mboya, 134; United Kingdom, *The Nigeria (Retirement Benefits) Order in Council, 1960* (L.N. 160 of 1960), first schedule.

19. Rothchild, 1969, 695, table 4.

20. For reference see Kenya, *Economic Survey,* 124, table 8.8. Nairobi: Government Printer 1969; also Rothchild, 1969-70.

21. Kenya, 1966b, 92-93, appendixes 8, 9; Kenya, *Economic Survey,* 1969, *loc. cit.,* 123, table 123; Kenya, 1969, 116-19 and tables.

22. Peter Garlick cited in Hunter, 1962, 140ff; Miracle in Robson and Lury, 229-30.

23. Miracle in Robson and Lury, 230.

24. Nkrumah, 1970, 11, 20.

25. Miracle in Robson and Lury, 225.

26. See pp. 249ff above.

27. Nafziger, 349-60.

28. Dotson and Dotson, chap. 3.

29. Amin, 1969, 183-84 (translation mine); Hoselitz, 1960, 139ff.

30. *West Africa,* March 26, 1971, 329; *ibid.,* week ending July 9, 1971, 784.

31. Amin, 1969, 182 (translation mine).

32. Odinga, chap. 5; also see Bing, on The Aborigines Rights Protection Association in Ghana, 43-46 and elsewhere.

33. Pfefferman, 1968, 60.

34. Amin, 1969, 184.

35. Nigeria, 1967, 49.

36. *West Africa,* January 10, 1970, 55; July 2, 1971, 763; July 9, 1971, 784. Ghana, 1964, vol. 4, tables 15 and 16; *ibid.,* Special Report "E", 48-53, table 9; Ivory Coast, 1967b, 43; American University, 1963 (Senegal, *Handbook*), 381.

CHAPTER 16

1. Holt and Turner, 78-82, 242-44, 868-88, 238-39.

2. This appears to be entirely foreign to African high-level civil servants. See, for instance, Adu; on the esprit de corps of the group, see D. J. Murray in Adedeji, 1968, 22; and Nigeria, Federation, 1971. *West Africa,* week ending November 19, 1971, 1345.

3. Kenya, 1967, 26; Nigeria, 1971, *West Africa,* July 15, 1971, 30.

4. *West Africa,* week ending July 16, 1971, 797-98.

5. This is balanced to an extent by the incompetence of the majority of government employees whose job security is rather low. See analysis of Adebo Commission in *West Africa,* week ending November 19, 1971, 1345.

6. *Nigeria,* Federation, 1971, 9, shows a 50 percent increase in the price of food and a 34 percent rise in the cost-of-living index in the cities.

7. IMF, 1968, 1969, 1970 (vols. 1-3), budget (expenditure) tables. In 1966 Chad showed 50 percent of total government expenditure, Central African Republic about 50 percent, Congo (K), (Zaire) 75 percent, and Gabon about 25 percent. France, 1969*b,* annexes 35-47, reveal a similar pattern for 1967.

8. Dumont, 78 and 80; by 1969, it had risen to about 64 percent, IMF, 1970 (vol. 3), p. 181.

9. E/CN.14/370, 98, table 62. The projection for 1968-69 was closer to 50 percent. France, 1969*b,* 292, annexe 40.

10. Kenya, 1967, 12.

11. Amin, 1971, 186-91; also Senegal, 1969, 21ff, 69-73.

12. *West Africa,* week ending August 20, 1971, 951.

13. Lee, 182; this is the prime reason why socialist regimes attempt to form civilian militias.

14. Some analyses of the African military seem particularly premature, considering the evidence on which they are based. For example, Nordlinger, 1970, 1131-48.

15. Lee, 92 and 94-95, table 5.

16. First 78-79; Van Der Meersch, chap. 22.

17. Lefever, 139-42.

18. Guttridge in Wood, 3.

19. Actually, with exceedingly few exceptions the early postcoup pronouncements reveal profound ignorance of social and economic reality on the part of the military. Miners, 167-73.

20. Ocran, 28-39; Price, 1971*a,* 364ff.

21. Miners, 174-75, 124-25.

22. Luckham in Panter-Brick, 68; Miners, 179ff.

23. Hunter, *Christian Science Monitor,* February 2, 1971.

24. Ocran, 49ff; Lefever, on the abortive 1960 Ethiopian attempt 145-49; Hunter, *op. cit.*

25. Lloyd in Panter-Brick, "The Ethnic Background to the Nigerian Crisis;" also Hunter, *op. cit.*

26. African Research and Publications Pamphlet, 68-69. First, 78-79. On Kenya, see Lee, 110, table 8.

27. The massacre of Acholi and Lango soldiers in the Uganda Army following the 1971 coup is reported to have been related to precoup tensions and plots. *Washington Post,* March 26, 1972.

28. Miners, 175-79.

29. Ocran, 49ff.

30. First, 363ff.

31. First, 398-401.

32. Ghana, *Economic Survey, 1967, op. cit.,* 111, table 5.

33. *West Africa,* week ending June 25, 1971, 737.

34. *West Africa,* week ending July 30, 1971, 881.

35. Lasswell, 1971, 62-79.

36. *West Africa,* week ending August 6, 1971, 911.

37. Nigeria, Federation, *Recurrent Estimates, of the Federal Government of Nigeria. 1970-71,* 13. Lagos: Federal Ministry of Information, 1970.

38. Nigeria, Federation, 1970, 35 and 89ff.

39. *Ibid.,* chap. 33.

40. Lee, 93, and 94-95, table 5.

41. *West Africa,* week ending August 6, 1971, 913; Nigeria, Federation, 1971, 36 makes pointed reference to this fact.

42. Lee, 96.
43. Lee, 90; also Wood, 29, appendix.
44. *West Africa,* June 1, 1968, 650; Miners, 273, note 13.
45. Mazrui and Rothchild, 87, note 16.

CHAPTER 17

1. E/CN.14/370, 9; cf. Helleiner, 1966, chap. 3.
2. Nkrumah, 1970, 75.
3. *Ibid.,* 76.
4. Potekhin, 59ff; Fougeyrollas, 46 argues that not the peasants but the farmers are the "true proletarians" of the third world.
5. E/CN.14/401, 58.
6. *Ibid.,* 58-59, tables 1 and 2.
7. Nkrumah, 1970, 75.
8. Review of Bretton, 1966, *The African Communist,* no. 31, Fourth Quarter, 1967, 87-88; Fanon, 1966, 99.
9. Nkrumah, 1970, 79
10. Odinga, chap. 6.
11. American University, 1967*b,* (Kenya, *Handbook*), 435.
12. United Kingdom, 1955, 214-223; and American University, *op. cit.,* 442-50.
13. Rosberg and Nottingham, 159-60.
14. Odinga, 259-63.
15. Kenya, 1966*a,* 154-55; Kenya, 1969, 200-208.
16. Nigeria, Federation, 1970, 103; Kenya, 1969, 132.
17. Helleiner, 1966, 78.
18. Hill, 1970, 21-29.
19. American University, *op. cit.,* 435; Meister, 53-54.
20. Odinga, 303.
21. Bauer and Yamey, 225-26.
22. Widstrand, 29-31.
23. Bienen, 271.
24. *Ibid.*
25. IMF, 1969 (vol. 2), 157-58; Meister, 56-69 for an excellent comparative analysis.
26. Ghana, 1967*d,* 45.
27. *Ibid.,* chap. 3, 14-21.
28. Nigeria, Western State, 1969, 85.
29. Goran in Widstrand, 64.
30. American University, 1969*c,* (Uganda, *Handbook*), 60.
31. Nkrumah, 1970, 75ff.
32. Suret-Canale, 93-116; Potekhin, 55-57.
33. Behrman, 124-219; also O'Brien, throughout.
34. Thompson in Carter, 1962, 253-54.
35. Ivory Coast, 1968, reflects that philosophy.
36. Odinga, 260-69.

CHAPTER 18

1. Davies, chap. 9; Berg; Fischer.
2. USSR, 192; Hodgkin, especially 118-20. Chaput, 109ff.
3. Pfefferman, 1968, 83-85.
4. Davies, 10.

5. Peter Cadogan, letter to *Times Literary Supplement,* November 20, 1970, 1359.

6. See, for example, Ghana, Central Bureau of Statistics, *Statistical Yearbook 1964,* 59, table 55, also 57, table 53. Accra: Government Printer 1967.

7. E/CN.14/INR/113, 4.

8. In Zambia, as everywhere else, the statistical rubric "wage and salary workers" included a far greater number, 349,000 in 1968, but the vast majority of these are relatively inconsequential in terms of power and influence potential. see Rothchild, 1971, 8, table 9, also Zambia, Mines Department, *Annual Report for the year, 1965,* 8. Lusaka: Government Printer, 1966; and Zambia Office of Vice-President, Development Division, *Zambian Manpower.* 2, 23, table 9. Lusaka: Government Printer, 1969.

9. Kilby, 267-73.

10. Kilby, 271-73; Zambia, Ministry of Labour, *Annual Report For The Year 1968,* 59, table 6 (for union membership as of December 12, 1968). Lusaka: Government Printer, 1969. American University, 1967b, (Kenya, *Handbook*), 520-21, table 39.

11. Kenya, *The Policy On Trade Union Organization in Kenya,* appendix 4, 33-36, table 9. Nairobi: Government Printer, 1965.

12. Davies, 106; *Christian Science Monitor,* March 19, 1971.

13. E/CN.14/401, 129.

14. For example, the Ghana strike, St. Clair Drake and Lacy in Carter, 1966, 67-118; Fitch and Oppenheimer, chap. 7.

15. Rothchild, 1971, 8, table 9. As virtually everywhere else, wage gains were eroded by price rises. Zambia, Office of Vice-President, *Zambia Manpower, op cit.,* 15, especially Figure 4.

16. IMF, 1968, 1969, 1970 (vols. 1-3), tables on government budgets. France, 1969b, annexes 35-47.

17. Kilby, 267.

18. Bretton, 1966b, 149-57.

19. Potekhin, 33-35.

20. Again Zambia's mine workers are the outstanding exception, although they, too, eventually encountered the universal restraint. Rothchild, 1971, 16 and 23ff.

21. Pfefferman, 1968, 85; Harries-Jones in Berelsford, 140-41, and 131, diagram #3.

22. Kilby, 296; Pfefferman, 1968, 83-85; Berelsford, 140-41.

23. Kilby, 273; Bretton, 1962, 136-38.

24. Cited in Kilby, 287; Melson.

25. IMF, 1969 (vol. 2), 168-69; Zambia, Office of Vice-President, *Zambia Manpower, op. cit.,* 15. and figure 4.

26. Harries-Jones in Berelsford; the tribal roots of union rivalry are concealed beneath a facade of party and personality conflicts. American University, 1969 (Zambia, *Handbook*), 346ff.

27. *Standard Bank Review,* November 1970, 25-26. (The cave-in occurred in September 1970).

28. IMF, 1969 (vol. 2), 166ff.

29. Kenya, 1969, 139.

30. Nigeria tightened antistrike measures after the civil war *West Africa,* December 20, 1969, 1541. Ghana moved to tighten controls in 1971. *West Africa,* week ending October 1, 1971, 1133; *ibid.,* week ending October 22, 1971, 1250; American University, 1968b (Tanzania, *Handbook*), 393.

31. Pfefferman, 1968, 87, and appendix "C", "Workers' Statements on Trade Unions", 265-68.

32. Berg, 10.

33. Atwood, 244-45.

34. Davies, 201-2.

35. E/CN.14/401, 48; and Zambia, 1966a, 14-16, sections 133-34, 135, and 149.

36. *Ibid.,* 10.

CHAPTER 19

1. Some of the analytical difficulties are illustrated in Donald L. Horowitz, *World Politics,* 23, 2 (January 1971), 232-44.

2. Suret-Canale, chap. 4; Potekhin, 55-57.

3. Austin, 1970, 3. We have referred elsewhere to the Luo-Kikuyu contests in Kenya, to the Bemba factor in Zambia, and, of course, to the Ibo-non-Ibo syndrome in Nigeria. It is of the essence to separate appeals *primarily* ethnic from appeals *primarily* directed at other issues.

4. Evidence is more implicit than explicit, for obvious reasons, but the demonstrable shortage of impartial and skilled observers strongly suggests that the special antifraud provisions found in electoral regulations in Ghana and Nigeria for example, parts 1 and 2, 26-29 (section 59), were difficult to enforce. Ghana, 1968c, is the best source; also Nigeria, Eastern Region, *General Election Report,* November, 1961, chap 4. Enugu: Government Printer, 1962; Nigeria, Federal Electoral Commission, *Review of the Federal Elections 1959,* 2 vols. declassified; Nigeria, Federal Electoral Commission, *Federal Election 1959, Instructions to Polling Officers.* Lagos: Federal Government Printer, 1959; Nigeria (*Electoral Provisions*), Order in Council, 1958. Lagos: Federal Government Printer, 1959.

5. Kenya, 1966, *Development Plan 1966-70,* 351-52, table 1; American University, 1967b, (Kenya *Handbook*), 438, table 28.

6. Rothchild, 1969; Zolberg, 1966.

7. Meisler demonstrates the power political edge of tribal conflict. See also Fernand Van Langenhove, *Conscience Tribales Et Nationales En Afrique Noire.* The Hague: Institute Royal Des Relations Internationales, 1960, for a general assessment of this factor.

8. For example, Odinga in Kenya and Kapwebwe in Zambia.

9. Chaput 36; and Rothchild, 1969, *op. cit.*

10. Berelsford, 138, 142.

11. *Ibid.,* 138, 140-41.

12. Zambia, Ministry of Labour, *Annual Report, For The Year 1966, op. cit.,* 12.

13. Nigeria Northern Region, 1958; also Lloyd in Panter-Brick.

14. Walker Connor, 1971, argues in support of the thesis that tribe preservation may be stronger than nation-building, "Nation-Building or Nation-Destroying," *World Politics,* 24(3) 1972, 352-354.

15. Zolberg, in Foster and Zolberg, 27.

16. Horowitz, *op. cit.,* 237-40.

17. *New York Times,* May 26, 1971; *Washington Post,* September 1, 1971.

18. See pp. 4-5 above.

19. *West Africa,* May 2, 1970, 485.

20. ST/ECA/109, 12.

21. E/CN.14/401, 176, table 15; also see 177ff.

22. "Lagos Descent Into Chaos," *West Africa,* February 13-19, 1971, 183.

23. Ghana, 1964, *Atlas,* 20 and 21; and Special Report "E", xlvi. The Nature of the problem is outlined in Nigeria, 1970, 217-18.

24. The 1971-72 Ibadan City Budget (Nigeria, Western State), provided a mere £1 million or about £1 per capita *West Africa,* February 20-26, 1971, 213. Given the high rate of corruption of city councils, it might well be prudent for central governments not to pour large sums into the cities.

CHAPTER 20

1. Commission On International Development, L. B. Pearson, Chmn., 1969, *Partners In Development.* 67-8. London: Pall Mall.

2. Marvick, 1.

3. *Ibid.;* Barkan.

4. NBC, "Today Show," May 1970, interview. See also Alain Touraine, "Note sur l'analyse international de formation des mouvements étudiants," *Social Science Information*, 8, 2, 31-47. For a different interpretation of the role of students, in connection with disturbances in the Sudan, see USSR, 1968, 173. In Zambia in 1971 students also assumed an active role for a brief moment. Letter by Ruth Weiss, *The Guardian* (Manchester), August 18, 1971; the campus was closed at once.

5. Marvick, *loc. cit.;* Hannah, in Coleman and Rosberg. The inadvertent fudging of the critical difference between "students" and "graduates" is illustrated in Moore and Hochschild, 24ff.

6. Chaput, 40; Finlay in Emmerson, 65.

7. Major student led or originated disturbances occurred in Algiers, Dakar, Abidjan, Accra, Ibadan, Kinshasa, Lusaka, Nairobi, Khartum, and Addis Ababa — all between 1964 and 1971.

8. Sir Arthur Lewis, lecture, Bowdoin College, April 25, 1968. Rockland (Maine) *Courier-Gazette*.

9. Pfefferman, 1968. 112.

10. Lewis, *op. cit.*

11. Y. P. Ghai and J. P. W. B. McAuslan, 402.

12. Ruth Sloane, *The Educated African.* New York: Praeger, 1962.

13. *West Africa,* August 2, 1969, 881.

14. Bienen, 265.

15. UN/FAO, *The State of Food and Agriculture 1970.* Rome: FAO, 1971; also Ralph Whitlock, "Back to the Land: The African Need," *Daily Telegraph,* September 14, 1971.

16. LeVine, 108, note 23.

17. Kenya, 1965, 4-5; Kenya, 1969, 125, paragraph 478.

18. Kenya, 1967, 6. Estimated requirements for the first independence decade indicated shortfalls in the high-level manpower sector as follows: Kenya, 14,000 by one count and 26,000 by another; Zambia, 16,000. E/CN.14/401, 232, table 9.

19. American University, 1969 (Zambia *Handbook*), 193.

20. Ghana, Parliamentary Debates, *Official Report,* 38, 8 (January 22, 1965), Cols. 228-66. On The Congo (Zaire), *Le Monde,* February 27-28, 1972.

21. American University, 1969 (Zambia, *Handbook*), 196 and 424.

22. P. 191. Also L. Behrman; American University, 1963 (Senegal, *Handbook*), 191ff. The potential of the mouridiya order is highlighted in the summary offered by Amin, 1969, 48:

> Les grand marabouts mourides sont avant tout des hommes d'État, la Confrérie ayant mis en place une société organisée de 500.00 habitants, communauté qui a ses régles propres d'organisation sociale et administrative. There are about 50 *grand marabouts* directing the society, recruited from the families, descendants, of the founder Bambia, the families M'Backe. It is administered by several hundred small marabouts in the villages, recruited from the rural area itself. The totality of the hierarchy lives off the income from agriculture (debts and gifts of the faithful), and income from the exploitation of the plantations 'des grand domaines.' Partly this income is utilized to administer the area, the administration of the mosques and koranic schools, social assistance, but partly it is used by the dignitaries themselves for private purposes, as personal income. (Translation mine).

23. Bienen, 263, 411.

24. E/CN.14/401, 183.

25. Bretton, 1966b. Richard E. Stryker in Foster and Zolberg, 91-2. The death of Tubman in Liberia suddenly brought to light the true nature of his political machine. *West Africa,* week ending October 15, 1971, 1195; *Washington Post,* September 20, 1971.

26. *West Africa,* week ending August 13, 1971, 927.

CHAPTER 21

1. Ekukinam, 43; also *West Africa,* July 4, 1970, 729.
2. Helleiner, 1966, 139.
3. Peccei, 21.
4. Ernest Benjamin, review of Bretton, 1966*b*, *American Political Science Review,* 63, 1 (March 1969), 228-29.
5. IBRD, February 1967, *Stabilization And Development In Ghana.* (Internal IBRD Paper Restricted), 3-5.
6. Nigeria, 1967, 233.
7. Interview with a bank officer in BCAO, Paris, May 1969.
8. "Cocoa Spies Cost Ghana a Fortune," *New York Times,* November 30, 1969; also Bing, 382-88.
9. Kaysen, 83.
10. Lewis, 28-35, 62.
11. Harsanyi, in Bruce M. Russet, *Economic Theories of International Politics,* 6-7. Chicago: Markham Publ., 1968.
12. Lange, 158, note 11.
13. Lindblom in Russet, *loc. cit.,* 479-480.
14. Frankel, 166-75.
15. David Butler and Donald Stokes, *Political Change in Britain,* chap. 2. London: Macmillan, 1969.
16. Andreski, 88.
17. Bretton, 1970*a*.
18. Simon, 1953, 504-5.
19. Hoselitz, 1960, 98.
20. Bretton, 1966*b*, 140-43.
21. *Africa Confidential,* no. 9, April 26, 1968.
22. Potekhin, 114.

CHAPTER 22

1. Schumpeter, cited in Stolper, 1966, 309.
2. IBRD, 1962, 48.
3. Lewis, 1967, 15-22.
4. Kenya, 1966*a*, 124. See also *ibid.,* 36; and E/3320-E/CN.14/54, ECOSOC *Official Record,* Thirteenth Session Supplement, no. 10, 10 and 86.
5. Kenya, University of East Africa Workshop. Communicated to author.
6. Lange, 146-47.
7. Marvin Howe, *New York Times,* January 3, 1971. See also Rothchild, 1969, 1.
8. Holt and Turner, 100.
9. *Ibid.,* 293-94.
10. Kindleberger, 226-27.
11. E.g., Robson and Lury, 40.
12. *Ibid.*
13. Kenya, 1969, 141.
14. Tripathy, 21.
15. The title of Stolper's book on his planning experiences in Nigeria.
16. Holt and Turner, 301.
17. "The reconciliation of the Main Bank Account has now been the subject of adverse comment in four successive reports by the Auditor-General," Zambia, Report of the Auditor-General on the *Public Accounts, For the Financial Year Ended 30th June, 1966,* 16. Lusaka: Government Printer, 1967.
18. Conclusions drawn by the auditor-general of Zambia, *ibid.,* 80.
19. E/CN.14/401, 182.

20. Tripathy, 72-73.
21. Heller, 61.
22. *Ibid.*
23. See Reginald Green in *Allen and Johnson*, 273-324.
24. Lewis, 1967, 64-65.
25. UN/ECA/FAO, 1964, 133.
26. Stolper, 1967, 9.
27. Rimmer, 190-204.
28. *Ibid.*, 198.
29. For a critical view on budget data, E/CN.14/370, 94ff.
30. Lee, 1969, 90.
31. Dina, 34-35.
32. Helleiner, 1966, 224. For general discussion of taxation in Africa, see Robson and Lury, 40-46; Alderfer, chap. 8.
33. Nigeria, Western State, 1969, 109-15.
34. Kenya, 1969, 2-6.
35. Kenya, *Estimates of Revenue, of the Republic of Kenya, for the year ending 30 June 1969,* Summary.
36. American University, 1968*b* (Tanzania, *Handbook*), 404-05; Bienen, 298.
37. American University, 1963 (Senegal, *Handbook*), 425.
38. American University, 1969 (Zambia, *Handbook*), 391-93.
39. Standard Bank, *Annual Economic Review, Zambia,* August 1971, 6.
40. Kamarck, 1967, 39.
41. Nigeria, Western State, 1969, 109; Staley, 207. As a result of stepped-up pressure for collection of taxes at the local level in Tanzania, the incident referred to as the "black hole of Mwanza" occurred in which a large number of allegedly delinquent taxpayers perished.
42. Schnittger 102; also Bienen, 296-98.
43. Ghana, 1968*c*, 45-49, provides ample clues on how this was done.
44. Due, 99-100.
45. Adedeji, 1969*a*, chap. 7 and 8, and 255-61; Dina; Lewis, 1967, 15-17.
46. E/CN.14/370, 14-15.
47. Due, 146-47.
48. Aboyade, 1969, 4-10. The doubt was expressed orally in an interview.
49. Rimmer.
50. Andrew Schonfield, *Modern Capitalism; The Changing Balance of Public and Private Power.* New York: Oxford University Press, 1964.
51. Kenya, 1969, 2.
52. Zambia, 1966*b*, chap. 2, 5; Nigeria, 1970, 36; also Ayida, 27-32.
53. Aboyade, 1969, 36-37.
54. Asiodu, quoting Heller, 4.
55. Ayida, 1969, 31.
56. Aboyade, 1968.
57. Olson, 1968, 106.
58. Peccei, 20-23; and Wildavsky, 100. Wildavsky asks: "Why should planning help secure radical change in Africa or Asia when it fails to secure more limited changes in France?"
59. Van Philips, 37-38.
60. Tripathy, 65ff.
61. ". . . while there may be many valid reasons — social, ideological, etc. — for establishing some economically inefficient plants, an entire industrialization programme run this way would bankrupt any country." E/CN.14/INR/141, 1-2. That report states further that "[e]ven the largest country of West Africa, Nigeria, consumes less than 10 percent of the non-food products and services consumed in Switzerland."
62. Kenya, 1966*a*, 36. The plan also notes that "Present projections of population growth suggest that Kenya may have little more than 1.3 acres per person of potentially productive land in the year 2000."

63. These difficulties not only impede planning but must be kept in mind in evaluations of the perpetually optimistic United Nations assessments. Attempts, for instance, to increase cocoa production by introduction of a certain hybrid crop in Ghana failed to yield expected results, because one-third or more of all cocoa produced there is wild, hence requires no production discipline and no labor. An experimental crop requires both if it is to be more than a mere experiment. The experience should not have come unexpectedly. Soviet experimenters have long been familiar with the tendency of farmers to defeat the best laid designs.

64. IBRD, February 1967, Africa Department. *Stabilization and Development in Ghana* (Internal Paper, Restricted), 65.

65. See, for example, A/6868/Add.1.

66. Nigeria, 1964, *First Development Plan, Progress Report,* 6-7. Lagos: Federal Ministry of Economic Development, 1965.

67. Daniel Bell, *Public Interest,* no. 15, (1969), 72; Aboyade, 1968, 275.

68. Nigeria, 1971. See *West Africa,* week ending November 12, 1971, 1337; and November 19, 1971, 1345.

69. Holt and Turner, citing Mason, 340.

70. Lewis, 1967, 36.

71. Samuelson, 750.

72. Dumont, 136-38; Amin, 1969, 182-83.

73. Samuelson, 750.

74. *Ibid.;* and Kindleberger, 74, 95ff.

75. *West Africa,* January 18, 1969, 73.

CHAPTER 23

1. Temporary relaxation of police control of potential consumer demand seems inevitably to trigger riots. Expectations that Africa's masses can be led to voluntarily accept deprivation seem unrealistic in light of riot potential and performance on the continent so far.

2. Pp. 122-31.

3. *West Africa,* week ending October 15, 1971, 1197.

4. UN Department of Economic Affairs. *Methods of Financing Economic Development in Under-Developed Countries,* 15. New York: United Nations, 1949.

5. Pfefferman, 1968, 91-92.

6. Kenya, 1966a, ix, and 77.

7. Kenya, 1969, 2-3, italics added.

8. *Ibid.,* 3.

9. Kenya, 1966a, 36.

10. *Ibid,* table 1. In this respect, Kenya ranked slightly above India but well below Zambia, Zaire (Congo, Kinshasa), Tanzania, or Brazil.

11. Kenya, 1967, 6.

12. *Ibid.,* 130-40.

13. Ghai, 3.

14. Rothchild, 1969, 3.

15. Estimates of revenue for the year ending 30 June, 1969, 1.
    K£ = Kenya pounds = U.S. $2.40.

16. E/CN.14/132 Rev. 1, 16, table 15; American University, 1967b (Kenya *Handbook*), 165.

17. Kenya, 1969, 67.

18. Jim Hoagland, *Washington Post,* January 30, 1970.

19. *Ibid.*

20. American University, 1969 (Zambia, *Handbook*), 278-80.

21. The productivity of the average Zambian worker was reported to have fallen by 12 percent while capital was being pumped into new industrial outlets. *Africa Research Bulletin,* November 15-December 14, 1969, 1537.

22. Nigeria, 1970, 71-72.

23. *Ibid.*, 72.

24. Helleiner, 1966, 206. Helleiner attributes the problem to the absence of records, the importance of subsistence production, and the corruptibility of tax collectors. Furthermore, partisan politics enters the picture on the local level, ensuring that politically motivated inequities are added to those already inherent in the economic environment. Highly mobile traders and lorry owners are reputed to have amassed fortunes while evading taxes (224). Dr. Diejomah, speaking at the Lagos Conference on Integration and National Unity observed that the rich shared the tax-free perquisites of the military (!). He also stressed that it was the producers of crops who bore the brunt of taxation via the arrangement with marketing boards — up to 40 percent of their income. *West Africa,* December 26-January 1, 1971, 1503.

25. Western Nigeria, *Statistical Bulletin,* vol. 8, nos. 1 and 2, (1966).

26. Nigeria, Federation, 1965, *Annual Abstract of Statistics,* 122, table 11.3; 124, table 11.4; 126, table 11.5. Lagos: Federal Office of Statistics, 1967.

27. Nigeria, *Recurrent Estimates* of the Government of the Federal Republic, 1970-71 (1970), *op. cit.* 13; Nigeria, 1970, 35.

28. Pfefferman, 1968, 249-50.

29. Diouf, 28-29.

30. *Ibid.,* 33-35.

31. Senegal, 1965, vol. 1, 19.

32. For European salaries, see *Marchés Tropicaux* I, cited in Diouf, Vermont-Gauchy, and Brun.

33. Senegal, *Rapport Générale Sur Les Perspectives De Développement Du Sénégal,* Premier Parti, 1-2 (17). Dakar: Bompard S.A., Janvier 1963.

34. *Ibid.,* 1-2 (18).

35. Amin, 1967, 298-299.

36. The article begins by recalling that "major producing areas in the South, and more particularly in the South-East, are more generously endowed and better incomes prevail there since the peasants in these regions shared the 29 billion CFA franc out of 46 billion paid for coffee and cocoa exports in 1964." Basing its estimates on the reported number of subscribers to electrical power, the article then notes that "[by] substracting the total number of European subscribers in the country (5,221 in Abidjan and 773 in Bouaké) we find that there were 20,000 African families who had an electric meter in 1964. This in turn would mean that there were about 20,000 Ivory Coast families living in the cities with a buying power of over 30,000 francs CFA per month."

The total picture based on these considerations, then is as follows:

No. of Families	CFA Francs
ca. 25,000	over 30,000
50,000	between 15,000 and 30,000
5,000	over 50,000

If one considers that 30,000 CFA francs converts to $125 per month, actually very little power and influence potential accrued to African families. *Marchés Tropicaux,* April 30, 1966.

37. E/CN.14/370, 14.

38. Amin, *op. cit.*

39. "The new and dangerous import — Inflation," *West Africa,* October 10, 1970, 1195.

40. Cited by Van Philips, 156.

41. Norris, in Farer, 94-105.

42. Helleiner, 1966, 138.

43. *Ibid.*

44. Cited by Schnittger, 39.

45. Ghana, 1968*b.*

Reference Bibliography

Aboyade, O.
    1968. "Industrial Location and Development Policy; The Nigerian Case." *The Nigerian Journal of Economic and Social Studies* 10 (3): 275-302.
    1969. "The Development Process." *Conference on National Reconstruction and Development, Ibadan* March 24-29, 1969. Unpublished paper (referred to below as *Ibadan Papers*).
Adedeji, Adebayo.
    1968. *Nigerian Administration and its Political Setting.* A collection of papers given at the Institute of Administration, University of Ife. London: for the Institute, Hutchinson.
    1969a. *Nigerian Federal Finance.* New York: Africana Publishing Co.
    1969b. "Federalism and Development Planning in Nigeria." Ibadan Papers.
Adu, A. L. 1969. *The Civil Service in Commonwealth Africa.* New York: Humanities Press.
Afana, Osendé. 1966. *Économie de l'Ouest Afrique.* Paris: Franco Maspero.
African Research and Publications Pamphlet. ca. 1960. *Congo, Prelude to Independence.* London: Goodwin Press.
Akyeampong, H. L. 1956. *The Doyen Speaks. Some Historic Speeches by Dr. J. B. Danquah.* Accra: West African Graphic Co.
Alderfer, Harold E. 1964. *Local Government in Developing Countries.* New York: McGraw-Hill.
Allen, Christopher, and Johnson, R. W. 1970. *African Perspectives. Papers in the History, Politics, and Economics of Africa Presented to Thomas Hodgkin.* Cambridge: Cambridge University Press.
American University, The *Area Handbooks.* Foreign Area Studies. Washington, D.C.: U. S. Government Printing Office.
    1963. Senegal, 550-70
    1964. Liberia, 550-38
    1967a. Angola, 550-59
    1967b. Kenya, 550-56
    1968a. Mozambique, 550-64
    1968b. Tanzania, 550-62

1969a. Burundi, 550-83
1969b. Rwanda, 550-84
1969c. Uganda, 550-74
1969d. Zambia, 550-75
1971a. Congo (Brazzaville), 550-91
1971b. Congo (Kinshasa), 550-67
1971c. Ghana, 550-153

Amin, Samir.
  1967.   *Le Développement du Capitalism en Côte d' Ivoire.* Paris: Les
          Éditions De Minuit.
  1969.   *Le Monde Des Affaires Sénégalaise.* Paris: Les Éditions De Minuit.
  1971.   *L'Afrique De L'Ouest Bloquée. L'Économie Politique De La Colo-
          nisation, 1880-1970.* Paris: Les Éditions De Minuit.

Andreski, Stanislav. 1969. *The African Predicament.* New York: Atherton
  Press.

Apter, David.
  1955.   *The Gold Coast In Transition.* Princeton, N.J.: Princeton University
          Press.
  1961.   *The Political Kingdom in Uganda: A Study in Bureaucratic Na-
          tionalism.* Princeton, N.J.: Princeton University Press.

Arrighi, G. 1967. *The Political Economy of Rhodesia.* The Hague: Mouton.

Asiodu, P. C. 1969. "Planning for Further Industrial Development in Nigeria."
  Ibadan Papers.

Atwood, William, 1967. *The Reds and the Blacks.* New York: Harper & Row.

Austin, Dennis.
  1964.   *Politics In Ghana, 1946-1960.* London and New York: Oxford Uni-
          versity Press.
  1970.   *Elections in Ghana.* New Delhi: India Council on Africa.

Awolowo, Chief Obafemi. 1968. *The People's Republic.* Ibadan: Oxford University Press.

Ayida, A. Akene.
  1965.   *Contractor Finance and Supplier Credit in Economic Growth.* Ni-
          gerian Institute for Social and Economic Research (N.I.S.E.R.) Re-
          print Series no. 18.
  1969.   "Development Objectives." Ibadan Papers.

Balandier, Georges. 1967. *Anthropologie Politique.* Paris: Presses Universitaires.

Barbe, R. 1964. *Les Classes Sociales En Afrique Noire.* Paris: Éditions Sociales.

Barbier, Jean. 1960. *L' Économie de l'Arachide Au Senegal.* Unpublished Doc-
  toral Thesis, Faculty of Law. Lille.

Barkan, Joel D. 1969. "The Political Socialization of University Students in
  Ghana, Tanzania, and Uganda." Paper delivered at the Sixty-fifth Annual
  American Political Science Association Meeting, September 2-6, 1969.

Bauer, P. T. 1963. *West African Trade: A Study of Competition, Oligopoly,
  and Monopoly in a Changing Economy.* London: Routledge & Kegan Paul.

Bauer, Peter T., and Yamey, Basil S. 1957. *The Economics of Underdeveloped
  Countries.* Chicago: University of Chicago Press.

Behrman, Lucy. 1970. *Muslim Brotherhoods and Politics in Senegal.* Cambridge,
  Mass.: Harvard University Press.

Bell, Roderick; Edwards, David V.; and Wagner, R. Harrison, eds. 1969. *Political Power.* New York: The Free Press.

Berelsford, W. V. 1965. *The Tribes of Zambia.* Lusaka: Government Printer.

Berg, Elliot J. "The External Impact on Trade Unions in Developing Countries: The Record in Africa." *Proceedings of the Sixteenth Annual Meeting, Industrial Relations Research Association* (IRRA), December 1963.

Bienen, Henry. 1967. *Tanzania: Party Transformation and Economic Development*. Princeton, N.J.: Princeton University Press.

Bing, Geoffrey. 1968. *Reap the Whirlwind: An Account of Kwame Nkrumah's Ghana from 1950-1966*. London: MacGibbon and Kee.

Birmingham, Walter; Neustadt, I., and Omaboe, E. N. 1966, 1967. *A Study of Contemporary Ghana*. Vol. 1, *The Economy of Ghana;* Vol. 2, *Some Aspects of Social Structure*. Evanston, Ill.: Northwestern University Press.

Blundell, Michael. 1964. *So Rough a Wind*. London: Weidenfeld and Nicholson.

Brett, Edwin A. 1969. "Politics, Economics, and Rationality." *Social Science Information* 8 (2): 49-66.

Bretton, Henry L.
   1962a. *Power and Stability in Nigeria: The Politics of Decolonization*. New York: Praeger.
   1962b. "United States Foreign Policy Towards The Newly Independent States." In *African Independence*, Peter Judd ed. 444-475. New York: Dell Publishing Co.
   1966a. "Political Influence in Southern Nigeria." In *Africa: The Primacy of Politics*, Herbert Spiro, ed., 49-84, 171-87. New York: Random House.
   1966b. *The Rise and Fall of Kwame Nkrumah. A Study of Personal Rule*. New York: Praeger.
   1970a. "Political Science Field Research in Africa." *Comparative Politics* 2 (3).
   1970b. "The Overthrow of Kwame Nkrumah." In *Problems in International Relations*, Andrew Gyorgy et al., eds., 277-99, 3d ed. Englewood Cliffs, N.J.: Prentice-Hall.
   1971. *Patron-Client Relations: Middle Africa and the Powers*. New York: General Learning Press.

Bryszinski, Z., ed. 1963. *Africa and the Communist World*. Stanford, Calif.: Stanford University Press.

Carothers, J. C. See Kenya, 1955.

Carter, Gwendolyn M., ed.
   1962. *African One-Party States*. Ithaca, N.Y.: Cornell University Press.
   1966a. *National Unity and Regionalism*. Ithaca, N.Y.: Cornell University Press.
   1966b. *Politics in Africa. Seven Cases*. New York: Harcourt, Brace & World.

Cartwright, Dorwin. 1965. "Influence, Leadership, Control." In *Handbook of Organizations*, James G. March, ed. Chicago: Rand McNally.

Cartwright, Dorwin, ed. 1959. *Studies in Social Power*. Ann Arbor, Mich.: Research Center for Group Dynamics.

Cartwright, Dorwin, and Zander, Alvin. 1962. *Group Dynamics: Research and Theory*. Evanston, Ill.: Row, Peterson & Company.

Chaput Michael. 1968. *Patterns of Elite Formation and Distribution in Kenya, Senegal, Tanzania, and Zambia*. Syracuse, N.Y.: Syracuse University Program of Eastern African Studies.

Clough, R. 1965. "Some Economic Aspects of Land Settlement in Kenya." Unpublished paper. Njoro, Kenya: Egerton College.

Coleman, James S. 1958. *Nigeria: Background to Nationalism*. Berkeley: University of California Press.

Coleman, James S., ed. 1965. *Education and Political Development*. Princeton,
    J.J.: Princeton University Press.
Coleman, James S., and Rosberg, Carl J. 1964. *Political Parties and National
    Integregation in Tropical Africa*. Berkeley: University of California Press.
Crowder, Michael. 1966. *A Short History of Nigeria*. New York: Praeger.
Dahl, Robert A.
    1957. "A Concept of Power." *Behavioral Science* Vol. 2 (2): 201-15.
    1963. *Modern Political Analysis*. Englewood Cliffs, N.J.: Prentice-Hall.
Darlington, Charles F., and Darlington, Alice B. 1968. *African Betrayal*. New
    York: McKay.
Davies. Ioan. 1966. *African Trade Unions*. London: Penguin Books.
Deutsch, Karl W.
    1963. *The Nerves of Government: Models of Political Communication
        and Control*. New York: The Free Press.
    1966. "External Influences on the Internal Behavior of States." In *Ap-
        proaches to Comparative and International Politics*, R. Barry Farrell,
        ed., 5-26. Evanston, Ill.: Northwestern University Press.
Dina, Chief I.O. 1969. "Fiscal Measures." Ibadan Papers.
Diouf, Coumba N.; Vermot-Gauchy, Georges; and Brun, Charles-Francis. 1965.
    La Question Des Salaires au Sénégal. Clairafrique — Supplement de Afrique
    — Documents, Numero 79. Dakar.
Dotson, Floyd, and Dotson, William O. 1968. *The Indian Minority of Zambia,
    Rhodesia and Malawi*. New Haven, Conn.: Yale University Press.
Drake St. Clair, and Alexander, Leslie. 1966. "Government Versus the Unions:
    The Secondi-Takoradi Strike, 1961." In *Politics in Africa. Seven Cases*, ed.
    G. M. Carter, 67-118. New York: Harcourt, Brace & World.
Dudley, B. J. 1968. *Parties and Politics in Northern Nigeria*. London: Cass.
Due, John. 1963. *Taxation and Economic Policy in Tropical Africa*. Cambridge,
    Mass.: M.I.T. Press.
Dumont, Rene. 1969. *False Start in Africa*. 2d rev. ed. New York: Praeger.
Easton, David. 1966. *Varieties of Political Theory*. Englewood Cliffs, N.J.:
    Prentice-Hall.
Ekukinam, A. E. 1969. "Main Trends in Banking and Monetary Policy to
    1968." Ibadan Papers.
Emmerson, Donald K. 1968. *Students and Politics in Developing Nations*.
    New York: Praeger.
Esseks, John D. 1968. "Economic Decolonization in a New African State:
    Ghana, 1957-1966. Unpublished paper.
Fanon, Franz. 1966. *The Wretched of the Earth*. New York: Grove Press.
Farer, Tom J. 1965. *Financing African Development*. Cambridge: M.I.T. Press.
Finlay, David; Koplin, Roberta E.; and Ballard, Charles A. 1968. "Ghana." In
    Students and Politics in Developing Nations, ed. Donald K. Emmerson, 64-
    102. New York: Praeger.
First, Ruth. 1970. *The Barrel of a Gun*. London: Allen Lane, Penguin.
Fischer, Georges. 1961. *Syndicats Et Decolonisation*. Paris: Foundation Nation-
    ales De Sciences Politiques.
Fitch, Bob, and Oppenheimer, Mary. 1966. *Ghana: End of Illusion*. New York:
    Monthly Review.
Foltz, William J.
    1964. "Social Structure and Political Behavior of Senegalese Elites." New
        Haven, Conn.: Yale University Press.

1965. *From French West Africa to the Mali Federation.* New Haven, Conn.: Yale University Press.

Foster, Philip, and Zolberg, A., eds. 1971. *Ghana and Ivory Coast.: Perspectives of Modernization.* Chicago: University of Chicago Press.

Fougeyrollas, Pierre. 1967. *Modernisation des hommes: l' example du Sénégal.* Paris: Flammarion.

France.

1969a. Caisse Centrale. *Recent Trends.* Paris.

1969b. Comité Monétaire de La Zone Franc. *La Zone Franc en 1967.*

Frankel, Joseph, 1963. *The Making of Foreign Policy.* London: Oxford University Press.

French, J. R. P., and Raven, B. 1959. "The Bases of Social Power." In *Studies in Social Power,* ed. D. Cartwright, 150-67. Ann Arbor: University of Michigan Press.

Frey, Frederick W. 1963. "Political Development, Power and Communications in Turkey." In *Communications and Political Development,* ed. Lucien W. Pye, 298-326. Princeton, N.J.: Princeton University Press.

Gamson, William A. 1968. *Power and Discontent.* Homewood, Ill.: Dorsey Press.

Genoud, Roger. 1969. *Nationalism and Economic Development in Ghana.* New York: Praeger.

Ghai, D. P. N. D. "Incomes Policy in Kenya." Unpublished paper.

Ghai, Y. P., and McAuslan, J. P. W. B. 1970. *Public Law and Political Change in Kenya.* London: Oxford University Press.

Ghana, Republic of

Ghana, *Area Handbook.* See American University.

1964. Survey of Ghana and Census Office, *1960 Population Census of Ghana, Atlas of Population Characteristics.* Also vols. 3, 4, 5, and Special Report "E." Accra.

1966. National Liberation Council. *Nkrumah's Subversion in Africa.* Accra.

1966-67a. Ministry of Information. *Report of the Commission . . . to Enquire into Affairs of NADECO Limited,* and White Paper no. 1/66 (Crabbe Commission). Accra: State Publishing Corp.

1966-67b. Ministry of Information. *Report of the Commission . . . to Enquire into the Kwame Nkrumah Properties (Apaloo Commission).* Accra: State Publishing Corp.

1967a. Ghana Information Service. Report of the Commission of Enquiry on the Commercial Activities of the Erstwhile Publicity Secretariat *(Ayeh Commission).* Accra: State Publishing Corp.

1967b. Ministry of Information. *Government Statement on the Report of the Committee Appointed to Enquire into Local Purchasing of Cocoa.* White Paper no. 3/67.

1967c. Ministry of Information. *Report of the Commission of Enquiry into Electoral and Local Government Reform.* Parts 1 and 2. Accra: State Publishing Corp.

1967d. Ministry of Information. *Report of the Commission on the Structure and Remuneration of the Public Services in Ghana (Mills-Odoi).* Accra: State Publishing Corp.

1967e. Ministry of Information. *Report of the Committee of Enquiry on the Local Purchasing of Cocoa,* and White Paper. *(De Graft-Johnson Commission).* Accra: State Publishing Corp.

1967*f*. Ministry of Information. *Summary of the Report of the Commission of Enquiry into Irregularities and Malpractices in the Grant of Import Licenses,* and White Paper. *(Ollenu Commission).* Accra: State Publishing Corp.

1967*g*. Ministry of Information. White Paper no. 1/68 on parts 1 and 2 of the *Report of the Commission of Enquiry into Electoral and Local Government Reforms (Siriboe Commission).* Accra.

1967-68. Ministry of Information. *Report of the Commission of Inquiry into the Circumstances Surrounding the Establishment of the Ghana Cargo Handling Company,* and White Paper no. 7/68. Accra: State Publishing Corp.

1968*a*. Ministry of Information. *Government Policy on the Promotion of Ghanaian Business Enterprises.* Accra: State Publishing Corp.

1968*b*. *The Proposals of the Constitutional Commission for a Constitution for Ghana.* Accra: State Publishing Corp.

1968*c*. Ministry of Information. *Report of the Commission of Enquiry into Electoral and Local Government Reform (Siriboe Commission).* Part 3. Accra: Ghana Publishing Corp.

1969*a*. Proceedings of the Constituent Assembly. *Official Report.* Accra: Government Printer.

1969*b*. Ministry of Information. *Report of the Jiagge Commission . . . to Enquire into the Assets of Specified Persons,* and White Paper no. 3/69. vols. 1-3. Accra: Ghana Publishing Corp.

1969*c*. National Liberation Council. *Political Parties Decree.* N. L. C. D. 345. Accra.

Gould, Peter.
1968. "Problems of Structuring and Measuring Spatial Changes in the Modernization Process: Tanzania 1920-1963." Unpublished paper.

1970. "Tanzania 1920-63: The Spatial Impress of the Modernization Process." *World Politics* 22 (2): 149-70.

Green, Reginald H.
1965. "Four African Development Plans: Ghana, Kenya, Nigeria, and Tanzania." *Journal of Modern African Studies.* 3 (2): 249-79.

1971. "Reflections on Economic Strategy, Structure, Implementation, and Necessity: Ghana and the Ivory Coast, 1957-1967." In *Ghana and Ivory Coast: Perspectives of Modernization,* eds. P. Foster and A. Zolberg, 231-64. Chicago: University of Chicago Press.

Green, Reginald H., and Seidman, Ann. 1968. *Unity or Poverty? The Economics of Pan-Africanism.* Baltimore: Penguin.

Gutteridge, W. 1962. *Armed Forces in New States.* New York: Oxford University Press.

Hance, William A. 1967. *African Economic Development.* Rev. ed. New York: Praeger.

Hanna, William J., and Hanna, Judith Lynne. 1967. "The Political Structure of Urban-Centred African Communities." In *The City in Modern Africa,* ed. Horace M. Miner. New York: Praeger.

Harvey, William B. 1966. *Law and Social Change in Ghana.* Princeton, N.J.: Princeton University Press.

Heidenheimer, Arnold J. 1970. *Political Corruption.* New York: Holt, Rinehart & Winston.

Heilbroner, Robert L. 1970. "On the Limited 'Relevance' of Economics." *The Public Interest* (21): 80-93.

Helleiner, Gerald K.
    1964a. *The Fiscal Role of the Marketing Boards in Nigerian Economic Development.* N.I.S.E.R. Reprint no. 5.
    1964b. *A Wide-Ranging Development Institution: Nigeria's Northern Region Development Corporation 1949-1962.* N.I.S.E.R. Reprint no. 11.
    1964c. *The Eastern Nigeria Development Funds, 1949-1962,* N.I.S.E.R. Reprint no. 8.
    1966. *Peasant Agriculture, Government, and Economic Growth.* Homewood, Ill.: Richard D. Irwin.
Heller, W. W. 1954. "Fiscal Policies for Under-developed Economies." In *Papers and Proceedings of the Conference on Agricultural Taxation and Economic Development,* ed. H. M. Wald and J. N. Fromkin, 61.
Hicks, John R. 1959. "A chapter in Federal Finance: The Case of Nigeria." In *Essays in World Economics,* 216-36. Oxford: Clarendon Press.
Hill, Polly.
    1956. *The Gold Coast Cocoa Farmers.* London: Oxford University Press.
    1963. *The Migrant Cocoa Farmers of Southern Ghana.* London: Cambridge University Press.
    1970. *Studies in Rural Capitalism in West Africa.* Cambridge: at the University Press.
Hodgkin, Thomas. 1957. *Nationalism in Colonial Africa.* New York: New York University Press.
Holt, Robert T., and Turner, John E. 1966. *The Political Basis of Economic Development.* Princeton, N.J.: D. Van Nostrand.
Hoselitz, Bert F., ed.
    1952. *The Progress of Underdeveloped Areas.* Chicago: University of Chicago Press.
    1960. *Sociological Aspects of Economic Growth.* Chicago: The Free Press.
Hunter, Guy.
    1962. *The New Societies of Tropical Africa.* London: Oxford University Press.
    1967. *The Best of Both Worlds? A Challenge on Development Policies in Africa.* London: Oxford University Press.
Huntington, Samuel P. 1971. "Does Foreign Aid Have a Future?" *Foreign Policy* (2): 114-34.
International Bank for Reconstruction and Development.
    1954. *The Economic Development of Nigeria.* Lagos: Federal Government Printer.
    1962. *The Economic Development of Kenya.* Nairobi: Government Printer.
International Monetary Fund (IMF). 1968-1971. *Surveys of African Economics.* vol. 1, 1968; vol. 2, 1969; vol. 3, 1970; vol. 4, 1971. Washington, D.C.: International Monetary Fund.
Ivory Coast
    1965. *Rapport sur l'évolution économique et sociale de la Côte d'Ivoire 1960-64.* Abidjan: Government Printer.
    1967a. Commission Interministerielle Pour Le Développement de la Region D' Abidjan. *Rapport préliminaire sur l' urbanisation D' Abidjan.* Décret no. 66-159 du Avril 1966. Abidjan.
    1967b. Ministère du Plan. *Cote D'Ivoire: Population. Etudes regionales 1962-1965.* Synthese. Abidjan.
    1967c. Ministère du Plan. *Perspectives décennales de développement économique social et culturel 1960-70* Abidjan: Ministère du Plan.

1968. *Premiere esquisse du plan quinquennal de développement 1971-75.* Abidjan: Ministère du Plan.

Johnson, Harry, ed. 1967. *Economic Nationalism in Old and New States.* Chicago: University of Chicago Press.

Jones-Quartey, K.A.B. 1965. *A Life of Azikiwe.* London: Penguin.

Kamarck, Andrew M. 1967. *The Economics of African Development.* New York: Praeger.

Kay, George. 1967. *Maps of the distribution and density of African population in Zambia.* Lusaka: University of Zambia.

Kaysen, Karl. 1968. "Model-Makers and Decision-Makers: Economists and the Policy Process." *The Public Interest* (12): 80-95.

Kenya

Kenya, *Area Handbook.* See American University.

1955. Kenya, Colony and Protectorate of Kenya. Dr. J. C. Carothers. *The Psychology of Mau Mau.* Nairobi: Government Printer.

1964. Kenya, Republic of. Ministry of Finance and Economic Planning. *Population Census, 1962.* Advanced Report of vols. 1 and 2. Nairobi: Government Printer.

1965. Ministry of Economic Planning and Development. *High-Level Man-Power Requirements and Resources in Kenya 1964-70.* Nairobi: Government Printer.

1966a. Ministry of Economic Planning and Development. *Development Plan 1966-70.* Nairobi: Government Printer.

1966b. Ministry of Economic Planning and Development. *Population Census 1962.* vols. 3 and 4. Nairobi: Government Printer.

1966c. Kenya, Republic of. *Report of the Maize Commission of Inquiry.*

1967. Kenya, Republic of. *Report of the Salaries Review Commission 1967.* Nairobi: Government Printer.

1968. National Christian Council of Kenya Working Party, Department of Christian Education and Training. *Who Controls Industry in Kenya?* Nairobi: East African Publishing House.

1969. *Development Plan 1970-74.* Nairobi: Government Printer.

Kilby, Peter. 1969. *Industrialization in an Open Economy: Nigeria 1945-1966.* Cambridge: at the University Press.

Killick, Tony. 1966. "The Economics of Cocoa." In *A Study of Contemporary Ghana.* Vol. 1, *The Economy of Ghana,* eds. W. Birmingham, I. Neustadt, and E. Omaboe, 236-49. Evanston, Ill.: Northwestern University Press.

Kilson, Martin. 1966. *Political Change in a West African State.* Cambridge, Mass.: Harvard University Press.

Kindleberger, Charles P. 1965. *Economic Development.* New York: McGraw-Hill.

Kuznets, S. 1960. "Economic Growth of Small Nations." In *Economic Consequences of the Size of Nations,* ed. E. A. G. Robinson, 14-32. New York: St. Martin's Press.

Laing, R. D. 1967. *The Politics of Experience.* New York. Pantheon.

Lange, Oscar. 1963. *Political Economy.* New York: Macmillan.

Lasswell, Harold. 1958. *Politics: Who Gets What, When, and How.* New York: The World Publishing Co. (1971 new ed.)

Lee, J. M. 1969. *African Armies and Civil Disorder.* London: Chattus and Windus.

Lefever, Ernest W. 1970. *Spear and Scepter.* Washington: Brookings Institution.

Leff, Nathaniel H. 1964. "Economic Development Through Bureaucratic Corruption." *American Behavioral Scientist.* 8 (3): 8-14.

Legum, Colin. 1961. *Congo Disaster.* Baltimore: Penguin Books.

LeVine, Victor T. 1967. *Political Leadership in Africa: Post-Independence Generational Conflict in Upper Volta, Senegal, Niger, Dahomey, and The Central African Republic.* Stanford, Calif.: Stanford University Press.

Lewis, Arthur W.
1965. *Politics in West Africa.* London: Allen and Unwin.
1967. *Reflections on Nigeria's Economic Growth.* Paris: Development Centre of the Organisation for Economic Cooperation and Development (OECD).

Leys, Colin, 1965. "What Is the Problem About Corruption?" *The Journal of Modern African Studies.* 3 (2): 215-30.

Lipset, Seymour Martin. 1969. "The Possible Political Effects of Student Activism." *Social Science Information* 8 (2): 7-29.

Mabileau, A., and Meyriat, J. 1967. *Décolonisation et Regimes Politiques En Afrique Noire.* Paris: Colin.

Mabogunje, Akin L. 1968. *Urbanization in Nigeria.* London: University of Ibadan.

Mackintosh, John P. 1966. *Nigerian Government and Politics.* London: Allen and Unwin.

Malmgren, Harald B. 1970-71. "Coming Trade Wars?" *Foreign Policy* (1): 115-43.

March, James G. 1955. "An Introduction to the Theory of Measurement of Influence." *American Political Science Review* 49 (2): 431-51.

Marchés Tropicaux Et Méditerranéens. April 30, 1966. Second Issue. The Ivory Coast Market.

Marvick, Dwaine. 1962. "Higher Education in the Development of Future West African Leaders." Conference On Education and Political Development, Lake Arrowhead, Calif. Unpublished paper.

Mazrui, Ali, and Rothchild, Donald. 1967. "The Soldier and the State in East Africa: Some Theoretical Conclusions on the Army Mutinies of 1964." *The Western Political Quarterly* 20 (1): 82-96.

Mboya, Tom. 1963. *Freedom and After.* London: Deutsch.

Meisler, Stanley. 1970. "Tribal Politics Harass Kenya." *Foreign Affairs* 49 (1): 111-21.

Meister, Albert. 1966. *Le Développement Économique De L'Afrique Orientale.* Paris: Presses Universitaires.

Melson, Robert. "Tribalism, Class-Consciousness and the Nigerian General Strike of 1964." Unpublished paper.

Miners, N. J. 1971. *The Nigerian Army 1956-1966.* London: Methuen.

Mitchell, William C. 1967. "The Shape of Political Theory to Come: From Political Sociology to Political Economy." *American Behavioral Scientist* 11 (2): 8-20, 37.

Moore, Clement, and Hochchild, Arlie R 1969. "Student Unions in North African Politics." Reprint no. 263. Berkeley, Calif.: Institute of International Studies.

Moran, Theodor W. 1971-72. "New Deal or Raw Deal in Raw Materials." *Foreign Policy* (5): 119-34.

Myrdal, Gunnar. 1969. *The Political Element in the Development of Economic Theory.* New York: Simon & Schuster.

Nafziger, E. Wayne. 1970. "The Relationship between Education and Entrepreneurship in Nigeria." *Journal of Development Studies* (4): 349-60.

National Christian Council of Kenya. See Kenya, 1968.

N'Diaye, Jean-Pierre, 1969. *Élites Africaine Et Culture Occidentale*. Paris: Présence Africaine.

Nettl, J. P. 1968. "The State as a Conceptual Variable." *World Politics* 20 (4): 559-92.

Nielsen, Waldemar. 1969. *The Great Powers and Africa*. New York: Praeger.

Nigeria

NOTE: References are to federal government 1960-1966, federal military government 1966 to the present. Subdivisions were regions until 1967 and states thereafter. Entries are arranged by publication date in the following order: federal government, regions, states.

Federation of.

1953.   *Native Courts Commissions of Inquiry 1949 to 1952*. Appendix and Summary of Recommendations. Lagos: Government Printer.

1957.   *Proceedings of the Tribunal appointed to Inquire into Allegations of Improper Conduct by the Premier of the Eastern Region of Nigeria in Connection with the Affairs of the African Continental Bank Limited and Other Relevant Matters* (1959). Lagos: Government Printer, 2 vols.

1960a. *Report of Elias Commission of Inquiry into the Administration Economics and Industrial Relations of the Nigerian Railway Corporation*. Lagos: Government Printer.

1960b. *Statement by the Government of the Federation of Nigeria on the Report of Elias Commission of Inquiry into the Administration* . . . Sessional Paper no. 7 of 1960. Lagos: Government Printer.

1962.   *Report of Coker Commission of Inquiry into the Affairs of Certain Statutory Corporations in Western Nigeria*. Vols. 1-4. Lagos: Federal Ministry of Information.

1967.   *Report of the Nigerian Railway Corporation Tribunal of Inquiry Appointed under the Tribunal of Inquiry Decree, 1966, to Inquire into the Affairs of the Nigerian Railway Corporation*. Lagos: Ministry of Information, Printing Division.

1968.   *Comments of the Federal Military Government on the Report of the Tribunal of Inquiry into the Affairs of the Nigerian Railway Corporation* . . . Lagos: Ministry of Information, Printing Division.

1970.   Second National Development Plan 1970-74. Lagos: Federal Ministry of Information.

1971.   *Second and Final Report of the Wages and Salaries Review Commission, 1970-71 (Adebo Commission)*. Lagos: Ministry of Information.

Northern Region.

1953.   *Report on the Exchange of Customary Presents*. Lagos: Government Printer.

1958.   *Memorandum to the Minorities Commission*. Kaduna: Government Printer.

Western Region.

1962.   *Report of a Committee Appointed to Consider the Registration of Title to Land in Western Nigeria*. P. S. Lloyd, Chairman. Sessional Paper no. 2 of 1962. Ibadan: Government Printer.

1967. Ministry of Economic Planning and Social Development. *Report of a Sample Survey of Unemployment Among School Leavers.* Vol. 2. Ibadan: Ministry of Economic Planning and Social Development, Statistics Division.

Western State.

1967. *Proceedings of Tribunal of Inquiry into the Assets of Public Officers and Other Persons in Western Nigeria.* vols. 2 and 3. Ibadan: Government Printer.

1969. *Report of the Commission of Inquiry into the Civil Disturbances which Occurred in Certain Parts of the Western State of Nigeria in the Month of December 1968, and Other Matters Incidental Thereto or Connected Therewith.* Ibadan: Government Printer.

Nkrumah, Kwame.

1965. *Neo-Colonialism. The Last Stage of Imperialism.* London: Nelson.

1967. *Challenge of the Congo.* New York: International Publishers.

1968. *Dark Days in Ghana.* New York: International Publishers.

1970. *Class Struggle in Africa.* London: Panaf.

Nordlinger, Eric A. 1970. "Soldiers in Mufti: The Impact of Military Rule upon Economic and Social Change in the Non-Western States." *American Political Science Review,* 64 (4): 1131-48.

O'Brien, Donal B. 1971. *The Mourides of Senegal.* Oxford: Oxford University Press.

Ocran, Major General A. K. 1969. *A Myth is Broken.* Harlow, Essex: Longmans Green.

Odinga, Oginga. 1967. *Not Yet Uhuru.* New York: Hill & Wang.

Olakanpo. O. 1966. *Monetary and Banking Problems in Nigeria.* N.I.S.E.R. Reprint Series no. 28.

Olson, Mancur, Jr.

1968. "Economics, Sociology, and the Best of All Possible Worlds." *The Public Interest* (12): 96-118.

1969. "The Relationship between Economics and the Other Social Sciences: The Province of a 'Social Report'." In *Politics and the Social Sciences,* ed. Seymour Martin Lipset, 137-62. New York: Oxford University Press.

Oser, Jacob. 1967. *Promoting Economic Development with Illustrations From Kenya.* Evanston, Ill.: Northwestern University Press.

Ostrander, F. Taylor.

1963. "The Place of Minerals in Economic Development." Presented to the Council of Economics at the Ninety-Second Annual Meeting of the American Institute of Mining, Metallurgical, and Petroleum Engineers. Dallas, Texas. Feb. 27, 1963. Unpublished paper.

1966. "The Role of Foreign Private Capital in Africa." In *Southern Africa in Transition,* eds. John A. Davis and James K. Baker, 347-61. New York: Praeger.

1967. "Zambia in the Aftermath of Rhodesian UDI." *African Forum* 2 (3): 50-65.

Panter-Brick, S. D., ed. 1970. *Nigerian Politics and Military Rule: Prelude to the Civil War.* London: Athlone.

Parsons, Talcott. 1963. "On the Concept of Influence." *Public Opinion Quarterly* (27): 37-62.

Pearson, Scott R. n.d. "Measurement of the Impacts of Petroleum Production on the Nigerian Economy: A Second Working Paper." Mimeographed, restricted circulation.

Peccei, Aurelio. 1968. "World Problems in the Coming Decades." *American Behavioral Scientist* 11 (6): 20-23.

Pfeffermann, Guy.
  1967.   "Trade Unions and Politics in French West Africa During the Fourth Republic." *African Affairs* July 1967, 213-30.
  1968.   *Industrial Labor in the Republic of Senegal.* New York: Praeger.

Pollock, James K. 1926. *Party Campaign Funds.* New York: Knopf.

Pool, Ithiel de Sola, ed. 1967. *Contemporary Political Science.* New York: McGraw-Hill.

Potekhin, I. 1968. African Problems. Moscow: Nauka.

Prest, A. R. 1963. *Public Finance in Underdeveloped Countries.* New York: Praeger.

Price, Robert M.
  1971*a.* "Military Officers and Political Leadership." *Comparative Politics* 3 (3): 361-79.
  1971*b.* "A Theoretical Approach to Military-Group Theory and the Ghanaian Case." *World Politics* 23 (3): 399-430.

Pye, Lucien, ed. 1963. *Communication and Political Development.* Princeton, N.J.: Princeton University Press.

Rimmer, Douglas. 1969. "The Abstraction from Politics. A Critique of Economic Theory and Design with Reference to West Africa." *The Journal of Development Studies* 5 (3): 190-204.

Robinson, E. A. G. 1960. *Economic Consequences of the Size of Nations.* New York: St. Martin's Press.

Robson, P., and Lury, D. C. 1969. *The Economics of Africa.* Evanston, Ill.: Northwestern University Press.

Rosberg, Carl, and Nottingham, John. 1966. *The Myth of Mau Mau.* New York: Praeger.

Rose, R., and Heidenheimer, A. 1963. "Comparative Political Finance." Reprinted from the *Journal of Politics* 25 (3): 644-811.

Rotberg, Robert. 1967. "Tribalism and Politics in Zambia." *Africa Report* 12 (9): 29-35.

Rothchild, Donald.
  1969.   "Ethnic Inequality in Kenya." *Journal of Modern African Studies.* 7 (4): 689-711.
  1969-70. *Citizenship and National Integrations: The Non-African Crisis in Kenya.* Studies in Race and Nations. University of Denver Reprints 1 (3).
  1971.   "Intersectional Conflicts and Resource Allocation in Zambia." Paper delivered at the African Studies Meeting, November 3-6, 1971, Denver, Colorado.

Russett, Bruce. 1963. "The Adoption of Political Styles by African Politicians in Rhodesia." Paper prepared for Annual Meeting of the American Political Science Association, New York, 1963.

Samuelson, Paul A. 1967. *Economics.* 7th ed. New York: McGraw-Hill.

Scarrit, James R. 1971. "Elite Values, Ideology, and Power in Post-Independence Zambia." *African Studies Review 14* (1): 31-59.

Schachter-Morgenthau, Ruth. 1964. *Political Parties in French-Speaking West Africa.* London: Oxford University Press.

Schatz, Sayre P.
  1963.   *Economic Environment and Private Enterprise in West Africa.* N.I.S.E.R. Reprint Series no. 6.

1964. *Development Bank Lending in Nigeria: The Federal Loans Board.* Ibadan and London: Oxford University Press.

1965. *The Capital Shortage Illusion: Government Lending in Nigeria.* N.I.S.E.R. Reprint Series no. 13.

1968. *The High Cost of Aiding Business in Developing Economies: Nigeria's Loan Programmes.* Extract from *Oxford Economic Papers* 20 (3).

Schätzl, L. H. 1969. *Petroleum in Nigeria.* Ibadan: N.I.S.E.R.

Schnittger, Lubbe. 1966. *Besteuerung und wirtschaftliche Entwicklung in Ostafrica.* Berlin: Soringer.

Scott, James C. 1972. *Comparative Political Corruption.* Englewood Cliffs, N.J.: Prentice-Hall.

Senegal, Republic of.

Senegal, *Area Handbook.* See American University.

1965. *Deuxième Plan Quadriennal de Développement Économique et Sociale.* vols. 1-3. Paris: Imprimerie Mozart.

1968. Ministère Du Plan Et De L' Industrie. *Situation Économique Du Sénégal 1967.* Dakar: Direction De La Statistique.

1969. *Troisième Plan Quadriennal de Développement Économique et Sociale, 1969-1973.* Dakar: Imprimerie A. Diop.

Sierra Leone. 1968. National Reformation Council. *Report of the Forster Commission of Inquiry on Assets of Ex-Ministers and Ex-Deputy Ministers.* Freetown: Government Printer.

Simon, H. H.

1953. "Notes on the Observation and Measurement of Political Power." *Journal of Politics* (15): 500-516.

1957. *Models of Man.* New York: Wiley.

Sklar, Richard. 1966. "Nigerian Politics: The Ordeal of Chief Awolowo, 1960-65." In *Politics in Africa,* ed. Gwendolyn Carter, 119-65. New York: Harcourt, Brace & World.

Smythe, H. H., and Smythe, M. M. "Subgroups of the New Nigerian Elite." Reprinted from *Dusquesne Review.* Pittsburgh, Pa.: Dusquesne University Press.

Soja, Edward W. 1968. *The Geography of Modernization in Kenya. A Spatial Analysis of Social and Economic Change.* Syracuse, N.Y.: Syracuse University Press.

Staley, Eugene. 1954. *Political Implications of Economic Development.* New York: Harper.

Stolper, Wolfgang.

1966. *Planning Without Facts; Lessons in Resource Allocation From Nigeria's Development.* Cambridge, Mass.: Harvard University Press.

1967. "Budget, Economic Policy, and Economic Performance." Paper delivered at the 1967 Annual Meeting of the American Political Science Association.

Strange, Susan. 1971. "The Politics of International Currencies." *World Politics* 23 (2): 215-31.

Suret-Canale, Jean. 1964. *Afrique Noire. L' Ère Coloniale, 1900-1945.* Paris: Éditions Sociales.

Thompson, Virginia. 1962. "The Ivory Coast." In *African One-Party States,* ed. G. M. Carter, 237-324. Ithaca, N.Y.: Cornell University Press.

Trimingham, J. Spencer, 1959. *Islam in West Africa.* Oxford: Clarendon Press.

Tripathy, Ram Niranjan. 1964. *Public Finance in Under-Developed Countries.* Calcutta: The World Press.

Union of Soviet Socialist Republics. (USSR). 1968. Institute of Africa. *A History of Africa 1918-67.* Moscow: NAUKA Publishing House.

United Kingdom.

    1955. East Africa Royal Commission 1953-1955. *Report* (Dow Report), Cmd. 9475. London: H.M.S.O.

    1958. Colonial Office, Nigeria. *Report of the Commission appointed to enquire into the fears of minorities and means of allaying them.* Cmd. 505. London: H.M.S.O.

    1960. *Historical Survey of the Origins and Growth of Mau Mau.* Cmd. 1030. London: H.M.S.O.

United Nations.

    NOTE: Only the more substantive reports or reference sources are given here. Other UN documents can be located by reference to the document number cited in the notes.

    E/CN.14/28, *Economic Survey of Africa since 1950.*

    E/CN.14/132 Rev. 1. *Economic and Social Consequences of Racial Discriminatory Practices.*

    E/CN.14/401. *A Survey of Economic Conditions in Africa.*

    E/CN.14/INR/1/Rev. 1. *Industrial Growth in Africa.*

    E/CN.14/L/320/Rev. 1. *Report of the ECA Mission on Economic Cooperation in Central Africa.*

    E/CN.14/SWSA/4. *Social Reconstruction in the Newly Independent Countries of East Africa.*

    ID/CONF. 1/RBP/1. 1966. *Industrial Development in Africa.*

    ST/ECA/109. *Economic Cooperation and Integration in Africa. Three Case Studies.*

    E/CN.14/370. *Economic Survey of Africa 1966.*

    E/4446. *Foreign Investment in Developing Countries.*

    E/CN.14/435. *Economic Conditions in Africa in Recent Years.*

    A/6868/ and A/6868/Add. 1. *Activities of Foreign Economic and Other Interests which Are Impeding the Implementation of the Declaration on the Granting of Independence to Colonial Countries.*

    UN/ECA/FAO. 1964. *Report of the UN/ECA/FAO Economic Survey Mission on the Economic Development of Zambia (Dudley Seers Report).* Ndola, Zambia: Falcon Press.

United States.

    1967. Department of the Army. *Africa: Problems and Prospects. A Bibliographical Survey.* DA-PAM-5, April 1967. Washington, D.C.: U.S. Government Printing Office.

    1971. Senate, *Hearings before the Subcommittee on United States Security Agreements and Commitments Abroad of the Committee on Foreign Relations, 91st Congress.* Vol. 2, parts 5-11. Printed for use of the Senate Committee on Foreign Relations. Washington, D.C.

Van Arcadie, Brian. 1963. "Gross Domestic Product Estimates for East Africa." *Economic and Statistical Review* 4 (9): ix-xii.

Van Den Berghe, Pierre L. 1967. *Race and Racism: A Comparative Perspective.* New York: Wiley.

Van Der Meersch, W. J. Ganshof. 1963. *Fin De La Souveraineté Belge au Congo.* Hague: Institut Royal Des Relations Internationales.

Van Philips, Paul A. M. 1957. *Public Finance and Less Developed Economy with Special Reference to Latin America.* The Hague: Martinus Nijhoff.

Vernon, Raymond. 1967. "Multinational Enterprise and National Sovereignty." *Harvard Business Review* 45 (2): 156, 158.

Wallerstein, Immanuel.
  1961. *The Politics of Independence.* New York: Vintage.
  1967. *Africa: The Politics of Unity.* New York: Vintage.

Weber, Max. 1956. *Wirtschaft Und Gesellschaft.* Tübingen: Mohr. 2 vols.

Welch, Claude E., Jr.
  1970*a*. "Civil-Military Relations in Commonwealth West Africa." Paper presented at the American Political Science Association Meeting, 1970.
  1970*b*. *Soldier and State in Africa.* Evanston, Ill.: Northwestern University Press.

Whitaker, J.C.S., Jr. 1969. *The Politics of Tradition. A Study of Continuity and Change 1946-1966.* Princeton, N.J.: Princeton University Press.

Widstrand, Carl Gosta. 1970. *Co-operation and Rural Development in East Africa.* Uppsala: The Scandinavian Institute of African Studies.

Wildavsky, Aaron. 1971. "Does Planning Work." *The Public Interest* 2 (24): 95-104.

Woddis, Jack. 1967. *Introduction to Neo-Colonialism.* New York: International Publishers.

Wood, David, 1966. "The Armed Forces of African States." *Adelphi Papers* no. 27. London: Institute of Strategic Studies.

Wraith, Ronald, and Simpkin, Edgar. 1963. *Corruption in Developing Countries.* London: Allen and Unwin.

Young, Crawford. 1965. *Politics in the Congo: Decolonization and Independence.* Princeton, N.J.: Princeton University Press.

Zambia, Republic of
  Zambia, *Area Handbook.* See American University.
  1966*a*. Manpower Report. *A Report and Statistical Handbook on Manpower, Education, Training and Zambianisation 1965-66.* Lusaka: Government Printer.
  1966*b*. Office of National Development Planning. *First National Development Plan 1966-1970.* Lusaka: Government Printer.

Zartman, I. William. 1966. *International Relations in the New Africa.* Englewood Cliffs, N.J.: Prentice-Hall.

Zolberg, Aristide.
  1963. "Second and Third Generation Elites in the Ivory Coast." U.S. Department of State. External Research Staff, Bureau of Intelligence and Research Policy Research Study. Unpublished.
  1964. *One-Party Government in the Ivory Coast.* Princeton, N.J.: Princeton University Press.
  1966. *Creating Political Order.* Chicago: Rand McNally.

PERIODICALS

Standard Bank, *Annual Economic Review.*
Standard Bank Review.
West Africa 1956-1972.

Index